THE CRUCIBLE OF WAR
VOLUME II
AUCHINLECK'S COMMAND

D1379819

Barrie Pitt served in both the European and Middle East theatres in the war, and later edited the enormous partwork *History of the Second World War*. He was also Editor-in-Chief of *Ballantine's Illustrated History of World War 11*. He is the author of *Zeebrugge, St George's Day, 1918, Coronel and Falkland, 1918 - The Last Act, The Battle of the Atlantic, Churchill and the Generals* and a novel, *The Edge of Battle*.

Auchinleck's Command is the second of the three volumes of *The Crucible of War.* Its companion volumes *Wavell's Command* and *Montgomery and Alamein* are published by Cassell in uniform editions.

THE CRUCIBLE OF WAR

VOLUME II
AUCHINLECK'S COMMAND

BARRIE PITT

CASSELL&CO

Cassell & Co
Wellington House, 125 Strand
London WC2R 0BB

The Crucible of War was first published in two volumes by Jonathan
Cape, 1980 and 1982
This three-volume edition published 2001

British Library Cataloguing-in-Publication Data
A catalogue record for this book is available from the British Library

ISBN 0-304-35951-3

Printed and bound in Great Britain by
Creative Print & Design (Wales), Ebbw Vale

To Nick and Jane
and Matthew and Carrie
with love

Contents

Illustrations

PLATES

ILLUSTRATIONS

MAPS

FIGURES

The author and publishers would like to thank Mr John Bachelor for permission to use his line drawings, figures 1–4.

Author's Note

Once again I must offer my thanks to the librarians, fellow historians, archivists and survivors of the various actions described herein, who have given me so freely of their time, their expertise or their memories. This second volume of *The Crucible of War* would have been, as the first one was and the others undoubtedly will be, impossible to write without them.

In particular I would like to thank the late Field Marshal Sir Claude Auchinleck and his erstwhile Chief of Staff, the late Major-General Eric Dorman O'Gowan, for the time they spent answering my questions and, in the case of General O'Gowan, dilating upon the answers. I would also like to thank Field Marshal Lord Carver and Major-General Douglas Wimberley, who were instrumental in correcting an egregiously biased impression I had formed of one of the principal characters in the story that follows, and to them and to both Lady Carver and Mrs Wimberley I must express gratitude for the hospitality they showed me while the operation was in progress.

To Major-General G. P. D. 'Pip' Roberts I must also express thanks for answering my questions and allowing me to quote from his answers, and, as in the first volume, I am again indebted to Generals Walther Nehring and Walter Warlimont. Professor Lucio Ceva too has earned my gratitude for his help in identifying Italian formations engaged in the Gazala battle, and also for elucidating the Italian Orders of Battle.

At a different level, Colonel D. T. L. Beath has been kind enough to read through the typescript and to point out various military solecisms I had committed, and to Mr John Keegan I owe an especial debt for his expert critique of the chapters dealing with *Operation Crusader*.

Finally, I must again thank Jane Caunt for retyping the book, Deborah Shepherd for so sympathetically editing it, and Frances Mary Moore for drawing some of the maps and compiling the index.

Prologue:
First Year of the Desert War

British troops began fighting in the Western Desert on June 11th, 1940 – twenty-four hours after Mussolini, in a hasty attempt to secure a position of advantage when the empires of France and Britain were divided up between the Axis Powers (a process which he thought might begin quite soon), had delivered an impassioned speech from the balcony of the Palazzo Venezia to a markedly unenthusiastic crowd, at the end of which he declared war on both of those 'effete democracies'.

The first troops into action had been those of the 11th Hussars – the reconnaissance regiment of what later became famous as the 7th Armoured Division – and during the weeks that followed their armoured cars and the cruiser tanks of 4th and 7th Armoured Brigades had carried out widespread and damaging raids on the Italian posts along the Egyptian–Cyrenaican border, between Sollum on the coast and Fort Maddalena fifty miles to the south. They had even carried out one raid down to Jarabub on the edge of the Kalansho Sand Sea, and had been defeated there more by the appalling heat than by any Italian military ardour.

Then in September, 1940, under increasing pressure from Mussolini, the Italian commander in North Africa, Maresciallo Rodolfo Graziani, had launched across the border an attack by the Italian Tenth Army, which advanced as far as Sidi Barrani where it halted, apparently lacking the equipment or fuel – or perhaps the energy or the will – to proceed further. The armour and infantry of the 7th Armoured Division had retreated slowly in the face of this advance, maintaining contact with the Italians and harassing them with minor but irritating attacks, and when Graziani's forces settled down and began building a series of what were evidently intended to be semi-permanent camps stretching in an arc south-westwards from Sidi Barrani, the 11th Hussars took up close observation positions and all began preparations for reprisal.

The Armoured Division had now been joined by the Sikhs, Punjabis, Rajputs, Mahrattas and the British battalions of the 4th Indian Division, the combination taking the name Western Desert Force and coming under command of one of Britain's most imaginative and competent soldiers, Lieutenant-General Sir Richard O'Connor. He by then had received orders from General Wavell, the

British Commander-in-Chief, Middle East, to expel the intruders as expeditiously as possible, despite the fact that he would have at his command only two divisions against the nine enemy divisions now spread over the desert between Sidi Barrani and the Egyptian frontier – a complication which apparently caused him but little apprehension.

Sir Richard O'Connor and his men began their attack on the night of December 9th, 1940, and such was the success which attended their efforts that by February 7th, 1941, they had not only expelled Graziani's forces from Egypt, but had also driven them back across Cyrenaica to the Tripolitanian border at El Agheila, thus completing the first lap of what later became known by the irreverent as the 'Benghazi Handicap'. They had advanced 500 miles in ten weeks, completely destroyed the Italian Tenth Army, and in the process captured 130,000 prisoners, including seven generals.

It was an extraordinary feat for so small a force, especially as their own casualties in killed, wounded and missing amounted to less than 2,000, but unfortunately for the men who had carried it out (they had been joined shortly after the beginning of the operation by the 6th Australian Division), decisions taken in London, Cairo and Berlin were to rob them of the fruits of their victory. In the face of the imminent invasion of Greece by twelve German divisions, Whitehall and Cairo headquarters now ordered all available trained and equipped forces across the Mediterranean, so the Australian and a New Zealand Division (which O'Connor had hoped would be available to speed his force onwards to Tripoli; but not, fortunately, the 7th Armoured Division, whose tanks were worn out, or the 4th Indian Division, which had been sent to Ethiopia to help reduce the Italian Empire there), were transported to the Balkans, and their unhappy destruction as fighting units followed quite quickly. Meanwhile, in Berlin, Hitler, unwilling to allow further military humiliation of his Italian ally, sent what he called a *Sperrverband* – a 'Blocking Force' – to North Africa, commanded by one of his favourite generals, Generalleutnant Erwin Johannes Eugen Rommel, who thereupon stepped on to the stage he was to dominate for many months.

It quickly became obvious that it was not in General Rommel's nature to hold defensive positions or even to fight defensive battles, especially when he had reason to believe that the enemy forces ranged against him were neither aggressively intentioned nor particularly well organised for their own protection. And of this he became more and more convinced.

Despite total lack of encouragement from his Italian allies in Tripolitania, and in blatant disobedience to orders from the *Oberkommando des Heeres* (High Command of the Army) in Berlin, he launched the armour of his own 5th Light Division and the armour and infantry of the Italian Ariete Division through the El Agheila defile on the morning of March 31st, 1941, and twenty-eight days later was occupying the old Italian positions on the Egyptian border at Fort Capuzzo and Sidi Omar, with a forward outpost at Halfaya Pass, ten miles inside Egypt. The second lap of the Benghasi Handicap had been even more spectacular than the first and, like the British advance westwards of three months before, his own to the east had been achieved with remarkably few casualties. Moreover, although his forces had captured only three British generals, these had constituted an even more significant 'bag' than his opponents', for one of them had been Sir Richard O'Connor himself, for whom General Wavell immediately expressed his willingness to offer six Italian generals in exchange. (The British Government quashed the idea on egalitarian grounds.)

The only circumstance that marred this lightning success was the failure to capture Tobruk, now some eighty miles behind Rommel's own front line and held in large part by the 9th Australian Division, determined not to lose the port captured by their brothers in 6th Division. It was to prove a continual distraction to Rommel's further ambition, and his attempts to storm its defences were to cause him serious losses in both men and material during the months which followed, though these were offset to some extent by the British losses in their own attempts to supply or relieve the garrison.

Of the first there were many by sea, and of the second two unsuccessful attempts by land. In May the aptly named *Operation Brevity* was launched, to be repelled easily by Rommel's Afrika Korps using for the first time in the desert war the remarkable 88mm. anti-aircraft gun in an anti-tank role; and then in June Wavell ordered Lieutenant-General Sir Noel Beresford-Peirse, now commanding XIII Corps (as Western Desert Force had been renamed) to attack again across the frontier, his force strengthened by over 100 new tanks which Prime Minister Churchill had insisted be rushed out across the Mediterranean, despite warnings from the Naval Staff of the risks of such a journey, despite also the shortage of arms in England for the Home Defences.

Operation Battleaxe was a disastrous failure. The new tanks were unfitted for work in desert conditions and their crews were unused to their machines and untrained in co-operation with accompanying infantry. During the first twelve hours over 50 per cent of the newly provided armour had been knocked out, and after three days' unavailing conflict Wavell called off the operation, his mauled forces retiring to their original position.

On the last day of the battle, Churchill, shaken by the accumulating evidence of the loss of what he had romantically come to look upon as his own contribution to a desert victory, left London and went down to his home at Chartwell, which he had shut up for the duration of the war, to roam disconsolately through the empty rooms and the once immaculate gardens, now shabbier, now showing the signs of less exact attention. It was not an atmosphere conducive to optimism, impartiality of judgement, or even of charity; and while he was there Wavell's report on the events of the last few days arrived, opening with the chilling sentence, 'I regret to report the failure of "Battleaxe".'

During the next few days the figures of British losses came in. XIII Corps had lost 122 officers and men killed, 588 wounded and 259 missing. The Royal Air Force had lost thirty-six aircraft and the artillery had lost four of their guns; but the figures that rubbed most salt into Churchill's wounds were the ones which revealed that of the hundred-odd Matilda tanks with which the battle had opened, sixty-four had been totally lost together with twenty-seven of the cruisers. He had not stripped Britain of her defences, ignored the advice of his Chiefs of Staff, and braved the dangers of the Mediterranean passage for results such as these.

Relations between the Commander-in-Chief, Middle East, and Mr Churchill had never been of the happiest. Wavell's taciturnity had reminded the Prime Minister too much of General Haig's attitude to his political masters of twenty-five years before, and Wavell's unwillingness to engage the Italian invaders immediately they had ceased advancing into Egypt the previous September – as Churchill had repeatedly urged – though perhaps justified by subsequent events, had left an atmosphere laden with bitterness and disappointment.

And now this latest, spectacular failure. Wavell must go.

But how? It would be better if it could be done with only the faintest hint of censure on Wavell's performance, for too many people would spring to his defence asserting that he was being made the scapegoat for the Government's own mistakes; and it would be better still if matters could be so arranged that Wavell did not return to London where he could well prove an embarrassment, and if questioned by the Press or by some of Churchill's parliamentary opponents might give answers that might best not be heard.

The solution was, in fact, quite neat and simple. Churchill wished command of the armies of the Middle East to devolve now upon the present Commander-in-Chief in India, General Auchinleck, who during the past months had many times demonstrated a generosity of spirit and a willingness to take risks which both impressed Churchill and appealed to his own nature. As Wavell had considerable experience of military service in India, the generals could simply exchange commands; Wavell would enjoy sitting under a pagoda tree – and he would be a long way from London.

The cables flew between Whitehall and Cairo, Whitehall and Delhi, Delhi and Cairo – polite, flattering, compliant. In due course aircraft bearing the new Commander-in-Chief, Middle East, and his personal staff arrived in Egypt, and after a few days of meetings and talks other aircraft flew in the opposite direction bearing the old one away. The talks between the two generals had been very friendly as they knew each other well, but undoubtedly Auchinleck had cause for a great deal of thought on many problems as he took up the reins of his new command. Those dealing with pure military tactics or strategy should pose no insurmountable obstacles, for he had spent his professional life coping with such matters; the present struggle in Syria, for instance, would not tax his competence unduly, though the launching of the vast German armies across the Russian frontier in *Operation Barbarossa* on the very day he was informed of his new appointment would call for fresh appraisal of many significant factors. But consideration of such matters must await their turn.

What he must do first of all would be to establish quickly and quite clearly the form of relationship to exist between his own headquarters in Cairo and those in Whitehall; more particularly those between himself and that brilliant, demanding, capricious but undoubtedly dominating figure – the Prime Minister, Winston Churchill.

According to what Wavell had intimated, differences between the two of them would inevitably arise, probably on basic issues. How soon? And how would they be resolved?

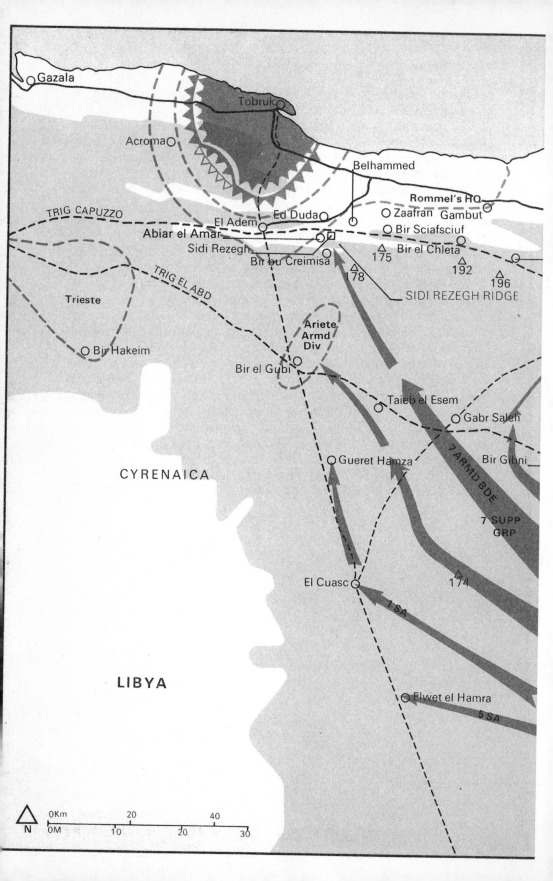

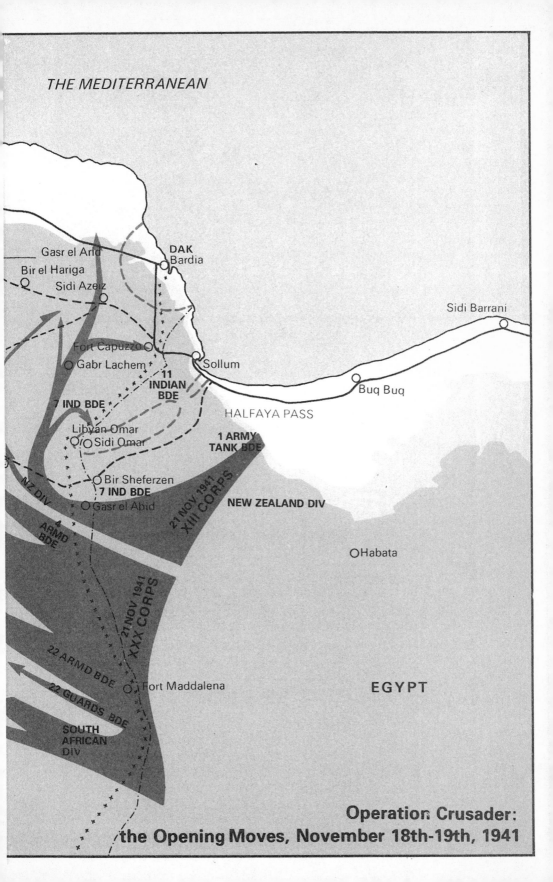

THE MEDITERRANEAN

Gasr el Arid

Bir el Hariga

Sidi Azeiz

DAK
Bardia

Sidi Barrani

Fort Capuzzo

Gabr Lachem

11
INDIAN
BDE

Sollum

Buq Buq

7 IND BDE

HALFAYA PASS

Libyan Omar

Sidi Omar

1 ARMY
TANK BDE

Bir Sheferzen

7 IND BDE

NZ DIV

Gasr el Abid

21 NOV 1941
XIII CORPS

NEW ZEALAND DIV

4
ARMD
BDE

Habata

21 NOV 1941
XXX CORPS

22 ARMD BDE

Fort Maddalena

EGYPT

22 GUARDS BDE

SOUTH
AFRICAN
DIV

**Operation Crusader:
the Opening Moves, November 18th-19th, 1941**

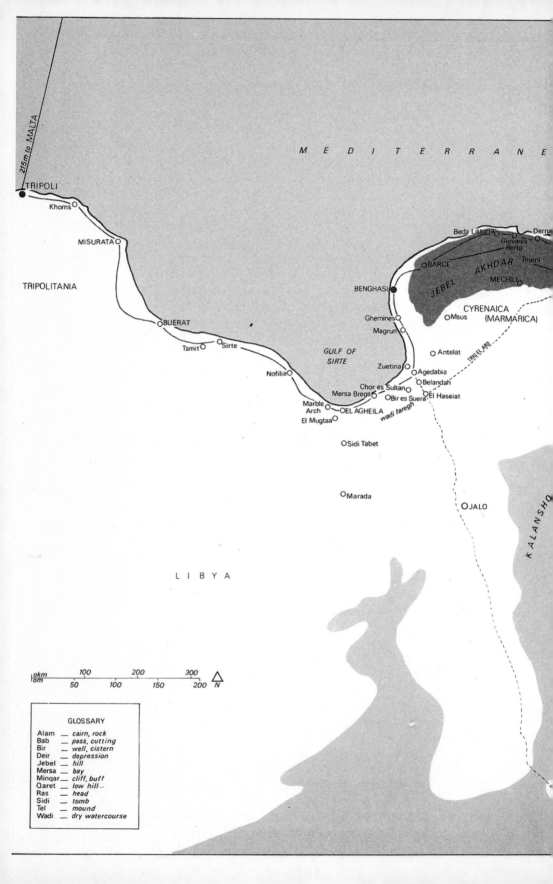

MEDITERRANE

215m to MALTA

TRIPOLI

Khoms

MISURATA

Beda Littoria
Giovanni
Berta
Derna
Tmimi

BARCE

JEBEL AKHDAR

MECHILI

TRIPOLITANIA

BENGHASI

CYRENAICA
(MARMARICA)

BUERAT

Ghemines

Msus

Magrun

Tamit Sirte

GULF OF
SIRTE

Antelat

TRIG EL ABD

Nofilia

Zuetina

Agedabia
Belandah

Chor es Sultan

Mersa Brega

El Haseiat

Bir es Suera

Marble
Arch

OEL AGHEILA

wadi faregh

El Mugtaa

Sidi Tabet

Marada

JALO

KALANSHO

L I B Y A

0km 100 200 300
0m   N
    50   100   150   200

GLOSSARY

Alam — cairn, rock
Bab — pass, cutting
Bir — well, cistern
Deir — depression
Jebel — hill
Mersa — bay
Minqar — cliff, buff
Qaret — low hill
Ras — head
Sidi — tomb
Tel — mound
Wadi — dry watercourse

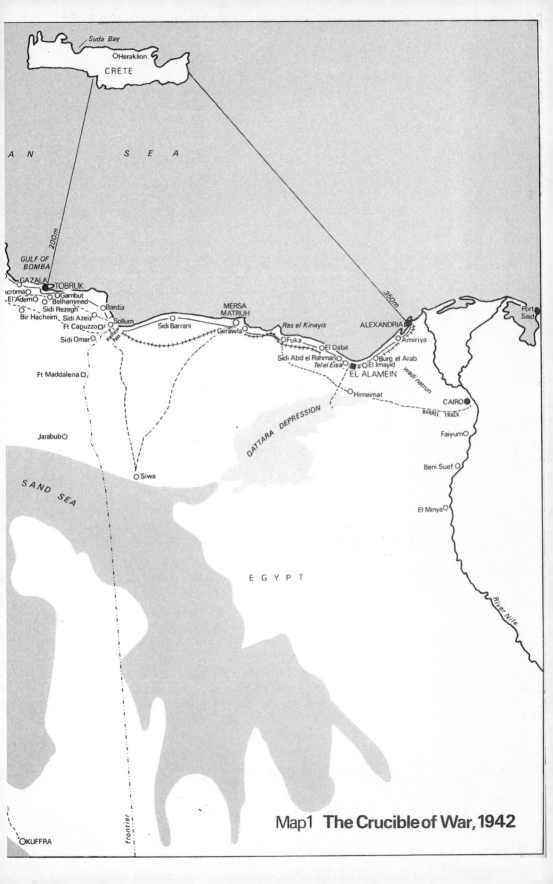

Map 1 **The Crucible of War, 1942**

1 · Auchinleck Takes Command

Plus ça change, plus c'est la même chose.

The most fundamental change in the situation in the Middle East as it had faced Wavell and as it now faced Auchinleck, was that brought about by the German invasion of Russia which, indeed, introduced an entirely new dimension into the war. What remained ominously the same was the total divergence of the conclusions drawn from that event in London and Cairo.

To Churchill and the Chiefs of Staff it seemed that Auchinleck was now presented with a golden – but fleeting – opportunity to strike at Rommel immediately while all Germany's attention was held in the east and not one tank, one fighter, one man or one shell could be spared to help the Afrika Korps in any danger which threatened. To Auchinleck it appeared as a heaven-sent release of pressure which would give him time to reorganise his forces, get to know his men and ensure that they were properly equipped and much better trained for the tasks he would set them, once he was confident of their prowess.

The scene was thus set for an immediate head-on clash. The first cable which Churchill sent Auchinleck began with the words, 'You take up your great command at a period of crisis,' and ended, 'The urgency of these issues will naturally impress itself upon you. We shall be glad to hear from you at your earliest convenience' – while Auchinleck's reply, after its opening politenesses, flatly declared, 'No further offensive in the Western Desert should be contemplated until base is secure.' It then went on to state that there was no possibility whatsoever of attacking Rommel until the vexatious affair in Syria had been brought to a successful conclusion.

Churchill, who had pinned all his hopes upon the tall, ruggedly handsome and until this moment apparently forthcoming and aggressive general, was bitterly disappointed. Had he exchanged an exhausted Wavell for an obstinate or pusillanimous Auchinleck? The thought that the second was as unlikely a prognosis as the first was unfair a judgment never crossed the Prime Minister's mind, for one of the qualities which gave him the strength to bear his enormous burdens was a profound belief in the acuity of his own opinions, and the correctness of his decisions. He could hardly have carried on without it.

But to Auchinleck, the barrage of cables he now received from London – urgent, abrupt, indicative of the Prime Minister's inclination to leave the absolute minimum to anybody else's judgment – did little but confirm the warnings he had received from Wavell (and later in a long letter from Sir John Dill) and strengthen him in his determination to exercise his command in his own way and to fight his battles, if not in his own time, at least at times which he himself felt gave the best chances of victory. And he did not consider that the forces now under his command could be welded into an army well-trained and powerful enough to defeat Rommel and expel the Axis forces from Cyrenaica – let alone from the whole of North Africa, which he considered to be his ultimate objective – until the end of the summer at the earliest, and probably not until well into the autumn.

But first of all there was this tiresome business up in Syria – which was, in the event, quite quickly concluded.

The second phase had coincided with *Operation Battleaxe* and by the end of it the Australians on the coast had reached Sidon and the British had reached Damascus – but Merjayun in the centre and Palmyra (under siege by Habforce which had come up from Baghdad) were still in Vichy hands. The fighting had been bitter in the extreme and of the Free French infantry only the Marine Battalion could still be relied upon, the others having lost their enthusiasm for battle against their fellow countrymen.

With the conclusion of *Battleaxe*, however, Air Marshal Tedder could release two fighter and three bomber squadrons to operate with the forces in Syria, and the 10th Indian Division (under Major-General 'Bill' Slim) came up from Baghdad along the valley of the Euphrates to take Deir ez Zor and threaten Aleppo. The Vichy French forces could thus see that odds were mounting against them from all directions, that no help could come to them from metropolitan France and that Germany's attention was elsewhere.

A fierce battle was fought on the coast at Damour during July 7th and 8th, Beirut was under close attack by the night of the 10th and on the evening of July 11th, Général Dentz was asking for an armistice to begin at midnight. The terms were agreed that night – Allied occupation of the country, the handing over intact of ships, aircraft, naval and air establishments, the release of all British, Indian and Free French prisoners; and the choice to be given to the officers and men of the Army of the Levant either to be repatriated to France or to stay and join the Free French.

The immediate results did little to encourage belief in any French desire to see the defeat of Hitler's Germany. Of the 37,736 officers and men offered this choice, only 5,668 opted to join De Gaulle's forces and of these only 1,046 were native Frenchmen, the rest being members of the Foreign Legion (mostly German or Russian), North Africans or Senegalese. Moreover, to the astonishment and disgust of the British and Australian commanders, and of the American Consul-General who had helped with the negotiations, it was discovered that *after the signing of the armistice terms*, Général Dentz had ordered the hasty removal via Athens, Munich and Lyons to the naval fortress at Toulon of thirty-eight captured British and Indian officers, one Free French officer and thirteen N.C.O.s of the Royal Fusiliers.

Cornelius Engert, the American Consul-General, wrote a tirade on the subject to his superiors in Washington containing such phrases as 'gross breach of faith' and 'indecent collusion between Berlin and Vichy', ending, 'The Nazis have found uncommonly apt pupils in the kind of moral turpitude which they themselves have so consistently displayed in their international relations.'

When the deception was discovered, Général Dentz, three other French generals and some thirty colonels and majors were promptly arrested (just as they were packing and ready for repatriation) and it was made clear to them and in due course to the authorities in France, that they would not be released until the missing Allied prisoners were returned – a move which brought violent expostulations from both Dentz and Paris with regard not only to the differences in rank between the French hostages and the Allied prisoners, but also upon the differences in colour, which apparently they felt most keenly.

At first the Vichy Government refused to believe that the British could be so uncouth as to hold French senior officers against exchange for British and Indian junior officers and other ranks, but when the facts of the matter were fully appreciated, they quickly discovered where the prisoners were being 'sheltered' (*hébergés*) and they were soon on their way back to Beirut, travelling in first class cabins.

But it had not been like that on their journey to France, during which they had been herded together in appalling conditions and made to eat with their fingers out of horse-troughs; which resulted in some bitter comments as they watched the French hostages leaving the comforts of a Carmelite convent near Jerusalem where they had been penned.

At a ceremony at Arles in October, Admiral Darlan decorated Général Dentz with the insignia of Grand Officer of the Legion of Honour and the returned hero referred to De Gaulle and his followers as 'the corrupt, debtors, place-seekers, the perpetually dissatisfied, the mismatched, the keepers of mistresses . . . ' and to the British as 'our secular enemies, who think only of finding France when peace comes without a Navy, colonies, or military traditions . . . They represent those things which almost destroyed us; democratic-masonic politics and judaeo-saxon finance.'

With senior officers such as Dentz, it is hardly surprising that France's armies put up so little resistance to Hitler's.

Once the Syrian campaign was successfully concluded, Auchinleck could turn his full attention to the Western Desert which in everyone's mind now appeared the most important theatre – at least until the possible arrival of German troops in the Caucasus. On July 15th, he sent a long and considered cable to Churchill in reply to the Prime Minister's urgent requests for immediate action, in which he stated that in his opinion not only was time needed for training tank crews in the use of their new tanks and in co-operation with both infantry and air forces, but also that a 50 per cent reserve of tanks should be available before any aggressive operations were commenced. In view of their breakdown rate en route to the battle-field this last point was perhaps not as unreasonable as it sounded.

According to his figures, therefore, if – as Churchill was promising him – by the end of July his tank strength in the Delta rose to 500 with another 75 in Tobruk, then by the end of October he should be able to open an offensive against Rommel with a striking force of about 350 tanks, supported by one infantry division. As in one of his first cables to the Prime Minister he had said that he needed two and preferably three armoured divisions plus a motorised infantry division to ensure success, the inference was that the 500 tanks which he had been promised was about enough to supply half the forces he considered necessary. And of course, if he did receive all the tanks he required, he would probably need more time to ensure the proper training of their crews, so the offensive would not be launched until even later.

'Generals only enjoy such comforts in Heaven,' wrote Churchill much later, when his blood-pressure had returned to normal. 'And those that demand them do not always get there.'

Auchinleck's stock at Downing Street after three weeks stood but little higher than Wavell's had after twelve months.

Auchinleck suffered from another disadvantage in addition to that of inexperience in dealing with politicians which he shared with Wavell. He had spent almost his entire military life serving in the Indian Army, and even the years of the First World War had been spent with Indian troops in Mesopotamia. Except for a ten-month period as a corps commander (end of January to mid-December

1940) in England, he had not served with the British Regular Army and he therefore did not know very well the men who made up that comparatively small group of senior officers from whom his immediately subordinate generals would be chosen. He thus had no knowledge of their strengths or weaknesses.

At an intermediate level, he was well acquainted with the officers and men of the 4th Indian Division (he had been commissioned, in 1902, into the 62nd Punjabis, now renamed the 1st/1st Punjab Regiment) and was glad to confirm Frank Messervy in command of it; but except for the personal staff he had brought with him from Delhi he was surrounded at the Cairo Headquarters by almost complete strangers – and perhaps most important of all, as there had been no armoured divisions in India (very few armoured cars even, let alone tanks), his main striking force in the field would be commanded by men of whom he knew little but their names when first they came under his command. The danger of mistaken choice at all critical levels was therefore present from the moment he accepted appointment as Commander-in-Chief.

The same was true at much lower levels, too. Auchinleck had little knowledge of the type of man who was flooding out to crew his tanks, to drive his armoured cars and lorries, to man his guns or to march forward into battle with nothing but his rifle and his trust in his comrades to protect him; but this he had in common with the other generals, for the men now arriving in the Middle East were no longer the professional, regular soldiers. They were the 'hostilities only' soldiers – civilians who had either joined the Territorial Army before the war and spent some of their weekends and two weeks every summer in keen but amateur military endeavour, or who had been called up under the National Service regulations and subjected to hastily organised training in little but the basic elements of their new craft.

The great majority of them were more than willing to serve; they were keen, they were intelligent, they would in time prove to be brave and hardy. But they still had a great deal to learn, especially about open warfare, as much of their preliminary training had been based on a belief that warfare in 1940 would not be markedly dissimilar to that of 1918. A large number of them also suffered from the great disadvantage that they did not believe that regular soldiers had much to teach them.

There was an enormous difference between the civilians who had flooded forward to join the British Army in 1914 and their sons and nephews who did the same in 1939, for the latter had read the books and seen the films which the embittered survivors of that first holocaust had wrung from their sufferings, and the message which stood forth from every page and every frame was that the High

Command from 1914 to 1918 had been incompetent, stupid, callous and unimaginative. Whatever the degree of fabrication or exaggeration in that judgment, there was a great tendency among the first of the hundreds of thousands of civilians who during the Second World War suddenly found themselves in uniform to accept it totally, to assume that the same situation applied now, and thus to regard the regular officers and men with whom they were thrown into contact with thinly veiled amusement, and to listen to their advice or instruction with scepticism. In their eyes, the regular officers were likely to be indolent, aristocratic and brainless, while the other ranks were assumed to have joined the army as a result of their inability to earn their livings amid the more rigorous competitions of civilian life. What could such people teach them that their own bright intelligences would not pick up on their own, probably more accurately and certainly more perceptively than their mentors would ever appreciate?

Evelyn Waugh wrote an account of his voyage aboard the converted merchantman *Glenroy* to the Middle East in February 1941, as a member of Number 8 Commando. The troop commanders were young, high-spirited and eager for adventure and one of the butts for their wit was the *Glenroy*'s captain, to whom they referred, to the extreme annoyance of the other naval officers aboard, as 'the old bugger on the roof'. But Captain Sir James Paget, whatever his shortness of temper or lack of social sophistication, was a long-serving, capable officer who knew exactly how to get a large ship filled with valuable men and materials from Greenock to Suez via the Cape of Good Hope, and 8 Commando should have been grateful to him for it. Instead they nicknamed him 'Booby', and were quite sure that given the shortest time to study the equipment on the bridge, they could do it themselves; and this was the attitude in which they would at first regard practically every professional officer placed in command of them.

The trouble was aggravated by the fact that many of the regular officers, especially at the top, felt a degree of sympathy with them. They had themselves fought in the Ypres and Somme trenches, had agreed with much that had been written between the two wars, and although they were determined themselves not to squander men's lives with the prodigality of Haig at Passchendaele or Mangin at Verdun, they were also aware that Government parsimony coupled perhaps with a degree of personal indolence (and who has worked so hard all his life that he knows for certain that he could not have worked harder?) might have left gaps in their professional competence which these brilliant young men would sense.

Some of them remembered 'Boy' Bradford who had won both the Victoria and Military Crosses by the age of twenty-four and before his death in 1917 had risen meteorically to the rank of brigadier-general. Perhaps one of these young prodigies would do the same?

The fact that by 1945 some of them would have done remarkably well by turning themselves into thorough-going professionals does not alter the fact that in 1941 they were still the veriest amateurs – dangerous amateurs, too, for some of them combined mistaken ideas of their own abilities with aristocratic, social or political influence enough to force those ideas through against the scepticism of more realistic professionals.

One of the results of this, in 1941, was the proliferation of 'private armies'.

There were undoubtedly times during the North African campaign – and to a lesser extent in the later campaigns in Europe and the Far East – when a few small unorthodox units, established upon unusual structures of rank and equipment, carried out valuable work behind enemy lines and thoroughly justified their independence of the more usual, tried and proved line of battle formations of Army Group, Army, Corps, Division, Brigade and Battalion. The Long Range Desert Group was arguably the most successful of these, but the Jock Column was the prototype and what was later to be called the Special Air Service the most enduring.

But there were other irregular units which had neither the professionalism of the Long Range Desert Group nor the necessity for existence of the first Jock Columns, and these were to drain off valuable men and materials from the regular formations by their demands, and lose a quantity of both through their inefficiency. The trouble was that service with them seemed so attractive, especially to the more romantically minded of the new arrivals in the theatre. They offered an escape from the regulation and discipline of battalion life, freedom for the young subaltern or private from the incessant disfavour of adjutant or regimental sergeant-major, and they were all at one time or another gilded with glamour. To have been able to boast in Cairo of taking part in some of the early Jock Column exploits could result in free drinks for an evening, and a place in the Long Range Desert Group was one for which captains would willingly drop to lieutenants and sergeants to privates; and those who failed to get into either, eagerly volunteered for any other formation which promised the same apparent freedom and cachet, however non-existent its record or doubtful its purpose.

From the point of view of the Cairo Headquarters, these formations were allowed to sprout because they seemed to promise a quick return for a minimal outlay, and if they had all performed as successfully as those first ones this could have been a profitable policy; but too often these *ad hoc* units were set up as a result of little but enthusiasm coupled with social salesmanship, and manned by youngsters with cheerfully vague notions of 'swanning around the blue', blowing up enemy dumps with loud bangs and spectacular pyrotechnics, and wearing unorthodox and somewhat flamboyant variations of uniform.

This matter of clothing was, on the surface, quite amusing, but in its way it was symptomatic of a malaise which had begun to infect the forces under Auchinleck's command, and would need the heat of action to burn it out.

The first troops to operate in the desert – the 11th Hussars, the R.H.A. batteries, the Rifle Brigade and K.R.R.C. – quickly found that many well-established ideas of uniform and equipment for hot climates were mistaken. Spine-pads, for instance, supposed to protect the nervous system from the harmful rays of the sun, gave the unfortunate wearers heat-stroke and those with sensitive skins an irritable rash. The solar topees may have given a little protection to the eyes against the desert glare, but proved impractical in the haste of battle, and were invariably crushed to pulp in the chaos of a lorry or truck body as the vehicle rocked and rolled over unmade or non-existent tracks.

Very quickly and to the dismay and frustration of the old-fashioned military medicos, the Australians first and the British afterwards demonstrated that after a comparatively short period of acclimatisation it was possible for men to work in the desert clad in nothing but shorts, boots and beret, with perhaps sun-glasses for those with sensitive eyes; and that in addition to turning mahogany they then exhibited all the other signs of robust good health.

But one very real problem was desert sores, which appeared when the cooler weather came especially around the neck and on wrists and hands. The collar of the serge battledress became impregnated with sand, and when the heat of exertion or midday caused sweat to run down the neck, chafing became unbearable and the tender skin raw and open; only the essential cleanliness of the desert prevented widespread infection. The solution was obviously to wear a scarf, and soon everyone was doing so – ranging from Paisley silks for the wealthy to soft yellow muslin made from illegally opened shell-dressings for those not so well-blessed. The more decorative scarves gave a welcome touch of colour to the drab desert scene and as long as the wearers still carried out their duties with professional efficiency, no one was bothered.

It was also quickly found that the serge battledress trousers were too hot during the day and too absorbent of sand, while khaki drill trousers or shorts were too light once the sun went down; so corduroys were increasingly worn 'up the blue' – and as army boots had a tendency to crunch gravel on a night patrol, these were often replaced by the rubber-soled boots, often of suede, which rejoiced in the name of 'brothel-creepers'.

Clad in beret (rust-coloured in the case of the 11th Hussars), khaki shirt with silk muffler, leather jerkin, corduroy trousers and suede boots, the old desert hand would still bring an admirable efficiency to his duties, an expertise with every weapon in his armoury against the enemy, and a tough realism to the business of war. But his appearance was seized upon with delight by the new arrivals, who added sheepskin coats and eau-de-Cologne, and once they were well sunburned believed – human nature being what it is – that they would be just as effective soldiers, when their chance came, as those they emulated.

In the meantime, a trip behind the Wire with this or that demolition squadron or somebody else's reconnaissance column (usually called a 'shufti-job') would give them experience, and also save them from the dull routine of drills, weapon-training, map-reading and vehicle maintenance under the instructions of those unimaginative fellows at the depot. One series of totally abortive coastal raids carried out in this spirit was most aptly code-named after the famous string of theatrical farces which had run during the 1930s at the Aldwych – Rookery, Nook, Cuckoo – and many of those who took part were to spend the rest of the war in German prison camps wondering what had gone wrong; of the remainder, some died, some obtained desk jobs on the Staff but the rest in time learned what soldiering was about and duly fulfilled their role. As it happened, their sheepskin coats proved excellent value, eau-de-Cologne was found beneficial for treating cuts and abrasions and if inhaled deeply during the stunning heat of a July midday, remarkably revivifying. But neither would replace professionalism.

One place where there were no silk scarves or eau-de-Cologne was in Tobruk. By July, the defences were firm, the tasks understood and accepted, the techniques of living and fighting in severely cramped and arid circumstances both well developed and well learned, and morale as high as anywhere in the Middle East – truly high, too; not just the journalist's delight of wise-cracking optimism and sing-songs around the camp fire, but the mood of grim determination which comes to men who have been told by their commander, 'There'll be no Dunkirk here. If we have to get out, we shall fight our way out. There is to be no surrender or retreat,' and have sufficient knowledge of and respect for him to know that he meant it.

Major-General Leslie Morshead was now in sole command of the Tobruk Fortress, Major-General Lavarack having left to command the Australians in Syria the day after Rommel's first attempt to take

Tobruk at Easter. Morshead was a man in the great civilian-soldier tradition of Australia's famous First World War general, Sir John Monash; a schoolmaster in 1914, a battalion commander in 1918 with the C.M.G., D.S.O. and Légion d'honneur, a shipping executive in 1939 and now in 1941 a major-general holding the most important Allied command in the Middle East after Auchinleck's.

For Britain, it was extremely fortunate that circumstances had combined to bring Morshead to that place at that time, for in addition to being extremely tough in both mind and body (he was known to his troops as 'Ming the Merciless') he was also highly intelligent and very perceptive. For instance, he had very quickly appreciated that however well conceived and soundly constructed the original Italian defences might be – and manned by Australians commanded by Morshead they were to prove very effective – they were essentially static, and if looked upon solely as a defence perimeter, could be cracked open by enemy pressure if this were allowed to come too close.

The defences must therefore be regarded as bases for offensive action and the no-man's-land beyond – as wide as it could be made and dominated by the Australians – was to be the only recognised perimeter.

'I was determined to make no-man's-land *our* land,' Morshead wrote later, and a keynote to his attitude was revealed by his reaction to a newspaper headline declaring 'Tobruk can take it!'

'We're not here to "take it,"' he announced angrily. 'We're here to "give it."'

At the beginning, of course, Rommel had been the first to attack, but after the initial attempt to rush the port, his troops found themselves up against defences growing in depth, manned by infantry who to their astonishment did not surrender as soon as the panzers had broken through, but stayed where they were and destroyed the German infantry and artillery crews trying to follow up the armoured spearhead. Even in the rear areas, the few panzers which got through found themselves furiously attacked by troops normally considered non-combatant, such as batmen, cooks and clerks, who had been told in no uncertain terms that whatever their nominal appointment their basic duty was to fight the enemy wherever they found him and never easily to yield a yard of ground. As a result of such Draconian commandments, many of the Afrika Korps troops who had taken part in the battle of the salient at the end of April regarded it as the most bitterly fought battle of the war.

In general, the Tobruk perimeter was held by Australian infantry, while the reserve positions and the vital defence of the port and harbour installations were in the hands of British tank crews and gunners. This was a combination which in the event proved very satisfactory, though it was the result of historical accident. The Australians had been the only combatant troops to arrive in Tobruk in large and still well-organised formations; the remainder had consisted either of base troops who had been sent up to administer the port after it had fallen to O'Connor's advance, or British and Indian troops who had avoided capture and made their way back piecemeal to Tobruk after the débâcle of Rommel's first advance.

When Morshead and Lavarack first surveyed their command after its hasty construction during the first two weeks in April, they discovered that of the 40,000-odd souls then in Tobruk and its immediate environs, some 15,000 were unlikely to contribute much towards its defence and should be moved out as soon as possible. Chief among these were 5,000 prisoners, but the majority of Corps troops – Ordnance, Pay, even Medical – could leave, and there was not even much point in keeping a strong complement of transport personnel as no one would be going anywhere. Those that did remain, however, were to be prepared to fight – and some Service Corps companies later fought so well as infantry that they won the right to retain the bayonets with which they had equipped themselves, and which are normally not carried by such second-echelon troops.

By the end of April, the garrison had been stripped down to 23,000 men, all armed and capable of fighting, of whom about 15,000 were Australian, 500 Indian and the rest British. The Australians were the men of the 9th Division – the 20th, 24th and 26th Brigades – plus those of the 18th Brigade from the 7th Division (whose other brigades were in Syria) together with divisional engineers, several anti-tank gun units, one artillery unit and an anti-aircraft battery. The British were the tank crews, the majority of the field and anti-aircraft gunners, a third of the anti-tank gunners and a battalion of the ubiquitous machine-gunners of the Royal Northumberland Fusiliers. The Indians occasionally manned the line with the Australians, and they played a vital role in the night patrolling.

Not surprisingly, garrison spirits had been somewhat cast down by the failures of both the *Brevity* and *Battleaxe* operations, so in order to keep everyone's mind off more depressing matters, Morshead immediately instigated a programme of extensive fortification and patrolling. The original Italian complement for each concrete-lined post in the outer defences had been two officers and twenty-five men with an orthodox scale of weapons; now the posts were meticulously cleansed of all the debris and filth of the previous battles and manned by half that number, but with their fire-power doubled and sometimes trebled by captured, reserviced and constantly checked and maintained Italian weapons. This was the Red Line, held by fire-power, continuously strengthened by the construction of new intermediate posts, and covered by an ever-widening band of mines.

Two miles behind it was the Blue Line, a series of platoon-held strong-points with a selection of heavier weapons including mortars, each surrounded by an anti-tank ditch and a zareba of barbed wire, its fire covering the wider and thicker minefields which by mid-summer extended forward almost as far as the Red Line. Behind them were the main field artillery batteries which it was their principal duty to protect, while the guns in their turn would protect the infantry from any panzers which reached this far – though their chances of doing so now were slim in view of the spreading mine-fields. These became eventually so omnipresent that a danger arose of the engineers losing track of them; before the end of the siege, to Morshead's fury, some Allied transport was blown up by Allied mines.

The whole of the defence system was dotted with what became known as the 'Bush Artillery' – Italian 37mm. and 75mm. anti-tank and field guns (there were even a couple of 105mm. guns in the coastal battery) which had been dragged from their original positions, or those in which they had been abandoned, cleaned, serviced and crewed by hard-swearing but enthusiastic infantrymen after but the briefest instruction from helpful gunners, who then retired, amused and somewhat shaken by the unorthodox fire instructions used.

'When they want to increase the elevation', one awed artillery subaltern later told his colonel, 'they say – "Cock the bastard up a bit!" – and the usual fire order is – "Let 'er go, mate!"'

At the beginning, the method of sighting was to peer along the barrel, for most of the Italian artillerymen had at least taken the precaution of destroying the sights before abandoning their pieces five months before, and despite this rough and ready method there is good reason to believe that one of the shells fired in this way killed General Prittwitz during the first enemy approach along the Derna road. By July, however, quite a number of sets of sights had been brought in at the earnest request of these amateur gunners by their infantry friends on patrol, for enemy gun-positions were a favourite objective, especially if they had been plastering the Red or Blue Lines.

The patrolling in no-man's-land went on night after night, and during the day when dust-storms were so thick that the enemy could be closing up unobserved. There were also continuous patrols between the Red Line posts, known as 'Love and Kisses' patrols. Pairs of men from each post would move out at given intervals to an agreed half-way point, where two sticks had been left; many factors could delay a team and the other had no wish to wait around, so if the first team to arrive were from one of the alternate 'Kisses' posts they would leave the sticks crossed. When the other team arrived they would know that their opposite numbers had been and gone and would leave the sticks parallel – the 'Love' position. If one team found the sticks in the same position three times running, there would be some urgent telephoning when they returned to their own post.

Other patrols watched the anti-tank ditches and the wire fences, while 200 or 300 yards further out patrols consisting of an N.C.O. and perhaps half a dozen men would lie in an observation or listening post, or cover a 'beat' of perhaps half a mile to give warning of any large-scale enemy approach or to shoot up any prowling enemy patrols.

These were the defensive patrols; but it was the offensive patrols which kept no-man's land under Australian domination and won for Tobruk its special fame. These could vary from a small patrol of just an officer or sergeant with ten men raiding a gun position, shooting up the crew, wrecking the gun with a grenade down the barrel and removing the sights, to a company-size attack taken out in carriers and accompanied by tanks to destroy a known German or Italian post.

Before a raid the men would have a hot meal and a tot of rum; then, dressed in one-piece patrol overalls reinforced at knee and elbow and either with soft-soled boots or with socks over regulation boots, they would set off, each man with two or three grenades, many armed with Tommy-guns, at least one Bren per section and the rest with rifle, bayonet or club. There was a great deal of personal selection and specialisation in the weapons each man carried, but the commando knife which was now coming into use so much in raids in Europe does not seem to have gained much favour among the Australians. The Indians were prepared to use the knife (although unfortunately there were no Gurkhas present to display their expertise with the kukri) but they patrolled in bare feet or made themselves sandals soled with strips of old tyres, moving down like ghosts upon their unsuspecting prey. One heart-stopping manoeuvre of theirs, to obviate the danger of killing the wrong people, was for two to creep up behind a sitting or standing sentry and while one pinned the subject's arms to his sides with a sudden embrace, the other slid a hand over his shoulder and felt for the collar badge. The only survivors of this chilling experience were Australians wearing their sun-burst badge, who then felt a re-assuring pat on the shoulder perhaps accompanied by a sibilant 'O.K. Aussie', release of the embrace and through the tumult of thudding heart an impression of flocks of large, dangerous birds flitting away into the darkness. One night, the Indians found three Italians asleep by their gun . . . and cut the throats of the two on the outside, deliberately leaving the one in the middle to a dire awakening.

Often the patrols would carry mines and plant them well to the rear of the German or Italian forward posts thereby catching the transport as it came up the following day, but on one occasion a large patrol with a high proportion of Sappers went out, lifted nearly 500 mines from a newly laid German field, brought them back and used them to cover a gap in front of their own southern sector. Mines were also taken at first from Italian fields, but the best hauls were made as a result of observation during the day of new Italian mine-laying, followed by a raid that night with the object of collecting the stocks as yet unlaid; it saved trouble, and occasional casualties.

Sometimes the patrols would lie up all day at carefully selected points, waiting for the enemy working parties or patrols to move at night, and ambush them . . . and sometimes they would themselves be caught by German patrols trying the same trick. Every night was punctuated by bomb-blast and split open with machine-gun and rifle fire . . . and every morning there would be more dead bodies in one uniform or another to lie rotting in the sun until either they were recovered and buried, or they burst and stank.

During the day, for everyone in Tobruk, the main curse was dust; and after dust the plagues of flies and fleas which inhabited every building, shack, strong-point or trench like a perpetual fifth column. The dust at Tobruk was as pervasive and all-encompassing as the mud had been at Passchendaele twenty-four years before, and still lives in the memory of every man who stayed there for more than a week. So much had happened within the confines of the Fortress even before the siege began, and so many men were now crammed inside it, that the surface clay was ground to powder even without the explosion of shell or vibration of gun which now pulverised deeper or shook more thoroughly. On average, at least every fourth day the wind blew and whipped up thick clouds in which men coughed and cursed and choked and wondered if they would ever breathe cool air again, and had hardly enough moisture left in their mouths to spit it out when evening came and the wind died.

Even when the wind dropped, the dust was still everywhere . . . in the food, in the weapons and weapon-pits, in boots, half-filling pockets, between the threads of shirts, under arms and under eyelids. You ate it, breathed it, rubbed it into your hair and scratched it into your flea-bites. And every time you slapped a fly to death, its squashed remains were coated in it.

Few men ever really gave up the fight against the flies, despite their continuous, monotonous pestering; perhaps because they gave you some peace at night (no one ever found out where they disappeared to) and thus you recovered your fury against them. During the day, they were there all the time, covering your food as soon as it arrived, accompanying it to your lips and into your mouth if you weren't careful; settling on every bead of sweat that appeared on your face, neck, hands or legs and trying to suck damp from the corners of your eyes. One particular brand would settle on your arms and legs and if you didn't slap it away quickly, seemed able to sink fangs into your flesh, brace its forelegs like a horse and rock on them until it had torn a lump away . . . at which all its friends would swoop down on the blood.

What was astonishing was that in addition to retaining their sanity, the Rats of Tobruk, as they were soon styled, remained in excellent health. Of course, the majority were young and in the prime of life and had been brought to a degree of fitness by army discipline and training before coming to the desert which, in the case of the British, they may not have known before – but one extra factor which was happily not present, the mosquito, could have nullified all natural advantages as it did later in the Far East theatre. In Tobruk, however, there was little enough water of any sort, so no stagnant pools and thus no malaria.

What water there was, either from the condensation plants by the harbour for those in the vicinity, or from artesian wells, was in short but regular supply – three-quarters of a gallon per man per day for all purposes – either brackish or chlorinated in taste and often medicinal in effect; an effect which if not carefully controlled could lead, ironically, to minor outbreaks of dysentery. After a time, the taste-buds adapted to tea reeking of sulphur or chlorine, but coffee was always a disaster – and the Germans who, after all, were sharing this particular aspect of the Tobruk siege were increasingly sardonic about it.

'Do not bother to try to make coffee,' one of them wrote. 'Just heat the water. The result will look like coffee anyway . . . and taste like sulphur, which every drink does out here!'

Chester Wilmot, an Australian journalist in Tobruk, recorded an occasion when someone arrived from Alexandria with a bottle of 'sweet' water which, after careful sampling by a select band, was shared out among them. Everyone drank his tot neat.

Food during the first few months had consisted of little but bread and bully beef with occasional tinned bacon or herrings; no butter, a little margarine but hardly any sugar or jam and no fresh vegetables at all. Ascorbic acid tablets were issued to combat vitamin deficiency but as soon as the siege settled into a pattern and shipping convoys could run with some degree of regularity, the dietary experts were called in and matters improved. Lime juice came up (and even the Australians would drink it in the absence of beer), fruit and vegetables usually tinned but occasionally fresh, and sometimes there was even real meat. Oddly enough, as the siege went on and boredom began to take its insidious hold, food became of little interest or importance (so long, of course, as there was enough to stave off hunger) and by August many of the front line posts held stocks of tinned bacon or fish because no one could be bothered to open or prepare it. So long as there was a good hot meal at night, the troops would exist during the day on bread and margarine, jam and cheese, washed down with chlorinated water.

What was essential, in almost everyone's mind, was the supply of cigarettes. The issue was fifty a week to each man and after June they were able to buy another fifty from the organised canteen, while the Australian Comforts Fund provided more (when the Navy could bring it in) and from the beginning, to the enormous appreciation of the British troops, it was agreed that everyone in Tobruk was Australian as far as Comforts were concerned.

Living conditions were rougher for the infantry than for the gunners or tank crews, but on the other hand the gunners – especially the ones around the harbour – were bombed and shelled much more often. There was no refuge in the Fortress from Rommel's heavy artillery, and his airfields at El Adem and Sidi Rezegh were so close that sometimes the infantry could hear the bombers take off and follow their entire flight until they had dropped their load over the harbour. Once Rommel had accepted that time must pass before his ground troops could hope to overrun the garrison, he concentrated all possible effort on disrupting the supply lines, and in his opinion the easiest place to do this was at the disembarkation point; as the months went by, the number of wrecks in the harbour grew, the devastation around it spread – but the anti-aircraft batteries thickened and the barrage which greeted the Luftwaffe pilots above the port claimed more and more victims.

At first, the raids had been carried out by dive-bombers in daylight, confident that history would be repeated and the anti-aircraft crews would take cover as soon as the howl of the Stuka dive reached its peak – but they were defeated by the realities of the situation. As there was nowhere for the besieged to run to in the long term, there was no psychological justification for running in the short term. So the gunners stayed at their posts, followed the dive-bombers down all the way and discovered to their astonishment that this was the safer procedure to follow, for it put the equally astonished pilots off their aim and eventually caused them to drop their bombs from a much greater height.

The Luftwaffe then tried different methods – high-level bombing, low-level strafing, both at once, low-level minelaying – and inevitably they scored some successes at the beginning of each new technique. But the officer commanding the artillery, Brigadier J. N. Slater, brought an immense enthusiasm to his command together with a great deal of originality, and so inspired his crews that each man came to regard the conflict as a direct contest between his own team and the Luftwaffe's, whose separate flights and indeed aircraft he quickly began to recognise. The gunners also began to appreciate that basic element of conflict which is so often overlooked in the heat of battle – that the enemy has problems too; and they planned to increase them.

They would vary the height of the barrage – one day at 4,000 feet, the next at 6,000 feet – and when the pilots learned to wait and not to come in until they had judged what that day's height was to be, the gunners mixed the heights so that although the concentration was not great at any one level, it was distributed up through a band. They learned to swing the block of the barrage together so that a pilot hoping to slip along the outer edge to find a place to dive in underneath would suddenly find himself in the middle with shells bursting above, below and all around. And when fighters tried to streak in low across the desert, they put up a barrage of Bofors and Breda fire along fixed lines, quite confident that they were not spraying their own infantry as the arcs of fire had been clearly worked out beforehand.

There was little the troops could do to protect themselves against long-range shelling except dig themselves fox-holes, reinforce their sangars or shelters with concrete slabs, steel beams from destroyed buildings and sandbags – or stake out claims in some of the deep caves with which the area had been honeycombed by the Italians. Quite a high proportion of the Rats of Tobruk lived in holes in the ground.

Protection of the Fortress from the land was therefore in the hands of the Australian and Indian infantry, and from the air in those of the mainly British artillery. From the sea, except for two 105mm. Italian guns, a few light guns and some Brens mounted for the protection of bathing parties, the defence was the responsibility of the Royal Navy – and as Tobruk also relied entirely upon the Navy for their supplies, the role played by the Inshore Squadron in the epic of the siege was critical.

Destroyers carried out the greater part of what became known as the 'Spud Run', for their advantages of both speed and fire-power took them quickly in and out of the danger zones and gave them good protection at the critical times, but a whole flotilla of smaller craft – lighters, South African whalers, captured Italian schooners

– all made their vital contributions. Every ship which visited Tobruk took in stores and took out men – in May 2,593 tons in and 5,918 men out, in June nearly 3,000 tons in and 5,148 men out. From July until September the majority of the men evacuated were wounded, but the supply tonnage mounted and on two occasions the petrol tanker *Pass of Balmaha* made the run, loaded with 750 tons of the vitally needed but appallingly dangerous fuel.

The Spud Run was in itself a very risky operation, without the additional hazard of a highly volatile cargo to escort. Chester Wilmot described a trip he made aboard the destroyer H.M.S. *Decoy* towards the end of the siege, with two other destroyers in company, each carrying some fifty tons of freight and about a hundred replacement or reinforcement troops.

They had left Alexandria early in the morning, were abreast of Mersa Matruh by 1530 and two hours later level with Sidi Barrani but well out to sea to avoid enemy aircraft based on Bardia. All hands were at Action Stations when the first aircraft appeared – to deep sighs of relief when these proved to be escorting Hurricanes – but speed was increased to thirty-two knots and the cramped and crowded decks throbbed as the ships tore through the water.

Air cover remained with them until just before dusk but then had to leave and the ships then ploughed steadily on for another four hours under a silver but waning moon, their crews praying that the enemy aircraft would stay out of sight of their phosphorescent wake until the moon had gone down. But with half an hour to go, the Stukas caught them and the next twenty miles were a journey of wide sweeps and sudden turns as the dive-bombers swooped and the destroyers twisted away. The decks became a chaos of sliding crates and ammunition boxes, of loose stretchers from a consignment which broke away, of cursing soldiers hanging on to stanchions and rails and equally vehement sailors intent on their duties of working the ship and fighting off the attackers.

At last the Stukas left to refill their bomb-bays, the two dim, shaded lights which marked the entrance to Tobruk harbour glowed greenly ahead, engine speed was cut, and slowly and with almost no wake the ships glided between them past a pair of blackly looming wrecks, and as *Decoy* slowed to a halt, two barges and two launches materialised from the shore and came alongside. Immediately, a frenzy of activity seized all aboard, but as most were old hands at this exercise it was an ordered frenzy. Troops clambered over the side, pitching their kitbags ahead of them; unloading parties demonstrated an enviable expertise as they manhandled crates and boxes, a tank track, a spare lorry engine, a new barrel for a Bofors, the stretchers, over the side and safely into a barge; then, from the other side, the wounded began their often pain-wracked lift up and on to the decks, helped by firm but surprisingly gentle hands. And by this time, the Stukas were back, knowing full well that their quarry was now in the tight confines of the harbour and that only the barrage could keep them away:

One stick of bombs screams down on the south shore of the harbour; the next is closer – in the water 500 yards away. The old hands continue working, unworried, but some of the new ones, like us, pause momentarily, shrinking down behind the destroyer's after-screen. From the man with the megaphone comes a sharp rebuke – 'What are you stopping for? Those bloody bombs are nothing to do with you.'[1]

The last man goes overboard, the barges pull away, the engines throb and the destroyer backs, turns and disappears into the blackness. Fifty tons of cargo and a hundred men disembarked, twenty stretcher cases and half a dozen walking wounded taken aboard; in and out in under half an hour.

Such episodes occurred every night during the dark period of the moon, but once the anti-aircraft batteries had demonstrated their ability to keep at bay the majority of the bombers, then the smaller, slower craft joined in, slipping into Tobruk just before dawn, lying close alongside the battered jetty or by one of the wrecks which had been roughly converted into a landing stage all day under heavy camouflage-netting while the cargoes were unloaded, and sailing again as soon as it was dark.

These craft were skippered and manned by a breed of staunch individualists who refused to be daunted by the enemy or restricted in any way by Authority. Their backgrounds were various and rarely respectable, their uniforms picturesque but practical, and their armaments unorthodox and usually of foreign make. The most famous was an R.N.R. lieutenant known as 'Pedlar' Palmer who at one time had commanded a company of Chinese Lancers in the Shanghai Volunteer Reserve, and who now ran a weekly service from Mersa Matruh to Tobruk in a captured Italian schooner, the *Maria Giovanna*. His navigation was of a rough and ready type, and after a wide sweep out to sea he would approach Tobruk preferably during the late evening so that his objective could be suitably illuminated by both bomb-flashes and anti-aircraft fire – through which he was quite content to sail unconcerned. On one dark night there was no air raid and he waxed indignant.

'How do they expect me to get in when there's no moon and no bloody air raid?'

The Italians got him in the end by fixing dummy lights about fifteen miles east of the Tobruk harbour entrance and the *Maria Giovanna* ended her days on the rocks with her skipper and crew in various prison camps; but 'Pedlar' had by this time taken some twenty cargoes into the Fortress and claimed to have shot down three aircraft with his motley collection of machine-guns. His Distinguished Service Cross was well earned.

As for the enemy, by midsummer the Italians were regarded by most with such amused affection that their working parties would be left in peace until they came too close, then sprayed with random machine-gun fire to make them retreat. The nearest Italian posts were visited most nights, and wrecked or despoiled with such regularity that they were soon abandoned; only if a prisoner were needed or if something had happened to anger the Australians in the sector would much blood be shed.

But the atmosphere along German sectors was different. Here, growing professionalism on both sides fostered a competition which relentlessly added to the casualty lists. Around the borders of the salient especially, the watch was never-ending, the thump of mortar-bomb, the crack of the sniper's rifle a continual punctuation. The commander of the 2nd Battalion of the German 115th Motorised Infantry Regiment, Major Ballerstedt, wrote:

> Enemy snipers achieve astounding results. They shoot at anything they recognize. Several N.C.O.s of the battalion have been shot through the head with the first bullet while making observations in the front line. Protruding sights in gun directors have been shot off, observation slits and loopholes have been fired on, and hit, as soon as they were seen to be in use (i.e. when the light background became dark). For this reason loopholes must be kept plugged with a wooden plug to be taken out when used so that they always show dark.[2]

On the other hand, such efficiency bred respect, and the adversity in which both sides dwelt produced a degree of fellow-feeling. After one particularly vicious battle at the beginning of August when a force of over a hundred Australians had been driven back to their starting-point, it was realised in the morning that more than thirty were unaccounted for and some of these must be lying wounded out in the minefields. In order to do something to help them, one of the Australian sergeants volunteered to be driven out sitting on the bonnet of a truck and waving a huge Red Cross flag, though no one had attempted such a move before. Some 400 yards short of the nearest German post, the truck stopped and the sergeant, accompanied by a stretcher-bearer and their Roman Catholic padre, walked forward another 100 yards until a German emerged from the post carrying a similar Red Cross flag and shouted to them that they were entering the minefield.

Two German engineers with mine-detectors then appeared and guided an officer and a German doctor towards them, and during the next half hour they all worked together to bring out four wounded and fifteen dead Australians, and the German doctor told them that already four other wounded Australians were being looked after in the German aid posts.

> When the last of our dead had been brought to us, the lieutenant told me we were not to move until they were all back in the post and had taken in their flag. He went back; his men went below. He lowered his flag and I lowered mine. I saluted him, and he saluted back, but he gave me the salute of the Reichswehr, not of the Nazis. Our armistice was over.[3]

In some parts of the sector, especially across and east of the El Adem road, a virtual armistice existed for two hours every night while men climbed out of their trenches to stretch their aching limbs, while water and food was brought up, the filth and debris of the day cleared and some relief from the heat enjoyed during the blessed cool of the first few hours of darkness; there would be little firing, and that generally vague and unaimed, and an unspoken agreement existed that this time should not be used for patrolling or even for swift preparation for any especially aggressive operation. That should wait until the signal was given to end the nightly peace – a burst of tracer fired vertically up into the sky, usually about midnight. By such unspoken agreements, life was made just a little less intolerable and respect between two opposing armies deepened.

Whether Rommel knew of such incidents and attitudes is difficult to say; one side of his nature would undoubtedly have sympathised, but on the other hand, the capture of Tobruk had become something of an obsession with him and his singlemindedness in such circumstances might have meant that any hint of compromise in its immediate achievement would provoke him to fury.

His position in North Africa had improved considerably, to a great extent, ironically enough, as a result of Halder's efforts to curb his activities. The arrival of General Gause and the posse of Staff officers had precipitated the change, for not only Rommel but also the Italian commanders had had no warning of the move and were immediately suspicious. Gariboldi as Italian Commander-in-Chief, North Africa (Comandante Superiore), protested vigorously at the introduction of yet another German general into his area of operations without consultation, and Generale Ugo Cavallero, the Chief of Staff in Rome (Comandante Supremo), was quite willing to forward the complaints to Berlin.

Although Hitler's attitude was one of apparent unconcern,

Halder was well aware of the high regard in which the Führer held Rommel and knew that he must act with caution; his explanation to Cavallero was subdued and couched in conciliatory tones so that the Italian Chief of Staff, who had his own ends to further and one important piece of inside knowledge, seized upon it, ordered Gariboldi to withdraw his objection and then, to everybody's surprise, proposed the establishment of a Group Headquarters in Africa to control the activities of all military formations, both Italian and German, and insisted that Rommel, despite his comparative lack of seniority, should command it.

He then drew Gariboldi's teeth by revealing to him that he was about to be recalled to Rome and replaced by Generale d'Armata Ettore Bastico, a close friend of Il Duce's and a man of such autocratic demeanour that he had made himself highly unpopular in practically all military circles; both Gariboldi and Cavallero would be delighted to watch him being ridden over by Rommel in one of his more implacable moods. As for Halder, he well knew that an appeal to Hitler to stop the promotion of a German general – especially one who was in many ways a protégé – to overall operational command in a theatre held until then to have been of major Italian concern, would fall on very deaf ears. The only success which Halder was able to snatch from the ruin of his plans to bring Rommel to heel was to insist that the new Army Group be called Panzergruppe Afrika and not, as was at first suggested, Panzergruppe Rommel.

Panzergruppe Headquarters were first of all set up at Beda Littoria, but Rommel quickly had them moved up to Ain el Gazala, with Advanced Headquarters – where, needless to say, he was to spend most of his time – further forward at Gambut, between Tobruk and Bardia. From there, by August he commanded all troops in the operational area and had also assumed territorial and administrative responsibilities as head of the 'Marmarica Command'. Considering that he had arrived six months before in charge of little but a single light division and that in mid-June he had been battling to defend his position as commander of all German troops in North Africa, his position now in command of all Axis ground troops facing the original enemy, Britain, was a remarkable achievement; and one revealing talents not always included among those expected in a plain, bluff, straightforward soldier. As Halder's fury increased, so did his sense of personal risk, for Rommel was proving a far more dangerous opponent in the convoluted world of Axis military politics than had been anticipated.

Promotion for Rommel had, of course, followed the extra responsibilities, but with the peculiar inconsequence which warfare brings about, Rommel first heard that he was a Panzergeneral from friends writing to congratulate him, having themselves heard it on the Berlin radio. It was mid-August before full confirmation of his new appointment arrived, and by that time the forces under his command, despite Halder's continual injunctions, had grown considerably and were in the process of redistribution and intensive training – especially the German formations, whatever their experience or prestige.

Generalleutnant Neumann-Sylkow's 15th Panzer Division was now complete, based on the coast at Marsa Belafarit and training hard in the desert to the south, while 5th Light Division had been built up, reorganised and renamed 21st Panzer Division, and was being put through its paces by its new commander, Generalleutnant Johan von Ravenstein, in the area just west of Bardia. Each division consisted of a panzer regiment of two battalions, each regiment with about 170 panzers – Marks II, III and IV, and a few captured Matildas – three battalions of infantry, an anti-tank battalion, a regiment of artillery, a reconnaissance battalion and the usual complement of engineer and administrative troops. These two divisions comprised D.A.K. – Deutsches Afrika Korps – Rommel's original responsibility in North Africa, now under command of Generalleutnant Ludwig Cruewell.

Another German formation which began arriving at the end of August and was eventually to win considerable renown as the 90th Light Division, was for the moment known by the cumbersome title of Division Afrika zur besondern Verfügung (shortened, not all that conveniently, to Div zbV Afrika), commanded by Generalleutnant Max Sümmermann and consisting of two infantry regiments, an engineer battalion, an anti-tank battalion and something called a 'Sonderverband' – which seems to translate most nearly to 'Special Service Unit'. What duties were intended for this formation remains uncertain, but some idea of the flavour of the Div zbV Afrika in its earliest days may be gleaned from the fact that one of its infantry regiments, Afrika Regiment 361, consisted mostly of ex-members of the Foreign Legion who had been collected during the sweep through France and had now come to Africa accompanied by the grim hint that this might be their last chance to rehabilitate themselves as 'good Germans'. As between them they had had considerable experience of desert fighting and their service for France had done nothing to promote pro-British sentiments, they were to prove a very valuable addition to Rommel's strength.

Finally, partly as a result of the sweeping success of German arms in Russia and the widening horizons for Hitler's ambition as the Wehrmacht swept down towards the Caucasus, opening his eyes to the possibilities of further advances down through Iran or perhaps

Anatolia to attack the Nile Delta from the north, the Führer ordered that a train of siege artillery was to be sent to Rommel in order to allow him to reduce Tobruk, thus freeing Panzergruppe Afrika to form the western arm of a pincer attack which would completely demolish the only hostile army left in the field after the obviously imminent collapse of Russia. This group, known to the Germans as Artillery Command 104 and to the British when they learned of it as 'Rommel's travelling circus', was centred at Belhammed five miles to the south-east of the Tobruk perimeter, and commanded by Generalmajor Karl Böettcher. It consisted of five artillery units and its armament included nine 210mm. howitzers, twelve French 100mm. guns and forty-six French 150mms, thirty-six Italian 105mms, eighty-four Italian 149mms, and twelve naval 120mm. guns. Once German thoroughness had mastered the problems posed by the diversity of ammunition, the train could lay down a most formidable barrage.

As for the Italian formations under Rommel's direct command in Marmarica, these were the four infantry divisions Bologna, Pavia, Brescia and Savona which made up Army Corps XXI commanded by Generale di Corpo d'Armata Enea Navarrini, three of which were used in the static investment of Tobruk, while Savona was disposed along the frontier. Here they held a line of well-prepared positions stretching from Sollum down past Sidi Omar, buttressed by German artillery posts including several of the precious 88mms and a large number of the salvaged Italian guns, all sheltered behind local and separate minefields while a further wide belt covered the front as a whole. And Major the Reverend Bach and his men still held Halfaya Pass.

Back in Cyrenaica was assembled the only Italian force with any pretensions to independence of Rommel, the Corpo d'Armata di Manovra XX – the Mobile Army Corps, known as C.A.M. – under command of Generale Gastone Gambara, consisting of one armoured division, the Divisione Corazzata Ariete, and a motorised division, the Divisione Motorizzata Trieste. Although the Comandante Superiore, Ettore Bastico (already nicknamed 'Bombastico' by Rommel's Staff), had intimated that it was never to be embroiled in any action without his own express permission, Generale Gambara was both experienced and realistic enough to know quite well where his orders would come from if emergency threatened.

Rommel, of course, was not to be satisfied for long with nothing but training programmes to occupy either his troops or his military ardour, and by early September he and the equally eager von Ravenstein had between them concocted a plan for a raid along the edge of the Escarpment towards what Intelligence believed to be a large British supply dump, possibly set up in preparation for a future attack. There were other reasons, too, for suspecting the British of aggressive intentions; until July, the two Afrika Korps Reconnaissance Battalions, numbers 33 and 3, had experienced no problems in keeping deep watches respectively in front of the Sollum–Sidi Omar line and along the open flank to the south, but recently their activities had been greatly curbed by the appearance opposite them of armoured cars of the 11th Hussars augmented by 4th South African Armoured Car Regiment, and some of the mobile columns which even they were beginning to call 'Jockolmnen'. The British air strength had grown considerably of late, too – thus even further blinding the view across the frontier – and their ground forces had reputedly grown even more. It was therefore imperative that information about British preparations be obtained, and if a solid blow could be delivered against such preparations at the same time, so much the better.

Operation Sommernachtstraum began at dawn on September 14th, as three columns from 21st Panzer Division moved through and past the Sollum–Sidi Omar line into Egypt, the northern column accompanied by Rommel himself, perched high up on the edge of the sunshine roof of his Mammoth, looking, as his A.D.C., Schmidt, recalled, 'like a U-boat commander on his bridge'. Battle Group Schütte was aimed along the line of the Escarpment, Battle group Stephan parallel and some ten miles south along the Bir Sheferzen–El Hamra track, and Reconnaissance Battalion 3 down along the Wire with instructions to raise as much dust as possible, thus creating the impression that the whole of the Afrika Korps was on the move. A large force of lorries followed the two main columns in order to collect the loot.

By midday the pincers had closed around the location of the presumed dump, to find little but a few empty bully-beef tins and some even emptier beer-bottles ('I noticed suddenly that my mouth was parched,' wrote Schmidt later) but one of the small outriding units came racing in with a captured lorry and its disconsolate driver and companion, which examination revealed to be the orderly room staff and truck of the 4th South African Armoured Car Regiment. The lorry was full of quite important documents and cipher material which von Ravenstein delightedly declared a prize quite sufficient to justify the raid on its own.

Rommel, of course, was by no means satisfied and urged the columns further on into Egypt, where they came up against ever-increasing opposition as the armoured cars and Jock Columns fell back upon the Support Group bases. By mid-afternoon both Schütte and Stephan columns were halted, and indeed out of petrol, south-east of Sofafi, where they were found by R.A.F. and

S.A.A.F. fighters and bombers and heavily attacked. As they were also being shelled by the Support Group 25-pounders, they experienced a very uncomfortable time during which they suffered some seventy casualties, including Rommel's driver, and a sliver of steel took off the heel of Rommel's boot.

The bombing and shelling continued and it was not until almost dusk that the columns were refuelled and could turn and make off back to the frontier – and it was during this race to the Wire that a front tyre of Rommel's Mammoth, which had been grazed by another splinter, chose to go flat. There was unspoken agreement among all the senior officers in the vehicle that the job of repairing it should fall to the A.D.C. and for some hours Leutnant Schmidt wrestled with the gigantic wheel while his Commander-in-Chief and staff sat around watching, and the wireless operator gloomily reported chit-chat on the British radio as the vehicles of the Support Group closed up. Rommel dared not send out a cry for help as this would undoubtedly be picked up by the enemy, and he had enough respect for the 11th Hussars to know that they would correctly interpret the situation and move very rapidly indeed to exploit it.

Map 3　*Operation Sommernachstraum*: September 14th–15th, 1941

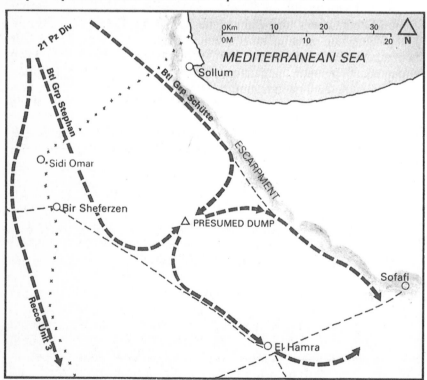

Eventually, with Rommel holding a shaded torch and other seniors helping as best they could ('which really just complicated the task,' as Schmidt rather sulkily reported) the wheel was fixed and, with Rommel driving, the Mammoth tore back through the gap in the Wire, to the evident astonishment of some Italian and German pioneers nearby. It had been a near thing, and Midsummer Night's Dream had at times held elements of a nightmare; but at least there was the consolation of the captured ciphers and orderly room papers. Further examination of these seemed to indicate that British forces in the area were being prepared, not for an advance into Marmarica, but for a retreat back behind Mersa Matruh.

This unexpectedly good news strengthened Rommel's determination to reduce the Tobruk Fortress, and warnings from Halder in Berlin and Bastico in Benghasi, that he should watch his back for an attack across the frontier immediately he began a main assault on the port, were rejected with disdain and a jet of caustic comment. The British in Egypt were not preparing to do anything significant; the Australians in Tobruk were the main enemy.

Rommel was quite wrong, of course, and Midsummer Night's Dream (or the 'El Hamra Scurry' as the British inelegantly dubbed it) did him far more harm than just the German casualties it caused, for it seriously misled him. The orders found in the orderly room truck had been for a temporary unit withdrawal, not a large-scale movement intended to change a strategic or even tactical pattern; and had Battle Groups Schütte and Stephan been allowed to progress much further, they would have uncovered some significant evidence of offensive preparations. General Auchinleck's plans for the Winter Battle were quite well advanced and both men and material were beginning to flood out to the area in unprecedented quantities.

Rommel was not even right in believing that when his attack on Tobruk was eventually launched, the main enemy would be Australian. Public opinion in the Dominion was demanding that their troops be relieved before conditions in the Fortress affected their health, and in July General Blamey had pointed out to General Auchinleck that the clear understanding that Australian troops would generally serve together was not being observed – so could the 9th Division be withdrawn from Tobruk and sent to join the 7th in Syria?

It was not a request which the Middle East Commanders-in-Chief could view with anything except apprehension – Auchinleck because of the risk and difficulty of replacing large numbers of experienced troops with large numbers of inexperienced ones,

Cunningham because of the extra strain which would be thrown on the already hard-pressed ships of the Inshore Squadron, and Tedder because although his air strength was increasing rapidly he would need everything which could fly when the main battle started, and between then and now he must use all available flying hours for training, for harassing the Luftwaffe airfields, for attacking the convoys bringing Rommel his essential petrol and ammunition and, most important of all, keeping the skies over the Western Desert clear of enemy reconnaissance planes, which, from mid-September onwards, would undoubtedly note the growing signs of offensive preparations.

But the Australian Government proved intractable, so during the dark periods of August, September and October the vast majority of the Australians (and the Indians) were replaced by the British 70th Division and the 1st Polish Carpathian Brigade – at some cost, it may be said, for during the operations the Navy lost three ships sunk, and two destroyers, a gunboat and a cruiser were badly damaged. The last attempt to evacuate the Australians was the most costly and had to be curtailed, with the result that the whole of the 2nd/13th Australian Battalion, two companies of the 2nd/15th and some men of the Divisional Headquarters were left behind; but an interesting facet of the siege is revealed by the bald figures of naval achievement during the period April 11th to December 10th. Including wounded and prisoners, the Royal Navy had evacuated 47,280 men and brought in 34,113, plus 33,946 tons of stores; and the price paid was 34 warships and merchantmen sunk, 33 damaged. As during the same period the R.A.F. and S.A.A.F. had provided air cover whenever possible over the sea approaches and the port itself, the Siege of Tobruk provides an excellent demonstration of the interdependence of the three services in modern warfare.

A most curious historical coincidence appeared to underline this. Mr Churchill had been pressing Auchinleck to appoint 'Jumbo' Maitland Wilson as commander of the rapidly growing army in the Western Desert (it had reached a size by the end of September to justify its assumption of the title 'Eighth Army') but either through a reluctance to have such matters dictated to him by Whitehall or through a genuine feeling that the northern front facing up towards the Caucasus might in the end prove more important, Auchinleck insisted on Wilson remaining in Syria in command of what became known as 'Ninth Army' with Headquarters near Beirut. For command of Eighth Army in the forthcoming offensive, Auchinleck chose General Cunningham, fresh from his triumphs in Ethiopia; so the two brothers Lieutenant-General Sir Alan and Admiral Sir Andrew were to hold high appointments in the same area; and as it happened the newly designated Western Desert Air Force at the

same time came under a new commander – a New Zealander, Air
Vice-Marshal Arthur Coningham. Even the same initial.

For Lieutenant-General Sir Alan Gordon Cunningham the future,
in August 1941, appeared very promising indeed. Fifty-four years of
age, in excellent health and giving everyone who met him an
impression of bouncing, bright-eyed vitality, he had just completed
one of the most successful and highly publicised campaigns in
British history and was as a result far better known to the British
public than O'Connor had ever been.

In eight weeks, Cunningham had led an army seemingly half
across Africa, crowning his achievements only the previous month
by replacing Haile Selassie, Lion of Judah and King of Kings, on
the throne from which the Italians had driven him five years before.
The speed and dash of the advance had impressed everyone – even
his military contemporaries, one of whom (Alec Gatehouse who
was about to serve under him) wrote, 'Cunningham was a mag-
nificent-looking chap. I thought, this is the man . . .'* Even
Churchill was prepared to be overridden in his favour.

Now he was to command the best-equipped army Britain had
managed to put into the field so far in the Second World War
against an opponent who, whatever his reputation or accomplishments, had at his disposal an army known to be numerically inferior
in men, armour and aircraft. Surely, Cunningham could not lose.

There were, as always, some flaws behind the impressive façade.
Cunningham was a gunner, and the divisions he had commanded as
a major-general had been infantry divisions. These quite important
factors in his military development had probably been an advantage
during his recent campaign through the close and broken country of
East Africa, but it was already being assumed that in the desert
armour would dominate or at least play the major role, and the
armoured formations themselves – especially those of the now-
famous 7th Armoured Division – were subtly (and perhaps un-
consciously) adopting a superiority of attitude which tended to
make those not wearing the black beret feel excluded. As
Auchinleck had already voiced the opinion that three armoured
divisions and not much else would be needed to win the war in
North Africa, Cunningham's lack of experience in handling armour
placed him at a psychological disadvantage, which may have been
increased by the thought of his elder brother watching his performance – however sympathetically – from a few miles away.

Moreover, upon taking up his command, he found that the main
outlines of two plans for the forthcoming offensive had already
been drawn up and his first duty would apparently be but to choose

*First quoted in *The Desert Generals* by Correlli Barnett (London) pp. 79–80.

between them. This did not take him long. The plan suggesting an advance deep down in the desert along the northern edge of the Sand Sea, from Jarabub through Jalo and then up to threaten Benghasi, would necessitate an unwarrantable logistics risk, however attractive the arrows might look on maps pinned to a Staff Office wall in Cairo. Moreover, even if the risks were taken, the difficulties overcome and the Eighth Army spearheads driven successfully through to their target, it might be some time before Rommel's supplies in the forward areas ran down, during which he might well be able to wreak considerable havoc across the Egyptian border. Being Rommel, he might even choose to ignore the force to his rear, drive aggressively eastwards and restock the Afrika Korps from British depots in the Delta. The second and less imaginative plan was far more practical, and with some modification was the one which Cunningham eventually put forward to Auchinleck and upon which *Operation Crusader* was launched.

Eighth Army consisted of two corps – XIII and XXX – and detached troops such as those in the Tobruk Fortress (now commanded by Major-General R. M. Scobie), the Matruh garrison, and forces held in reserve. XIII Corps, now under command of Lieutenant-General A. R. Godwin-Austen (an appointment looked upon with some suspicion and resentment by Churchill), consisted of 4th Indian Division under Frank Messervy, the New Zealand Division under Bernard Freyberg and 1st Army Tank Brigade (with 135 tanks, half Matildas and half the new, faster infantry tanks, the Valentines) under Brigadier H. R. B. Watkins.

XXX Corps consisted of 7th Armoured Division now commanded by Strafer Gott promoted Major-General, made up of the Support Group under Jock Campbell, and two armoured brigades, 7th and 22nd; the 1st South African Division under Major-General G. E. Brink, the 22nd Guards Brigade whose task would be basically to protect the Field Maintenance Centres (a development from O'Connor's Field Supply Depots) set up behind the advance; and Alec Gatehouse's 4th Armoured Brigade Group.

The basic plan was for the infantry divisions of XIII Corps to mask, then surround and capture from the rear the static defences along the frontier between Sollum and Sidi Omar, while the armour of XXX Corps crossed the frontier south of Sidi Omar, swung up towards Tobruk where, after defeating the Afrika Korps panzers en route, they would join hands with the Tobruk garrison and together sweep westwards, to break through the Axis forces in the Gazala line defences, and repossess themselves of Cyrenaica.

A detached force known as the Oasis Group was to stage a demonstration down in the Jarabub–Jalo area to distract Rommel's attention at the crucial moment, and to this end flocks of dummy

lorries and tanks were already assembled there, while the surrounding atmosphere was filled with fake signal communications and
general wireless traffic; and other, smaller-scale diversions had also
been organised. But the main passage for the Eighth Army was to
be close along the coast, and its main force was assembled there.

During the conferences and deliberations which had preceded the
final decisions, there emerged some significant divergences of
opinion, the main one concerning the employment of Alec Gatehouse's 4th Armoured Brigade Group. Consisting basically of 4th
Armoured Brigade strengthened with extra artillery and infantry, it
had at first been cast in the role of a 'Centre Force' charged with the
duties of guarding the left flank of the XIII Corps infantry as they
advanced across the Wire to get behind the static defences, at the
same time maintaining contact with the right wing of XXX Corps.
In such a geographic situation, it could also find itself fighting a
main engagement with 21st Panzer Division should von Ravenstein
choose to bring that formation south from its base area near Bardia.
At first, Gatehouse's force had been part of XIII Corps but
Cunningham decided that its mobility made it more suitably part of
XXX Corps, a decision which brought protests from the infantry
commanders. Later, Bernard Freyberg was to write:

> When the Planning Conference was being held at Army Head-
> quarters on the 6th October I listened in cynically. The proceed-
> ings bore a close resemblance to the talk I had with the Com-
> mander of Western Desert Force . . . before the 'Battleaxe'
> disaster. I did not take any part in the discussions until the
> employment of the New Zealand Division was discussed . . . at
> once I made it clear that I did not agree with the plan to go into
> the blue against unbeaten armoured formations unless I had
> tanks under my immediate command.[4]

Cunningham quickly pointed out that 4th Armoured Brigade
Group would be alongside in support, but this statement was met
with the cold inquiry as to who would give Gatehouse the final
order if 4th Armoured was wanted both forward with 7th Armoured
Division engaging perhaps Neumann-Sylkow's 15th Panzer Division,
and at the same time back on the New Zealanders' wing threatened
by von Ravenstein:

> I made it clear that that [support from 4th Armoured] meant
> nothing to me, as they could be ordered away in a crisis and
> under the circumstances that unless we had tanks under our
> immediate command we should not be moved across the wire
> until the armoured battle had commenced. In this I was quite
> precise. I was not popular.[5]

Freyberg was by no means alone among infantry commanders in his desire for armour whose duty would be specifically to protect his troops against panzers, so much so that after the war one of the Royal Tank Regiment officers there, Michael Carver, was to write:

> The 'Crusader' operation was fought to an unending accompaniment of screams from one infantry division, headquarters, or field maintenance centre after another for tanks to come and protect them against the presence or threat of enemy tanks.[6]

Perhaps the armoured formations should not have been so loud in their protestations of omnipotence for they now found themselves fighting to maintain the concentration of force vital to their allotted task of destroying Rommel's armour; any requirement for them to act as watch-dogs for helpless flocks of infantry they considered not only a waste of battle-strength, but also something of a slur upon their role as Monarch of the Battlefield.

As the main lesson of *Battleaxe* – that the greatest potential for the destruction of the Afrika Korps panzers the British possessed at that time lay with their artillery, not with their tanks – had apparently not yet permeated upwards even as far as brigade and divisional commanders, it is hardly surprising that it had not reached Cunningham either, and that the basis of his plan remained for 7th Armoured Division to meet and vanquish Rommel's two panzer divisions.

His confidence that his own armour would be strong enough to carry out this vital role was based upon the British superiority in numbers of tanks, and on paper this appeared undeniable. According to Intelligence estimates, Panzergruppe Afrika could put into the field about 240 mixed Marks II, III and IV panzers and an additional 150 Italian M13s; the 160 Italian light tanks, Cunningham was assured, could be safely ignored. Against these figures, XXX Corps alone could field some 475 tanks, while the Army Tank Brigades with XIII Corps and in Tobruk held a total of 261 tanks of which 201 were 'I' tanks – Matildas and Valentines.

But of course such purely quantitative calculations ignored other equally crucial factors. In view of the cavalier attitude adopted towards the Italian light tanks it might, for instance, have been more realistic to discount some of 7th Armoured Brigade's ninety-four cruiser tanks of marks earlier than the Crusader, many of which – as should have been foreseen – would be in the workshops until a few days before the operation began. Moreover, Churchill's habit of assuming that the arrival of a tank at Suez would precede its employment on the battlefield by a fully capable and experienced crew merely by the time taken to transport it there, was here being accepted by men who should have known better. Owing to a continued lack of communication between Cairo and London, all the new Crusaders for 22nd Armoured Brigade had perforce gone straight from ships to engineering sheds, where they spent valuable weeks (to the perturbation of Admiral Cunningham as he considered the effects of a really heavy air attack on Alexandria) undergoing essential modification to air and lubrication systems before they could be sent up into the desert – thus drastically reducing the time in which their crews, straight from England, could adapt to desert conditions and tactics.

However, the dictum remained that British armour should destroy the German panzers and it seemed that the Tank Corps had won the argument; they were thus somewhat bemused when the details of Cunningham's plan emerged to find that they were not maintaining to any great extent that concentration of armour which they had demanded. Although, despite Freyberg's protests, Gatehouse's 4th Armoured Brigade Group remained a part of XXX Corps, it was still ordered to remain in the neighbourhood of the New Zealand Division close to the Wire, while the experienced 7th Armoured Brigade, accompanied by the inexperienced 22nd Armoured Brigade (it was the first brigade of the 1st Armoured Division to arrive in the Delta, the other brigades having been delayed in England by shipping shortages), pressed on up towards Tobruk, with the South Africans to their left rear.

However, they would not drive immediately all the way to Tobruk, but at the end of the first day dispose themselves in a triangle around Gabr Saleh, an insignificant landmark in an otherwise featureless desert about a third of the way between XXX Corps's crossing-point of the Wire and Tobruk itself, the points of the triangle being just over twenty miles apart. The 7th Armoured Brigade (with a high proportion of the early mark cruisers) would be at the apex of the triangle pointing towards Tobruk with the Support Group just behind them, 22nd Armoured Brigade with their 155 newly modified Crusaders and Yeomanry crews on the left, and 4th Armoured Brigade Group, now totally re-equipped with American Stuarts (regarded by the Americans as light tanks and dubbed 'Honeys' by the British tank crews who were delighted by their reliability), held back on the right to afford the protection to XIII Corps.

Here, according to the official 'Preliminary Narrative', 'the enemy armour would be compelled to fight on ground of XXX Corps' choosing' – a piece of casuistry whose hollowness would have been revealed had anyone braved Cunningham's growing irritability by asking who in XXX Corps chose that particular piece of ground, and why? The area around Gabr Saleh was just as flat, stony and open as any other part of the adjacent desert, and if the strategy was to tempt the Afrika Korps forward to its destruction, then 'ground of XXX Corps' choosing' should surely have some natural defensive advantages.

In fact, the area was not 'chosen' by anyone, but dictated by Cunningham's attempt to compromise between the armour's wish to stay concentrated, and the infantry's wish to have armour protection on its flank. Lieutenant- General C. W. M. Norrie, who found himself unexpectedly in command of XXX Corps just six weeks before *Operation Crusader* was launched (owing to the death in an air accident of the intended corps commander, General Pope), was most unhappy about the plan. Not only was there in his eyes an unnecessary dispersion between the brigades at the points of the triangle, but

> . . . in order to make the enemy fight I considered it essential for our forces to secure ground vital to him. I did not consider Gabr Saleh of any real importance to the enemy. In fact, if we went there, there was no real reason why he should attack us and we were in danger of handing him the initiative . . . I suggested we would do better to threaten the enemy L of C about Sidi Rezegh from the word 'Go'.[7]

But Norrie's reservations and suggestions were dismissed and the concept of the clash of armour developed, best described in the most detailed account of *Operation Crusader*, by the South African historians J. A. I. Agar-Hamilton and L. C. F. Turner:

> After 30th Corps had made its penetration, the *Afrikakorps* would present itself at Gabr Saleh and be soundly beaten. The remaining stages would follow decently and in order – the march to Sidi Rezeg, the break-out of the Tobruk garrison (with the seizure of the Sollum–Sidi Omar positions as a picturesque parergon), and the rounding-up of the broken remnants of the *Panzergruppe* between Acroma and Ain el Gazala. It was hoped that the port of Tobruk would be available as a supply base on D3 and the permanent water of the Jebel el Akdar at the end of a week. The smooth flow of events could not possibly be hindered by so perverse a circumstance as a rebuff to the Eighth Army, and even the German armour would not be so ill-mannered as to be late in attending its rendezvous with destiny. The detailed provisions of the Corps Operation Orders . . . confirmed the sense of inevitability, until even those who originally disliked the plan were bemused into acceptance.[8]

The employment of the South Africans on the outer flank of the advance was another matter of doubtful prescience. General Brink's division had arrived in Egypt with an immense reputation as a result of their splendid achievements in Ethiopia, but their first employment in the area had been to restore the fortifications at Mersa Matruh in the face of Rommel's advance to the Wire, for these had been allowed to deteriorate after O'Connor's victories. Even after the immediate threat had died away, 1st South African Division were kept at the task of extending the Matruh defences even deeper, and the time and energy which could and indeed should have been spent learning the differences between warfare in desert and warfare in bush and mountain were instead spent digging. Not only did this affect their efficiency for the coming battle but it obviously affected the morale of men who had volunteered for active military duties, and now found themselves continually employed as static labourers.

Moreover, the reinforcements sent up from the Union to replace the casualties suffered in the Ethiopian campaign were so inadequate in both quantity and training that the decision had to be taken to go into battle with only two instead of three brigades, and for even this weakened division there was not enough transport until early October. Even then, a large number of the lorries and their drivers were commandeered by Eighth Army Q side to help build up the supply dumps in the forward area, and thus were not available for training. This circumstance not only increased the risk of faulty navigation at crucial moments, but allowed little or no time to rehearse the vital and often complex routines of supply under battle conditions.

General Brink on several occasions pointed out these deficiencies in the training of his command to Cunningham, and as late as November 2nd General Norrie after an inspection reported, 'I must again bring to your notice that I am not at all satisfied with the progress of training of 1 SA Div due to factors beyond their own control . . . '[9]

The South African troops themselves were keen, tough and only too eager to undertake any operations allocated to them, and there is no doubt that they were more than competent to carry out some of the more static duties required in *Operation Crusader* – such as the investment of the defences south of Sollum with which 4th Indian Division, the infantry with more experience of desert warfare than any other, had been charged. But Cunningham had intimated to Brink that he wanted the South Africans in the forefront of the battle, and when Brink reiterated that his men required more time, presented him with a virtual ultimatum. Brink must let him know by a stated hour whether his division was in a fit state to play an important part in the battle or not; if not, its role would be reduced.

This was surely a most unfair burden to place upon the shoulders of a subordinate commander, especially of a Dominion formation anxious to uphold its reputation and again prove its loyalty to the Mother Country. That night Brink wrote in his diary:

> There was no time to ponder or to argue. The Army Commander was applying the acid test. I was not happy about the state of training of my Division and in my heart I felt that it was not in a fit state, tactically, and did not possess the hitting power to engage in serious operations. We have splendid fighting material, well led and ably commanded, but the best human material in the world requires careful moulding and must have the wherewithal to engage a tough and determined enemy such as the *Afrika-Korps*. The die was cast, however, the Division was already on the move to its concentration area and the honour of South Africa was at stake.[10]

Thus the formations given the specific task of seeking out the two panzer divisions of Rommel's Afrika Korps consisted of three armoured brigades of which one – the 22nd – was totally inexperienced but comparatively well-equipped, one – the 7th – was experienced but equipped in large part with out-dated tanks (described by General Norrie as being in a state of 'general debility') and the third – the 4th – was both experienced and equipped with new tanks, but held back from the most likely area of battle by its requirement to protect infantry divisions; all protected on the outward flank of their advance by an understrength division of troops who, in the opinion of their commander, were inadequately trained.

But at least the 4th Indian Division and Bernard Freyberg's New Zealanders were more than capable of discharging their duties of pinning down and then cutting off the Axis troops along the frontier. Perhaps they might also help in the destruction of the panzers.

Moreover, a considerable degree of surprise would be achieved, for not only had the combined R.A.F. and S.A.A.F. kept the skies above the concentration areas clear of German or Italian reconnaissance aircraft, but the British intelligence services under Brigadier Shearer had achieved a coup as remarkable in its way as the repeated cracking of the Enigma codes by the Bletchley Park organisation in England.

It had all begun in July when a Palestinian farm-worker reported that he had seen a parachutist descend to the ground near Ramleh and had later observed him digging holes nearby as though to bury something. The parachutist was eventually caught and upon close investigation proved, despite a remarkably Jewish appearance, to be, of all people, the Gauleiter of Mannheim, dropped into

Palestine by German Intelligence with a view to increasing anti-British sentiment among the Arabs.

In the holes he had dug were found a bundle of Palestinian currency and a short-wave transmitter complete with codes, identification signals and specified times of transmission, and it was not long before Shearer and his team were exchanging routine and fairly harmless messages with what seemed likely to be their opposite numbers in Bari. Then, with more devious ploys in mind, they sent out details of troop movements which they guessed could be adequately confirmed by other espionage networks in the Delta and were soon receiving congratulations upon the accuracy of their information, together with the news that Rommel was most grateful for it and would welcome more.

With the forthcoming major operation in mind, Shearer now decided upon a more ambitious piece of deception.

Auchinleck was persuaded to pay an obviously very official visit to Ninth Army H.Q. in Palestine, dust columns were seen moving east across Sinai and northwards through Palestine giving the impression of heavy traffic driving wide to escape observation – and Bari were dramatically informed by this valued new source that Britain's real immediate intentions were to move as much strength as they could spare up towards the Caucasus to help Russia, and thus safeguard her own oil supplies in the Persian Gulf. The apparent preparations for an attack in the Western Desert were a cover, and could safely be disregarded.

This was indeed news to gladden Rommel's heart, feeding his almost fanatical obsession to capture Tobruk. From then on, no report or suggestion of aggressive intentions by the British against Panzergruppe Afrika was listened to with anything except irritation, and on one occasion he contemptuously threw aerial photographs of the extension of the British rail-line westwards from Mersa Matruh to the floor, refusing even to look at them. On November 14th he telephoned Berlin to complain of continuing harassment by his worried Italian allies (presumably, for security reasons, he could not reveal the source of his own confidence) and he gave the Chief of the Wehrmacht Operations Staff, Oberstgeneral Alfred Jodl, his personal guarantee that no danger existed on his front. He even informed Gambara that his next attempt to reduce Tobruk could begin on November 20th without the slightest risk of serious interference, and at the beginning of that month flew off to Rome to spend a fortnight with Dearest Lu.

Operation Crusader, or the Winter Battle as the Germans were to call it, was not to be distinguished by great perception or even competence at the highest level on either side; only the fighting troops were to win renown.

Shortly before Eighth Army began moving to its battle positions, two small-scale operations were mounted to divert Axis attention from the main fronts, by parties made up from officers and men who had come out from England with the Special Service Brigade, originally intended for the attack on Rhodes. The brigade had played a somewhat inconclusive role in the opening stages of the Syrian campaign and was now being disbanded, many of the men having already returned to their regiments. Some, however, had been retained to form the nucleus of what was to prove the most durable of the private armies.

On the night of November 16th, five Bristol Bombay aircraft took off from a small airfield near Fuka carrying fifty-seven men and three officers, whose aim was to carry out raids on Luftwaffe airfields in the Gazala–Tmimi area, their special targets being the new 109F fighters which were proving a hazard to the R.A.F. Tomahawks and Hurricanes.

Meteorological forecasts were excellent at take-off, visibility perfect, and during the early part of the journey there was little wind to confuse the navigation. But as the five planes droned westwards over the sea, conditions worsened rapidly and by the time they were due to turn south to cross the coastline, they were flying in thick turbulent cloud which bucketed the aircraft around the sky until all were separated and lost. Soon it was evident that even if the correct dropping zone could be found, cloud base was so low that for the parachutists to be dropped at the minimum safe height of seven hundred feet, they would have to be dropped blind in thick fog. One pilot who did venture down to try to pick up a landmark, found cloud base at 200 feet – registered on his altimeter just seconds before it disintegrated in a burst of anti-aircraft fire which came up to greet him. Incredibly, that aircraft survived for the moment, to fly in a gigantic circle as a result of a jammed compass, until it ran out of petrol and after further misadventures was shot down and its passengers and crew either killed or taken prisoner.

But in the meantime, the other four pilots had all pressed on separately through the appalling conditions until they felt that they were over the correct destination, whereupon they dropped their parachutists – disastrously. Many of the men were never seen again, some on landing were dragged by their canopies – caught open by the powerful ground wind – along the bumpy and rock-strewn desert floor to broken and agonising deaths, and no one escaped the ordeal entirely unscathed. Morning revealed not only that the supply chutes were so dispersed over the desert that, for instance, although much explosive was recovered no one could find the fuses, but also that the party had been dropped so far south that there was no chance of any of them reaching their objectives in either time or condition to carry out their allotted tasks.

Tacitly, the operation was abandoned, and the twenty-two survivors set out for their rendezvous with the Long Range Desert Group at the Rotunda Segnale. Fortunately, they arrived there safely and even more fortunately among them were two men – Captain David Stirling and Lieutenant Paddy Mayne – who were able to draw the correct conclusions from their experiences and thus keep alive the basic concept behind the Special Air Service Regiment.

The second operation held, even by 'private army' standards, bizarre elements in both concept and conduct.

Early in October, six officers and fifty-three men from No. 11 Commando (which had taken part in the landings at the mouth of the Litani River in June) had congregated in the Canal Zone and there practised the techniques of landing on open beaches at night, in rubber dinghies and canvas-covered canoes, called 'folboats', launched from the slippery decks of submarines.

On the night of November 13th/14th, they attempted to do this off the coast of the Jebel Akhdar, some twenty miles west of Appollonia, but in a howling gale very different from the calm in which they had continually trained. The result was that it took seven hours instead of the planned ninety minutes to get twenty-eight men (including the operational commander, Lieutenant-Colonel Geoffrey Keyes) ashore from the first submarine, *Torbay*, and when the second submarine, *Talisman*, closed the shore to disembark her commandos, she touched bottom and in the subsequent turmoil seven boats and eleven men were swept overboard and several never seen again. At this, *Talisman* withdrew with many of the raiding force still aboard, so that in the morning when Keyes assembled his force – wet, chilled to the bone and short of vital weapons and equipment – it was already considerably under strength for the operations for which it had been landed. One person who was present, however, was Colonel Robert Laycock, the original commander of the Special Service Brigade, who had accompanied the force as 'observer', and now decreed that in the circumstances the objectives must be curtailed.

These had originally been four in number – to attack the Italian Headquarters at Cyrene and cut all telephone and telegraph installations, to attack the Italian Intelligence Centre at Appollonia, to wreck communications around El Faidia, and to attack the German Headquarters at Beda Littoria and Rommel's personal villa to the west of the village. Who originally proposed this last objective is a mystery lost in time and perhaps the files of the Cairo

Headquarters, but as the only possible reason for attacking a small private villa would be to capture or kill the occupants – and as the improbability of Rommel allowing himself to be captured and then transported from a point so far behind his own lines to Egypt, or even to Tobruk, must have been recognised – there can be little doubt that the purpose behind this part of the Keyes Raid was assassination. Perhaps Laycock's presence was intended to relieve the young man (Keyes was only twenty-four) of an agonising decision should Rommel indeed be taken alive, and then stand in chance of rescue.

In the face of the major depletion of forces, however, it was now agreed that only two of the objectives would be pursued – the attack on the telegraph and telephone systems at Cyrene, and the attack on the German Headquarters at Beda Littoria. Only if the German Commander-in-Chief was in that particular building would he be in danger, and the idea of an attack on his private villa was tacitly dropped.

It took the party until the night of November 16th to reach a small cave some five miles from Beda Littoria, where they passed the whole of that night and most of the following day in uncomfortable and odorous surroundings, but at least sheltered from the torrential rain which had plagued them almost continuously since their landing. They spent the time drying their clothes, cleaning their weapons and gradually thawing out from the debilitating cold which had gripped them from the moment they had emerged from the submarine hatches, wondering what had happened to the blazing, sub-tropical sunshine in which, reputedly, the southern Mediterranean shore was continually bathed.

At about 1800 Keyes, who had carried out a short reconnaissance during the afternoon, briefed the whole party, divided it in two and sent one half off to blow up the communication pylon near Cyrene while the rest listened to his detailed plans for the attack on the German Headquarters. Then, with blackened faces, clad in combat gear and wearing plimsolls, they all set off on the final stage of the attacks.

By midnight, Keyes and his party were at the outskirts of Beda Littoria and the first nerve-shattering experience occurred when one member tripped over a tin can, to produce a frenzied barking from every dog in the neighbourhood and hysterical screams from at least one of the inhabitants. Two of Mussolini's soldiers who investigated the uproar were arrogantly bullied in fluent German by Keyes's second-in-command, Captain Robin Campbell, until they retired wearing a decidedly disgruntled air and doubtless reflecting upon the disagreeable truculence of some of their allies.

Keyes by this time had himself cut through the wire surrounding the Headquarters Building – a six-storey house standing away from the main village – to find that the rain, which had made their journey so uncomfortable so far, now yielded a dividend by confining all of the sentries except one to their tents. This exception Keyes silently killed and the rest of the party now joined him, bringing with them sufficient explosive to wreck both the building and the electric power plant close by.

As investigation revealed no easy access to the building, Campbell hammered on the front door and demanded entry in his excellent German, and when eventually the door opened, Keyes jammed his revolver in the ribs of the startled soldier behind it – who was, however, sufficiently well-trained and brave as to grab the gun, begin wrestling with Keyes and to shout warnings at the top of his voice. Surprise now lost, Campbell shot the struggling German over Keyes's shoulder, Keyes flung the door back and the six men making up the assault party stormed inside. The next few minutes were a chaos of sub-machine-gun and pistol fire, of shouts of anguish and alarm, of slamming doors and running footsteps on stone steps.

On the left of the main hall, a door started opening and Keyes kicked it wide to see inside about ten Germans frozen in startled shock; he was emptying his revolver into the room when Campbell appeared at his elbow with a grenade so Keyes pulled the door shut while the pin was pulled and the fuse burnt down, then opened it again. A crash as the grenade went in, a burst of Tommy-gun fire into the room as well – and then a single shot back from some more than usually quick-witted German and Keyes was flung away by a bullet which hit him just over the heart. He was dead within seconds.

An uncanny silence now fell upon the building as every light went out. Campbell dragged Keyes's body outside, checked back in the house for further signs of hostile activity, then ran around to the rear where a covering party had been left. Too late he remembered he should have shouted a password; sub-machine-gun bullets smashed into his leg and the party at the Rommel-haus was now without an officer capable of leading. Sergeant Terry took over, brought up enough explosive to blow up the entire building – only to discover that the fuses were rain-soaked and unusable and that the only damage the party could still inflict was by way of dropping a grenade down the breather pipe of the main generator, which thus at least kept the place in darkness.

The fit men then withdrew, justifiably believing that the Germans would not ill-treat their wounded, and by the following evening had made contact with Colonel Laycock at the beach. There then followed hours of frustration while their signals to *Torbay* – lying fully surfaced about 400 yards out – were unacknowledged and *Torbay*'s belated signals to them were largely incomprehensible and certainly did not result in boats coming in to fetch them. The twenty-two survivors moved just before dawn into a wadi to lie up for the day, but there they were first attacked by Arabs and then by Italians, so Laycock gave orders for them to split into small groups before a more serious attack by Germans developed.

In the end, all except two were captured; Laycock and Sergeant Terry got clear and after forty-one days made contact with the British near Cyrene. Campbell was well treated by his captors though his leg had to be amputated, Keyes and four Germans were buried with full military honours by Rommel's chaplain, and in due course Keyes was awarded a posthumous Victoria Cross. It had undoubtedly been an operation upon which great courage had been exhibited, and a certain amount of skill.

But not enough, for important aspects of training had been neglected. There is no point in arranging a pick-up from a beach unless each side can read the other's signals, and even less in carrying explosive for miles without two methods of detonating it – and preferably more. And a number of questions yield only unsatisfactory answers.

Why should a party of at maximum sixty men be commanded by a lieutenant-colonel, however young?

Why was a full colonel accompanying the party?

Why, as a full colonel was present, did he allow the landings to continue in the face of such appalling weather conditions, with the consequent loss of time, and the deterioration of both men and material?

Every answer obtainable to these questions, from whatever source, is coloured by reference to such admirable qualities as courage, leadership, imagination, devotion to duty and to one's men; by the sceptical listener the trumpet tones of romantic excitement can clearly be heard. What still seems to have been missing was hard professionalism and an acceptance of the grim realities of war.

And of course, Rommel had moved his headquarters from Beda Littoria weeks before, and that night was nowhere near the place.

2 · Crusader: The Clash of Armour

During the weekend of November 16th and 17th, 1941, the whole of the Eighth Army was on the move – 100,000 men, 600 tanks, 5,000 assorted cars, trucks and lorries; and although the troops accepted the resultant tribulations with their usual sardonic good humour, the administrative staffs were shaken by the ordeal.

The South Africans probably had the worst time of it as a result of their enforced lack of training, and after the last short move to the concentration area, deliberately undertaken at night, General Brink declared, in heartfelt tones, 'Never again!' Units became entangled, men were lost and run over, vehicles overturned; and the tally of broken springs, axles and propeller shafts, for which spares were almost unobtainable, was deeply worrying. The most frightening revelation of all, however, was the figure for petrol consumption. The vehicle average, estimated at eight miles per gallon, proved during that last chaotic phase no higher than two miles per gallon – a situation perceptibly worsened by the fact that three of the overturned vehicles had been petrol carriers and 1,500 gallons of precious fluid had been poured into the sand. The spectre of the division stalled and isolated in the desert haunted the South African command for the rest of the operation.

Even the move forward of the New Zealand Division, by now as well trained and experienced as any in the desert, had not been without difficulties, again due to the absolute aridity of the desert. Even at the low ration of a gallon of water per day per man, each brigade needed to take with it enough to fill a small reservoir – and water was only one of the vital necessities. Each brigade required 1,000 vehicles to carry the men, weapons, ammunition and stores – and spread out at ten vehicles to the mile, this gave a tailback 100 miles long which took six and a half hours to pass any given point. On the last seventy-mile move up to the concentration area the leading vehicles of each brigade arrived at their destination before the last had left the starting-point. It was, indeed a quartermaster's nightmare come to life, and a nightmare unrelieved by any awakening to a world of sanity when morning came.

Altogether there were fourteen brigades of one sort or another on the move, picking their slow, dusty, frustrating and often inexpert ways across the Egyptian desert towards the Wire and the enemy beyond, and it is astonishing that the morale of everybody concerned was as high as it was. Inexperience and the optimism of youth played a very great part (they are qualities of inestimable value to an uncertain military command) and Churchillian rhetoric had also helped. Before the major moves had taken place, a message from the Prime Minister had been read to them all:

> For the first time British and Empire troops will meet the Germans with an ample equipment in modern weapons of all kinds. The battle itself will affect the whole course of the war. Now is the time to strike the hardest blow yet struck for final victory, home and freedom. The Desert Army may add a page to history which will rank with Blenheim and with Waterloo. The eyes of all nations are upon you . . . May God uphold the right![1]

Despite passages in that exhortation which struck a rather hollow note in the minds of some senior officers, the men of the Eighth Army accepted the spirit of the message and even added to it from their own happy confidence. According to one of the New Zealand historians, ' . . . the morale of the Division was at its peak, a level never surpassed,' and Desmond Young, the biographer of Rommel, wrote of this approach march to *Crusader*, 'The battle that ensued was desperately fought by both sides. On ours there was an exhilaration, a will to victory that I had not seen equalled since the final battles at the end of the first war.'

This was as well, for the spirit was to be severely tested almost immediately. That night the hitherto mild November weather broke, the wind rose and at first whipped up a sandstorm distinguished by the perverse quality of being bitterly cold, followed shortly by the most spectacular thunderstorm to burst upon the desert within local memory. Jagged flashes of lightning ripped open the Mediterranean skies, and as the clouds built up thicker and thicker, each acted as both electric pole and light reflector until the entire horizon sparked and crackled, floodlighting the desert with an almost continuous, cold, green, flickering radiance, while overhead the thunder boomed and roared, then crashed out with the startling suddenness of cannon-fire.

And then the rain came. Squalls of bitter sleet swept across the huddled army, lancing down through every tear in fabric, gap in lacing, open windshield or gun-port; soaking inexorably through serge or drill to transform it into icy poultices to chill the flesh and blood beneath – and to turn the desert dust to mud. Along the Escarpment, wadis flooded and cascades washed away not only rocks and clumps of scrub but men who had thought to find cover and shelter in them, and their weapons and equipment too. The rain flooded the whole of the desert from Tobruk across to Sidi Barrani and down in a triangle whose apex was well south of Fort Maddalena, collecting in flat pans, turning sand-stretches into spongy marshes, and totally washing out Air Vice-Marshal Coningham's airfields and any chance of R.A.F. covering operations until they dried. It even put a stop to a proposed bombardment by the Royal Navy of the Reverend Bach's positions around Halfaya, as the spotting planes could not take off.

The only consolation for the Eighth Army was that the Luftwaffe was similarly grounded, and that Rommel's forces, poised for their concentrated attack on Tobruk, were just as severely discomforted as themselves.*

The storm ended before dawn, though all next day the sky remained overcast with dark, sullen clouds; but exercise and movement soon warmed the waiting soldiers. The armoured cars moved first through the Wire – 11th Hussars on the left leading the Yeomanry of 22nd Armoured Brigade (11th had been patrolling on both sides of Fort Maddalena for nearly a week), 4th South African Armoured Car Regiment in the centre leading 7th Armoured Brigade, and the 1st King's Dragoon Guards (less one squadron in Tobruk) on the right; by midday they had all fought brief, sporadic actions with Axis armoured cars which had then retired.

The armour of XXX Corps then followed, 4th Armoured Brigade Group and the New Zealanders wheeling on the inside rim. Despite the conditions of the night before, high spirits quickly returned and confidence surged through the vast procession – though at certain levels, new doubts arose. One of Freyberg's battalion commanders, Howard Kippenberger, wrote:

> This great approach march will always be remembered by those who took part in it though the details are vague in memory. The whole Eighth Army, Seventh Armoured Division, First South African Division, and the Second New Zealand and Fourth Indian Divisions moved westwards in an enormous column, the armour leading. The Army moved south of Sidi Barrani, past the desolate Italian camps of the previous year, along the plateau south of the great escarpment, through the

*For a map of the opening moves of *Operation Crusader*, November 18th–19th, 1941, see the back endpaper.

frontier wire into Libya, south of the enemy garrisons in the Sidi Omars, and wheeled north. Then, just as we were rejoicing in the conception of a massive move on Tobruk, disregarding the immobile frontier garrisons and crushing everything in our path, the whole Army broke up and departed different ways.[2]

Not so many people, however, noticed the fragmentation; besides that extraordinary amalgam of fear and excitement, of frantic activity and tense waiting, of hoarse direction and sweating obedience which makes up the first moves into battle, those who travelled in the midst of the slow swing across the frontier were treated to a memorable series of mirages. Alan Moorehead was there:

> At times you could see on the horizon a towered city that floated on a lake and undulated as you watched like a stage back-cloth blown in the wind. Small bushes looked in the distance like great trees, and each truck was a two-storied house passing through the dust. Often we saw groups of castles on the horizon. As we approached, these turned to battleships and then at last from a mile away they resolved into the solid shapes of tanks.[3]

Shortly after midday, it became evident that enemy forces in front were beginning to stand and that the armoured cars could go no further forward on their own (11th Hussars on the outer flank of the advance had by this time driven sixty miles into enemy territory) and the armour came up. In the centre, the cruisers of 2nd R.T.R. came through and before the impressive sight of them moving apparently invincibly forward, the cars of Rommel's Reconnaissance Battalion 33 retired and very soon the spearheads of 7th Armoured Brigade had crossed the Trig el Abd and reached their rendezvous for the day, about ten miles north-west of Gabr Saleh. On their right, Alec Gatehouse's 4th Armoured Brigade Group had also reached their day's objective across the Trig el Abd, level with and about ten miles east of Gabr Saleh, having pushed back elements of Reconnaissance Battalion 3 (which had reported back in some agitation that they were being attacked by over two hundred heavy tanks). Only on the outer rim of the wheel had there been delay, for 22nd Armoured Brigade had had the usual poor luck which accompanies inexperience, and stopped at dusk some ten miles short of their objective. Outside them, 1st South African Brigade had overcome their recent lack of training and covered sixty miles to reach the track running south from Bir el Gubi down to Jarabub at El Cuasc, with 5th South African Brigade another twenty miles south at Elwet el Hamra.

All in all, XXX Corps had advanced very satisfactorily, meeting nothing but armoured screens and suffering very little from enemy action. And if breakdowns had reduced the number of tanks with 7th Armoured Brigade from 141 to 119, and with 22nd Armoured Brigade from 155 to 136, this was set off by a discovery of German inadequacy which heightened even further the air of general euphoria. During the advance of the 2nd R.T.R. cruisers, they had overrun and captured one of the famous German eight-wheeled armoured cars, and during the evening tank enthusiasts flocked in from miles around to inspect it. Brigadier G. M. O. Davy, now commanding 7th Armoured Brigade, was amused:

> One used to hear of primitive people being impressed by visiting warships, not because of their speed, armour or fire-power, but for the number of their funnels. The German eight-wheeler had somehow acquired an importance, in the imagination of its opponents, which nothing but its eight wheels could have justified. It was a poor thing, with thin armour and few weapons, and in the light of day the once formidable myth collapsed.[4]

A cold comfort, though, to men such as Sergeant Wood and his crew of the 11th, who in their Marmon-Harrington had been shot to death twelve weeks before by the highly efficient crew of one of these eight-wheelers.

To General Cunningham, the events of the day had been mildly irritating and its very success provided a mixture of both satisfaction and uncertainty; and the uncertainty was growing.

He had set out before first light and it was unfair that a sticky patch of soft sand had so engulfed his car that he arrived at General Norrie's Corps Headquarters (at which he intended to spend this first day of *Operation Crusader*) an hour late. Fortunately, Norrie had allowed a margin for emergencies, and they had moved off on time, crossed the Wire amid the bulk of XXX Corps B Echelon supply vehicles and by evening had settled down at Point 174, south of Gabr Saleh, due east of El Cuasc, and thus central to the northern and western faces – surely the most vital – of the deployment of the armoured force with which he intended to annihilate the Afrika Korps.

As the signals came in – and they were laconic in the extreme, for one lesson at least had been learned from *Battleaxe* and British wireless discipline greatly tightened – he could build up a picture of all that had happened that day, and see how smoothly his plans had gone.

All armoured brigades, including 4th Armoured Brigade Group and Brigadier Campbell's Support Group were, if not in exact position, certainly in sufficient approximation to give cause for satisfaction, while the New Zealanders had crossed the Wire south of Bir Sheferzen, regrouped and were ready to advance northwards to take the enemy static defences in rear when called upon to do so. As for the 4th Indian Division, 7th Brigade was closed up around Bir Sheferzen occupying the doubtless watchful attention of German and Italian units in the Sidi Omars, 11th Brigade was on the coast opposite Sollum while between the two the cars and carriers of Central India Horse kept watch and the Matildas of 1st Army Tank Brigade waited ponderously for their call to action.

All had gone according to the book.

The only missing element was the enemy.

Where was Rommel?

Rommel was at his advanced headquarters at Gambut and had not the slightest intention of reacting seriously to what he was certain was nothing but a diversion staged by the British Command in order to frighten the Italians at El Gubi and Bir Hakeim, causing them in their turn to distract his attention from his main purpose, the final reduction of Tobruk. To suggestions by Cruewell and his Chief of Staff, Oberstleutnant Fritz Bayerlein, that 15th Panzer Division should at least be put on the alert and Panzer Regiment 5 from von Ravenstein's 21st Panzer Division sent down towards Gabr Saleh to check on the reports of British armour in that neighbourhood, he replied brusquely, 'We must not lose our nerve' – a rebuke which ruffled the feelings of the Afrika Korps command, and added to the tensions at Gambut.

For although the attacks on the south-east face of the Tobruk perimeter were planned to commence in some sixty hours' time, there were many at headquarters, especially among the Quartermaster Staff, who felt that insufficient fuel and ammunition had been collected. Rommel might appear unconcerned about the intentions and capability of the British Eighth Army, but even he had to recognise the recent accomplishments of the Royal Air Force and the Royal Navy. Since September, port installations at Tripoli and Brindisi had been under constant attack by Wellingtons based in Egypt and Malta, and the supply convoys across the Mediterranean upon which Panzergruppe Afrika had to rely for existence, just as much as Eighth Army had to rely upon the rail and lorry trains from the Delta, had been harried mercilessly.

Ten Axis ships had gone down in September, seven in October and the tally so far in November was already ominous; and of late the concentration by the R.A.F. on less remote targets such as the Luftwaffe bases at Derna, Barce, Benina, Berka and Tmimi – and the roads and tracks in between – indicated not only that the British were aware of the impending attack on Tobruk (as how could they be ignorant?) but that they also knew the most vulnerable aspect of Afrika Korps's deployment, the jugular vein of communications guarded for the most part by the troops of the uncertain ally, Italy. Twenty per cent of the vital supplies sent from Germany, including the most precious of all, petrol, was ending either in flames or at the bottom of the sea, and if this proportion continued and the battle for Tobruk should be prolonged, then a most critical situation would arise.

In the Oberquartiermeister's offices, Q Branch, then, there was just as great a concentration upon capture of the all-important town and harbour as there was in Rommel's mind; and those who heard of yet another piece of evidence purporting to demonstrate immediate British aggression on land, tended to agree with Rommel's terse disposal of it. On the first night of *Crusader* (November 18th) according to the Afrika Korps War Diary:

> The German Liaison Officer with Savona Division reported results of the interrogation of an English soldier captured at Sidi Omar. It appeared from this that 7th Armoured Division had already advanced west of the Wire, 4th Indian Division was on either side of the Wire and two South African Divisions were moving west from Mersa Matruh.[5]

Obviously, this was a deliberate attempt to deceive, reminiscent of the famous trick played by Colonel Lawrence in the Syrian desert twenty-three years before, when he gulled the Turkish Command into a mistaken view of the axis of the British advance on Damascus. If anything, it confirmed opinion at Gambut that no serious threat to the assault on Tobruk existed, and that the empty manoeuvrings by the British around Gabr Saleh were a bluff which could safely be ignored.

The cloak of secrecy which had been thrown over Eighth Army intentions by a combination of radio discipline and freakish nature, and then perfected by Brigadier Shearer's deception, was making available enormous military advantages for General Cunningham to exploit. It was a pity that this situation was not one for which his plan had provided. In the event, having arrived on the 'ground of their own choosing' XXX Corps was finding itself blandly ignored and in exactly that danger of losing the initiative of which Norrie had warned his superior. There is indeed the faintest suggestion of crocodile tears about Norrie's expressed regrets that, to urgent requests for information upon which to base future plans, he had to reply that evening that he had none.

One result of the uncertainty thus generated was the issue of two sets of orders which although apparently in some agreement, differed in one vital respect. Strafer Gott, who had no intention of allowing 7th Armoured Division to lose the momentum they had acquired during the first day of the operation by hanging about doing nothing on the second, issued orders that on the morrow the armoured car screens were to probe forward both north and west, that the Support Group with the 22nd Armoured Brigade in close attendance should investigate Bir el Gubi where it was known that Bersaglieri of the Ariete Armoured Division were in strength, and that 7th and 4th Armoured Brigades should be prepared for battle with the Afrika Korps to the north.

Two hours later, XXX Corps issued orders upon Cunningham's direction, that 7th Armoured Division would secure *both* Bir el Gubi *and* Sidi Rezegh on the direct line towards Tobruk, and that the 1st South African Brigade would move up to take over Bir el Gubi, with their 5th Brigade moving to Gueret Hamza some ten miles south along the same axis. As the message ended with the statement that bomber support had been requested for the following day above both Ed Duda and El Adem, and that the Army Commander was 'anxious to stage relief' – presumably of Tobruk – it seemed that the decision had been taken to go straight for the port without achieving that 'destruction of the enemy armour' which had previously been considered so vital. But as the message also precluded any move by 4th Armoured Brigade Group much further westwards, it seemed that this amendment to the original *Crusader* plan envisaged two brigades, one totally inexperienced and the other equipped largely with outdated tanks, between them brushing aside the Ariete formations at Bir el Gubi and advancing to Tobruk against whatever resistance Rommel could organise; and presumably the bland indifference with which Afrika Korps had regarded Eighth Army moves to date would not continue once their vital communications between Sidi Rezegh and Ed Duda were threatened.

Whatever the thinking, Gott accepted that 22nd Armoured Brigade's blooding in battle would now be as leaders instead of in support, and that its support in turn would come from the South Africans, while Jock Campbell's more experienced force remained close to Gabr Saleh ready to follow 7th Armoured Brigade north towards Sidi Rezegh and Tobruk beyond. A matter not greatly considered was that however derisory the performance of the Italian M13s might be, they would fight a defensive battle and thus be well supported by their artillery; and another was the inadequacy of the communications system. The orders for the moves of the South African brigades up towards El Gubi only reached General Brink the following morning, and he understood them to mean that his men would only move into and occupy the location *after* the armour had captured it.

The move against Bir el Gubi by 22nd Armoured Brigade began early in the morning, and by noon the Crusaders of 2nd Royal Gloucester Hussars were on the outer defence line, driving the first enemy tanks their crews had ever seen back into the perimeter. It was an exhilarating experience for them. There was then a pause, more Crusaders from the 4th County of London Yeomanry (C.L.Y.) came up on their left, and despite warnings from one of the 11th Hussars' squadron commanders, a full-scale copybook attack was launched against what the Brigade Staff thought was a mobile defence post five miles east of El Gubi, but which proved to be a heavily fortified main line screened by dummies, behind which sheltered, in fact, the whole of the Ariete Armoured Division.

It was extraordinary that the Crusaders did so well. One observer said that the main attack was 'the nearest thing to a cavalry charge with tanks seen during this war', and its very unlikelihood may have given it a first spectacular advantage during which 34 M13s and 12 Italian guns were knocked out, and over 200 of the Bersaglieri killed or taken prisoner – a score which might indeed have been larger. One of the 4th C.L.Y. squadron commanders, Viscount Cranley, later wrote:

> The enemy seemed somewhat daunted by this spirited, if not very professional, attack and were coming out of their trenches in considerable numbers, offering to surrender, but thanks to brigade headquarters not having listened to the 11th Hussars, there was no infantry close enough to take over, and the bulk of my tanks were by now knocked out. The enemy quickly appreciated the position and, bobbing back again, started to shoot us up once more.[6]

By 1630, both the Gloucester Hussars and the 4th C.L.Y. had run into severe trouble against artillery and in minefields, and the 3rd C.L.Y. who had mounted a relieving attack to the north-west, had also suffered heavily in a counter-attack by the main body of the Italian 132nd Tank Regiment; blazing Crusaders littered the area around Bir el Gubi, grounded tank crews ran for shelter towards anything which moved and might be friendly, while isolated tanks, the rest of their troop burnt out or trackless, collected together and moved slowly and uncertainly back out of range of the still efficient and relentless Italian gunners. Wireless communications had long since broken down.

That evening, 22nd Armoured Brigade reported that they had lost half their tanks, though the Italians only claimed that they had destroyed fifty so perhaps the other thirty-two had merely broken down; but the fact remained that one of the three brigades with which Cunningham intended to destroy the Afrika Korps armour had been very roughly handled – and Bir el Gubi was still firmly held by the Ariete Division.

The advance of 7th Armoured Brigade northwards was, however, attended by success. During the morning they had pushed away elements of the German Reconnaissance Battalion 33 (which had leaguered virtually alongside them during the night) and, preceded by their screen of South African armoured cars, pressed on over the ridge of what became known as the Southern Escarpment. They saw before them running east–west a sloping valley, gradually rising on the far side to the Escarpment crest upon which stood the white, square tomb of Sidi Rezegh, and beyond which lay the Trig Capuzzo; on the floor of the valley lay the airfield, upon which were dispersed several aircraft of the Regia Aeronautica with, for the moment, unsuspecting ground personnel unhurriedly moving between them.

It looked an enticing and indeed promising prospect and the events of the next hour or so were to justify the impression. With an hour to go before sunset, the Crusaders of 6th R.T.R. preceded by the South African armoured cars swept down and across the valley to charge the airfield with most satisfying results. Many of the aircraft were shot down as they tried to take off, some were even shot down as they gallantly turned and tried to beat off their assailants, but many were caught on the ground and either crushed by the tanks or later hacked to pieces by exultant crew members.

One squadron of tanks was ordered further forward to take the crest of the main Escarpment, but there they found two battalions of the ex-Foreign Legionnaires of Afrika Regiment 361 well entrenched, and as there were no accompanying British infantry (for the Support Group was still beyond the southern escarpment) the squadron retired back to the airfield, as did the armoured car patrols which had explored westwards towards the El Adem–El Gubi track until they ran into fire from the Italian Pavia Division. By nightfall, therefore, 7th Armoured Brigade was solidly in leaguer on the Sidi Rezegh airfield.

This was, of course, the location at which Norrie had wanted to concentrate the whole of XXX Corps armour as soon as possible after the crossing of the Wire, feeling that Sidi Rezegh was indeed of vital importance to Rommel; now, if Norrie's judgment proved correct, he could find himself facing the massed panzers of the Afrika Korps with the armour of just one brigade – and the most ill-equipped one at that. Little support could be given it, for as the evening reports came in it seemed that 22nd Armoured Brigade was too badly mauled to be of much use, and Cunningham's injunction against moving up 4th Armoured Brigade was still in force. Not that Gatehouse's command had come through the day unscathed, for at last Rommel was beginning to take notice of the British presence west of the Wire.

During that second morning (November 19th) von Ravenstein had become more and more conscious of strong British forces to his immediate south, and when General Cruewell came to see him he repeated his request of the previous day to be allowed to send a strong panzer force down towards Gabr Saleh. The commander of the Afrika Korps, though he agreed with von Ravenstein's point of view, was still smarting under Rommel's suggestion of weakening nerves so he drove back to Gambut and placed the situation before his commander again. This time Rommel proved more amenable and by 1145 orders had been issued for a reinforced Panzer Regiment 5 (the reinstated Battlegroup Stephan) to attack and destroy 'the enemy threatening Reconnaissance Battalion 3'.

It was, in fact, the reports from this reconnaissance unit which had prompted a more reasonable attitude on Rommel's part, for since early morning he had been reading accounts of a delaying action by them against armoured cars of the King's Dragoon Guards and American Stuarts of 3rd R.T.R., who had been endeavouring to push the German patrols back northwards. There were even reports coming in of British armoured cars or light tanks advancing as far north as the Escarpment overlooking Bardia. The British were apparently putting more into this diversionary raid than had been expected.

Battlegroup Stephan, consisting of eighty-five mixed Panzers III and IV plus thirty-five Panzers II, complete with an artillery component of twelve 105mm. howitzers and four 88mm. flak or anti-tank guns, moved off shortly after midday and reached the area north-east of Gabr Saleh by 1430 to find the fifty Stuarts of 8th Hussars deploying rapidly to meet them.

What followed was the infinite confusion of the first purely panzer versus tank encounter on a large scale to take place in the desert, and it bore little relation to any previously held theories on armoured warfare. Instead of troops or squadrons manoeuvring together in mutually supporting teams, it became a frantic scurry of individual tanks fighting individual battles amid a cloud of sand and smoke, which blotted out visibility beyond a few yards and formed a choking fog illuminated sporadically by the flare of exploding ammunition and often by the flash of cannon much too near for comfort.

The Germans relied upon their drill and routine, the British upon the speed and manoeuvrability of their Honeys together with a

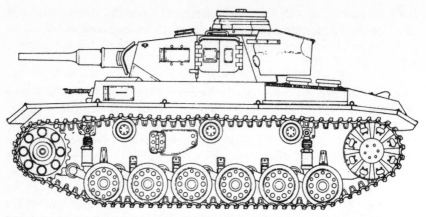

Figure 1 Panzerkampfwagen III (Ausführung F): weight 20 tons; armour 12mm.–30mm.; engine 300 h.p.; maximum speed 25 m.p.h.; armament one 5cm. (L/42), two 7·92 m.g.; crew 5

certain native quickness of reaction, and during the battle no one could tell which combination was proving the more effective. The first charge of the Hussars took them clean through the German formation and they then turned and swept back in again in a manner reminiscent of the charge of the Heavy Brigade at Balaclava, the action being at such close range that the inadequacies of their main armament were unnoticeable. An American observer of the battle (Colonel Bonner Fellers, who had attached himself to XXX Corps Headquarters and was watching with considerable interest the performance of the Honeys) noted that the German anti-tank guns co-operated superbly on the flanks of their panzer columns, but were handicapped by the fog and confusion and suffered losses from the machine-guns of the marauding Hussars as these briefly emerged from the murk, and more later when the Honeys of 5th R.T.R., which had also been detached northwards after the K.D.G.s came hurrying back to join the battle.

It was all, as Alexander Clifford who was also watching it, commented, 'utter, indescribable confusion':

> There was something in it of a naval battle, something of a medieval cavalry charge, but all speeded up madly as you might speed up a cinema film . . .
>
> Inside that frantic jumble tanks were duelling with tanks in running, almost hand-to-hand fights, firing nearly point blank, twisting, dodging, sprinting with screaming treads and whining engines that rose to a shriek as they changed gear. As each new tank loomed up ahead gunners were swinging the muzzles of their guns automatically, eyes strained behind their goggles, fighting through the smoke and dust to discriminate friend from foe . . .

Men told me afterwards that they were not even conscious of the two-pounders going off almost in their ears, so tense was their concentration.[7]

But a strange incident towards the close of the battle served to highlight grave and significant deficiencies in the British approach to armoured warfare. Either as a result of wireless requests or of routine practice, a German petrol and ammunition column arrived on the horizon about an hour before sunset, and as if at a signal the panzers drew off and clustered around it like bees around a honey-pot; and the British could do nothing but stand and watch, for the German guns could pick Honeys off long before their own guns could register effectively. As for the British artillery, it was too scattered, it took too long to get into action and out again – and it still lacked the spirit and training of close co-operation with armour.

The battle was renewed briefly before sundown, but the two sides then drew apart, the Germans to remain on the battlefield (and thus to be able more easily to recover their damaged panzers) the British retiring.

They both claimed victory, and both overestimated the number of hostile tanks destroyed – the first example of a persistent habit which was to play havoc with operational planning on both sides for most of the campaign. Colonel Stephan claimed twenty-four Honeys destroyed and although this figure was close for Honeys knocked out, many had been towed away and were repaired and back in action within twenty-four hours, giving an actual loss to 4th Armoured Brigade of but eleven. The British claimed 'between nineteen and twenty-six' panzers knocked out, but in fact Battle-group Stephan left only two Panzer IIIs and one Panzer II wrecked on the battlefield, while their admirable recovery service took away four damaged Panzer IIIs, and any other damage was sufficiently slight either to be reparable by the crews or left until the battle was over.

There is today no doubt as to which side had come off best in the first armoured mêlée between German panzers and British tanks in the desert, but at the time the true facts were not known and thus had no impact on that vital ingredient in battle, morale.

The tank crews of the 4th Armoured Brigade were delighted anew with the performance of their Honeys and were quite certain that they themselves were the equal of Rommel's panzer crews; and as for the reflections of their commander, from the reports coming in he was certain that his brigade was more than holding its own, and that when the fighting was renewed the next morning the destruction of the nearby enemy force was inevitable. By then the 3rd and 5th Royal Tank Regiments which he had sent off to the north that morning towards Sidi Azeiz and Bardia would have rejoined, bringing between them over a hundred more Honeys, and his concentrated brigade would be irresistible.

The idea of a concentrated *corps*, whether at Gabr Saleh or Sidi Rezegh, seems to have disappeared from everyone's mind.

November 20th was surely the day upon which tactical command on the desert battlefield – on both sides – was at its nadir.

Rommel, still the victim of British deception and ignoring the warnings from his intercept service that the whole of 7th Armoured Division was now west of the Wire, was still intent upon the reduction of Tobruk, and in order to protect himself against further interference he most uncharacteristically gave Cruewell a free hand to use his armour to clear up this intrusion behind the frontier. As for the reports of British troops near both Sidi Rezegh and Bir el Gubi, Sümmermann's Div zvB Afrika could deal with the first and the Ariete of Gambara's C.A.M. the second. Meanwhile, the deadline for the great assault – dawn tomorrow – was fast approaching.

Perhaps Cruewell did not see the reports of the intercept service which gave the probable positions of the left and right wings of the 7th Armoured Division at Bir el Gubi and Gabr Saleh respectively but he did know about those of the previous day from Reconnaissance Battalion 3 which had told of British tanks at Sidi Azeiz and above Bardia. Deciding that here must lie his greatest danger, he sent Neumann-Sylkow's 15th Panzer Division eastward along the Trig Capuzzo and ordered von Ravenstein to drive with the rump of 21st Panzer Division south-eastwards to Sidi Omar, rendezvousing en route with Battlegroup Stephan after the latter had disengaged itself from whatever formation it had been fighting that evening. Thus the intrusive British armour close behind the frontier would be encircled from both north and south, and cut off in a classic German military manoeuvre from both its supplies and its escape route.

Gatehouse's detachment of armoured cars and tanks on the previous day was therefore reaping a temporary, and totally undeserved, reward.

As for Cunningham's plans, these too were based upon misconception. Although he had been startled by the reports that 22nd Armoured Brigade had already lost half their tanks, the equally mistaken reports of 4th Armoured that they had administered a trouncing to the Afrika Korps were adequate compensation. At one moment it had even begun to look as though the original plan for *Crusader* – the destruction of the Afrika Korps in the neighbourhood of Gabr Saleh – was to be realised, and the fact that it was now being undertaken by one brigade group instead of by the whole of XXX Corps, does not seem to have perturbed anyone. But it was the success of 7th Armoured at Sidi Rezegh (in doing nothing but occupy a virtually unprotected airfield) which really excited him.

Here, he felt, was where concentration should take place (without exposing the flank of XIII Corps, of course) and success be exploited. The dominant point of the main Escarpment overlooking the airfield was Point 175, and 7th Armoured Brigade should send out a force to capture this as soon as possible. Meanwhile, Campbell's Support Group would cross the southern escarpment and join them on the airfield and 22nd Armoured must disengage themselves from Bir el Gubi and move northwards to add what was left of their strength to the force in the main battle area. In addition, to provide extra infantry for holding the line along the main Escarpment once the Afrika Regiments had been ejected, 5th South African Brigade was to leave Gueret Hamza, swing in a semicircle to the west around Bir el Gubi, cross the southern escarpment and also make for the airfield, while the remaining force in the area, 1st South African Brigade, took over the task first allotted to 22nd Armoured.

This, it will be remembered, had been to occupy and hold Bir el Gubi which, as events had proved, would entail the prior defeat and ejection of the Ariete Armoured Division from well-fortified defences. Even Corps Headquarters admitted that the situation there was 'obscure', but optimism ruled to such an extent that it was felt that the losses sustained by 22nd Armoured *must* be offset by a corresponding weakening of the Ariete, and the destruction of the remainder should be well within the capability of so doughty a formation as 1st South African Brigade. This atmosphere was somewhat chilled by the reaction of its commander, that staunch individualist Dan Pienaar, who forcefully rejected the argument, pointing out that failure by an armoured brigade was no guarantee of success by infantry; his orders were soon modified to that of just 'masking' the stronghold, his protest being perhaps the one note of realism in that night's communications.

The Germans moved first, 15th Panzer duly debouching on to and moving along the Trig Capuzzo, and the infantry of 21st Panzer (Battlegroup Knabe which had remained behind when Battlegroup Stephan had been detached) moving south-eastwards towards the rendezvous with Stephan at Gabr Lachem, prior to the joint advance on Sidi Omar. But by 0830, Knabe was reporting a strong enemy tank force in front and calling for help from both sides, in response to which von Ravenstein ordered a quicker move north by Stephan but Neumann-Sylkow took no notice. In this he was fully

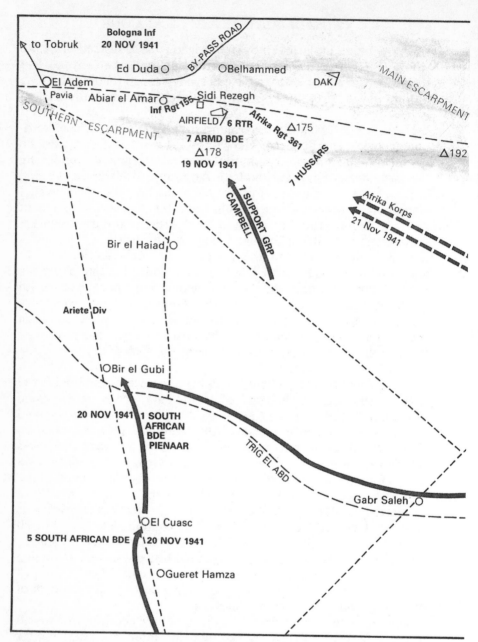

Map 4 *Operation Crusader*: November 20th–21st, 1941

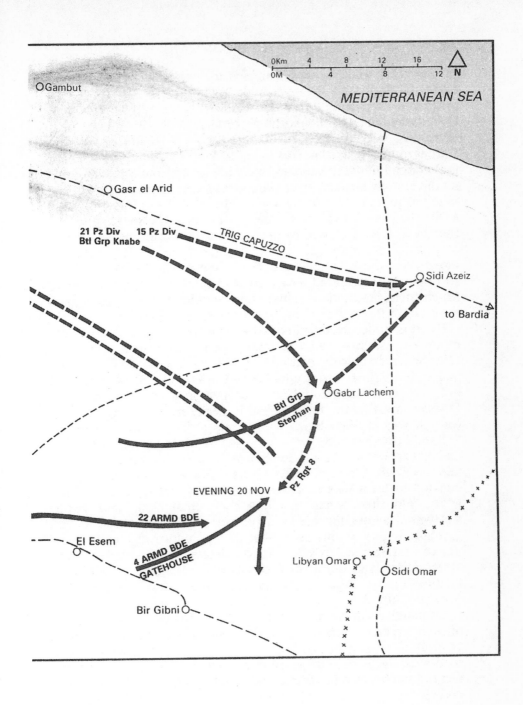

justified, for when Cruewell hurried to the scene, he quickly and correctly diagnosed the opposition as nothing more than a few armoured cars (King's Dragoon Guards) and coldly ordered continued obedience to the morning's orders.

In this, 15th Panzer encountered no opposition at all, but Battlegroup Stephan, having been delayed by late arrival of their fuel and ammunition supplies, was only saved from serious trouble by the equally late arrival of Gatehouse's tank regiments which had failed to join him during the night. The result was a running battle as Stephan first moved across the front of both the 8th Hussars and the 5th R.T.R., followed by the breaking off of the engagement by Stephan on receipt of the hastening order from von Ravenstein to move northwards to meet Knabe – a move which Gatehouse not surprisingly interpreted as a retreat in the face of superior force. Much encouraged, 4th Armoured pursued for about six miles, then leaguered to complete their long-delayed concentration.

By this time, Neumann-Sylkow had reached Sidi Azeiz unmolested and reported the total absence of British armour to Cruewell, who quickly realised his error and concluded that the main axis of the British advance had been the Trig el Abd after all, and not the Trig Capuzzo. Thus the spearhead of 7th Armoured Division must be the force at Sidi Rezegh, and whatever covering force it was at Gabr Saleh was merely a flank guard. Neumann-Sylkow's division had by this time swung south around Sidi Azeiz and met groups Knabe and Stephan at the Gabr Lachem rendezvous, and it was while the combined Afrika Korps was here that Cruewell decided to launch its concentrated strength first against the flank guard and then, when this had been eliminated, back north-westwards across the desert in pursuit of the spearhead at Sidi Rezegh. It was at this point that he was informed that the now united 21st Panzer Division was completely out of both petrol and ammunition, and unless they could be supplied by air would be unable to move until the next day. And the Luftwaffe was already fully committed.

Cunningham in the meantime, beginning to despair of the arrival of that crucial moment in battle upon which the commanding general of one side or another (preferably one's own) can seize and so decide the issue, had early that morning left XXX Corps and returned to his own headquarters east of Maddalena. There he was greeted by reports from Coningham that bombers on the way back from operations over Cyrenaica the previous evening had seen Axis traffic streaming back westwards from Tobruk to Gazala, from El Adem to Acroma and from Bardia towards Tobruk. What this traffic was is now irrelevant, but it could have been anything from empty supply vehicles going back for refill, to Galloway's suggestion that it was Italian administrative troops moving out of critical areas to leave room for operations by German armour; but in the mood of euphoria which had overtaken Eighth Army Headquarters as a result of the advance to Sidi Rezegh and the possibility of the imminent relief of Tobruk, it was interpreted with only the minimum of hesitation as the first move in a general evacuation of Marmarica by Panzergruppe Afrika. This reading of events was to influence thought at the top at several crucial moments during the next few days.

In the immediate future, however, it was to receive something of a setback, for at 1100 Norrie signalled the content of the latest British intercepts of messages between Cruewell and Rommel, which included the exchange setting out Cruewell's new and more accurate understanding of the situation, but not that concerning 21st Panzer Division's enforced immobility. According to these intercepts, 4th Armoured Brigade would by noon be under attack from the entire Afrika Korps, and with sudden appreciation of the fact that Rommel's armour would then be concentrated whilst his own was dispersed, Cunningham sent off urgent signals instructing 22nd Armoured Brigade to ignore its previous orders to join the forces at Sidi Rezegh, and instead to move smartly eastwards and reinforce Gatehouse's brigade. As 22nd Armoured was at this time still embroiled with Dan Pienaar's cautious take-over of the positions around Bir el Gubi and, moreover, itself in need of refuelling and resupply, it would be some while before it could arrive anywhere near Gabr Saleh, so 4th Armoured's fate, had Cunningham's information been correct, might have been sealed; and probably 22nd Armoured's as well, had it run into a combined Afrika Korps just emerging from the triumphant destruction of Gatehouse's force.

Not that this possibility was in any way apparent to Gatehouse or his tank commanders, still brimming with confidence in their own invincibility. Only ten miles away from them to the south-east lay the bulk of 2nd New Zealand Division, its three brigades fully assembled, in battle order and with its full complement of divisional artillery and a battalion of the new Infantry tanks, the Valentines, attached from 1st Army Tank Brigade – all under command of its famous and aggressive commander Bernard Freyberg, already finding the waiting somewhat irksome. But of course, the New Zealanders were an infantry division and a part of XIII Corps, and when the Corps B.G.S., John Harding, suggested that the two formations might find mutual benefit in co-operation, it was an idea which fell on one set of deaf ears.

Freyberg and his men were more than willing to help Gatehouse and the dashing Hussars and tank regiments, but these on their part were unconcerned with the odds which might be against them and wished to fight their own armoured battles without assistance from pedestrians. Cunningham was not entirely to blame for the unco-ordinated lurches into danger of parts of XXX Corps.

As it happened, Cruewell, too, now failed to see the advantages of concentration and co-operation and, ordering 21st Panzer to refuel as quickly as possible and join 15th Panzer the following day in the chase along the Trig el Abd to Sidi Rezegh, he directed Neumann-Sylkow's division south to clear away the 'flanking force' on their own. At 1600, Panzer Regiment 8 set out with two infantry regiments in echelon to the left and a powerful artillery force behind, and half an hour later came upon 4th Armoured Brigade in a sound defensive position on a slight rise, with the sun behind them and full ammunition racks.

For the next thirty minutes a slogging battle between tanks was fought out in which the British advantages of hull-down positions and light were matched by numerical superiority on the German side which gave 15th Panzer an overlap; and then the German artillery component came up and amid the crash of howitzer and 50mm. P.A.K. could be heard the whiplash crack of the 88mms. Soon smoke and flame were erupting from some of the front line Honeys and inevitably the weight of the German attack drove 4th Armoured slowly back down the reverse side of their slope.

Then, as the panzers advanced and light began to fade from the sky, the first hurrying Crusaders of 22nd Armoured appeared to the west, and Neumann-Sylkow threw out an artillery screen to guard his main attack against what might be a strong attack in flank; and by the time the bulk of 22nd Armoured survivors had arrived, darkness had fallen and the night rituals begun. The panzers leaguered where they were, their recovery teams began work on their own casualties while their medical and engineer teams removed the British wounded from the knocked-out Honeys and then blew up the wrecks.

The British brigades withdrew south of the Trig el Abd with 4th Armoured on the right of 22nd Armoured, formed leaguer, reported their tank strengths at respectively 97 Stuarts and 100 Crusaders, and prepared themselves for what the morrow might bring. There was still no thought in anyone's mind of co-operation with the New Zealanders, perhaps because, for the first time since crossing the Wire, two of XXX Corps's brigades were at last within supporting distance of one another.

This meant, however, that the other two components of 7th Armoured Division, 7th Armoured Brigade and the Support Group – the 'spearhead' aimed at what had now become the main target of the operation, Tobruk – although themselves concentrated, were at least thirty miles ahead of the division's best-equipped armoured units and supported only by one infantry brigade, with another held back by its task of 'masking' a hostile armoured division.

Moreover, during the previous night (November 19th/20th), while 7th Armoured Brigade and the South African Armoured Cars had leaguered on the airfield and considered how successfully they had conducted themselves, Panzergruppe Afrika had been making strenuous efforts to reinforce the Afrika Regiments of Sümmermann's Division along the main Escarpment in front of them. Some 100mm. guns had been rushed across from Bardia, a battalion of Bologna infantry with a German engineer battalion and some more artillery were moved up to the eminence at Belhammed from which, although north of the Trig Capuzzo, it could certainly shell the airfield; and the German infantry along the main Escarpment grouped for a dawn attack on 7th Armoured Brigade's positions.

This, covered only by the attackers' anti-tank guns, was quickly beaten back, but at 0800 another attack was launched under cover of a much heavier barrage from the force at Belhammed, and although the German infantry was again held by the British artillery and the tank guns, the position of 7th Brigade on the exposed and open plain clearly left a great deal to be desired. The armoured cars, for instance, if they were not to disperse away from the airfield altogether, could do little or nothing to protect themselves. According to 4th South African Armoured Cars' War Diary:

> R.H.Q. had (rather rashly perhaps) parked next to a battery of 25-pounders, which were severely shelling the enemy position on the Sidi Rezegh ridge to the N.W. This idyllic state of affairs came to an end at 0830 hours when the enemy Artillery got the range of these guns (and incidentally of R.H.Q.) with unpleasant accuracy. A rapid move of a few hundred yards became necessary, and such was the urgency of the case that R.H.Q.'s tea and sausages . . . were left to waste their sweetness on the desert air. The 25-pounders were forced to pull out also, but not so fast but that a gunner (evidently a man of unusual presence of mind), contrived to carry off R.H.Q.'s breakfast with him. He undoubtedly deserved the tea and sausages, but he might perhaps have left (or anyhow returned) the plates and the mugs.[8]

The shelling continued on and off throughout the day, but there were no more attempts at infantry assault on the position, and in their turn 7th Armoured quickly decided that the attack ordered by Cunningham on Point 175 would need more infantry support than they had available – even after the whole of the Support Group had closed up. This should therefore await the arrival of 5th South

African Brigade which would not reach the southern escarpment until late in the afternoon. As its commander, Brigadier B. F. Armstrong, was understandably reluctant to move into the danger area at night, it was obvious that Afrika Regiment 361 would remain undisturbed by anything except minor harassment by light units until the next day.

The rest of November 20th thus passed comparatively uneventfully at Sidi Rezegh. Sporadic shelling by German artillery certainly made the place uncomfortable for the occupants and a Stuka attack during the afternoon added to the noise and fury, but there were few casualties to report at the end of the day.

Then, in the evening, General Gott arrived with plans for the next day – November 21st – and revealed that the decision had been taken to order the break-out of the Tobruk garrison to be launched at dawn. Norrie had in fact given the code-word ('Pop') during the afternoon, and plans were now laid for the infantry on the Sidi Rezegh airfield to clear the ridge to the north so that the armour could then make its way down the Escarpment at Abiar el Amar to the west, to reach and cross the Trig Capuzzo and the Axis by-pass and meet the Tobruk Matildas of 32nd Army Tank Brigade at Ed Duda after their break-out. In due course, they would all be joined by Armstrong's 5th South African Brigade which should have crossed the airfield during the morning, and together the combined armour and infantry would advance westwards and secure the ground between Ed Duda and the main Tobruk–El Adem road.

It all promised very well, and no one there was to know of another factor about to be introduced into the situation. The obvious need for secrecy to shroud all such ploys as Brigadier Shearer's will on occasion itself contribute to their failure or untimely end. That evening in its normal news bulletin, the British Broadcasting Corporation had joyfully announced that the Eighth Army, with some 75,000 excellently armed and equipped men, had invaded Libya with the object of destroying the remainder of the Axis forces in Africa, and that the operation was proceeding successfully; and when Rommel heard of it, the scales dropped from his eyes. He abruptly abandoned the proposed assault on Tobruk, approved Cruewell's orders to the Afrika Korps for the following morning and urged action at the earliest moment and with the greatest speed. As a result von Ravenstein's refuelled division was moving by 0300, and an hour later Cruewell received a further spur to action from his Commander-in-Chief.

The situation in this whole theatre is very critical. In addition to the strong enemy force south-east of Tobruk, 500 or 600 enemy cars are moving through the desert towards Benghazi from the south-east. On 21 November *Afrikakorps* must begin moving in good time and follow the enemy tanks which have advanced toward Tobruk. Objective the centre airfield at Sidi Rezegh.[9]

The feint moves of Oasis Group between Jarabub and Jalo were at last having an effect, and it was rather a pity that it was not – as had been intended – towards a dispersion of Rommel's forces, but towards a greater concentration.

Inside Tobruk, the news that at last the moment for the break-out had come generated immense excitement, lifting the spirits of the garrison, especially those of the crews of the thirty-two cruisers and sixty-nine Matildas who were to lead the sortie, with their attached infantry. Although the patrolling across the no-man's-land on the south-east sector had not been pressed of late quite so vigorously as it had been when the Australians were there, it was felt that sufficient was known of the enemy posts which made up the first objectives – 'Butch', 'Jill', 'Jack', 'Tiger' and 'Tugun' – their surrounding minefields and their Italian occupants, for it to be assumed that they would all be captured within the time schedule. The 'I' tanks would then press on and, despite their lack of speed, most probably reach Ed Duda before the cruisers of 7th Armoured Brigade coming up from the south. Anyway, it would be a healthily competitive race, and in the meantime the hours of darkness must be used by engineers to gap the minefields, open the wire and bridge the anti-tank ditches along the break-out sector.

It all began very well, D Squadron, of 7th R.T.R. leading through the gap, swinging left to assault 'Butch' and – with some losses on minefields of which they had inexplicably received no briefings – completely surprising the occupants who were being marshalled and led back towards the perimeter by 0900. The R.T.R. tank crews were rather surprised, too, for the occupants proved to be Germans from the Afrika Regiment and not Italians from the Bologna Division as they had been led to expect.

Half an hour later, C Squadron of the 4th R.T.R. was in trouble. Not only had they been delayed by a bottleneck on their own side of the break-out gap, but their start line had been laid askew and many of the flank tanks had run on to mines and been variously knocked out of the fight; by the time they had covered the mile and a half approach to their objective, 'Jill', they were not only behind their schedule but also behind their infantry, the 2nd Battalion the Black Watch. These, however, with a fine disregard for the advantages of armoured protection, pressed on through the murk, rushed the minefield surrounding the post, broke through the wire and to the thrilling skirls of their pipes stormed the post at point of bayonet. Such actions exact their price, however, and though the Afrika Regiment survivors here were also soon on their way into Tobruk, white and shaken by the ordeal they had just experienced, they could console themselves with the numbers of dead Highlanders lining their route.

Their blood up, the remnants of the battalion immediately rallied behind the 4th R.T.R. and moved towards the main objective of the first phase of the break-out – 'Tiger'. Among the Highlanders was a

Map 5   Tobruk break-out: November 21st, 1941

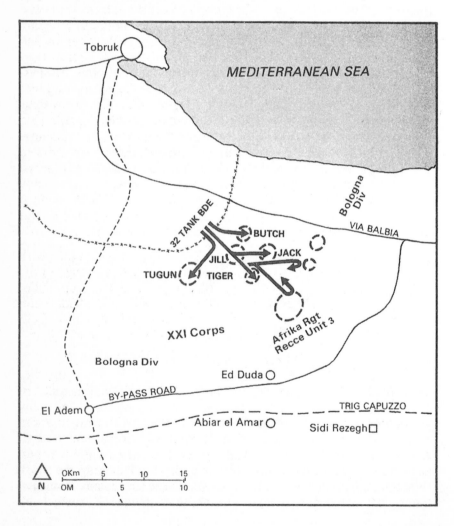

Rhodesian who had chosen to fight with the men from whom his ancestors had come:

> The enemy held his fire until we were past the wire. And then his machine-guns let go. Such of us as survived at once fell flat to take what cover we could; but our Adjutant, who had been wounded, crawled to where we were lying and got to his feet. 'Isn't this the Black Watch!' he cried. 'Then – charge!' He waved us on with his stick and was instantly killed. We rose and took 'Tiger' with the bayonet . . . but of our battalion that evening only 8 officers and 196 men were able to answer to their names. [10]

'Jack' was captured by 1030, but 'Tugun' proved a very hard nut to crack and the assault had faltered by mid-afternoon with tanks held up by minefields or anti-tank guns, and infantry completely pinned down. Moreover, other assaults to take secondary objectives beyond 'Tiger' were thrown back, and by the time set for the final drive to Ed Duda (1430) 32nd Army Tank Brigade was, in fact, bitterly fighting to retain the ground won so far against rapidly assembled and robust German counter-attacks, organised by Rommel who by this time was personally directing the battle alongside four 88mms which he had rushed across from Gambut.

Then just before 1600, a message came through that the juncture with the XXX Corps troops from Sidi Rezegh must be put off at least until the next day. At Sidi Rezegh also, the battle had not gone quite as General Gott had hoped.

As with the break-out, it had started off well enough. One of the artillery commanders wrote of the dawn of that epochal day:

> The slow first light of November 21st, 1941, broke on the usual desert scene at Sidi Rezegh. Leaguers were dispersing. From every quarter came the noise of transport starting up, guns rumbled slowly and cautiously into battle positions; chilled, silent men with sleep-heavy eyes moved mechanically into their appointed places. Everywhere full use was being made of the valuable 30 minutes of half-light, when visibility was too poor for the enemy to pick out a target.
>
> Support Group of the 7th Armoured Division was preparing for battle . . . [11]

Under the cover of a four-minute concentrated barrage by the 25-pounders, three companies of the 1st King's Royal Rifle Corps and one of the 2nd Rifle Brigade, with tanks on each flank and carrier platoons to the front, formed up on the exposed ground to the south of the airfield and at 0830 began their advance, with no more substantial shield than a smokescreen, against Italian and

German infantry well dug in along the line of the Escarpment in positions with excellent fields of fire. The carrier platoons, who had raced forward so fast that they caught up with the tail of the barrage and were fortunate in suffering no casualties at that stage, overran many forward German and Italian gun positions, and then the platoons in the centre reached the lip of the Escarpment to see a 100-yard-wide slope in front of them beyond which the ground dropped almost vertically. The slope was peppered with enemy posts ensconced in small wadis and birs from which came a hail of small-arms fire, so the line of carriers wheeled right and swung sheer across the width of the slope to reach a wadi running across its eastern edge, where the riflemen swarmed out, cleared the wadi and began pouring enfilade fire across the slope; but many of the enemy posts were out of range or covered by dips and bumps in the slope. On one side of this central thrust, carriers of D Platoon had run into concentrated anti-tank fire and been virtually wiped out; on the other side C Platoon reached their objective unscathed.

On the airfield, the main bulk of the riflemen began to march forward. There was still enough dust and fog to screen them from anything but the artillery fire as they crossed the airfield, but once they were in the ground to the north they were in open view of the German and Italian posts along the line of the Escarpment, and the closer they got to the lip the more they were exposed to posts further back on the reverse slope.

Now was fought a pure infantry battle in which platoons edged up to defensive posts under cover of fire from neighbouring platoons and the age-old leap-frog tactics, sparked by leadership, engineered by training and routine, and sustained by unbelievable courage, gradually closed the gap between attackers and objectives until the last charge with bomb and bayonet could be mounted. A posthumous Victoria Cross was won by Rifleman Beeley, who when the time came for the final assault against his platoon's target found himself the only unhurt survivor, so he raced across the last stretch alone firing his Bren-gun from the hip and with that uncanny combination of luck and accuracy which is occasionally bestowed on high enterprise, wiped out seven occupants of the post who between them had been manning an anti-tank gun and two machine-guns. He was himself killed by a grenade when about twenty yards from the post.

By noon, the whole of the lip of the Escarpment was in the hands of the riflemen, some 600 mixed German and Italian prisoners were being led back towards the airfield while the bodies of nearly 400 more littered the battlefield. But of the 300 officers and men who had mustered on the airfield at dawn, 84 were not present at the subsequent roll call.

Now the armour could go forward, and with a great deal of panache the Crusaders of 6th R.T.R. swept across the ridge past the tomb of the prophet, down towards the Trig Capuzzo and Ed Duda beyond; and straight on to the anti-tank guns of Reconnaissance Battalion 3, reinforced by the four 88mm. guns which were later to halt the 'I' tanks breaking out from Tobruk, all under the personal command of Rommel himself.

As on Hafid Ridge during *Battleaxe*, the Crusaders which reached the reverse slope were knocked out to a tank, those lucky ones behind rapidly retiring as soon as the sight of the blazing hulls and the sound of high velocity shell revealed the situation; but in any case they would have had to be recalled, for the leading panzers of the combined 15th and 21st Panzer Division – the entire Afrika Korps, in fact – were in sight to the south-east and 7th Armoured Brigade and the Support Group were in danger of annihilation.

Perhaps the main trouble with the British command of the battle on November 21st was that 7th Armoured Division were fighting two battles thirty miles apart, and however talented General Gott may have been, he could not exercise close control in both places at once.

Brigadiers Gatehouse and Scott-Cockburn (of the 22nd Armoured Brigade) had spent the night preparing their battle positions for what promised to be the long-expected clash of armour the following day, still with undiminished confidence in their ability to fight the whole of the Afrika Korps and destroy it on their own, despite their previous experience against, respectively, one panzer division and one Italian armoured division in which each had suffered casualties and been forced to retire. They certainly felt no need for help from Bernard Freyberg's infantrymen away to the south, and a great deal of their planning was directed towards a relentless pursuit of a beaten enemy once he turned and ran.

It thus came as little surprise to either of them, or to their tank crews, when after a night spent listening to the sounds of armoured movement to the north and to reports from 11th Hussars of a strong concentration of panzers north-east of Gabr Saleh, in the morning the wide spaces in front of them emptied after but the briefest exchange of fire, and the Afrika Korps was seen streaming off over the horizon to the north-west. Scott-Cockburn's Crusaders raced across to catch the enemy in flank but mistimed the strike and hit only a rearguard and then thin air, while Gatehouse's Honeys were a little slow getting away and despite their speed never managed to catch up in force.

The Crusaders did manage to check their first lunge, regroup, swing forward and launch another attack in flank later during the morning, but they came up against some 88mms with Afrika Korps H.Q. in the centre of the column and lost, according to Oberst Kriebel who was with Neumann-Sylkow's H.Q., seven of their number before the rest retired out of range. For the next hour 22nd Armoured hung on the flanks of 15th Panzer, during which time according to their reports they destroyed about 200 German trucks and cars (there is no mention of these losses in the Afrika Korps Diary) and then, because of a 'hitch in the petrol supply', they had to break off the action and refuel. The short range of the Honeys had already forced a similar check on the 4th Armoured Brigade, but as they watched what they considered to be a thoroughly beaten enemy disappearing over the north-western horizon, few doubted that a great victory had been won or paused to wonder what might be happening to their comrades-in-arms away towards Tobruk. Most of them, at that point, had never heard of Sidi Rezegh.

By this time, in fact, one formation of the 7th Armoured Brigade was already in process of annihilation. In the face of what he at first thought was but a minor threat, Brigadier Davy had hastily thrown the thirty-odd old cruisers and twenty Crusaders of the 7th Hussars in front of the approaching enemy, while he rethought the day's engagements:

> From the point of view of the 7th Armoured Brigade the problem was clear-cut. The sortie from Tobruk . . . had already begun, and the leading troops of the 70th Division should now be approaching Ed Duda. The attack [to the north] must take place as planned. But the arrival of German armour from the south-east was a threat to the main project and had to be dealt with at once. Other troops, known to be operating farther to the south, would soon be able to intervene and it was important that the smallest possible number of troops should be diverted from the attack towards Ed Duda.[12]

His own H.Q. was still south of point 178 on the southern escarpment, and having deployed a battery of Royal Horse Artilley and his reserve force of 2nd R.T.R. cruisers close by, as an outer shield to the Support Group forces still occupying the ground around the airfield, Davy accompanied the Hussars on their allocated task 'to locate and delay the advance of the enemy tanks'. Although he was sceptical of reports from the south that the Afrika Korps had been defeated, and somewhat surprised by the continued absence from the battlefield of both 5th South African Brigade and 22nd Armoured (he had not known of the switch across by Scott-Cockburn's brigade the previous evening) he still thought that he was faced at the most with only one panzer division, and that 4th Armoured Brigade would be aggressively snapping at its heels.

As it was, the combined force of the most famous armoured corps in the world at that time was sweeping down upon two regiments of outdated tanks, spread across some ten miles of desert with a single battery of artillery somewhere between them.

Davy and the Hussars first saw the oncoming hordes about 0830, but even then considerable doubt existed as to their identity for the head of the attack was wreathed in lorries of the Support Group's B Echelon, swept up in the course of 21st Panzer's advance and now – ignored by the panzer crews – endeavouring frantically to get out of the way. Among them, coolly and efficiently, the German anti-tank gunners had infiltrated their mobile 50mm. P.A.K. guns and with these they opened fire on the Hussars, who could not reply at that range anyway and were hindered by the swarm of British soft-skinned transport even when the range shortened.

During the holocaust which followed, all but ten of the old cruisers (and these the ones that had broken down before battle had joined) and all the Hussars' Crusaders were destroyed; not just knocked out with some possibility of recovery and repair, but completely wrecked as the panzers rode over their positions and pumped shell after shell into their smoking and immobile hulls until they were reduced to scrap iron. Between the wrecks, surviving crew members dodged from cover to cover, carrying wounded, dragging burnt and pain-wracked comrades out of hatches, falling under the hail of machine-gun fire; 7th Hussars was not to be seen again in the desert, although re-formed, it fought in Burma.

Two miles to the west, Davy's reserve cruiser force from 2nd R.T.R. was held off by the inevitable German anti-tank screen, its early efforts to intervene having merely served to push 15th Panzer to the right so that its weight was added to that of 21st Panzer as they crashed together down on the Hussars. During the morning, therefore, 2nd R.T.R. suffered little damage – a piece of good fortune which they owed, though they did not know it, to what had now become the overriding aim behind the Afrika Korps advance: to sweep down the gentle slope westwards between the southern and main Escarpments to Abiar el Amar obliterating whatever force held the airfield, then across the Trig Capuzzo to Ed Duda, eventually to make contact with Artillery Group Böttcher at Belhammed. In this way they would eliminate the British forces threatening the besiegers of Tobruk, Rommel's command would again be concentrated and could then turn and clear up the remaining Allied units littering the desert between Tobruk and the frontier. But first, the panzer divisions must halt to refuel and replenish their ammunition racks from the supply vehicles now congregating at the head of the valley down which they intended to charge.

The Support Company of 2nd Rifle Brigade were to be the first to feel the weight massing against the British force around Sidi Rezegh, for they occupied the eastern end of the southern escarpment and it was in this direction that the first of the panzers to complete refuelling decided to investigate:

> Sixteen tanks appeared over a ridge moving slowly westwards about eight hundred yards away into the valley to the north-east. The two 2-pounders on the ridge to the north under command of Ward Gunn opened fire on them. The 25-pounders of the 60th Field Regiment engaged them over open sights. Four of them went up in flames. The remainder halted, dodged about and, finding that they could make no headway against our fire, but having had a good look at our positions, withdrew just out of sight. They had returned our fire and the two anti-tank guns had been knocked out. It was quite clear that the enemy's retirement was only temporary . . . Everyone in the Battalion knew that the Germans were choosing their own time and their own place of attack and that not sixteen but sixty tanks might appear at any moment over the ridge.[13]

During the short interval before the onslaught, frantic efforts were made to dig just a little deeper into the unyielding rock, and messages were sent off to Davy's H.Q. warning them of the developing situation and asking for any available tank protection – messages which were greeted with frank incredulity by the brigade major who indignantly accused them of firing on 7th Hussars. This was not a comforting reaction for the riflemen and their gunners, now becoming acutely aware of their isolation in the face of ominous German preparations.

First came a series of Stuka attacks (not very effective once fox-holes were deep enough for men to lie in them), followed by some concentrated shelling – and then the panzers moved in. There was nothing the riflemen could do but shrink lower into their weapon pits, and the only three vehicles still with them – the signals trucks – were soon under fire, two in flames while the other, by some incredible miracle, was driven unscathed out of danger by a quick-thinking and dauntless corporal. They had, however, sent off signals to Brigade Headquarters couched in such terms as to persuade the brigade major that friends were not being mistaken for foes, so five Crusaders arrived on the edge of the battalion area – to be totally destroyed well before their 2-pounders could be brought into effective range. And all the while a little dog ran pathetically from slit trench to slit trench seeking its master and attracting a hail of fire to any spot where it stopped and made obviously friendly overtures to some subterranean figure.

This stage of the battle was thus fought out between panzer crews and gunners who, despite the flimsiness of their gun-shields where they existed at all, remained coolly at their posts until, separately and inevitably, they were killed or too badly wounded to continue serving their weapons. Two 2-pounder anti-tank guns and a Bofors anti-aircraft gun were at one moment the only weapons capable of engaging effectively and one of their officers was Lieutenant Patrick McSwiney:

> At 1130 hrs the enemy came on again and were engaged by the anti-tank guns in front of my troop and were halted after six tanks had been put out of action . . . only one member of the troop survived. A few minutes earlier Colonel de Robeck had appeared and found me lying full length on the ground whilst moving between my guns. He was standing in the front of his truck waving his fly whisk – presumably at the bullets which were flying thick and fast from the machine-guns of the leading enemy tanks! We passed the time of day from our respective positions and I asked for permission to withdraw. I was informed that this was a case for no withdrawal![14]

One of the anti-tank guns commanded by Second Lieutenant Ward Gunn was soon put out of action and when the crew of the other had all been killed or wounded, the driver began backing it away. At that moment, Gunn was joined by Major Bernard Pinney who shouted to him, 'Go and stop that blighter!' – which seemed a little hard on the chap even at the time – and Gunn, the wounded driver and Pinney together cleared the 2-pounder and got it back into action until Ward Gunn was himself killed and the ammunition set alight. Pinney put the flames out and continued firing until another hit finally wrecked the gun, whereat he reversed and drove it out of danger; he was killed the following day in not dissimilar circumstances, and Ward Gunn was later awarded a posthumous Victoria Cross.

But in the meantime, the 25-pounders of the 60th Field Regiment just to the north of the Rifle Brigade positions were themselves being slowly but surely overwhelmed, as panzers of 21st Panzer Division came across from their refuelling point and began the move down the valley between the southern and main Escarpments. Gun after gun fell silent as the crews were picked off, as the guns were hit, as the ammunition blazed or ran out; between the panzers the German infantry were moving insidiously but inevitably forward, and it seemed that all too soon the last artillery screen would be thrust aside and only the Support Group headquarters units and the survivors of 6th R.T.R.'s morning attempt to reach Ed Duda would stand between the Afrika Korps and their objective at the bottom of the valley across the airfield.

And at this point, 21st Panzer ran short of ammunition, while 15th Panzer on their left flank and still south of the southern escarpment became conscious not only of 2nd R.T.R. pressure, but also of 'a fresh armoured force superior to ours' manoeuvring away to the south-west. This was, in fact, 22nd Armoured Brigade who had swung westwards after their pause for refuelling. They had no sense of urgency – for how could there be a crisis to the north with the Afrika Korps so badly beaten that they had turned and run but a few hours before? As for 4th Armoured Brigade, they too were in no haste to move after their quarry, and when they did so found themselves delayed by patches of boggy sand caused by a sudden mid-morning rain storm. In the event, both British brigades were to take several hours in their much faster tanks to cover the same ground that Afrika Korps had covered in just over one, and their comrades in 7th Armoured Brigade and the Support Group were to see little of them before darkness fell; but at least their reported presence now gave respite to the hard-pressed men in the valley.

And one small action fought against the panzers was crowned with success, though its lessons seem not to have been appreciated for far too long. When the panzers withdrew again to cluster around their petrol and ammunition lorries, two troops of South African armoured cars went forward to observe them and on their way up passed a squadron of 2nd R.T.R. tanks lying hull-down behind a ridge:

> Both troops moved closer to the enemy column, in spite of heavy shell fire, and were busy counting enemy tanks when a party of 25 of them detached themselves from the main enemy concentration and came straight for our patrols.[15]

These manoeuvred carefully and with forethought, gradually enticing the panzers forward out of support of their own guns until they suddenly found themselves under those of the hull-down 2nd R.T.R. cruisers. The result was the destruction of five panzers and damage inflicted on six more without the slightest loss or damage to the British or South Africans; and, as the South African history says, 'an object lesson in what could happen if the British tanks caught their opponents without their regular anti-tank screen'.

The fighting for the rest of that day was concentrated around the eastern end of the southern escarpment, where 2nd R.T.R.'s screen of elderly cruisers was gradually whittled away until by nightfall only six were still in action, and the full weight of the attack fell upon the survivors of the Rifle Brigade Support Company. Their attached artillery now destroyed, one platoon totally eliminated and the others all severely reduced in strength, the order was given for the survivors to make their own separate ways out of danger:

> Under cover of a few wisps of smoke from the burning vehicles and the occasional distraction of friendly aircraft flying overhead, most of Battalion Headquarters and subsequently most of 'S' Company crawled away, all being shot at as they did so.[16]

By nightfall, the eastern end of the southern escarpment was in German hands, and with all the evidence now available it can be seen that November 21st, 1941, was a day of some achievement for the Afrika Korps. They had destroyed the 7th Hussars, inflicted considerable damage on two Royal Tank Regiments – the 2nd and the 6th – destroyed a large number of the Support Group's guns and wiped out the Support Company of the Rifle Brigade. Moreover, on the other side of the battlefield, the Afrika Regiment and Reconnaissance Battalion 3 had stemmed both the break-out by the Army Tank Brigade from Tobruk and the attempt by 7th Armoured Brigade to push forward to join hands with them, and as this portion of the day's battle had been under Rommel's personal direction, one would think that he had by evening good cause for satisfaction.

He was, in fact, deeply worried – both by the apparent weight of forces between which he and his immediate command were sandwiched, and by Cruewell's failure to bring the Afrika Korps down through the valley to take some of that weight away. His messages to Cruewell had held during the latter part of that day a note of irascibility which did nothing to ease Cruewell's own problems, or to soothe the worries with which the commander of the Afrika Korps was beset – for he, too, had little idea of the true picture.

In Cruewell's mind, his famous corps was almost completely encircled by forces 'immeasurably superior' – to quote the Afrika Korps Diary – to his own, with an apparently inexhaustible supply of fresh reserves to throw against him whichever way he turned. His route to Ed Duda was blocked by the powerful artillery formations of the Support Group which had beaten back his panzers; to the south-west were the armoured formations of which he had received late intelligence, and beyond them, according to Italian sources, another strong force of British or South African infantry was containing the Ariete Armoured Division and awaiting opportunity to pounce upon his flank if he ventured too far west; while he knew that behind him was the 4th Armoured Brigade Group closing up from Gabr Saleh after the morning's disengagement.

Although he was more than willing to accede to his Commander-in-Chief's instructions to concentrate with the other forces of Panzergruppe Afrika nearer to Tobruk, it seemed to him that he could not, after all, do so by the direct route down the valley. He would have to regroup to the east and then send aid to Rommel along the Trig Capuzzo, having extricated his forces from between the British brigades and regained that freedom of manoeuvre which was the constant desire of the well-trained panzer leader.

Spurred on by another missive from Rommel which reached him at 2240 and opened with the instruction, 'On 22 November, D.A.K. in conjunction with Pavia Division will hold the area reached today, as well as Belhammed. The Corps will prevent enemy tank forces on its front from pushing through to Tobruk,' Cruewell ordered 15th Panzer away eastwards to regroup seven miles due south of Gambut around Point 196, and von Ravenstein to take his 21st Panzer Division down the Escarpment near Point 175 and along the Trig Capuzzo to Belhammed, where he would also assume command of Afrika Regiment 361 and an infantry regiment, Number 155, whose main duty would be to expel the British from the Escarpment as soon as possible.

Thus, during the night of November 21st/22nd, for the third time in three days, the Afrika Korps vacated the field before XXX Corps formations which had little chance of defeating or even resisting them had they stayed. No wonder the British remained confident of victory, only the remnants of 7th Armoured Brigade and the Support Group registering even surprise as they watched the German infantry and armour stream away from the ground they had won so doughtily.

At Eighth Army Headquarters, the atmosphere by the evening of November 21st was filled with that supreme confidence which is based upon solid and predicted achievements. As foretold, XXX Corps had met and thoroughly defeated the Afrika Korps. Simply by adding up the figures of panzers destroyed coming in from the brigade headquarters (and according to that day's figures alone 170 panzers had been 'hit' – a phrase which in that air of euphoria was interpreted as damaged beyond repair), it was evident that Rommel's armour had been reduced by over 50 per cent. This was further borne out by the figures of XXX Corps's casualties – for they could surely not have lost as many tanks as that without inflicting comparable losses on the enemy? In any case, it all fitted in with the belief sparked by the R.A.F. reports of the westward flow of Axis traffic two days before, that Rommel was pulling back out of Marmarica and was more than ready to evacuate the area at least as far back as Gazala.

That evening a Press cable was sent from Cairo which read:

It is authoritatively stated that the Libyan battle, which was at its height this afternoon, is going extremely well. The proportion of Axis tank casualties to British is authoritatively put at three to one. General Rommel, the German commander, is trying to break through, but his situation is becoming more unfavourable . . . [17]

Many people who read it took even greater heart from the slightly guarded tone of the last sentence, confidently assuming that total victory, though not yet fully established, would be consummated within a matter of hours.

The only question causing General Cunningham great concern was the failure of the link-up with the Tobruk break-out. Here there seemed definite indications of a check to his plans (for the schedule still called for the use of the port facilities to fuel the general advance by Day 3) and he had already put measures in hand to help in that area. Since early that morning, XIII Corps had been implementing their portion of the *Crusader* plan, for Cunningham had phoned Godwin-Austen just before 0900 and suggested a move northwards by the New Zealanders and the 7th Brigade of 4th Indian Division, although he emphasised, somewhat uncharacteristically and surely unusually for one in his position, that he 'was not going to press XIII Corps Commander if XIII Corps Commander was against the project'.

But Godwin-Austen was as eager to see his corps into action as Bernard Freyberg was to lead his division, and by noon the New Zealand brigades were all across the Trig el Abd with two-thirds of the Matildas of 1st Army Tank Brigade, while 7th Indian Brigade and the rest of the Matildas were abreast on their right. By late afternoon, New Zealand Division Cavalry had reached Sidi Azeiz where they took fifty-five very surprised Germans and Italians prisoner, 4th New Zealand Brigade were moving up through them across the Trig Capuzzo towards the heights above Bardia, 5th Brigade had swung right along the Hafid Ridge towards the rear of Fort Capuzzo and 6th Brigade had swung the other way towards the Trig Capuzzo in order to concentrate at Bir el Hariga, some ten miles west of Sidi Azeiz.

Meanwhile, the Punjabis, Sikhs and Royal Sussex battalions of 7th Indian Brigade were moving in behind the two Omars, Libyan Omar and Sidi Omar, in order the following morning to attempt to repeat their successes of almost a year before at Nibeiwa, the Tummars and Sidi Barrani. They were imbued now with as much confidence as they had been then, with perhaps more justification than the rest of Eighth Army.

By the evening of November 21st, then, three brigades of XIII
Corps were poised to fall on the rear defences of the frontier while
one – 6th New Zealand – was pointed away from that battle area
towards Tobruk; and with the delay in link-up with the Tobruk
garrison in mind, Cunningham had sent a message to Norrie
offering this extra infantry reinforcement should he feel he needed
it. Unfortunately, there was an ambiguity about the message which
gave Norrie the impression that the New Zealanders would be
coming up along the Trig el Abd instead of the Trig Capuzzo, and,
mindful of the communications of his over-extended corps and
conscious of the presence already of the two virtually unemployed
South African infantry brigades, he rejected the offer on the
grounds that he already had enough infantry above the Escarpment
– a rejection which elicited the decidedly huffy comment from
Cunningham that if, in that case, Tobruk were not relieved soon, he
would 'certainly require to see the Corps Commander tomorrow'!

The armour was beginning to reap the consequences of its own
hubris.

Throughout this period – and indeed until the end of the year and
well into the next – the troops were living in conditions of acute
discomfort. Although in the daytime some warmth was engendered
by action and the bright but often watery sun, the nights were
bitterly cold and rain always fell at some point, so that during that
brief spell of half-light in which every day's 'stand-to' took place,
the desert was spotted with clumps of bone-chilled, unshaven,
unwashed men groping clumsily for their weapons, for their water-
bottles, for any remnant of their rations which they had saved, for
their boots if they had cared to take them off before they had fallen
asleep.

If their days had not been riven by battle, pain, fear and the
deaths of comrades, then they had been spent either in dry, dusty,
flea-bitten and scorpion-ridden boredom, or in equally dusty and
much more thirst-making hard labour at the wheel of a lorry, at the
shaft of a spade or pick-axe, or confined within the shaking, reeling,
jolting box of some vehicle or other as it swayed across the lunar
landscape with such inconsequential and unpredictable jumps and
drops that it was necessary to cling fast all the time to some
comparative fixture in order to avoid not only painful knocks but
the ever-present risk of broken bones.

Thirst, fleas, grit, sweat-caked clothing, cuts, bruises and desert
sores, sanitation at its most rudimentary; this was life in the desert
for men of both Eighth Army and Panzergruppe Afrika during the
last days of 1941. The only comfort, even for those whose sense of
privacy and individuality was the most developed, was the pro-

pinquity of lives circumscribed by the walls of a lorry, the hull of a tank, or for infantry in defence posts the line of weapon-pits or the chasm of a wadi. Even for the formations which had not yet seen action with the enemy, such as those of the 22nd Guards Brigade organising and watching over the Field Maintenance Centres by now well established south of the Trig el Abd, the aridity of life drove men in upon themselves, limiting their horizons to the world of platoon, battery, tank troop or even just tank crew; and if memories now recall the comradeship and the flashes of excitement and occasional triumph, they forget the fear, the cold, the aching guts, the dreadful sights, the stench, the disgust.

The night of November 21st/22nd was no different from the others; it rained everywhere almost continuously so that in the morning hard pans had been converted into large sheets of water and, according to Alexander Clifford, sandy wastes reduced to the 'consistency of cold cream'. Behind the Omars waited the British and Indian infantry of the 7th Indian Brigade with the Matildas of 42nd R.T.R., overlooking a minefield of uncertain position and magnitude.

The attack went in on time with armour and infantry carriers racing in together, and supporting infantry following:

> But there *was* a minefield! . . . just forward of the enemy's foremost posts – a narrow belt of mines hidden in the sand; and the first wave of tanks ran slap on to it. It took more than a mine to knock out a Matilda but tracks were blown off and sprockets damaged, and nearly all the leading tanks were brought to a sudden halt in full view of the enemy. Worse was to follow, for behind the minefield, carefully sited on rising ground with a good field of fire, well dug in so that their muzzles almost rested on the sand, was a troop of the dreaded 88 mm. guns. Their first shot went clean through the front of Lieutenant Hembrow's tank, set it on fire and killed the entire crew; and they followed this up by engaging all the first echelon of tanks lying crippled on the minefield. The Matilda carried no H.E. with which to reply; and though they engaged them with their Besa machine-guns, they were unable to silence them.[18]

But another Matilda squadron found a way through the minefield and the Royal Sussex then 'poured over the position' which surrendered early in the afternoon.

This was the post of Sidi Omar, and later that day the 4th/6th Punjabis with their escorting Matildas repeated the operation at Libyan Omar a few miles to the west – repeated also the experience of watching their tanks shot up by well-sited 88mm. guns, and paid for their victory with the same proportion of casualties.

Away to the north, 5th New Zealand Brigade had stormed into Fort Capuzzo early in the morning and proceeded to rip out the telephone lines and wreck water-pipes and any other permanent installations they could find; 4th Brigade had reached the outskirts of Bardia and captured a German transport park with all its vehicles and personnel, and 6th Brigade – after a hair-raising night journey – reached the Trig Capuzzo about 1000 and an hour after received orders to move further westwards. Cunningham and Norrie had resolved their misunderstandings and XXX Corps could certainly do with more infantry fed into the gap north of the main Escarpment up towards Belhammed, so the New Zealanders should move first of all as far as an obscure point named Bir el Chleta, just six miles south-west of Gambut. As this was the area in which Afrika Korps Headquarters had been stationed for some time, and to which Cruewell had directed 15th Panzer the previous evening, it seemed likely to become crowded.

But not as soon as it might have done, for Rommel was now in control of the battle from the Axis side, his preoccupation with Tobruk for the moment forgotten, replaced by an acute sense of the passage of time and a determination to make up for any that had been lost. The crews of both panzer divisions were quickly disabused of their belief that the morning of November 22nd could be devoted to rest and maintenance, those of 15th Panzer soon finding themselves probing back westwards along the crest of the main Escarpment overlooking the Trig Capuzzo, searching for British armour whose presence around Point 175 had been reported by Reconnaissance Battalion 33.

As for von Ravenstein's 21st Panzer, they had hardly deployed their infantry and artillery (with General Böttcher's) on the southern slope of the Belhammed position – from which defence line they expected to repulse the next attempt by the British on the Sidi Rezegh ridge to link up with the Tobruk break-out – when Rommel was amongst them, issuing orders for an immediate assault by Battlegroup Knabe on the ridge itself to drive the Support Group riflemen from the positions they had so gallantly won the previous morning. In addition Infantry Regiment 155 was sent with supporting artillery and some armour to the southern escarpment around Bir bu Creimisa from where they were to push off any British or South Africans they found there eastwards and into the open desert.

Panzer Regiment 5, having refuelled its tanks and restocked its ammunition racks, was to make its way carefully by the northern route under cover of Belhammed itself on to the by-pass road, then along to Ed Duda, across to Abiar el Amar and thus around the western end of the main Escarpment. From here, with the German infantry holding the attention of the enemy along both flanking escarpments, they would sweep up the valley which the previous day they had failed to sweep down, and this time, under Rommel's eagle eye, they were expected not to halt until the British on and around the airfield had been annihilated.

According to one of the panzer crews, although they were desperately tired, dirty, thirsty, and somewhat shaken by their repeated experience of battering their heads against a wall compounded of British stubbornness and an apparently immense material superiority, they all felt a wave of reassurance sweep over them with the realisation that Rommel was now again firmly in control – even if this meant yet another commitment to a battle they did not seem to be winning.

For the British around the airfield, the morning passed comparatively peacefully. At dawn the South African armoured cars had reported the impending departure of the last of von Ravenstein's panzers (they had been delayed in their movement across and down the Escarpment near Point 175 by lack of fuel) and at 0730 some of 22nd Armoured's Crusaders attempted to close with them but were fought off effectively by the inevitable rearguard anti-tank screen; and 4th Armoured Brigade, having completed the early morning rituals, had moved off to attack German armour which they had seen the previous evening leaguering nearby, only to find that the enemy leaguer was not there. After trouble caused by bogging in the soft ground, 4th Armoured rallied back in its previous night's position. Eventually they received orders to make for Point 175, from where, at about midday, the Honey crews watched the last details of Panzer Regiment 8 making their way down to the Trig Capuzzo – and were themselves seen by men of Reconnaissance Battalion 33.

Other than these activities, the British troops between the two escarpments occupied themselves with nothing more aggressive than reorganising the remnants of their formations, tending their wounded and arranging their evacuation, repairing and refuelling their vehicles as far as was possible, and restocking ammunition racks. And well away to the south of the Trig el Abd, XXX Corps Headquarters made itself ready for what it referred to, even in its report, as 'General Cunningham's threatened visit'.

This, however, proved quite a painless experience, for Cunningham contented himself with expressing guarded satisfaction with progress so far, and delivering himself of the opinion that with the New Zealanders moving along towards Tobruk it seemed likely that *Operation Crusader* would develop more and more into an infantry battle, in which case he hoped that South Africans would soon be able to play a more significant role than they had to date. With this hint in mind, Norrie requested General Brink to concentrate both his brigades and move them up into the Sidi Rezegh area (presumably this meant at least up to and across the southern escarpment) while 22nd Guards Brigade should move in bulk to Bir el Gubi to take over the tasks of 'masking' the Ariete, leaving only token screens with the Field Maintenance Centres. Obviously Pienaar could not move his 1st South African Brigade until this take-over was complete, but Armstrong's 5th South Africans should move as soon as was convenient towards Point 178, on the left flank of the positions held by the survivors of the Rifle Brigade Support Company, now reinforced by some of Jock Campbell's headquarter troops. There were, however, reports of German infantry on the crest of the southern escarpment here, and good grounds for believing that they might be growing in strength – so the South Africans should be prepared for some opposition; it might indeed be a good thing for them to move as soon as possible, for if the enemy were allowed to consolidate there, they would overlook the concentration of the 22nd Armoured Brigade with the remnants of the 7th Armoured Brigade taking place just below them in the ground to the south of the airfield.

This was a point which was exercising Strafer Gott, and shortly after 1300 he held a conference on the landing ground where it was declared that no attempt would be made that day to link up with the Tobruk garrison (which was, of course, the main reason for the British presence in the area) but that everything possible must be done to ensure the progress northwards of 5th South African Brigade so that Armstrong's men would be available, with the riflemen already on the Sidi Rezegh ridge and the Support Group artillery, to undertake the advance to Ed Duda early the following morning. Just before 1400, he left the airfield to drive to Armstrong's H.Q. to make certain that the South Africans themselves appreciated the need for movement.

He thus missed the opening of the first battle of Sidi Rezegh.

The first wave of the panzer attack was seen massing for an advance up the valley even while General Gott's conference was taking place, but warnings only reached the gunners along the western flank who then so busied themselves with preparations to withstand the assault that the message seems not to have been passed on; but by 1415 everyone on the airfield could see what was happening. At least fifty panzers were coming implacably up the slope towards them, more were moving up behind, and the attached and ubiquitous German anti-tank screens were weaving between the column and along the flanks.

The 25-pounders of 4th Royal Horse Artillery were the first to open fire, and soon all the guns of the Support Group were in action, the crews, half-naked, caked in dust runnelled with sweat, crouched either in the open or behind the derisory gun-shields as they slaved with automaton precision to pump their shells out at the advancing panzers. Smoke and the crash of battle engulfed the airfield, shot with the fire of explosion as shells from the Mark IVs erupted among the guns and, as the panzers edged in, machine-gun bullets whined close and too often cut down the unshielded crew members. And now, unlike during the previous day's fighting on the other side of the airfield, there was no sign of an easement of the pressure as panzers, flak guns, the crouching, leap-frogging knots of German infantry edged inexorably forward despite the weight of steel flung against them. Desperately, the gunners waited for help from someone – more gunners, some tanks or even the orderly-room clerks from the Support Group Headquarters who were almost the only infantry left on the airfield.

Suddenly it arrived; Crusaders from 22nd Armoured Brigade had come up from their new positions under the southern escarpment, passed through the waiting gunners of the 60th Field Regiment,

Map 6   The first battle of Sidi Rezegh: November 22nd, 1941

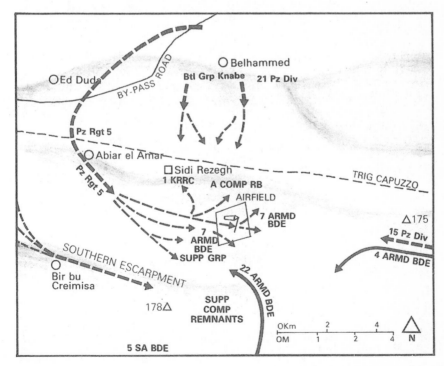

wheeled across the airfield and then through the R.H.A. gun-line and into battle. The exhausted gunners relaxed briefly and used the respite to clear away debris and collect the ammunition from the guns already out of action. But, in the words of one of the official accounts:

> The relief was very short. With horrified eyes they saw tank after tank go up in flames, hopelessly out-gunned. Sadly, but with grim determination, the gunners took up the battle again, while the tanks re-formed under their protection. Bravely our tanks went into the unequal contest again, and for a while armour fought armour. But the end was inevitable, and when the remnant of our tanks limped out of battle, the field was left once more to the gunners.[19]

Now the military exploits of Brigadier Jock Campbell reached their zenith. Not only was it his own command, the 7th Support Group, which was the principal – indeed at times the only – British formation in action, but the most committed arm in the airfield was the artillery and he was himself a gunner, his own regiment the Royal Horse Artillery. That afternoon he was everywhere – standing upright in his unarmoured staff car and holding nothing more lethal in his hand than a red flag, he time and again rallied the few survivors of the 7th Armoured Brigade and of the Yeomanry of the 22nd, to lead them forward through the gun-lines and into the chaos and confusion of the armoured battle. Shells burst alongside him, machine-gun bullets, shell-splinters and pebbles pock-marked his car, but wherever the action was most furious, the tall figure was there, stiff, aristocratic features more and more obscured under the cake of dust and grime, the voice hoarser, but the energy never flagging.

But by now the cumulative tank losses of *Operation Crusader* were taking their toll – of morale. Too many British tanks were now battered and smoking hulks, and too many tank crew members had been shocked by the sight of comrades burnt to death and by the realisation that despite the exhortations of higher authority, there was something lacking in their armoury against the Afrika Korps; they tended now to come out of the battle more quickly than before and were more reluctant to turn and go back in again. In the lengthening time-gaps between their appearances, the panzers and the German infantry were reaching nearer and nearer to the British guns, and these were falling silent or drawing back. As they did so, they were pressed south-east by the first wave of panzers, while the second wave swung north-east against the rear of the British infantry now holding the Sidi Rezegh ridge against the assaults of

Battlegroup Knabe supported by the heavy artillery of Böttcher's siege train on Belhammed.

Overrun unexpectedly from the rear, their ammunition shot away and without protection against panzers, the riflemen of the 1st King's Royal Rifle Corps and of A Company, the Rifle Brigade – many of whom had fought in every major engagement since Sofafi and a host of minor skirmishes with the Jock Columns – were hunted through the wadis as daylight faded and all were either dead or prisoner by 1600. By dusk the length of the Sidi Rezegh ridge was back in German hands.

But the battle in the valley had still to be decided. If by this time the airfield itself seemed to have been lost by the British, the 60th Field Regiment had formed another gun-line to the south and behind it Jock Campbell was still rallying, exhorting, bullying the desperate tank crews to further efforts, often succeeding by nothing more than his own example and refusal to believe they would not follow when he led the way back into the conflict.

'What could we do?' one exasperated Crusader driver said afterwards. 'We couldn't let the bastard go back on his own, could we? Not in that bloody silly little staff car?'

So they went out again and again, and braved the fire of the 50mm. and 88mm. anti-tank guns, and watched their own 2-pounder solid shot ricocheting away from the panzer armour unless a lucky strike gave it a head-on impact. By 1530, help was at hand; 4th Armoured Brigade was moving slowly across from Point 175 (and being rather more slowly followed by the leading panzers of Neumann-Sylkow's division, still searching for them) but were in some doubt as to what was happening. According to the first official account to be written after the battle:

> to 4 Armd Bde, the situation was obscure; 'the aerodrome, which could be seen in the centre of a large depression, was covered with derelicts. The enemy appeared to be on the north-western edge, 7 Sp Gp and 22 Armd Bde on the south.' The strength of 4 Armd Bde at this time was a hundred and eight tanks.[20]

These were, of course, Honeys which were really no match for the panzers – but they were armoured vehicles and as such grist to the battle's mill and strength to Jock Campbell's purpose. Indifferent to other orders which their leading troops (of 3rd R.T.R.) might have been given, Campbell drove up, leapt from his car, hammered on the sides of the tanks until the tank-commanders threw back the hatches and looked out, shouted his orders, leapt back into the car and, according to one observer, 'led them in a sort of cavalry charge waving a red flag . . . '

Among them was Cyril Joly, already shaken by the scenes around him.

I was appalled at the extent of the devastation and carnage, which seemed to spread as far as the eye could see. It was a frightening and awesome spectacle – the dead and dying strewn over the battlefield, in trucks and Bren-carriers, in trenches and toppled over the trails of their guns, some silent and grey in death, others vocal with pain and stained by red gashes of flowing blood or the dark marks of old congealed wounds. Trucks, guns, ammunition, odd bits of clothing were smouldering or burning with bright tongues of fire. Here and there ammunition had caught fire and was exploding with spurts of flame and black smoke . . . [21]

Now, with the other Honeys of his squadron, he followed this 'large man standing unprotected in an open car flying a brigadier's pennant on the bonnet' and found himself almost immediately blinded in 'a vast synthetic sandstorm caused by the medley of charging tanks and bursting shells which soon blotted out the scene . . .'

Nobody has ever been able to describe in detail what happened under that dense cloud, for nobody outside it could do anything but stare in astonishment at the blank phenomenon and nobody inside it could see what was happening beyond a very limited, and itself confused, circle. But one section of the combatants in that extra-ordinary mêlée was becoming increasingly conscious of a crucial factor; both battalions of Panzer Regiment 5 and their anti-tank batteries were by now short of ammunition, and if the pitch of battle remained as high as this for much longer their racks would soon be empty. Slowly, and almost unbelievably to the watchers, the cloud began to extend northwards back across the airfield, and as it did so it thinned to reveal the panzers withdrawing towards the main Escarpment, now – although this was not yet known to the British – in the hands of Battlegroup Knabe.

On the southern borders of the airfield, the Honeys and the few remaining Crusaders halted and waited while a few guns and infantry came up and the fog dissipated; and just before last light, General Gott, who had returned to the sound of the guns, held a conference with Gatehouse, Scott-Cockburn and Campbell (who had at last been slightly wounded, under the right arm, probably as he waved forward yet another attack). Despite the improving visibility the situation was still obscure, for even though the panzers appeared to be withdrawing, Gott and his brigadiers were all too aware of the weaknesses behind them. To all intents and purposes, 7th Armoured Brigade no longer existed, its survivors together with those of 22nd Armoured Brigade mustering only 49 tanks between them; and if 4th Armoured Brigade still had 100 tanks, these were Honeys, outgunned and outranged by the panzers. As for the Support Group, no one yet knew the price they had paid for the fame which was to be theirs once the story of that afternoon became known.

In the circumstances, withdrawal appeared the most sensible course – withdrawal from a position which had never been easily defensible and which now, with an unbeaten enemy panzer force this side of the only natural barrier – the Sidi Rezegh ridge – appeared untenable. Somewhere to the south – surely by now at least on the southern escarpment – lay the virtually unscathed 5th South African Brigade with beyond it the equally sound and unharmed 1st South Africans under Dan Pienaar. These brigades should form the nucleus of a new force with which to continue the battle, and the men and armour in the valley should fall back towards the most northerly of them (Armstrong's 5th Brigade) with the Support Group to the east and the two armoured brigades forming battle positions by 'first light 23 November, to protect the two flanks of this leaguer'.

This apparently logical and wholly reasonable plan would have held greater chance of success had 5th South African Brigade actually been able to clear the German infantry off the southern escarpment, and thus to join forces with the Rifle Brigade companies holding the eastern end. As it was, they had been unable even to reach their first objective, Point 178.

The first advance towards this point, by 3rd Transvaal Scottish, had begun at about 1300 with artillery support from eight field guns, across 1,000 yards of open desert against a wadi just to the east of Point 178 which was 'believed to be held by the enemy' – but, they hoped, not in great strength.

The hopes were not justified.

Even before they became fully aware of the strength and determination of the men of Infantry Regiment 155 in front of them, the marching South Africans suffered casualties from a sudden Stuka attack, and when they had approached to within 500 yards of the lip of the wadi, heavy machine-gun fire was opened on them and they soon found themselves pinned to the desert floor by a tremendous concentration of rifle and Spandau fire, supported by both artillery and mortars from well-concealed positions in the other wadis which seamed the escarpment. One observer wrote of the Transvaal Scottish:

These magnificent infantry advanced in widely extended lines

of riflemen followed by man-handled mortars and other weapons
– a text-book show of 1914–15 vintage. Magnificent but not
war.[22]

It was certainly not war in 1941; even the British riflemen who had
taken the Sidi Rezegh ridge the previous morning had been
supported by forty-two field guns, covered by a smoke screen and
preceded by assault platoons in carriers.

There was little the South Africans could do but stay where they
were and endeavour to burrow into the ground, while the only units
which could help them – artillery and a few valiantly manned
armoured cars – drew such sustained and accurate fire on both
themselves and the infantry that their efforts soon petered out.
Transvaal Scottish lost both their colonel and second-in-command
that grim afternoon, and when they were withdrawn after dark their
strength had been whittled down by twenty-five men killed, nine
missing and eighty-three wounded.

The failure to take Point 178 had other repercussions too. Across
the ridge from the South Africans and equally engaged with the
staunch and efficient German infantry, were B Company of 1st
Battalion Rifle Brigade, the remaining guns of 4th R.H.A. and the
batteries at the western end of the 60th Field Regiment line.
Through this line the British troops on the airfield and just south of
it began to withdraw and with that expert sense of opportunity
which characterised units under Rommel's command and with
which the British were to become only too familiar, the refuelled
panzers, artillery and infantry groups came hurrying down to take
the fullest advantage of an enemy in retreat.

The men of the Rifle Brigade had watched the first battle for the
airfield, the cloud which screened the 4th Armoured when they
joined the battle and the return up as far as the southern edge; now
they watched the slow inexorable creep of action back towards
them as the Honeys dropped back through the gun-line, as the
75mm. shells exploded again around the unprotected 25-pounders
and the panzers closed in. One of the artillery observers later
described the scene as darkness fell:

> Under cover of artillery concentrations and supported by tanks
> the German infantry advanced on the gun positions. Orders were
> given for a withdrawal on to the South African Brigade, which
> was in action three miles to the south. Troop by troop, under
> covering fire from the remainder, the guns, or what was left of
> them, moved out as the day drew to a close. Officer casualties
> had been heavy but N.C.O.s rose magnificently to the occasion
> and withdrew in good order. Towards dusk the last remaining
> guns of a troop of 60th Field Regiment and a troop of 3rd R.H.A.

seemed doomed. The advancing German infantry were almost on them. Firing at point-blank range, with apparently no hope of survival, these indomitable men still fought their guns. Suddenly a troop of light British tanks roared out of the gathering gloom, charged straight into the German infantry and, firing with every weapon they had, halted the enemy attack long enough for the gunners to hook in and pull out.

The final scene was awe-inspiring enough. In the light of burning vehicles and dumps our guns slipped out of action, leaving the field to a relentlessly advancing enemy, who loomed in large, fantastic shapes out of the shadow into the glare of bursting shells.[23]

Thus the valley was emptied of British troops as darkness thickened on the evening of November 22nd. Just below the southern escarpment, the 5th South Africans drew together and ruefully considered the day's events while the weary Crusader crews of 22nd Armoured formed a leaguer on their western flank and the grim remnants of the Support Group clustered around Jock Campbell's H.Q. to the east, sure in the knowledge that no one would ever call their military worth into question. Further out in the desert to the east lay the headquarters of 4th Armoured Brigade awaiting the return of their commander, Gatehouse, while the squadrons of the 3rd and 5th R.T.R. sorted themselves out after the confusions of both their advance to the airfield and their withdrawal. Among them, still, was Cyril Joly:

As usual, the leaguer seemed to be ringed with enemy, whose presence was always marked by an astonishing display of coloured Very lights. But it was not these nor the failure of the supply column to arrive that caused my worry. For no accountable reason I felt that something was wrong somewhere . . .

With Kinnaird I was no nearer finding a solution, except that I heard that the Brigade was still not fully accounted for and that tanks, some in fairly large numbers, appeared to be wandering aimlessly about the area in which the units had leaguered. While I stood by Kinnaird's tank and listened to the flurry of orders and information being passed on the Brigade forward control, I suddenly heard, quite distinctly, at no great distance, the muffled note of the engines of a column of tanks and the accompanying clank and creak of tracks. For a moment I nearly shouted . . . But some instinct restrained me, and I listened to the column move past without even disturbing Kinnaird.[24]

This was unfortunate, for what Joly heard were the advance units of Panzer Regiment 8 of Neumann-Sylkow's 15th Panzer Division at last catching up with the British armour they had set out to find some hours before. They had had little contact all day as their progress westward had been no faster than that of the armour they were looking for, except that as daylight faded the noise of battle in front of them had suddenly increased, and their commander, Oberstleutnant Cramer, reacted in the traditional way by driving towards the sound of the guns. But darkness was upon them before they could reach the valley and for some time they probed slowly and carefully forward. At about 1700 they saw in front of them a congregation of dark shapes from which suddenly erupted a white Very light (fired, in fact, to guide Gatehouse back to his H.Q.) and in its glare the battalion commander recognised the vehicles as English tanks at ten yards. According to the War Diary of 15th Panzer:

> [Cramer] burst through the enemy leaguer in his command vehicle and ordered No 1 Company to go round the left and No 2 Company round the right to surround the enemy.
> The tanks put on their headlights and the commanders jumped out with their machine-pistols. The enemy was completely surprised and incapable of action. Thus far there had been no firing. A few tanks tried to get away, but were at once set on fire by our tanks, and lit up the battlefield as bright as day. While the prisoners were being rounded up an English officer succeeded in setting fire to a tank.
> This *coup* on our part got the rest of 4 British Armoured Brigade with light casualties to ourselves. The Brigade Commander, 17 officers and 150 other ranks were taken prisoner. One armoured command vehicle, 35 tanks, armoured cars, guns and self-propelled guns, other fighting vehicles, and some important papers fell into our hands.[25]

This tally of success is not quite accurate, since not Gatehouse but his second-in-command was taken, and it was, in fact, only the headquarters of 4th Armoured Brigade which had been rounded up, the operational squadrons being still dispersed at varying distances away. Nevertheless, from the British point of view it was a devastating blow, for it meant that for the next few vital hours, indeed perhaps days, the only substantial armoured formation left to XXX Corps would be without a head, incommunicado until an emergency signals framework could be set up, and with all its own internal and XXX Corps's codes hopelessly compromised.

There was another spurt of confused action when Cramer and his men stumbled across some 5th R.T.R. tanks as the panzers were feeling their way out of the ring with their captures and the Honeys were groping around to find their own command; but with the lack of directives and the general incomprehension of events on all sides which now shrouded the night's activities, they both broke away for fear of finding when daylight came that they had been firing on their own units. Neither Neumann-Sylkow nor Norrie, at that point, was aware of what had happened – Norrie at least being much more concerned with plans for the following day.

He had already approved Gott's plans for the concentration of the remaining armour around 5th South African Brigade south of the southern escarpment, and indeed was determined to strengthen it further. The New Zealanders and a squadron of Valentines had begun their move along the Trig Capuzzo early in the afternoon and their leading elements, now aware that they might meet strong German forces at Bir el Chleta, were planning to diverge around them when orders came (from Cunningham) that they were to advance as fast as possible to Sidi Rezegh and assist the hard-pressed Support Group. To do this, they must climb the Escarpment (quite gentle this far east), concentrate above it and then move to Point 175 prior to the last step down to the valley. These orders had been received by the New Zealanders at 1615; since then they had been making their way westwards at maximum speed (eight miles per hour), and no further information or instructions had reached them.

And in addition to the New Zealand brigade, Norrie felt that with 22nd Guards Brigade moving up towards Bir el Gubi, the 1st South Africans should get away to join their sister brigade immediately, leaving only the sketchiest masking force behind. General Brink received instructions to this effect by 1445 and duly passed them on to Dan Pienaar, though Brink's acknowledgment to Norrie expressed doubts both as to the speed with which 1st South African Brigade could disengage from the Ariete, and the advisability, in view of this probable delay, of the brigade attempting to move up towards the southern escarpment until daylight the following day.

As for the brigade commander's reactions, as the South African historians put it so delicately:

It was not Brigadier Pienaar's habit to allow the orders of any superior to pass without thorough examination and discussion, and he now proceeded to indicate the difficulties that lay ahead. He

pointed out to Div . . . that, in the light of information regarding enemy dispositions in the intervening area, it would be most dangerous and inadvisable for a motorized infantry column to move during the hours of darkness beyond the 38 Northing Grid Line [i.e. within 15 miles of Sidi Rezegh air-field].[26]

Pienaar requested permission instead to move due east for some eight miles, then to turn north, leaguer for the night and move up towards 5th South African Brigade the following morning (of November 23rd). It has never been ascertained what the 'information regarding enemy dispositions in the intervening area' between Bir el Gubi and 5th South Africans consisted of, for there were no German units there – but Brink loyally supported his brigadier and Norrie, conscious of Dominion susceptibilities, reluctantly agreed but stressed the urgency of the situation.

As a result, the bulk of Dan Pienaar's brigade arrived at their turning-point at dusk and moved about a mile northwards, but orders to stop and leaguer there until the following morning failed to reach the soft-skinned B Echelon supply transport and also the men of the 10th Field Ambulance, and these proceeded happily throughout the night, eventually settling down for breakfast but two miles south of the southern perimeter of 5th South African Brigade, an area also occupied by soft-skinned B Echelon units. With the panzers away to the north and British armour on each side, it seemed quite a sensible arrangement that the dispositions of Armstrong's artillery and anti-tank screens should be along the western, northern and eastern sides of a box with the southern side left open to receive any support which might come up.

Thus, with some degree of concentration but with a vulnerable 'soft' space between the two vital infantry brigades, began for the South Africans and the British the morning of November 23rd. For the New Zealanders some seventeen miles away to the north-east, it was proving rather more exciting.

They had been delayed by minefields during their move along the Trig Capuzzo in the afternoon, and their commander, Brigadier Barrowclough, halted them just after 2000 for a hot meal and rest, for the Valentine crews had been on the move for many hours (they had been late coming up to the start point and had thus delayed the whole brigade) and in any case if battle threatened it would be as well to replenish fuel tanks and feed the men. The supply transport arrived after midnight, a conference was held between the unit commanders and at 0300, shivering with the cold and half asleep, the soldiers climbed back into their lorries and the journey began again. It was very dark, the drivers could hardly make out the jolting, heaving shapes of the vehicles in front and progress was very slow. At dawn the main columns halted while reconnaissance parties were sent out to establish their position. According to the New Zealand history:

> The men were cold, tired, and hungry, and lost no time in dismounting to set up burners, boil billies, and get something to eat.

Daylight always reveals in a great laager an apparent confusion with vehicles of many kinds facing in all directions, each like a domestic household – waking, washing, cooking and not minding its neighbours. And so it was this morning . . . The war could wait until after breakfast.[27]

It was at this point that two important discoveries were made. The first was that the guides had veered off the course during the night and instead of avoiding Bir el Chleta, the brigade was precisely there; and the second was that sitting in the middle of the brigade leaguer were Cruewell's Afrika Korps headquarters, complete with almost all his wireless vehicles and the whole of his cipher staff. There was also part of a German mobile column within the mêlée which promptly developed and this put up most resistance to capture – but the end was certain and swift. Within a few minutes some 200 German prisoners were being rounded up and the staff vehicles ransacked for the vital information they contained.

Gatehouse was not the only commander to face the coming day's trials without a headquarters and, indeed, the loss of Afrika Korps H.Q. was obviously more serious to Rommel than the loss of 4th Armoured H.Q. to Cunningham.

General Cruewell, accompanied by his Chief of Staff, Oberstleutnant Bayerlein, had only left the headquarters half an hour before the arrival of the New Zealanders, and although the loss of his staff undoubtedly occasioned him much inconvenience, the thought may have crossed his mind that there were advantages to be abstracted from every situation.

Just before he had left his H.Q., according to Bayerlein, 'D.A.K. received a long wireless message for the deciphering of which General Cruewell had not time to wait. He had to act on his own initiative.'

Certainly, the message contained a great deal of administrative detail which was of little interest to the commander of the Afrika Korps, but it began with Rommel's orders for battle on the following day, and whether or not Cruewell knew of the general outline of those orders, it is evident that he disagreed with them. The relationship between Rommel and Cruewell at this time may have borne some resemblance to that between Sir Hyde Parker and Nelson during the Battle of Copenhagen, the loss of Cruewell's cipher staff providing him with a conveniently blind eye, for he now issued orders to 15th and 21st Panzer Divisions which differed in marked degree from Rommel's intentions.

To Rommel, the situation was at last clear and he felt he controlled it. The airfield at Sidi Rezegh was held by Panzer

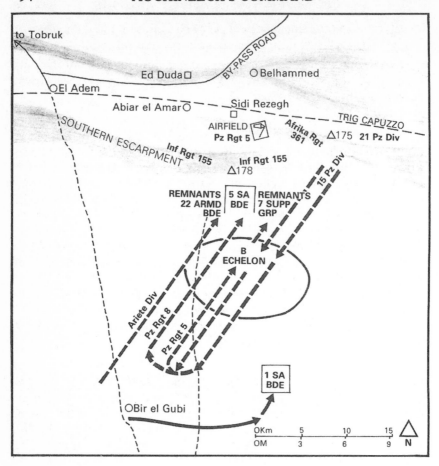

Map 7   *Totensonntag*: November 23rd, 1941

Regiment 5 (21st Panzer Division's armour) with their own divisional infantry of Battlegroup Knabe holding the Sidi Rezegh ridge. The infantry and armour of 15th Panzer Division were grouped south-west of Point 175 which was itself held by Infantry Regiment 361, while Infantry Regiment 155 held the southern escarpment, just to the north of the main British and South African concentration. Accordingly, he issued his orders, beginning:

On 23 November, *Panzergruppe* will force a decision in the area south-east of Tobruk, by means of a concentric attack by *D.A.K.* and parts of Corps Gambara. With this object, Corps Gambara will advance from El Gubi at 0800 hours with elements of Panzer Division Ariete in the direction of Gambut. At 0700 on 23 November, *D.A.K.*, effectively concentrating its forces, will advance in the general direction of El Gubi – with main effort on the left wing, encircle the enemy and destroy them.[28]

Again the classic German manoeuvre of encirclement was intended or, to use a different metaphor, the enemy were to be smashed between the hammer of the German panzer regiments and the anvil of the Ariete.

For reasons at which one can perhaps guess, Cruewell seems to have felt that both hammer *and* anvil required a German component, and his instructions to 21st and 15th Panzer Divisions were to the effect that the panzer regiments should amalgamate south of Point 175 as quickly as possible and, accompanied by the infantry of 15th Panzer Division, cut through the enemy's lines of communication in a drive to Bir el Gubi. There they would join up with the *Ariete*, turn, and *then* crush the opposition against the anvil of Infantry Regiment 155 – with a secondary anvil waiting further back in the shape of Battlegroup Knabe on the Sidi Rezegh ridge in case the overstrained steel of 155 should fracture under the impact.

A glance at the map will reveal the interesting possibilities open to an armoured force following the shortest route on the first leg of that journey.

The combination of Cruewell's modification of Rommel's concept and the German habit of rising and going to work rather earlier than their opponents resulted, from about 0800 onwards on the morning of November 23rd, in some quite extraordinary scenes. Men in every stage of dress and undress, caught at their morning rituals, scampered about the desert racing for their weapons, their vehicles or their slit trenches, and as the armour and infantry carriers of 15th Panzer Division (21st Panzer armour were late off the mark and came through afterwards), with Cruewell, Bayerlein and Neumann-Sylkow in the first wave, crashed through the soft-skinned B Echelon transport which occupied the gap between 5th and 1st South African Brigades, British lorries, staff cars, ambulances, trucks, pick-ups and motor-cycles bolted in all directions like a stampeding herd in a Western film.

Some raced for the security of the two South African Brigade perimeters but others went helter-skelter out into the desert in whichever direction took the fancy of the driver – west, south-east or around and back towards the Wire. The supply vehicles for Jock Campbell's Support Group were the first to see the danger and feel the shock, and quite naturally the majority moved first to rally to that stalwart figure, only to find that he wished them for the moment away and over the horizon while he amassed around his own person whatever fighting force was available.

Sitting on top of his A.C.V. waving alternate red and blue flags – made from his scarves – for 'Stop' and 'Go' . . . he started to rally every [fighting] vehicle he could find to turn and face the German tanks. He had 23 people in the A.C.V., all urging the driver to go like hell, while Jock kept shouting down that he was not to go faster than 8 m.p.h. and to stop when he was told to. To one Troop of guns . . . he gave the classic order: 'Expect no orders. Stick to me. I shall advance soon!'[29]

And advance in due course he did, surrounded by a miscellaneous collection of old cruiser tanks, a few repaired Crusaders which had not managed previously to report back to Scott-Cockburn, parts of both B and C Squadrons of the 11th Hussars, and guns from both 60th Field Regiment and his own beloved Royal Horse Artillery. However, by the time this motley collection had assembled and moved into action, the bulk of the panzers were through and wreaking havoc among the South African supply vehicles – and with the incongruous perversity of war, Campbell led his force through the tail of the onslaught, on into a patch of soft ground where many of his heavier vehicles promptly bogged down.

But the fighting by no means ended with Campbell's temporary disappearance, for Armstrong had posted artillery out as a screen for his transport, and this was soon joined by some Support Group guns which had been north of the axis of Cruewell's advance and now raced across to attack it in flank.

One of the South African B Echelon sergeants later wrote:

British artillery kept rushing from one side of our lines to the other. Pandemonium appeared to have broken loose. We all fired with our rifles and a tommy-gun on German tanks which we saw not far distant. The firing was passing continually over our heads. One British tank ran right over the shell slit in which our driver was crouching, next to the truck, covering him with earth. A British anti-tank gun took up its position right next to us, firing over our heads. The ground shook with the reverberations of the heavy firing and the falling of shells all around us and we saw German tanks on all sides.[30]

Everywhere, men caught in trenches were blazing away fruit-lessly with small arms at the shut-down, implacable panzers as they drove past, but these – except for a burst of machine-gun fire at some unusually reckless and exposed figure – were concentrating their attention and fire on the fleeing trucks and lorries and the occasional gun or tank which dared to stand in their direct path. But behind the panzers came the German infantry carriers, and these had much more time and attention for the men who had not leaped aboard the escaping transport.

Short, fierce infantry fights developed as isolated Bren-guns opened up the carriers, which slowed to a halt to spill their cargoes out in a flood which then rushed the defiant post and wiped it out. Many of the B Echelon units, including 10th Field Ambulance which of course bore no arms heavier than the officers' pistols and the drivers' unbayoneted rifles, were rounded up almost complete and taken prisoner; but many were later to find themselves abandoned by their captors as their growing weight of numbers slowed the advance and menaced the redeployment for the main attack; and in this theatre at any rate, there was to be no indiscriminate slaughter of prisoners.

But the panzers did not have it all their own way. According to 15th Panzer's War Diary, 'Again and again strong enemy battle groups with tanks, anti-tank guns and artillery came out of the desert and tried to take the Division in flank to divert it from its objective.'[31]

One of these 'battle groups' consisted of a detachment of Honeys from 4th Armoured Brigade which had become so hopelessly lost the previous evening that it had leaguered with some South Africans – a happy coincidence as their commander was Major Bob Crisp, a well-known South African cricketer who had elected to join the British Army.

After spending a convivial night with them, he and his tanks had left the leaguer shortly before the German attack developed, and after a brief period of confusion in the opening mêlée, he noticed a battery of four German field-guns for the moment isolated in an otherwise empty patch of desert, firing over the battle area and into 1st South African Brigade zone.

'It seemed to be a monstrous bit of cheek,' related Crisp later, 'and got my back up!' Despite the danger he would face if any of the gunners noticed the Honeys streaking upon them from the rear, he ordered a charge – across nearly a mile of open desert – and fortunately for him, he was not seen until his tanks were within 300 yards of the guns and he could then see the panic on the faces of the Germans as they frantically swung the nearest gun around. There was a flash and a cloud of black smoke, but 'I could afford to laugh at this, and I believe I actually did, as the gun was pointing upwards at a range of about 6,000 yards, and there I was not 100 yards away. I knew I had them.'

But not for long. Although Crisp took the whole battery prisoner and ordered them to march away to 5th South African Brigade area, he had no way of enforcing his order once circumstances distracted his attention from them; and as no member of his command possessed the technical knowledge necessary to wreck the field guns, these were, according to 15th Panzer War Diary, later brought back into action. The morning of November 23rd, though sparkling with myriad deeds of valour and enterprise, was not distinguished by remarkably high military expertise.

Even on the German side, this was so. By 0900 Neumann-Sylkow had watched the chaos spreading in front of him for long enough to sense further opportunity for immediate exploitation; he could see now the southern borders of the 5th South African Brigade area and had a shrewd idea of the confusion which must reign therein. Surely the time had arrived for a change of plan, a decision to do without the Italians at El Gubi entirely, and a switch of course which would take his armour without the slightest check to their momentum straight up through the open side of the South African box into its soft centre?

But Cruewell would have none of this. Perhaps because, having made up his own plan in defiance of Rommel's ideas, he would now brook no interference from a subordinate, or perhaps because of the strength of these isolated (and indeed uncoordinated) flank attacks, he ordered a continuation of the advance towards Bir el Gubi, his only additional instruction being to 21st Panzer infantry which he now ordered to move down towards the southern escarpment to buttress Regiment 155 and increase the threat to the South Africans from the north. To 21st Panzer's armour he sent word that they should hurry along to take up their prescribed position with 15th Panzer and himself for the afternoon attack.

Thus the Afrika Korps armour plus the 15th Panzer's infantry swept on towards Bir el Gubi and the Ariete formations, leaving in its wake the dispersed, badly shaken and in no small part destroyed supply trains of two South African Brigades and Jock Campbell's Support Group, and to the rear two astonished infantry brigades, one on each side, each still virtually untouched so far as its fighting strength was concerned but with one of them at least acutely aware of the danger which would soon be threatening from the south-west. They may have been half asleep when the Afrika Korps first approached that morning, but they were wide awake now, and they knew where their gun-lines must lie if many of them were to see the sun set that evening.

The lull which followed was certainly not wasted by the British and South Africans of 5th Brigade.

The first to move in was D Battery of 3rd R.H.A. from the Support Group, followed shortly by all the remaining artillery from 22nd Armoured Brigade and two more R.H.A. batteries with 25-pounders. These took up positions on the south-west corner of the brigade area, and General Gott, who was now advising Armstrong and at the same time trying to organise a defence of the whole 7th Armoured Division area, brought across the 2nd Battalion of the Scots Guards from 4th Armoured Brigade. He then instructed a reluctant Jock Campbell to release the 4th R.H.A. batteries (originally from 7th Armoured Brigade but collected that morning as a result of what one surely carping critic referred to as the brigadier's 'predatory instincts') to guard the eastern flank of the 5th South Africans, but allowed Campbell to keep the rest of his motley collection of guns and fighting vehicles. With the survivors of the Support Group headquarters, these set off to the south-east, where to Campbell's annoyance many of the heavy vehicles promptly sank up to their axles in yet another bog.

Meanwhile, twelve 25-pounders of the South Africans' own artillery came hurrying down from their previous positions as Armstrong stripped his eastern and northern sectors of as much as he dare, plus two 18-pounders firing solid shot and nine 2-pounder anti-tank guns. But as the ground was so hard and time was so short, many of the 2-pounders remained portée'd on their lorries.

And all the time, with the B Echelon traffic which had found refuge inside the brigade perimeter thickening the target, Böttcher's heavy guns on Belhammed some eight miles away were lobbing their great shells into the area, to explode with shattering force and random effect, sometimes to obliterate lorries and trucks, sometimes scything down anything which stood higher than two feet above the ground in the path of their wayward shards – but quite often doing no more harm than making a big bang. In such circumstances heavy artillery is like a primitive god – uncertain, inconsistent and unjust; and hateful. And very wearing on the nerves.

Away towards Bir el Gubi, Cruewell had by 1235 made contact with the Ariete divisional commander and ascertained that he was willing for nearly two-thirds of his division's armour to take their place in Cruewell's attack. Some explanation and indeed persuasion had been necessary because Ariete was part of Generale Gambara's Corpo d'Armata di Manovra and as such did not come under Panzergruppe Afrika command (though Rommel was, at that moment, engaged upon clandestine manoeuvres which resulted in it doing so on the following day) – but by 1300 clear understanding had been reached and the amalgamated armour of Afrika Korps and Ariete was being marshalled for the attack.

It must have been a remarkable sight. Cruewell's intention was that the three armoured formations would form a long line with 120 panzers of Panzer Regiment 8 grouped in the centre, 40 panzers of

Panzer Regiment 5 on the right and 100-odd M13s of the Ariete on
the left; and with them all moving together at their joint maximum
speed, they would sweep down on the 5th South African Brigade
and the remnants of the 7th Armoured Division, and consign them
all to oblivion. Some 200 yards behind the lines of armour, the
infantry of Rifle Regiment 115 and Infantry Regiment 200 would
follow in their carriers, their orders being that they were to remain
in the vehicles at least until they were under heavy fire and
preferably until they had followed the panzers well into the enemy
positions. Such manoeuvres were, as Panzergruppe's Chief of
Intelligence was later to write, with marked reserve, 'an innovation
in German tactics', and as the men and vehicles of the assault force
lined up almost as though on parade for inspection by a Prussian
Generalfeldmarschall, many of them must have wondered whether
Rommel would have approved had he been there; and some, what
price would have to be paid for so unsophisticated an approach to
modern battle.

For the introspective or superstitious there was another cause for
thought. Every day is a bad day upon which to fight a battle, but for
Christians Sunday is probably the worst; and for those who were
sensitive to such matters this particular Sunday was the worst of all.

November 23rd, 1941, fell on the last Sunday of the ecclesiastical
year, known in the English Church calendar as the 'Sunday next
before Advent'. But for German Protestants it was the Sunday
upon which they prayed for the souls of the dead, and its very name
of *Totensonntag* holds the chill of sorrow and the grave. Assuredly,
it was not a day upon which to fight any battle, let alone one in
which the evident intention was the total annihilation of all the
combatants on one side or the other.

Whatever the private thoughts of the German soldiers, however,
they seem not to have affected their sense of duty and obedience.
Even as they formed up for the attack, Panzer Regiment 5 on the
right of the line was under fire from artillery with the 1st South
African Brigade, who had withdrawn slightly after the events of the
morning and were now watching the German deployment with
considerable interest. But these harassing tactics made no difference to the forty panzers and at 1500 when Cruewell signalled
the order to advance, the whole line moved forward, gradually
increasing speed until the ground shook under the massed steel
charge.

Almost immediately, it met a storm of fire from the opposing
guns, firing over open sights. On the left, the Italian M13s were late
off the mark, slow to catch up and suffered such severe casualties
when they did so that their line dropped back, exposing the flank of
Panzer Regiment 8 which thus became more vulnerable to the

South African fire; but their commander, Oberstleutnant Cramer, in the leading tank held an undeviating course towards the enemy, spurring his armour on with brief exhortations over the air. Oberstleutnant Kriebel was also there:

A terrific fire front of well over 100 guns [*sic*] concentrated on the two attacking panzer regiments and the two rifle regiments following close behind in their vehicles. A concentration of anti-tank weapons unusual in this theatre of war, and cleverly hidden among enemy vehicles which had been knocked out during the morning, inflicted heavy losses . . . [32]

And if the panzers were able to withstand at least some of the shock of the fire, the soft-skinned vehicles crammed with infantry behind had nothing but their speed and good fortune to protect them. Jock Campbell's example of uncaring courage was repeated now on the opposite side by at least one commander, for Oberstleutnant Zintel led his men of Rifle Regiment 115 standing upright in his car, apparently unconcerned by the shot and shell which screamed past him.

Heinz Schmidt had some time before managed to persuade Rommel to release him from his duties as A.D.C. and was now commanding an anti-tank company in Zintel's regiment:

The regimental commander led, standing erect in his open car. The Major's car followed, with me right behind him. We headed straight for the enemy tanks [*sic*]. I glanced back. Behind me was a fan of our vehicles – a curious assortment of all types – spread out as far as the eye could see. There were armoured troop carriers, cars of various kinds, caterpillars hauling mobile guns, heavy trucks with infantry, motorized anti-aircraft units. Thus we roared on towards the enemy 'barricade'.

I stared to the front fascinated. Right ahead was the erect figure of the colonel commanding the regiment. On the left close by and slightly in rear of him was the Major's car. Tank shells were whizzing through the air. The defenders were firing from every muzzle of their 25-pounders and their little 2-pounder anti-tank guns. We raced on at a suicidal pace.

The battalion commander's car lurched and stopped suddenly – a direct hit. I had just time to notice the Colonel steadying himself. He turned sideways and dropped from the car like a felled tree. Then I had flashed past him. The Major was still ahead.

I recognized infantry positions in front of me. There was a tall, thin fellow out in the open, running backwards as if impelled by a jet from a hose. I heard bursts behind me and followed the tracer as it whipped past me into the distance ahead. How slowly tracer seems to travel! The tall fellow dropped . . .

The Major's car lurched and went over on its side. I was alone out ahead in this inferno now. In front I saw nothing but belching guns.

Then suddenly there was a violent jolt, a screeching and a hiss, and my car stopped dead. I saw a trench immediately ahead, leaped from the car, and plunged towards the slit.[33]

Oberleutnant Schmidt was lucky for very few of the officers and N.C.O.s of Regiment 115 had reached even this far alive and unwounded. But the panzers had broken through the gun-line and were now wheeling to the support of their infantry (which in this and other cases had actually beaten the armour to the first enemy positions, so acutely had they realised that in speed lay their only safety) and as the British and South African guns were put out of action or hastily dragged back by their tows, the German infantry could come out of whatever shelter they had found and fight the opposing infantry, by this time attacking the German artillery units as these came up. Fierce, isolated fights broke out along the length of the southern border of the brigade area, confused, shrouded in sand and smoke, fought most often to the death of either or both sides.

On the left, where the Ariete had still failed to catch up, Crusaders of 22nd Armoured Brigade were seen massing for a charge against the left flank of 15th Panzer's infantry, and their anti-tank platoons swung around to help the divisional screen which had ridden as usual along the flank of the charge. And when the British tanks had been fought off, there followed a duel with South African guns on the south-west corner of the box until, tardily, the M13s of Ariete again came up and for a short while relieved the pressure, until they were themselves reduced to smoking hulks.

On the right flank, the outer units of 21st Panzer Division had at first found themselves with apparently no opponents ahead, for their line of march took them past the eastern flank of the box – but Jock Campbell's miscellany, despite its troubles with the desert bogs, regained for itself sufficient mobility to make threatening drives towards its flanks. This in turn drove the forty-odd panzers which were all that Panzer Regiment 5 had left northwards, where they wreaked havoc among the 5th South African B Echelon vehicles now endeavouring to escape the fury developing inside the box.

For by 1600, leading troops of 15th Panzer Division were deep into the heart of the 5th South African Brigade, the gun-line along the southern border smashed, its ammunition gone, its gun crews dead or prisoners, the portées almost all in flames for too little time had been given for digging in. With the disintegration of the opposing artillery the first wave of Panzer Regiment 8 had been able to reassemble and methodically work their way to the north through the inside of the box. The first effect was to start a stampede among the B Echelon vehicles, but when the majority of these had fled or been destroyed some of the Crusaders from 22nd Armoured, having been driven away from the western flank of the attack, came across and tried to delay the implacable advance of the Panzers. One observer of this stage was Major Melzer, commanding 11th South African Field Ambulance whose Main Dressing Station lay at first behind the screen of Crusaders:

> As the battle developed they kept on their patrols, but were gradually being pushed back closer and closer to us. After a while they were about 300 yards away, then 200 yards, then 100 yards . . . Eventually they reached us, and our tanks actually worked their way between the groups of casualties lying on the ground.[34]

The line of British tanks was forced back behind the M.D.S. which then had an uncomfortable time between the two lines of manoeuvring and embattled armour until, inevitably, the panzers were also fighting among the lines of casualties and Melzer became worried about the danger to the wounded men:

> My fears, however, were quite unfounded, because the German tanks kept clear of the persons lying on the ground, and not one of the casualties or personnel was run over by a tank. Eventually the front line of the German tanks had the M.D.S. behind them, and they kept on the advance until all their tanks had passed us.[35]

Shortly afterwards German infantry posted guard over the Field Ambulance and all within knew they were prisoners, but no attempt was made to interfere with their ministrations to the wounded. During the two hours when the M.D.S. had been in the front line of the conflict, only two men had been wounded and no one believed that the injuries had been caused by anything except accident; the desert bred a chivalry of its own.

Beyond the Field Ambulance lay the Brigade Headquarters and by 1615 these had been taken – to the astonishment of the Staff who had been curiously out of touch with the German progress. Shortly afterwards Brigadier Armstrong, his brigade major, intelligence officer and signals officer were all taken prisoner, while away to the north near the southern escarpment the last battles were taking place; but even at this stage it was to be by no means a simple roll-over for the panzers. Panzer Regiment 8 found themselves alone in the middle of the enemy, whose fierce, determined resistance still persisted. The shell-fire continued to fall on the tanks without abatement. At this stage the regimental commander personally summoned his last reserves, the regimental engineers, in their troop carriers and what escort tanks were available, to join II/8 and attempt to decide the day without the infantry. This was an epic of courage and soldierly sacrifice. The tanks charged forward ruthlessly: the engineers followed close and dug out of their holes the crews of the field and anti-tank guns which had been overrun by the tanks.[36]

Then there was little but the infantry of the 3rd Transvaal Scottish ahead of the panzers, virtually defenceless against them, especially as they were now being overrun from the rear. Although some groups managed to slip off into the gathering dusk, those nearest the panzers and the German engineers were quickly rounded up and marched back towards the centre of the box, forming in the gloom that saddest and most dispiriting sight of all – amorphous clumps of beaten men deprived of their weapons and for the moment of their purpose.

There was one final burst of action across the desolate scene as the last remaining tanks of 22nd Armoured Brigade made a dash for the haven of a link-up with Campbell, or whoever now lay to the south-east of the battle area. They had watched the gradual disintegration of the South African brigade, the escape of the surviving Scots Guards, the last defiant shots from the few isolated South African guns before ammunition ran out. Now they felt that a surprise burst of energy might cause sufficient confusion for some of the prisoners to slip away:

> The final rush through the camp and the German tanks was thrilling: Lt. Col. Carr was at the head. Towards the end his tank was set on fire, but he and Major Kidston got on to other tanks and went on. Major Kidston's tank again became knocked out and he had to spend the night in the enemy lines, eventually creeping out next morning on Lieut Melville's tank.[37]

But Carr and the others broke through the German agglomeration and emerged on the far side of the box – to see in the gloom ahead dark, looming shapes at which they promptly opened fire. Fortunately, only two hits had registered and no one killed before it was realised that the shapes were those of some 7th Hussar relics, and that the 22nd tanks had broken through to the British forces concentrated around the Support Group. These lay just to the east of 1st South African Brigade, which had taken but little part in the day's fighting and were now anxiously watching the fires to the north and speculating on the fate of their friends.

Away to the north, the leading panzers of 15th Panzer Division had reached the southern escarpment and made contact with Infantry Regiment 155, who had spent their day watching the holocaust to the south and making such threatening moves as were necessary to hold the attention of the South Africans in the northern flank of the box.

They could now look back across a scene of harrowing desolation – harrowing even for those who could count themselves the victors, for if it was evident that the 5th South African Brigade had been destroyed, the litter of smashed panzers and the toll of grey-clad corpses pointed to the fact that the price was so high as perhaps to have been Pyrrhic. Among the groups of battle-tired infantry and disconsolate prisoners, between the burning lorries and exploding heaps of blazing ammunition, around the dark clumps of doctors and orderlies still intent upon their ministrations, the German staff officers walked or drove, muttering between themselves, counting, asking their questions and gradually piecing together the events of the day; and adding up the butcher's bill.

Totensonntag had proved a day of grievous cost to all.

3 · Crusader: The Infantry Take Over

As Rommel was not to become aware of the full cost of the fighting on *Totensonntag* for some days, it is not surprising that on the evening of that fateful day he arrived at the headquarters at El Adem greatly excited, announcing news of a decisive victory over the British.

He had been out of direct touch with Cruewell for nearly twenty-four hours but had gathered from various sources the extent of the fighting and had received via 21st Panzer Headquarters a message from Afrika Korps to the effect that a 'large enemy force' had been destroyed. This news when confirmed and amplified together with the reports of British armour destroyed on previous days surely added up to a tale of the virtual destruction of the larger part of Cunningham's army? On November 21st, the British 7th Armoured Brigade had been wiped out, during the evening of the 22nd the reports from 15th Panzer indicated destruction of the 4th Armoured Brigade, and now came news from Bayerlein that 'the remains of the 7th Armoured Division and the main body of 1st South African Division [*sic*] were destroyed. There is no further danger to Tobruk.'

At El Adem there was also news for Rommel of another, more personal victory. Only that morning he had sent a complaint to Mussolini about Generale Bastico's lack of personal involvement in the battle, with its resultant hesitancy on the part of Italian formations to move into action; already, to his surprise, Il Duce had responded by placing the whole of Gambara's Corpo d'Armata di Manovra at Rommel's disposal and directly under his command. With such an increase in the striking power available, coupled with the day's victories, should it not now be possible, to use his own words when writing of *Battleaxe*, 'to decide the issue of a battle merely by making an unexpected shift of one's main weight'?

As Rommel saw it on the evening of *Totensonntag*, at least half of Cunningham's army – and the important armoured part of it at that – was spread-eagled over the desert, much of it destroyed, the rest disorganised and split into a hundred fragments, all short of the necessities of battle and probably in many cases of life itself – and if he could strike quickly, its total annihilation would be certain. But speed was essential. The British had on previous occasions revealed a power of recuperation and a talent for improvisation which could snatch victory from defeat, and this might still happen if those isolated units were given opportunity to coalesce, and if they could be resupplied.

In supply lay their hope and therein also lay their vulnerability. Now, therefore, was the time to cut their lines of communication and by rapid and violent movement, to increase their disarray and block their withdrawal routes to Egypt. It must not take long, and to his patient staff he announced that he intended to place himself at the head of the Afrika Korps and lead it, with Ariete on the right flank, in a lightning stroke to the frontier which would not only paralyse the enemy forces in between, but relieve the frontier garrisons (including the one at Halfaya still under command of the redoubtable Major Bach) which had been holding out so valiantly during the last four days.

As he intended to take with him his Chief of Staff, General Gause, Headquarters control would remain in the hands of the Operations Chief, Oberstleutnant Westphal. To the latter's protests on the question of British intentions regarding Tobruk, Rommel promised that he would return within twenty-four or at the most thirty-six hours, and said he was sure Westphal was more than capable of managing on his own until then.

To his Quartermaster at El Adem he also announced that he hoped to capture the British supply dumps along the way, and when in his attempts to make contact with Cruewell he arrived at Neumann-Sylkow's headquarters at about 0400, he gave orders for an advance guard to move off as soon as possible towards Sidi Omar, perhaps as a result of a plaintive request for help received from the commander of the Savona Division there the previous afternoon. In the absence of Cruewell, Rommel also assumed command of Afrika Korps – which might have been a cause of tension at Kilo 13 on the Tobruk by-pass two hours later when the two at last made contact.

Not that Rommel was in a mood to notice other people's hurt feelings or even contrary opinions. Cruewell's suggestions that the following day might be better spent reorganising the Afrika Korps and assessing the cost of the recent fighting, in clearing up the litter of enemy units still at large in the space between the Trig Capuzzo and the Trig el Abd and, more especially, in salvaging the vast stocks of captured and abandoned enemy material before the enemy could reclaim them, were brushed aside as restricted and unimaginative. According to Bayerlein, who had remained at Cruewell's side all the time, Rommel summarised the whole situation in the following words:

> The greater part of the [enemy] force aimed at Tobruk has been destroyed; now we will turn east and go for the New Zealanders and Indians before they have been able to join up with the remains of their main force for a combined attack on Tobruk. At the same time we will take Habata and Maddalena and cut off their supplies. Speed is vital; we must make the most of the shock effect of the enemy's defeat and push forward immediately and as fast as we can with our entire force to Sidi Omar.[1]

In the van would be 21st Panzer Division which had apparently suffered less than 15th Panzer during *Totensonntag*'s battles, and Afrika Korps H.Q. with both Rommel and Gause in attendance would accompany them; 15th Panzer would bring up the rear, with Ariete on the flank. As for Cruewell's excellent suggestions regarding salvage, Infantry Regiment 155 and the Afrika Regiment could undertake this chore, and in so doing motorise themselves – perhaps in time to follow the main thrust and help exploit it. But at this moment all that mattered was speed, speed, speed . . . and everything must be sacrificed to it!

Needless to say, both 21st and 15th Panzer Divisions had ended *Totensonntag* short of ammunition and fuel and although much had been done during the night to repair the situation, neither division was ready to move as soon as their Commander-in-Chief would have liked. Eventually his patience wore thin and Panzer Regiment 5 was peremptorily ordered off, with von Ravenstein in the lead and Rommel and Gause urging on the following units. By 1100 the Mammoth was well up with the leaders, Rommel himself perched up on the edge of the roof in his usual position, filled with the excitement of the chase and his hopes for such a victory as would put the recent conquest of France in the shade and silence once and for all his critics in Berlin.

From the top of the command vehicle, the view must indeed have given added zest to his excitement and foundation for his hopes, for now he was treated to the kind of spectacle which the previous day had been witnessed by Neumann-Sylkow's staff as they crashed through the supply trains of the two South African brigades on their way down to Bir el Gubi. On each side he could watch the British and South African B Echelon leaguers explode into activity as the leading panzers drove down on them, the startled crews hurling partly cooked meals, tins of food, petrol and water-cans, weapons and clothing into their lorries before leaping into the cabs and driving furiously away from the wrath which threatened.

Isolated figures blazed angrily but unavailingly back with Bren-guns at the oncoming hordes, then ran out of the way and threw themselves into fox-holes or passing vehicles, or into the shelter of the wrecks which littered the area; and the leading panzers ploughed indifferently on, aware only of the spreading chaos in front of them and the eager, eagle eye of their commander immediately behind.

Unknowingly, they crashed through one corner of the 1st South African Brigade box (the brigade had just withdrawn southwards to Taieb el Esem, west of Gabr Saleh and on the Trig el Abd) and for a few unheeded minutes they might have caught Dan Pienaar himself as he careered with considerable panache back through their ranks on his way from General Brink's H.Q. about four miles to the east. They drove straight across the triangle contained within the points Bir Berraneb, Bir Taieb el Esem and Gabr Saleh and in so doing pushed out of their way the headquarter units of XXX Corps, 7th Armoured Division, 1st South African Division (General Brink's H.Q.), 7th Support Group and the relics of 7th Armoured Brigade, and had it not been for that acute sense of survival which marks headquarter personnel and Rommel's own insistence upon speed, there is no doubt that the Afrika Korps could that morning have made a most notable haul of prisoners.

Map 8   Rommel's 'Dash to the Wire': November 24th–27th; 1941

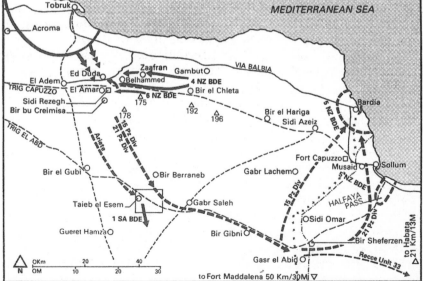

As it was, most of the headquarter units skipped out of the way to find shelter amid the Support Group artillery and some armoured formations which had hastily rallied along the flanks of the advance, and were intent on doing what they could to hinder it.

This was not very much and by noon von Ravenstein and the leaders were past Gabr Saleh and had reached the Trig el Abd, along which they moved with gathering speed towards the frontier. Directly in front of them they could watch, fleeing in chaos and confusion, literally hundreds of British and South African vehicles from mobile workshop pantechnicons to bucking motor-cycles and scurrying pick-up trucks, all bearing frustrated, frightened, angry and bewildered officers and men whose most coherent thoughts were probably best summarised by one exasperated wail overheard emerging from a rapidly accelerating truck:

'Christ Al-bloody-mighty! Not again!'

One officer had been taking advantage of what promised to be a relaxed and peaceful morning to indulge in a complete sponge-down in a basin of carefully saved water when the area he was occupying was deluged with scurrying transport, and when its cause became apparent he had just time to abandon all and leap into his staff car and drive it away. He managed to make two small adjustments to his comfort during the frantic drive which followed, but when several hours later he brought his vehicle to a halt and alighted, he did so wearing nothing but one unlaced boot, his steel helmet and an expression of such unmitigated ferocity that two private soldiers who witnessed his emergence and had been about to offer comment and even some unsolicited advice, instead stiffened to attention and remained rigidly at the salute until he had pulled on another boot and stamped away towards the reporting centre.

To Rommel, driving at a furious pace with the most advanced units of 21st Panzer, exhilaration at the prospect of victory was a continual urge to even greater effort, and by 1600 he was at the Wire near Gasr el Abid directing von Ravenstein up towards Halfaya without waiting for either the rest of the division, or even the presence of the official Corps Commander.

So General Cruewell, travelling well behind the leaders, was in fact both worried and annoyed by the time he arrived at Gasr el Abid an hour later.

He had not had nearly such an exciting journey as his Commander-in-Chief, perhaps because he lacked Rommel's optimistic temperament and flexibility of vision, but also because he had been able to watch those British and South African formations pushed aside by the column's spearhead rapidly reorganizing themselves and, indeed, causing casualties among the panzers in the second and third waves of the advance. Moreover, the further along the route he had travelled, the more evident it had become that whatever confusion the advance might be spreading in enemy ranks, an uncomfortable degree of disorganisation and disarray was now affecting his own.

The Afrika Korps now presented a decidedly ragged appearance, the prime cause being the speed of the head of the column resulting in growing attenuation in the body. In any column, even when speed of march is carefully controlled, concertina-ing is a well-known phenomenon – but when the speed at the head is continually increasing *as a result of direction at the head*, the tailing-out behind becomes more pronounced every minute. Had the distance to the Wire been much greater the separate parts of Afrika Korps would undoubtedly have lost not only contact, but also cohesion, and when Cruewell eventually reached Gasr el Abid it was to find his corps spread out from just south of Halfaya Pass back in a fifty-mile hook to Gabr Saleh, with a vehicle casualty rate for the day's advance to make him blench.

Panzer Regiment 5, which had led the column in the morning, had been forced to halt for refuelling back along the Trig el Abd (the lead had then been taken over, to the armour's mortification, by the infantry and artillery of Battlegroup Knabe now driving on up after von Ravenstein) and its first reports gave a figure of only thirty vehicles still in running order. Worse was to come, and four hours later at von Ravenstein's H.Q. Cruewell was faced with the fact that of the 170-odd panzers with which 21st Panzer Division had entered battle five days before, only four Pz IIs, fifteen Pz IIIs, one Pz IV and a command vehicle could still be considered battle-worthy! Panzer Regiment 8 with 15th Panzer had not suffered so severely, losing only seven tanks during the day's travel, but the division's Reconnaissance Battalion 33 had now lost all its remaining armoured cars – a revelation which threw a light of startling clarity on the effect of two days' violent action.

At last the details of the losses suffered the previous day in the attack on the 5th South African Brigade were emerging, and back at El Adem, Oberstleutnant Westphal was examining them with growing horror.

Over seventy panzers had been knocked out during the fighting on *Totensonntag* and even the Afrika Korps's recovery service could do nothing to help, for they were themselves now part of the 'Dash to the Wire' and (though Westphal did not yet know this) had been badly shot up by South African armoured cars and by low-flying aircraft; and this destruction of armour, in Westphal's opinion, did not even constitute the most crippling loss. It was the cost in senior and experienced officers and N.C.O.s which presented the darkest item in the balance sheet for *Totensonntag*, for Panzer Regiment 8 had lost two battalion commanders and five out of six of its company commanders, while many of the officers and N.C.O.s of Rifle Regiment 115 had been killed including the regimental commander and one battalion commander, and most of the remainder wounded. Figures for 21st Panzer were not so stark for they had been on the fringe of the *Totensonntag* fighting; but today they had been in the lead . . .

Oberstleutnant Westphal was by no means a happy man at the end of his first day as *de facto* commander of Panzergruppe Afrika, and his task of providing support to his Commander-in-Chief, by now some seventy miles away, was made more difficult by another piece of news which filtered through that evening. The Ariete Division, although they had started out more or less on time, had run full tilt into a large and stationary enemy formation well back along the Trig el Abd and were apparently unable to break through it, to push it aside or even to go around it. Il Duce's gesture of co-operation did not, in the circumstances, seem likely to aid the Afrika Korps to any immediately noticeable degree.

Not that Rommel was as yet aware of this. Even as Westphal was absorbing this latest piece of dire information, Rommel was issuing his orders for the following day by which he intended to destroy the remnants of Cunningham's army – an operation in which both Ariete and Trieste Divisions were meant to play crucial parts, as were non-existent cars of Reconnaissance Battalion 33:

> *Afrikakorps'* task is to co-operate with the [Italian] Motorized Corps, bottle up and destroy the enemy east of the Sollum front, west of the Sollum front and at Bardia. For this purpose 21 Panzer Division will swing east from the Sollum front; 15 Panzer will close the enemy's route southward, with half its forces on either side of the Wire and its centre in the Gasr el Abid area. Ariete will adjoin it on the west, with Trieste on the flank of Ariete. 21 and 15 Panzer will force the enemy into the minefields on the Sollum front and compel him to surrender. Reconnaissance Unit 33 will push forward to Habata to block the descent from the escarpment so that the enemy will be unable to use it for withdrawal or replenishment.[2]

Any modifications suggested by Cruewell on the grounds either of exhaustion of German forces or unreliability of Italian support were brushed aside, and he was persuaded to issue orders hurrying 15th Panzer and Reconnaissance Battalion 33 forward to their designated positions and then to set off himself, accompanied again by Bayerlein, to catch up with von Ravenstein and direct him to concentrate his division in readiness for an attack at dawn next day (November 25th) to 'drive the New Zealanders into the minefields'.

But of course, the New Zealanders were by now miles away to the west and Rommel was 'building pictures', totally disregarding unwelcome intelligence from any source. Convinced that XIII Corps was still sandwiching his frontier garrisons between its Indian half to the east and its New Zealand half to the west, and apparently unaware that the Sidi Omar position, most of the Libyan Omar position and all of Fort Capuzzo had been lost some thirty-six hours before, he envisaged the formation of two more outside layers to the sandwich with which he would squeeze the enemy infantry between the concrete of the garrisons and the steel of Afrika Korps and Ariete, blowing up any who might survive the pressure on the double line of minefields stretching from Sidi Omar to Sollum.

And the state of mind which allowed Rommel to brush aside unpalatable news and ignore such facts as overstrained logistics would also not allow him to remain at even his advanced headquarters if everyone else was further forward; so having dispatched Cruewell northwards he then took Gause and his A.D.C. to drive eastwards through the Wire, past a number of the rear units of 4th Indian Division and in the general direction of Habata, possibly in search of some of those British supply dumps which he had promised his Quartermaster but which he had as yet signally failed to discover.

The search proved fruitless, and eventually he ordered a return through the black, empty, early Egyptian night towards the Wire; and some miles short of it, at about 2000, the car broke down and no efforts on the part of any of the occupants could get it moving again. They now became suddenly conscious of the fact that they were to all intents and purposes lost in enemy territory, and that the night, in addition to being dark and starless, was extremely cold.

Fortune, however, had not yet deserted Rommel. After about an hour's acute discomfort, they heard the approach of a heavy vehicle and to their gratified astonishment saw Cruewell's Mammoth lumbering towards them out of the darkness on its way back from von Ravenstein's headquarters. It was sheer coincidence that brought them together in that virtually trackless expanse, and it was with a degree of satisfaction that Bayerlein later related how Rommel and Gause, shivering with cold, respectfully asked for a lift.

But the night's adventures were by no means over for when they reached the Wire they could find no gap through it, and the Mammoth by itself was not the vehicle to force a passage. An impatient Rommel then insisted on taking the wheel himself – but to no purpose, and after spending some hours 'banging fruitlessly against the Wire like a bewildered bee on a window-pane, even

Rommel gave in, and the accumulated authority of the *Panzergruppe* settled down for a night in the open desert'.[3]

The Mammoth had in fact hit the Wire well south of its destination and even Rommel's legendary sense of direction, according to Bayerlein, was of no effect.

> To make matters worse they were in an area completely dominated by the enemy. Indian dispatch riders buzzed to and fro past the Mammoth, British tanks moved up forward and American-built lorries ground their way through the desert. None of them had any suspicion that the highest officers of the German–Italian Panzer Group were sitting in a captured command vehicle, often only two or three yards away. The ten officers and five men spent a restless night.[4]

But when daylight came, they soon established their position and drove sedately northwards to the Gap and through the Wire, doubtless watched on occasion by British and Indian junior ranks who had no intention of approaching a command vehicle of known British design (and the black German crosses had faded to virtual invisibility) and perhaps incurring the wrath of the high-ranking brass within.

Rommel and his senior commanders were back at Gasr el Abid by 0700.

To General Cunningham the events of the last two days had, not surprisingly, now composed themselves into a picture of almost unmitigated disaster made blacker by the euphoria of the previous period. If at midday on November 22nd he could still adopt at Norrie's headquarters an attitude of relative satisfaction with the progress of the battle – despite the criticism of the armour implied by his prognosis that the relief of Tobruk would probably have to be undertaken by the infantry of XIII Corps – by that evening, as news of the massacre of 7th Armoured Brigade at Sidi Rezegh came in, he was becoming sufficiently worried to urge Freyberg to send as much more of the New Zealand Division as he thought wise westwards towards Tobruk, leaving the 'minimum troops necessary' at the frontier to keep the Capuzzo–Bardia area under observation.

Freyberg's reaction to this was to take his 4th Brigade hurriedly after Barrowclough's 6th, leaving the 5th New Zealand Brigade around Bardia and Sollum. By the evening of *Totensonntag* he had established his own H.Q. at Bir el Chleta, the scene of the capture of Cruewell's.

Cunningham now decided to recast the *Crusader* plan fundamentally, giving Godwin-Austen not only responsibility for the relief of Tobruk, but also command of the Tobruk garrison, the 5th South

African Brigade and perhaps also of the 1st South Africans. Norrie's armour should guard the inner flank of the infantry and 'continue the destruction of the enemy armour'. But, even before the events of that Sunday afternoon were to reveal the hollowness of the premises upon which those orders were based, the figures of tank losses at Sidi Rezegh the previous day had so depressed Cunningham that he sent an urgent request to Cairo asking that Auchinleck should fly up at once.

That this request was not totally the result of momentary panic is demonstrated by the fact that Cunningham's B.G.S., the sardonic but undeviatingly resolute Brigadier Galloway, also telephoned his opposite number in Cairo about the same time, indicating that another influence at Eighth Army Headquarters would be necessary if the battle in Libya were not to get out of hand.

In the meantime, Cunningham had held a midday conference with Godwin-Austen at which he suggested that Norrie should be asked to decide either to break off the battle or to retire and stabilise on a line from Point 175 to Bir el Gubi, and even raised the question as to whether it was wise to continue *Operation Crusader* at all. As Godwin-Austen's corps was still virtually untouched, its commander reacted vigorously with the suggestion that now was the time to press forward with his infantry towards Tobruk, and as soon as Cunningham had left he made contact by radio-telephone with Norrie whom he found unruffled by events and confident of his ability to handle any immediately foreseeable situation.

No one on the British side, however, had foreseen the grim battle that took place that afternoon, and the destruction of the 5th South Africans and the immobilisation of 4th Armoured as a result of the amputation of their H.Q. were sufficient to dent (temporarily) even the imperturbability of Generals Freyberg and Godwin-Austen. The effect upon Cunningham was to convince him that *Operation Crusader* had been a failure. When Auchinleck descended from his aircraft at Maddalena that Sunday evening, Cunningham insisted that all forces in Libya should be withdrawn immediately in order to form a shield to keep Rommel from the Nile.

He found himself faced with friendly, cool but quite unyielding opposition from two strong men. Auchinleck had learned many years before the undoubted truth that nothing is either as good, or as bad, as it appears at first sight, and Galloway, as B.G.S. to General Wilson in Greece, had recently seen and weathered far worse situations than the one facing the British on the evening of *Totensonntag*. They could both accept the military realities of enormous tank losses in XXX Corps, but they also both saw that the unscathed XIII Corps – which itself contained over a hundred 'I' tanks in 1st Army Tank Brigade – was certainly capable of driving forward to Sidi Rezegh and Ed Duda and, if given the opportunity, perhaps of breaking into Tobruk and thus releasing the 'I' tanks of the 32nd Tank Brigade. And with Tobruk open both XXX and XIII Corps could be fed with Auchinleck's carefully husbanded reserves, with much greater speed and efficiency than across the open desert as at present.

What was needed, of course, was a firm grip at the top, and Auchinleck's presence was enough to provide it for the time being. By 2230 on *Totensonntag*, Cunningham had been sufficiently reassured as to issue orders instructing Godwin-Austen to push the New Zealanders further westwards (their 25th Battalion had taken Point 175 that afternoon during very heavy fighting with the Afrika Regiment) and to Norrie telling him to reorganise his remaining armour as quickly as possible and to use it to protect Dan Pienaar's South African brigade in the south and the New Zealanders in the north. Nevertheless, he still proclaimed in his instructions to Norrie that the main role of armoured forces was to destroy enemy tanks – an attitude with which both Auchinleck and Galloway agreed at that time – so an element of compartmentalisation was still present in the planning for the next day.

In the event, Rommel's 'Dash to the Wire' put paid to all Cunningham's plans and forced a greater degree of co-operation upon armour and infantry in the immediate neighbourhood than had been achieved before. But it also gave Cunningham's nerves an even more severe jolt, and the unkind ribaldry which greeted the news that many headquarters staffs had been forced to make hurried and undignified scrambles to safety reached its climax when it became known that Cunningham himself had escaped capture by the narrowest of margins.

He had visited Norrie's XXX Corps Advanced Headquarters that morning and then gone further forward to 7th Armoured Division's H.Q. where, in the words of one observer, he, Norrie and Gott settled down to 'cook up the next battle'. They had not been so engaged for very long when shells began to drop among the dispersed vehicles, whistles blew and everyone began throwing equipment into lorries and driving smartly away. Brigadier Clifton, XXX Corps's Chief Engineer, drove Cunningham at furious speed across hummocky desert and through a 'thickening mob of run-aways' back to the Advanced H.Q. airstrip, where the pilot was already revving up the engines as Cunningham arrived. He then took off before his passenger was comfortably seated (missing a lorry crossing the airfield by about three inches as he did so) and from that moment the Eighth Army Commander had little to do but watch the stampede of vehicles taking place underneath him and reflect upon the perils of a military career. But not for long afterwards; he arrived back at his own H.Q. to find that Auchinleck had spent the morning in calm analysis of the situation and had drawn up the following document:

To:– Lieut.-General Sir Alan Cunningham,
     K.C.B., D.S.O., M.C.
Commander,
EIGHTH ARMY.

1. Having discussed the situation with you and learned from you the weak state to which 7th Armoured Division has been reduced by the past five days' fighting, I fully realize that to continue our offensive may result in the immobilization, temporarily at any rate, of all our cruiser and American M3 tanks.

2. I realize also that should, as a result of our continued offensive, the enemy be left with a superiority of fast moving tanks, there is a risk that he may try to outflank our advanced formations in the Sidi Rezegh–Gambut area and cut them off from their bases in Egypt. I realize also that in this event, there would remain only very weak forces to oppose an enemy advance into Egypt. On the other hand, it is clear to me that after the fighting of the last few days, it is most improbable that the enemy will be able to stage a major advance for some time to come.

3. There are only two courses open to us:
   (i) To break off the battle and stand on the defensive either on the line Gambut–Gabr Saleh or on the frontier. This is a possible solution as it is unlikely that the enemy would be able to mount a strong offensive against us for many weeks and would enable us to retain much of the ground we have gained, including valuable forward landing grounds. On the other hand it would be counted as an Axis triumph and would entail abandoning for an indefinite time the relief of Tobruk.
   (ii) The second course is to continue to press our offensive with every means in our power.

There is no possible doubt that the second is the right and only course. The risks involved in it must be accepted.

4. You will therefore:
   (i) Continue to attack the enemy relentlessly using all your resources even to the last tank.
   (ii) Your main immediate object will be as always to destroy the enemy tank forces.

    (iii) Your ultimate object remains the conquest of Cyrenaica and then an advance on Tripoli.

5. To achieve the objects set out in para. 4 it seems essential that you should:

    (i) Recapture the Sidi Rezegh–Duda ridge at the earliest possible moment and join hands with Tobruk garrison. It is to my mind essential that the Tobruk garrison should co-operate to the utmost limit of their resources in this operation.

    (ii) Direct the Oasis Force at the *earliest possible moment* against the coast road to stop all traffic on it and if possible capture Jedbaya or Benina, neither of which is strongly held apparently.

    (iii) Use the Long Range Desert Group patrols offensively to the limit of their endurance against every possible objective on the enemy lines of communication from Mechili to Benghazi, Jedbaya and beyond to the west. All available armoured cars should be used with the utmost boldness to take part in this offensive. The advantages to be gained by a determined effort against the enemy lines of communication are worth immense risks which will be taken.

C. J. Auchinleck
General
C.-in-C. M.E.F.[5]

In the circumstances reigning at the Maddalena Headquarters at noon on November 24th, even the ebullient Dan Pienaar would have hesitated to question so lucid and explicit a direction, and, repressing his doubts, Cunningham loyally set about expediting his Commander-in-Chief's intentions. Another trip to Godwin-Austen's H.Q. reassured all concerned that a XIII Corps drive to Tobruk would be supported at all levels, but the trip back took Cunningham over a triple column of Axis transport moving eastwards from Gabr Saleh, which worried him again until he had returned to the reflective calm engendered by Auchinleck's presence.

By now, darkness had fallen, Rommel's car had broken down (less than thirty miles from where Auchinleck was sitting), von Ravenstein was planning the drive intended to take him north past Halfaya Pass towards Capuzzo, Cruewell was on his way back to Gasr el Abid; and back in the desert reaches lining the Trig el Abd, Allied and Axis formations were still blundering about trying to avoid each other and find their own friends. Typical among the adventures of that confused night were those of the remnants of 7th

Support Group and 7th Armoured Brigade, who had been ordered
to move south across the Trig el Abd and reach Field Maintenance
Centre 62 which, like No. 63 even further south, had been
completely missed by Rommel's drive. According to the Rifle
Brigade historian, the whole march was a nightmare:

> It was pitch dark. The column which formed up, close together
> and four abreast, contained various extraneous elements. Jock
> Campbell sat astride the bonnet of his armoured command vehicle,
> hoarse with energy expended, so that his voice reverberated like
> a ghost's whenever the engines were turned off. At intervals Very
> lights would go up, showing that there were parties of Germans in
> every direction.The column moved by fits and starts. At halts
> other vehicles would be heard approaching, sometimes the
> ghastly clanking of tanks, quite unidentifiable until they were
> right on top of the column. Once a German motor-cyclist shot
> through the column and away before anyone could engage him.
> One party of Germans met our column about half-way up and in
> the confusion and shooting and excitement many vehicles went
> astray. But as dawn broke the Support Group found themselves
> on the edge of the vast dump on which the continuance of the
> offensive depended. The Germans in their rush towards the wire
> had left it a few miles to their south.[6]

Gradually, during the night, groups sorted themselves out,
formations coalesced and attained some degree of internal reorganisation, headquarter units found their subordinate echelons
and sometimes even found their generals – though Norrie, who had
spent most of the day driving around with Gott, is reported to have
remarked pensively that there was much to be said for fighting a
battle with only an A.D.C. in attendance as it saved so much
paperwork.

But by the morning of the 25th, a great deal of both literal and
figurative dust had settled, and if the mixture of German combatant
and British non-combatant units east of the Wire was still confused
and lacking sound direction, the British, South African and New
Zealand fighting units west of the Wire were settling themselves
down and making ready to continue the battle. For them, Rommel's
'Dash to the Wire' had been of almost unalloyed benefit.

Two brigades of the New Zealanders – the 4th and the 6th – were
by now driving westwards together towards Tobruk, the 4th along
the Trig Capuzzo and the valley on each side, and the 6th along the
Sidi Rezegh ridge. At dawn on the 25th, the 4th Brigade had
reached Zaafran, and the 6th, after a hard battle for a blockhouse
some two miles west of Point 175 which had further reduced their

strength, already severely diminished by the fighting on *Toten-sonntag* for Point 175, sent their 26th Battalion on and across the landing-field 'littered with the wreckage of German and Italian planes, burnt-out and abandoned tanks, a few trucks and some field guns'.

Late in the morning came more orders from Godwin-Austen. With Rommel and the Afrika Korps engaged around the frontier, now was the time for the link-up with the Tobruk garrison, and the first move for the New Zealanders would be to occupy the dominating heights in the area – Zaafran itself, Belhammed, Ed Duda and the length of the Sidi Rezegh ridge. General Freyberg, perhaps with memories of infantry fighting in 1918 and certainly with a sceptical attitude towards the tactics adopted so far by the armour, decided that night should provide the cover for his eager troops to go in with the bayonet, leaving Matildas and Valentines to follow in a supporting role. At 2100 six battalions crossed their start lines.

Freyberg's faith in his men's courage was certainly justified, but darkness and broken country over which no reconnaissance had been carried out form a recipe for confusion, and both brigades ran into trouble. Headquarters of 4th Brigade veered too far right and found themselves at one point on the Via Balbia and out of touch with their battle formations which were engaged in vicious (and eventually successful) fighting on the summit of Belhammed; 6th Brigade ran into the Bersaglieri around the Sidi Rezegh tomb, and these fought them off with such determination that two of the attacking battalions found themselves floundering down the Escarpment on to the Trig Capuzzo (from which they had to crawl back up the wadis the following day) while the other two battalions were still pinned down on the landing-ground at dawn. It looked as though 26th November would be a bad day for the Kiwis.

However, General Scobie's men inside the Tobruk perimeter were as anxious as ever to escape the increasing claustrophobia of life within the perimeter, and more especially in the 'appendix' which had been formed during their first break-out attempt. The code-names of the Axis strong-points which had been the targets for the first drive had been changed, for security reasons, to those of the more squashily-sentimental characters of a well-known film, and 'Doc', 'Bashful', 'Happy' and 'Sneezy' had all been bloodily eliminated during the previous week; and while 4th New Zealanders had been wresting Belhammed from Group Böttcher, a combined armour and infantry attack had ejected the Bologna Division from 'Grumpy'. A counter-attack was beaten off during the morning of the 26th, and by midday the thirty-seven Matildas, fourteen cruisers and twenty light tanks of 32nd Army Tank Brigade under Brigadier

Willison, supported by the 25-pounders of 1st R.H.A., were poised on the edge of 'Bashful' for the four-mile plunge across the desert to Ed Duda.

In all, it took them just short of an hour and a half, during which time they were subject to sporadic and almost random shelling from various points in a quadrant from below Belhammed to just west of Ed Duda, but very little from Ed Duda itself where units of Trieste Division seem to have been taken by surprise – and by 1320, muffled in a thick dust-cloud, the Matildas were on top of the feature for which both the Tobruk garrison and Norrie's armour had been aiming for days, with advanced patrols down to the Trig Capuzzo and infantry of the 1st Essex Battalion coming up in support.

From four miles away to the east, the pinned-down New Zealanders watched not only the capture of Ed Duda but also the excellent fighter cover provided by the R.A.F., followed by direct bombing support by Marylands of the S.A.A.F. which, however spectacular it might have been, was misdirected and fell upon the advancing Essex who lost half their carrier platoon as a result.

Nevertheless, the excitement of beating off the inevitable German counter-attacks on Belhammed and the news of the taking of Ed Duda was enough to spur the New Zealanders to even greater efforts, and that night 6th Battalion went in again with the bayonet in what their historian called 'the hardest, bloodiest and most deadly attack ever staged by our unit'. By morning on November 27th, the whole of the Sidi Rezegh ridge was in New Zealand hands, the 9th Bersaglieri were wiped out as a fighting unit and the 26th New Zealand Battalion had lost another eighty-four men.

But their 19th Battalion, accompanied by tanks of the 44th R.T.R., had flanked the main opposition and marched through the night to Ed Duda. Just before midnight, the link-up with the Tobruk garrison was made and the 'Tobruk Corridor' had been formed – 'for whatever', as the South African historians say, 'it was worth'.

Further west at El Adem, Oberstleutnant Westphal was watching developments with ever-increasing anxiety. He had been unable to communicate with either his Commander-in-Chief or the commander of the Afrika Korps for over twenty-four hours, the only wireless link still open being to von Ravenstein who was as ignorant of Rommel's whereabouts as Westphal himself. Aircraft sent out to find Rommel had failed to return or even to report back (they had been shot down by marauding R.A.F. fighters) and Westphal had an uncomfortable feeling that dispatch riders or even escorted Staff Officers sent to establish communication would likewise disappear. All through November 25th and 26th, he had been sending signals via 21st Panzer to Rommel and Cruewell until, apparently despairing of ever receiving answer or even acknowledgment from the highest level, he sent a résumé of the situation to von Ravenstein late on the afternoon of November 26th, suggesting that 21st Panzer Division at least had better move as quickly as possible towards Tobruk and attack the New Zealanders from the rear before the whole of the Tobruk front disintegrated.

Von Ravenstein, tired of sitting in the Egyptian desert out of touch with both Corps and Army Commander, moved with admirable celerity, slipping between 4th Indian formations and the New Zealanders of 5th Brigade at Capuzzo, around and into Bardia where he intended to refuel and refill his ammunition racks before continuing towards Tobruk. To his surprise, he met 15th Panzer just as they were emerging from the fortress, having gone in for exactly the same reasons, and some hours later he discovered that Rommel was there as well. Feeling with some justification that he had done rather well to extricate himself from Egypt so smartly, von Ravenstein reported to his Commander-in-Chief, to be greeted at once with astonishment and rage. Roundly declaring at first that the message von Ravenstein had received had been nothing but an enemy ruse, Rommel then took such strong exception to Westphal's action that that officer's career was undoubtedly in the balance for several days – until, in fact, Rommel reached El Adem and could examine the situation maps and read the reports upon which Westphal's decision had been made; after which he apparently made no comment but went to lie down for a few hours, never mentioning the matter again.

But in the meantime, his attention had been drawn back towards the crucial area, and during the early hours of November 27th he spent some time drawing up plans for the renewal of the Battle of Sidi Rezegh, and the destruction of yet another large formation of Dominion troops. By 0200 the first directives were sent out, ordering the dispatch westward along the Via Balbia of von Ravenstein's H.Q. and Battlegroup Knabe, and Neumann-Sylkow to clear up the situation on the frontier as quickly as possible and then to follow von Ravenstein for a combined attack on the New Zealanders.

A note of protest was struck by Neumann-Sylkow at the time schedules to which he was expected to move but Rommel insisted upon a further attack on the frontier positions before 15th Panzer returned to Tobruk. There then followed such a sequence of events as to cause the student of military affairs to wonder if there is much point in careful planning.

Panzer Regiment 8 moved off towards Sidi Azeiz, again became thoroughly entangled with 21st Panzer Division outside Bardia, extricated itself after the loss of much valuable time and then moved on. At 0600, Neumann-Sylkow received from Westphal an impassioned signal, 'C-in-C cannot be contacted at moment. *Panzergruppe* orders your immediate start to relieve the Tobruk front. Situation grave. *Achtung!*' – which, in the circumstances, he ignored, moving off instead after his panzer regiment who were already, much to his surprise, reporting a strong enemy force in front of them.

There then followed a sharp and bitter fight during which 15th Panzer Division captured some 800 prisoners, a huge supply dump of whose existence Panzergruppe had been unaware, six field guns and the entire headquarters of 5th New Zealand Brigade including its commander, Brigadier Hargest. And while they were counting their spoils, Rommel, at last convinced of the danger threatening to the west, arrived to cancel his previous orders and dispatch the bulk of the division back towards Tobruk. 'Order, counter-order . . . ' had thus resulted not in 'disorder' but in a very handsome profit.

Still stranded much further south at Gasr el Abid, Cruewell was at this time completely in the dark as to even the whereabouts, let alone the objectives, of his armoured divisions, neither had he any late news of the position around Tobruk although he suspected this to be serious. He therefore decided to move up towards Sidi Azeiz where he hoped to find at least some of his units. On the way up he unexpectedly came across the Ariete Division which had the previous evening managed to disengage itself from the force blocking its route down the Trig el Abd (Dan Pienaar's 1st South Africans) and set out towards the frontier. Cruewell found the Ariete artillery busily shelling the post at Bir Ghirba, but on his own responsibility he instructed the division to break off the action and proceed at once towards Tobruk – an order which came as a relief to the headquarters of the Savona Division who had been the only occupants of Bir Ghirba for weeks past.

Later that day the last Afrika Korps detachment – Group Wechmar, which on the morning of the 25th had been ordered south along the Wire to mask the activities of the Oasis group at Jarabub but had never moved because of petrol shortage – after an abortive attack on the Indians at Sidi Omar was also ordered up to Sidi Azeiz, then to follow 15th Panzer westwards; and so the 'Dash to the Wire', 'Rommel's Swan' or 'The Matruh Stakes' as the venture became variously known to the more irreverent of Eighth Army's junior ranks, came to an end, its sole tangible result the fortuitous capture during its dying spasms of 5th New Zealand Headquarters.

It did, however, have another, less concrete but more significant result. To borrow a metaphor from a distinguished authority on the Afrika Korps, Mr Ronald Lewin, the spectacular nature of the Afrika Korps manoeuvrings was itself throwing up its own anti-bodies, first in the form of the grip which Auchinleck had taken on the battle at a crucial juncture, and now in that of a change of command which Auchinleck felt himself compelled to make.

During the morning of the 25th had come news to Maddalena of the advance of a large panzer formation southwards towards them from Gasr el Abid. This was, in fact, Panzer Regiment 5 looking for a gap in the Wire through which it could make its way up to join its commander, but to Cunningham and his staff it looked rather like a direct attack on themselves, and all agreed that Auchinleck's presence there constituted an unnecessary risk. The Commander-in-Chief was therefore hurried away aboard an aircraft, and on the long flight back to Cairo he had had ample time for reflection. Twice he had listened to exhortations from Cunningham in which extreme anxiety had been the keynote, twice he had had to use his authority to calm exaggerated fears, to overrule the Army Commander's suggestions and to insist that the battle should continue – and although Cunningham had immediately and loyally accepted the directions which Auchinleck had given him, there was little doubt that those directions were now being obeyed by a man who held reservations as to their wisdom.

Cunningham's mind, in fact, had been set by recent circumstances into a *defensive* mould and he was endeavouring to obey *offensive* instructions. It was hardly a pattern for success. The atmosphere when Auchinleck had left Maddalena, if not one of panic, was decidedly one of 'flap' – a state of affairs which must be put right and not be allowed to recur, so a new figure must be placed at the head of Eighth Army.

But who? The next senior officer in the theatre was Godwin-Austen and after him was Norrie – but to change Corps Commander at this juncture would surely be even more upsetting than changing the Army Commander. One change at that level was bad enough, two could be disastrous.

The ideal of course would be for Auchinleck to take over himself, but, aware that his eyes must continually sweep a wider horizon than just that of the Libyan theatre, he concluded that he must appoint instead a man of his own cast of mind, not only already imbued with his own ideas but also fully cognisant of his plans for the immediate future; someone, in fact, already on his Staff.

His choice fell on Major-General Neil Ritchie, then Deputy Chief of the General Staff at the Cairo Headquarters – a big, cheerful, beefy man of conventional military looks who had already commanded the famous 51st Highland Division after its re-formation after Dunkirk, and had since served very efficiently on the Staff. He would have been a natural choice for promotion to Corps Commander had such an opening been available but now he would have under him two Corps Commanders each of longer service than he was. In the circumstances, they would undoubtedly understand and support him, and his appointment as Army Commander would, at least until he had proved himself, be temporary.

The change-over took place at Maddalena in the early afternoon of November 26th, and General Cunningham flew back to Cairo in the plane which had brought Ritchie up; after which Cunningham went into hospital suffering from severe exhaustion.

It seemed at first that Ritchie had taken over at a most propitious moment, for that evening the link-up at Ed Duda occurred and by the morning of the 27th it had become evident that the tank strength of XXX Corps was higher than could have been expected. Industrious recovery on the battlefield together with some excellent work by the Tank Delivery Section had raised the strength of Gatehouse's 4th Armoured Brigade to 77 Honeys, while 22nd was now possessed of 42 assorted cruisers. These 119 tanks, however, comprised the sum total of 7th Armoured Division's tank strength, for the survivors of 7th Armoured Brigade had retired to the Delta and the formation was not to see action in North Africa again.

But with this reinforcement and reorganisation, both Norrie and Gott felt that the time had come for XXX Corps to re-enter the battle, and for a start the armour should do something about the strong enemy column reported moving along the Trig Capuzzo. From Bir Sciafsciuf 22nd Armoured should move down the Escarpment and form an ambush to stop the head of the column, while from Bir Berraneb twenty miles to the south 4th Armoured's Honeys should race up as quickly as possible and attack the main enemy body which they should catch strung out on the road; and in order to clear up the area behind the frontier and ensure that no significant German force was lurking behind the main battleground, the Support Group should send out various columns from Gabr Saleh in a fan from Sidi Omar up to Gasr el Arid. In other words, a degree of concentration in the north and dispersion to the east was ordered.

Scott-Cockburn's Crusaders were in position by 1330 and in action by 1342, their hulls well screened in wadis, their 2-pounder anti-tank guns effective against the armoured cars and soft-skinned transport at the head of Neumann-Sylkow's force, and their attached eight 25-pounders enough to keep the panzers back for a while; and just as the inevitable and efficient German redeployment was likely to bring overwhelming pressure against them, the

Honeys of 4th Armoured appeared over the ridge and began pouring their shot in against the flank. Further back, Major Crisp even took his troops down the Escarpment and wrought a degree of havoc among the supply train until two *Batterien* swung their barrels around and effectively drove them off; and even while this was happening Hurricanes and Marylands of the R.A.F. and S.A.A.F. arrived overhead and caused many casualties and much damage to 15th Panzer's already exiguous transport.

Ritchie had kept well in touch with developments despite the distance between Trig Capuzzo and Maddalena, and now made his first personal intervention in the *Crusader* operation at 1845 by signalling XXX Corps that it was imperative that the sealing operation by the armour was continued and that 15th Panzer was prevented from all further advance westward and, should they attempt it, southwards as well across the ridge.

Unfortunately, his instruction arrived after darkness had fallen, at which point the British armour had followed their usual practice of breaking off the action and retiring some five miles southwards into the desert. Surprised and extremely gratified, 15th Panzer had pressed forward again and, despite losses during the day (not excessive for six hours of battle) covered another seven miles, thus reaching their day's objective before calling a halt. They were then almost next door to the New Zealanders' B Echelon, and as Cruewell had by this time ordered 21st Panzer to come across from the Via Balbia and Ariete were coming up also from Sidi Azeiz, Freyberg's men were very soon going to find themselves under extreme pressure.

By this time, 4th New Zealand Brigade with the 'I' tanks of 44th R.T.R. were at Belhammed, 6th Brigade held the Sidi Rezegh ridge between Point 175 and the Tomb, while the infantry and tanks of the garrison were at Ed Duda and by a singular coincidence of objective not previously much in evidence at any stage or level during *Crusader*, the headquarters of the New Zealand Division, of XIII Corps and of 1st Army Tank Brigade were all clustered together on the Trig Capuzzo at the eastern end of the New Zealand positions. Much time was being spent trying to eliminate small German units between Belhammed and the Sidi Rezegh escarpment, and 24th and 26th Battalions of 6th Brigade reluctantly concluded that after their quite heavy casualties of the previous two days they were unable to occupy the southern escarpment upon which the regiments and most of the artillery of Group Böttcher were congregated, west of Bu Creimisa. The New Zealanders therefore spent the night of November 27th/28th clearing up their area, burying their dead, resting and preparing for the morrow with a fair degree of confidence. They were for the most part unaware of the danger threatening from the east, and considered that their next move would be either into Tobruk or on towards El Adem. In any case, if serious fighting became necessary again, 1st South African Brigade were somewhere close at hand to the south and would be joining them soon.

During November 28th, in fact, little fighting took place around Sidi Rezegh – an advance from the southern escarpment by the infantry of Group Böttcher collected another 200 New Zealanders and reduced the strength of 24th Battalion to about 100 men, while to the south of Sciafsciuf the British armour, somewhat disgruntled by the manner in which Panzer Regiment 8 had pressed on the previous evening instead of waiting for the next day's play, attacked sporadically in the late afternoon, lost several more of 22nd Armoured's cruisers and then retired again into the desert as darkness fell. Further east, Support Group's Jock Columns felt that they had had a hugely successful day, having made offensive moves against Ariete and the tail of 15th Panzer and watched them both disappear westwards – though Italian reports do not mention the attacks, claiming that they were moving instead in accord with Cruewell's instructions, while Heinz Schmidt, commanding two rearguard companies of the 15th Panzer, remarks:

> The desert was alive with small mobile columns of the enemy – 'Jock Columns' they were called – which were a nuisance, as mosquitoes are, but in the end no more violent in their sting. They were never really strong enough to do irreparable damage.[7]

That night, in view of the evident build-up of German pressure westwards along both the Trig Capuzzo and the ridge, the three British headquarter formations threaded their way along the valley past Belhammed and into the comparative haven of Tobruk, Godwin-Austen signalling his safe arrival to Ritchie, 'Corridor to Tobruk perfectly secure and open to passage our troops and will be kept so. Have arrived there without incident. Press may now be informed that Tobruk is as relieved as I am.'

Conditions were not, however, as cosy as that message may seem to indicate, if only because of the appalling weather conditions. Much further south the 1st South Africans were engaged in a series of peripatetics of which historians have since found difficulty in making much sense:

> We bedded down at night under four blankets and although we were fully dressed and wearing greatcoats and balaclava helmets, the icy wind swept right through us. We got filthier every day. Even if we could have spared water for washing it was too cold to undress . . . rations were finished. We [his section] lived for days

on rice begged from passing Indians, and biscuits ground to powder, with which we made a hot, tasteless porridge that warmed our insides for an hour or two . . . [8]

It was all a far cry from the popular picture of golden sand dunes, green oases and tropical heat.

The day was not totally devoid of significant events, however. After an absence of four days, Rommel had returned to Panzergruppe Headquarters at El Adem and was securely back in command again, intent upon resealing the Tobruk perimeter, reopening the Battle of Sidi Rezegh and destroying the New Zealanders.

· The first move in the battle began late the following morning (November 29th) when 15th Panzer, which had climbed the Escarpment east of Point 175, swept down the Sidi Rezegh valley to turn north around Abiar el Amar in a move reversing the sequence with which 21st Panzer had opened their first attack on the airfield seven days before. By mid-afternoon they were facing north-east towards the defences of Ed Duda, which consisted of the infantry of 1st Essex, 2nd/13th Australians, a company of 1st Royal Northumberland machine-gunners and twenty-six 'I' tanks of 4th R.T.R. all under command of Lieutenant-Colonel Walter O'Carroll of the R.T.R. In a three-hour attack, the leading panzers rolled over two companies of the unfortunate Essex infantrymen, destroyed all the anti-tank guns in the area and knocked out fifteen tanks, but fortunately for O'Carroll, just behind his headquarters was a battery of Royal Horse Artillery. When, shortly after 1700, the panzers advanced again, they found themselves pinned down by a storm of fire which took them totally by surprise.

Map 9   The ordeal of the New Zealand division: November 28th–December 1st, 1941

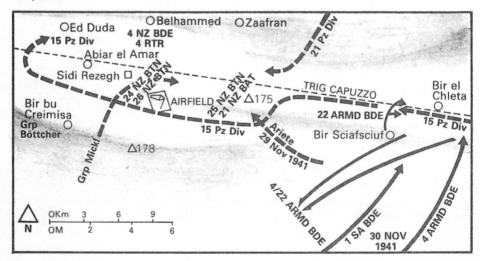

Moreover, the bombardment increased as darkness thickened, for Brigadier Willison arrived and decided that shock tactics alone would rectify the situation. Just before midnight, after yet another crashing barrage from the R.H.A., the eleven remaining tanks of 4th R.T.R. lined up abreast with only a foot between their horns and advanced directly forwards with every gun firing as fast as it could be reloaded and two companies of Australians charging with the bayonet immediately behind. By 0200, the Essex positions were re-established, 167 German prisoners were being led back towards Tobruk and the bodies of many more littered the area. Panzer Regiment 8 had been bloodily repulsed and the Tobruk 'Appendix' still existed.

At the eastern end of the New Zealand pocket, November 29th had brought mixed fortunes to the defenders. Just after dawn they had been astonished by the approach of a convoy of about 200 unidentifiable trucks and lorries which made its last run to the New Zealanders' position under the impartial artillery fire of both sides. It proved then to be a supply column brought up by XXX Corps's indefatigable Chief Engineer, Brigadier Clifton, who had disdained such aids to travel as recognised tracks and driven through the night in a roughly northerly direction, confident that he would hit the Escarpment eventually as long as he avoided the German leaguers, illuminated as usual by their unending flare pattern. When he came to the Escarpment, he just led the convoy straight down it, vehicles crashing from rock to rock and slithering down the scree slopes with remarkably few total catastrophes, though none of the vehicles was ever quite the same again, a qualification also applicable to the drivers. But they brought Freyberg's men much-needed food and ammunition, eight armoured cars, two anti-tank guns and seventeen Honeys intended for Gatehouse's brigade which remained for the moment in the pocket.

Then came an even more unexpected bonus.

Just after 0800, an outpost of 21st Battalion on Point 175 was surprised to see approaching them a German staff car which, when but twenty yards away, obligingly pulled up so that its occupants could make inquiries as to their position from what they obviously expected to be friendly troops. The New Zealanders quickly disabused them of their illusion, and when they inspected their haul, found that they had captured an obviously high-ranking German officer who gave his name and rank, perhaps unimaginatively, as Colonel Schmidt, together with his driver, 'a tin of Aulsebrook's biscuits, some cartons of South African cigarettes, a case of Crosse and Blackwell's tinned delicacies, a bottle of Greek brandy, and a jar of rum' – plus an extensively annotated map showing German and Italian positions and a collection of papers which revealed among other things the daily cipher changes for 21st Panzer Division for the next few days.

Retaining such items as they did not consider of great military significance, the fortunate members of the outpost sent the staff car and personnel onwards to Divisional Headquarters, where German etiquette promptly betrayed the unfortunate 'Colonel Schmidt'. Confronted with General Freyberg, he saluted, clicked his heels together, bowed shortly and announced, 'Von Ravenstein, General!'

He was the first high-ranking Afrika Korps officer to become a casualty of the *Crusader* operation, and proved such a charming and honourable man that everyone who met him was glad that he had not become the victim of a more fatal miscalculation.

Throughout the day, however, there was one continual disappointment for the New Zealanders in the non-arrival of Dan Pienaar's 1st South Africans, whose assistance had been promised and whose appearance was expected hourly by every one of Freyberg's men with some of the eagerness of beleaguered Western pioneers awaiting the U.S. Cavalry. This gave rise in the early evening to an unfortunate and even ludicrous episode when 21st Battalion on Point 175 was informed that a column, 'probably the South Africans', was approaching from the east, and the men swarmed out to give a warm welcome to high-turreted vehicles which they assumed to be Marmon-Harrington armoured cars. These proved, however, to be the leading tanks of the Ariete, the Italian commanders standing in open turrets waving their berets in the equally mistaken belief that Point 175 was held by *their* allies – and it was probably the enthusiasm of the welcome which astonished the Italians and made them the first to appreciate the true situation; another 200 New Zealanders found themselves 'in the bag' as a result.

The Ariete also took over a fully equipped New Zealand field hospital which had been captured the previous day by the Germans. It must be said that their treatment of the 1,000 patients and 400 medical personnel entirely lacked the chivalry with which the original captors had behaved.

As for the 1st South Africans, a curious malaise seems to have affected them, and also the remaining British armour in 4th and 22nd Brigades.

Admittedly the experiences of Dan Pienaar's South Africans so far in *Operation Crusader* had been unlikely to inspire confidence either in the higher direction of the battle or in their own fortune. Their journey across the frontier had been a nightmare, the first operational order they had received after arrival in the battle area

had been to undertake a task – the elimination of the Ariete at El
Gubi – at which the 22nd Armoured Brigade at its full strength had
failed, and of the subsequent modification of the order one of the
critics of the battle has since written, 'It would be interesting to
have some enlightenment on the tactics which should be adopted by
an infantry brigade when called upon to "mask" a hostile armoured
division in the desert.'

Nevertheless, they had taken up static positions around Bir el
Gubi where they had been subject to sporadic shelling and
occasionally fierce Stuka attacks for three days, until given the
order to move up close to the 5th Brigade – a night move despite
their previous experience, and one which Pienaar again caused to
be modified. And from the position in which the modified order left
them on the morning of *Totensonntag* they had witnessed the
destruction of their brother South Africans – a sobering experience
which strengthened Pienaar's determination that his 'boys', as he
affectionately referred to the troops under his command, should not
be unnecessarily exposed to risk.

Like the 'Pals' Battalions' of the First World War, many South
African formations were composed of men all from one district, and
when the news of the destruction of the 5th Brigade reached home,
there would be many localities plunged into deep mourning. Dan
Pienaar had no intention of allowing the same pall of sorrow to
blanket the areas of Natal and the Transvaal from which the 1st
Brigade men came – a natural feeling with which one can sym-
pathise, though not one likely to lead to speedy victory in battle. As
a result of these sentiments, Pienaar repeatedly interpreted orders in
such a way as to keep his men away from the battle areas, a course
he was enabled to follow both by the astounding degree of
ambiguity in the phrasing of the orders he received, and the marked
reluctance of British senior commanders at this time to press their
demands too hard upon Dominion troops.

After *Totensonntag*, 1st Brigade had moved to Bir Taieb el
Esem, south of the Trig el Abd, where they had missed the rush of
'Rommel's Swan' but then found themselves blocking the route of
the Ariete, a situation in which both formations appear to have
found some satisfaction, for they remained virtually static for
twenty-four hours doing little but shell each other at comparatively
long ranges, while the Ariete M13s and the South African
armoured cars manoeuvred circumspectly between. The appearance
of the Italian tanks was enough, however, to cause Pienaar to send
out signals indicating heavy engagement and requesting armoured
support, with the result that Alec Gatehouse was sent across with
Honeys from his brigade and two batteries of R.H.A., arriving,
according to one South African account:

... just in time ... in sailed Brig Alex [*sic*] Gatehouse, that gay
cavalier of the armour. His top-booted legs dangled from the
turret-top, a Scots plaid travelling rug lay across his knees, for the
day was cold; later one was to see Gatehouse with that rug belted
round his waist like a kilt, riding into battle seated in an arm-
chair strapped to the top of a tank. Gatehouse of the heavy head,
the hawk nose and deep-set eyes, was a man after Pienaar's
heart, and in later days he often remarked: 'Alec Gatehouse is a
great tank commander, the best in the Desert – I will fight with
him anywhere in tanks.'[9]

This encomium did not, apparently, strike any responsive chord in
Gatehouse's breast; much later he was to write of his arrival at
Taieb el Esem that he 'could see nothing which justified the
prevailing view that we were "just in time". Nor did I see any signs
... that the 1 S.A. Bde had already been fiercely attacked twice
that morning ... Brigadier Dan Pienaar was, in my opinion, in a
highly excitable state, and it was very difficult to discover what he
wanted ... '[10]

What he wanted was to get his brigade out of whatever danger
they then stood in. That night, despite repeated orders to stand firm
and, to use his divisional commander General Brink's words, 'scrag
them [the Ariete] hard', he pulled out in pitch darkness, made a
highly efficient night march south to the protection of the nearest
Field Maintenance Centre – and let Ariete through to the frontier.

This occurred on November 26th, and on the evening of the
following day began the series of signals intended to move 1st South
African Brigade up to the assistance of the New Zealanders on the
Sidi Rezegh ridge.

It is a fascinating and, at this remove, entertaining, exercise to
follow the movements of 1st South African Brigade during the next
few days (unless, perhaps, you are a New Zealander). Orders to
move them nearer to the battle area seem to have arrived almost
invariably either too late or not at all, those ordering a change of
direction or suggesting a temporary halt being acted upon with
remarkable celerity; and there were also several clashes with hostile
forces which have found no mention in German or Italian histories
but which – according to Pienaar's later accounts – further delayed
the South African arrival at Sidi Rezegh.

But no means all the responsibility for the extension of the New
Zealanders' ordeal on the ridge rests in South African hands. On
one occasion, Norrie halted a South African move on receipt of a
signal from Godwin-Austen of which no trace has subsequently
been found, and early on the morning of the 29th, Pienaar received
the following signal from XXX Corps:

Information Rome [Point 175] area obscure. Your task join
Bernard [General Freyberg] earliest but do NOT repeat NOT
move from present position until contacted Bernard's boys with
own recce and consider move feasible.[11]

It was late in the afternoon before one of the South African
armoured cars made contact with the New Zealanders, and
Freyberg's immediate request that Pienaar move as quickly as
possible to Point 175 was negated by the arrival there instead of the
Ariete; so 1st South Africans again remained where they were,
despite further instructions from Freyberg (under whose command
they had now been placed) that they were to press on and either
recapture Point 175 or by-pass it and enter the pocket by another
route. Unfortunately, in the early evening, wireless communication
between the two bodies of Dominion troops broke down before
Pienaar could explain fully the reasons why such a move would be
impracticable; and indeed, Freyberg was to die many years later
without thoroughly appreciating them.

General Ritchie had also felt that the early presence of 1st South
Africans at Sidi Rezegh was essential – so strongly that he sent
messages to Norrie suggesting, indeed urging, their immediate
move further forward which were in due course passed on to the
errant brigade; but as the South African historians delicately
remark, 'Pienaar, having braved the wrath of the redoubtable
"Bernard", was not likely to be disturbed by the reported sentiments of more remote members of the military pantheon.'[12]

So he remained where he was, his brigade formed into what
Norrie referred to as a 'South African huddle', their day's peace
disturbed only by their own airmen, who showered them with
pamphlets in Italian and German and caused four casualties by
indiscriminate machine-gun fire.

The British armour was not acquitting itself much better, either.

Having failed to halt the progress of 15th Panzer along the Trig
Capuzzo on the 28th, on the following day it missed all but the tail
of the move down over the landing-ground and instead had a brush
with what could only have been elements of the Ariete, about which
the best which can be said is that the results were inconclusive. As
the main 7th Armoured artillery support was still dispersed over the
desert in random Jock Columns, they borrowed some of Dan
Pienaar's guns and used these to shell the Italians from quite long
range, while the Honeys and cruisers milled about between.

Early in the afternoon, Strafer Gott somewhat impatiently
ordered a concentration of both guns and armour to carry out a
direct assault towards Point 175, but it cannot be said that this

assault was pressed home with any worthwhile degree of determination. The Honeys came to a halt soon after their first move, upon the appearance to the west of 'a force of up to forty tanks' – presumably Ariete M13s and as such no opposition to the seventyplus Honeys, especially as these were soon joined by the cruisers of the 22nd. Yet both brigades remained virtually stationary while the guns continued banging away until light faded – whereupon the British armour retired as usual some seven miles into their night leaguer.

The men were undoubtedly very tired, perhaps more tired than the Italians as they had been moving about much more; and the tank crews had certainly become much more conscious of shortcomings in their vehicles, and especially their guns, than they had been when they crossed the Wire ten days before. It also seems that by this time their disillusionment was spreading upwards to more senior levels, where officers were questioning the very doctrines in which they had been trained. Vocal expression of these doubts came most often in contemptuous remarks about their own 2-pounder solid shot armament, and envious ones about the German artillery, especially the 88mm. – but underlying these comments was a growing admiration for the military expertise of the Afrika Korps and exasperation at the repeated failures of their own concepts and techniques to beat them.

Perhaps, as Howard Kippenberger had felt at the beginning of *Crusader*, the whole of Eighth Army, armour and infantry, should have remained together, co-operating and concentrated? Perhaps it was *not* the task of armour to destroy armour? Although the questions may not have been asked outright, seeds of doubt were already planted deep in the minds of men who, though willing to risk their lives in battle for their country, were unwilling to have them thrown away by incompetence.

On the last day of the month – a week after *Totensonntag* – Scott-Cockburn handed over the remaining twenty-five cruisers of 22nd Armoured to Gatehouse, and retired with his headquarters back to Egypt leaving Strafer Gott with but one composite brigade of 120 tanks in place of the three brigades with which 7th Armoured Division had crossed the frontier so confidently eleven days before. Gott's orders to his armour for that day were 'to harass and destroy the enemy as opportunity occurred and to protect 1 S.A. Inf Bde Gp which was under orders to advance and regain from the enemy Point 175 hill' – orders which may have been framed to give tank commanders an enviable freedom of action, but which, containing as they did a choice of roles, gave instead to the tired and disillusioned men the opportunity to avoid the hazards of aggression.

The protection of the 1st South Africans was given priority over the harassment and destruction of the enemy, and as Dan Pienaar was still employing Fabian tactics to avoid confrontation with either Afrika Korps or Ariete, this allowed the British armour to settle down on the South Africans' right flank to ward off enterprising – but in different circumstances surely ineffective – attacks by the Ariete M13s. These continued on and off during the day, and some M13s were destroyed – one account claimed sixteen for no British loss – but Point 175 overlooking the New Zealanders' eastern flank stayed in Italian hands, and darkness found the South Africans and the British armour but little nearer the besieged force than they had been at dawn.

The South Africans had made one move. In the morning, Pienaar had detached an infantry battalion and a field battery off towards Point 178 on the southern escarpment in response to orders from XXX Corps that he should again change direction of advance so that he could attack the flank of 15th Panzer Division (with an infantry brigade!) but after it had run into strong opposition from what was now called Group Mickl (General Böttcher had taken von Ravenstein's place in command of 21st Panzer) it was recalled and by mid-afternoon was safely back inside the 'huddle'.

But Norrie had become so concerned at the lack of movement that he decided personally to 'apply a little ginger' and went down to Pienaar's position where he found the brigadier 'in an affable and

Figure 2 Carro armato tipo M13/40: weight 14 tons; armour 14mm.–30mm.; engine 105 h.p.; maximum speed 20 m.p.h.; armament one 47mm., three 8mm. Breda m.g.; crew 4

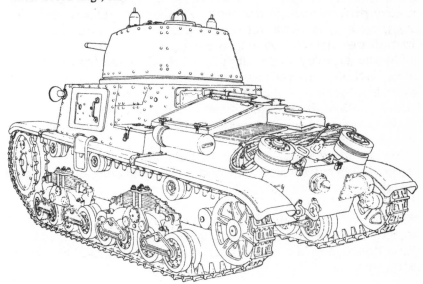

pleasant mood but . . . insufficiently conscious of the urgency of the situation . . . '

After some discussion, it was decided that Point 175 was, after all, the true objective for 1st South Africans, but that instead of proceeding directly there (after all, the armour had failed to get through so how could a soft-skinned infantry brigade?) Norrie should himself lead them to a point overlooking the Trig Capuzzo near Bir Sciafsciuf, and that the brigade should then approach its objective from the east along the line of the Escarpment. By noon, the line of march had been agreed and Norrie led off with his own Battle H.Q. and three armoured cars, only to find after some time that he was out on his own again. Rude but encouraging signals were dispatched and in due course

> the leadings tps of 1 SA Bde came slowly into view and halted, so I sent back Brigadier Aikenhead (my C.C.R.A.) to Brigadier Pienaar with orders that he was to push on immediately . . . The momentum was soon re-established, only to be followed by some quite accurate and heavy shelling of the column from a west and NW direction. This unexpected development again caused the leading tps to pause and some men actually got out of their trucks, with the apparent intention of digging in.[13]

In his efforts to get the column moving forward again, Norrie came to the conclusion that although the troops themselves were anxious and indeed eager to get on, they had been given no idea of what was expected of them.

It was thus nearly dark when, with Norrie himself leading them in a recce car, 1st South African Brigade eventually reached the Escarpment at Bir Sciafsciuf some ten miles east of the nearest New Zealanders, in time for their artillery to join forces with the guns of one of the Jock Columns in the neighbourhood in harassing the enemy transport moving along the Trig Capuzzo below. But the effort of reaching the Escarpment had apparently exhausted the brigade's strength – or perhaps its brigadier's spirit of co-operation – and to Norrie's extreme irritation, yet another South African huddle was soon only too evidently in existence, exhibiting all the familiar signs of gluey immobility.

As for 4th/22nd Armoured Brigade, this was still out in the desert, five miles south of Point 175, taking up night leaguer positions.

The failure of both the South Africans and the British armour to reach Point 175 on November 30th and take the pressure off the New Zealanders had resulted in the loss for the second time of the main length of the Sidi Rezegh ridge.

The last ordeal for the battered 6th Brigade began at about 1400, after a comparatively peaceful morning, when the guns of Group Mickl began a bombardment from their positions on the southern escarpment which by 1500 had become very severe. According to the 26th Battalion history:

> A large-calibre gun was firing and its shells left huge craters in the rocky ground. Eight men had been killed and seven others wounded . . . One soldier who had been blown out of his trench during the morning suddenly went berserk. The men on the higher ground watched with dismay enemy tanks converging on the sector. Infantry were crossing down the southern escarpment and moving northward through the wadis. The 25-pounders had practically ceased firing . . . One by one the anti-tank guns were knocked out. Two more sent up by Brigade HQ suffered a similar fate after they had fired a few shots . . . Enemy infantry moved in from the south. As they neared the sector and crossed the ridges the tanks opened fire . . . Firing as they came, the enemy armour breasted the escarpment and fanned out across the lower ground. The 24th Battalion was overrun, then A and B Coys of 26th Battalion. A few men made a break and escaped.[14]

By dark, the main body of the attackers had swept eastwards along the ridge almost as far as Point 175, while some of the panzers had gone down to the Trig Capuzzo across which, after a brief battle with New Zealand artillery, they could see the rising ground opposite leading up to the summit of Belhammed still in the hands of Freyberg's 4th Brigade. Of 6th Brigade, only the headquarters, the field regiment of artillery, a machine-gun platoon and the battered remnants of 25th Battalion still grimly hanging on just west of Point 175 remained – and Brigadier Barrowclough's request that they all be allowed to retire into Tobruk was refused on the ground that the South Africans had been ordered to join them during the night, and the armour to attack the Ariete at first light. Not surprisingly, this information was greeted with scepticism, and General Godwin-Austen was left in no doubt that he would be held responsible if the gallant survivors of the brigade were not extricated from their perilous positions.

Pienaar did in fact send out three companies of infantry towards Point 175 during the night, but they found themselves being accompanied by unidentified vehicles to the north and as a result managed only to mount a two-platoon attack on their objective, which not surprisingly failed; after which they returned to their huddle. Gatehouse's armour, however, did move up to the rescue at dawn on December 1st. They drove northwards along the eastern edge of the landing-ground, being fired upon by Group Mickl from the west and Ariete from the east to such effect as to give them a distinct feeling of the Light Brigade charge at Balaclava, and several Honeys were knocked out by the time the main body reached Barrowclough's H.Q. – where they found themselves excitedly welcomed by the eighty-odd 'riflemen, drivers, cooks and clerks' who were all that remained of 24th and 26th Battalions, and who now rushed forward to join what they thought would be a victorious break-out charge to regain the lost ground.

There followed a brief interlude of discussion and explanation, but in the end it was realised that discretion would be the better part of valour and the disappointed Kiwis accepted their lot. There was at first some misunderstanding about the precise direction of withdrawal, but eventually the 6th Brigade survivors made their way north-eastwards towards Zaafran, under the noses of both Ariete and the 21st Panzer Division – who had remained curiously muted since the capture of von Ravenstein, despite his replacement by Böttcher. Behind them, 4th/22nd Armoured remained as shield against possible attack by 15th Panzer until just after midday, under sporadic fire from Ariete and occasionally sallying forth against small groups of panzers and armoured cars of one or other of the reconnaissance battalions, which all apparently retired hastily. During the afternoon, the Honeys climbed back up the Escarpment and regained first their night leaguer, and later went even further back to spend the next night at Bir Berraneb.

By now exhaustion was affecting almost everyone in the battle area, and one of the New Zealand historians who had been taken prisoner and was in the hospital wadi now in the hands of Ariete noted that German troops in the neighbourhood were walking like zombies. The 'Dash to the Wire' had not only reduced 21st Panzer to less than half its strength in men and less than a third in equipment, it had also worn what remained down almost to the limits of physical endurance; and General Böttcher does not seem to have been the man to rejuvenate them. During the morning of December 1st he signalled Cruewell complaining of continual harassment on flank and rear (from the Jock Columns) and asking permission to march away from the danger area and find haven with Corps H.Q. at Bir bu Creimisa – a request which brought a sharp rebuke from Cruewell, especially as Böttcher had had the presumption to send a similar signal in clear to Panzergruppe H.Q. over Cruewell's head.

But 15th Panzer still possessed reserves of energy upon which to call, and Rommel, who was in the area, ensured that they did so by assigning to them the attack intended to complete the annihilation of the New Zealanders.

They were on the move by 0400 on December 1st, infantry and

machine-gun units making their way up the southern slopes of Belhammed under cover of darkness – a cover continued after dawn by a thick mist. Then as light increased, a heavy barrage opened behind them both from their own divisional artillery and that of Group Mickl, the summit of Belhammed disappeared under a cloud of black smoke, and the armour of Panzer Regiment 8 came up through the murk. As the panzers rolled forward, crushing the flimsy sangars which were all the protection the New Zealand infantry had been able to erect, fierce fighting again broke out – but only at infantry level, for the New Zealand and British artillery could see nothing of the battle and even the Valentines and Matildas on the western flank were blinded by mist and smoke. By 0830, the survivors of Kippenberger's battalion – now reduced to nine officers and 286 other ranks – were faced with the alternatives of surrender or slaughter by the panzers (and wisely chose surrender), 18th Battalion had lost all its anti-tank guns and retreated westwards into the Tobruk garrison area, while Freyberg himself had missed capture by a hair's breadth and slid off with his Battle H.Q. and that of 4th Brigade to Zaafran, where eventually he was joined by the survivors from 6th Brigade.

The Tobruk corridor had been cut and the port was under siege again.

Freyberg's position was bitter indeed. His division had been the instrument by which Rommel's frontier garrisons had first been bottled up, had been the one by which the siege of Tobruk had been lifted, and for four days his men had fought to hold a pocket against increasing pressure from two panzer divisions and a siege train – while an unscathed infantry brigade and an armoured formation with over a hundred tanks manoeuvred gravely in the far reaches of the desert without, as far as he could see, attempting to do anything to help him. It is not surprising that his opinion of the reliability of armoured formations had not been raised by the events of the last few days, that he did not regard Dan Pienaar with much affection, and that his wireless conversations with his Corps and Army Commanders were curt and much to the point. That night he talked to Norrie about plans for the evacuation of the remnants of his division back across the border, and the history of the New Zealand Divisional Signals has an enlivening account of the event.

The GOC called up Headquarters 30 Corps by RT and spoke to General Norrie about his intentions. Sergeant Smith stood by the set while the General spoke and listened in horrified silence while he described his plan in the plainest of plain language, quite unblemished by the merest pretence of RT procedure or security precautions. Smith bounded over to OC A Section: 'Did you hear what he said? Did you hear?' he yelled and, without waiting for an answer, 'Tiny said that we are going to break out at dusk – four miles east, nine miles south-east over the escarpment and then flat out for the wire! *And all in clear!*' The last words were almost a shriek. Throwing out his arm in the direction of the sinister black shapes squatting on the distant skyline . . . , he turned and peered earnestly into the face of Lieutenant-Colonel Agar, who had come up to see the fun. 'And what does he think those bastards out there are going to do about it, sir?' As he sauntered off dejectedly, fragments of his mournful soliloquy floated back to his hearers: ' . . . nine miles to Point 192 . . . east to the wire . . . nine miles to Hell, more like.'[15]

There is, however, despite the sergeant's gloom, a Destiny which guards people like 'Tiny' Freyberg (who in the First World War had won three D.S.O.s in addition to his V.C.) and it was still working effectively on December 1st, 1941.

Despite Rommel's clear and forceful instructions to Afrika Korps that the remains of the New Zealand Division were to be found and annihilated, despite also Cruewell's strict injunction that 21st Panzer Division were to stay where they were blocking the Trig Capuzzo at the eastern end of the pocket, General Böttcher decided that the sudden disappearance of all enemy presence immediately in front of him constituted an open invitation for his armour and infantry to advance westwards, towards Afrika Korps H.Q. and home. By dusk, Panzer Regiment 5 had moved five miles along the Trig and were climbing the Escarpment west of the landing-ground, and by 2000 they had ensconced themselves with their protective infantry in defensive positions around the Mosque, while behind them followed the vehicles of their supply echelon.

Much further back, the tired but gratified survivors of the 2nd New Zealand Division, led by their general and including a doubtless sceptical and puzzled signals sergeant, were making their unobstructed way through the gap so obligingly left for them, rendezvousing thirteen miles further east with Norrie just before midnight, and then pressing on as far as Bir Gibni by dawn. They crossed the Wire the same day and reached Baggush before the end of the week – accompanied all the way by sixty Italian prisoners who, once they had realised what was happening, had hastily repaired some trucks and lorries in the neighbourhood of Zaafran so as to ensure that they would not be left behind.

As the South African brigade had also moved on the night of December 1st/2nd and by dawn were safely back in their old leaguer around Taieb el Esem, Tobruk was now isolated once more, with the nearest friendly formations twenty-five miles away,

and Ariete, the Afrika Korps, the siege train and General Sümmermann's Division zbV Afrika (retitled that day 90th Light Division)
firmly ensconced between.

Thus it would seem that the courage, determination and tran-
scendent military expertise of the Afrika Korps, coupled with the
resilience and drive of their redoubtable commander, had in twelve
days defeated the far greater numbers and heavier weight of
armament which Eighth Army had flung against them in *Operation
Crusader*. They had destroyed one South African brigade and two
of the three British armoured brigades, and so battered the New
Zealand Division that it had retired from the fray; there seemed to
be every justification for the jubilant note in a signal which Rommel
sent off that night to the High Command:

> In the continuous heavy fighting between the 18th November
> and the 1st December, 814 enemy armoured fighting vehicles and
> armoured cars have been destroyed, and 127 aircraft shot down.
> No estimate can yet be given of the booty in arms, ammunition
> and vehicles. Prisoners exceed 9,000, including three generals.[16]

Yet that picture was false, the jubilation unwarranted.

In addition to the purely factual error in the signal (brigadiers do
not count as generals in the British Army; and one of the supposed
generals had been a full colonel), there were other factors to be
taken into account before a true balance could be struck, and if
Rommel had not as yet appreciated the realities of the situation,
there were others who had.

Some hours before Rommel had sent off his signal, Lt-Colonel
Howard Kippenberger, wounded and a prisoner in the wadi
hospital, was sadly contemplating the scene of the destruction of his
own battalion (20th) on Belhammed, when he was approached by a
German artillery officer.

'We have taken Belhammed,' he said, 'and our eastern and
western groups have joined hands.'

As this was confirmation of Kippenberger's suspicion of the
resealing of the Tobruk perimeter, he expressed his regret.

'But it is of no use,' answered the German. 'We have lost the
battle.'

To this the New Zealander replied with some reserve, suggesting
that if this were true, the Germans could at least console themselves
with the reflection that their enemies would judge that they had
fought well.

'That is not enough. Our losses are too heavy. We have lost the
battle.' And the German officer went despondently on his way.

But to Rommel a victory had been won and must now be exploited
– and there were still the courageous garrisons on the frontier to
whom succour and encouragement must be given; so he now
proposed a second 'Dash to the Wire'. A battalion group was to be
detached from each panzer division and sent off immediately along
the two northern routes towards Bardia and Sidi Azeiz, to be
followed at the latest by dawn on December 3rd by a reinforced
regiment with tanks, and backed up as far as Gasr el Arid by
Ariete, and as far as Bir el Chleta by Trieste. The remainder of the
Afrika Korps would join forces with the Italian XXI Corps divisions
still holding the Tobruk perimeter to the west, in order, with 90th
Light Division attacking from the north, to eliminate the British
positions at Ed Duda; and the reconnaissance battalions would
probe south from Group Mickl positions on the southern escarpment to find out what the recently dispersed British armour was
doing beyond the Trig el Abd.

Even Cunningham would hardly have dispersed his forces wider
than that and it is not surprising that Panzergruppe staff and the
Afrika Korps command were appalled by Rommel's proposals. The
only consolation they could draw would be that enough might be
discovered of the enemy dispositions for them to be able to discern
the intentions behind them.

Little but probing movement therefore occurred during December
3rd, though reports from the first battalion groups to set out
indicated that they had come up against shields barring the way to
their objectives and were awaiting the heavier support, and in the
evening a signal from Gambara reported that Italian units around
El Gubi were being harassed by shell-fire which Rommel interpreted as nothing more than activity by yet another Jock Column.

But the morning of December 4th presented him with an
ominously different picture. For one thing, his staff had been able
to provide him with figures of German losses since the beginning of
the battle, and these made sombre reading indeed. Sixteen commanding officers had now been killed or seriously wounded, the
losses of junior officers had been in proportion, and 3,800 other
ranks were also out of action. In addition, 142 panzers, 25 armoured
cars and 390 lorries had been destroyed, while of the artillery, eight
88mms, 34 anti-tank guns, ten heavy guns, seven medium, 24 field
guns and 60 mortars had been lost, and although at least the
transport position was eased by the capture of vast numbers of
British trucks and lorries (it had long been virtually impossible for
aircraft or reconnaissance patrols to distinguish between Allied and
Axis columns on the move), this potential advantage was limited by
dwindling petrol and diesel stocks.

Moreover, whether the 'harassing' to which every movement was subject was being carried out by formations no more lethal than Jock Columns or not, the effects were cumulative and beginning to assume significant proportions; already Ariete were complaining of shell-fire from the line of the Escarpment which slowed up their movements along the Trig Capuzzo, while that same morning Gambara reported anxiously that one of the largest Italian fuel dumps nearly twenty miles north-west of Bir el Gubi had been blown up, apparently by a squadron of King's Dragoon Guards. This was bad enough, but then came news that *Indian* troops had captured another dump six miles north-west of Bir el Gubi and that Camerons were attacking a position held by a Young Fascist battalion close by. Obviously, 4th Indian Division had moved up from the frontier – but hopes that this might make the relief of the frontier garrisons easier were dashed by news that the 15th Motor-cycle Battalion moving along the Via Balbia had been virtually wiped out by New Zealand Cavalry and a Maori battalion.

To complete the morning's doleful picture, a well-mounted attack by elements of 21st Panzer, Group Mickl and Engineer Battalion 200 on the appendix at Ed Duda had been halted and pinned down by artillery fire, and then after an hour of increasingly heavy bombardment the supporting 21st Panzer artillery had been suddenly blanketed by shell-fire from the *south* – where another Jock Column had attacked Pavia in Group Mickl's place around Bir bu Creimisa, capturing their anti-tank guns and a large number of prisoners.

From what Panzergruppe Afrika could see on the morning of December 4th, Eighth Army was exhibiting some of the more dispiriting characteristics of the Lernean Hydra, and Afrika Korps's recent successes in hacking off heads had nevertheless left the main body active, if not intact. Even Rommel showed signs of frustration that morning, and the final blow fell shortly after midday with the arrival at El Adem of a report that Bir el Gubi itself was being attacked by a brigade group with artillery and over a hundred tanks.

Hastily, the exiguous remains of Panzer Regiment 5 were sent across the Sidi Rezegh landing-ground towards the southern escarpment to regain command of those vital heights, and Rommel – realising that after all the main area of conflict must still remain south of Tobruk – sent orders recalling the patient and long-suffering Neumann-Sylkow and all his mobile forces from the frontier, so that Afrika Korps would be concentrated to deal with this freshly developing menace; and to increase the chances of success, he also ordered 90th Light Division and the Bologna Division down from the north of the appendix, thereby stripping the eastern end of the Tobruk perimeter of besieging forces.

This was indeed a significant development. For the first time in eight months, one flank of the Tobruk perimeter was open – and if no one was immediately interested in moving out through it, this was only because the attentions of the garrison were engaged elsewhere.

The Duke of Wellington, when talking about the French and British armies of the Peninsular War, is reputed to have compared Napoleon's to a superbly balanced team of horses working together in well-designed linking harness, whereas his own consisted of a mixture of nags tied together with ropes. But when the French leather harness broke the team was thrown into confusion, whereas if the British rope broke – as it frequently did – it was only necessary to tie another knot and the jumble would carry on unconcerned.

It was, of course, a parallel which omitted mention of the figure on the driver's seat, but some of the explanation of the strength still left in Ritchie's hands after the débâcles of the last days of November may be found in it. If the destruction of the 5th South African Brigade had lowered the morale of the 1st Brigade, it had had little effect upon the New Zealanders – whose destruction in turn was of little concern to Norrie's armour, to the 4th Indians or to the 2nd South African Division, already under orders to move up to relieve the Indians on the frontier. Auchinleck and Ritchie might have been worried by the arithmetic of the battles (though they had far less cause than Rommel) but the fragmentation caused by differences in attitude between Imperial and Colonial troops, between armoured elite and pedestrian infantry, between regular officers with private means and 'hostilities only' officers and men with nothing but their pay, though it badly hindered co-operation during the build-up for an attack, gave to each isolated – even 'tribal' – section a degree of bloody-minded independence which was proving useful in the shadow of catastrophe.

'I'm all right, Jack!' was a common attitude at this stage of *Crusader* throughout Eighth Army, and if it reflected adversely on the effectiveness of political and military command, it now provided Ritchie with a number of formations with which he could at least keep punching the Panzergruppe Afrika bag, even though the fists might not be working in conscious co-operation. His instructions to his Corps and Divisional commanders had been that at all costs pressure on the Axis forces must be kept up, and his own pressure on the commanders themselves was strengthened by the arrival of Auchinleck at his headquarters on December 1st, and the re-assuring presence of the Commander-in-Chief there in the background for the next ten days.

One of the first moves had been the bringing forward of 11th

Indian Brigade and the arrangements for the relief by the 2nd South African Division of the other two Indian brigades, so that they could move up later. Another had been the appointment of 1st South African Brigade to take over protection of the Field Maintenance Centres thus releasing the 22nd Guards Brigade for a more active role, and then the direction of both 11th Indian and the Guards Brigade towards El Gubi. This was in fact intended as a clearing operation which would then allow 4th Armoured Brigade – now up to a strength of 136 Honeys, though the quality of the new crews was suspect – to sweep forward and take El Adem, afterwards driving on towards Gazala if the opportunity arose; and all the while the Support Group Jock Columns would harry and observe the Axis movements.

The result of these arrangements was that by the evening of December 4th the Mahrattas, Camerons and Rajputana Rifles were either in possession of or attacking Italian positions north of El Gubi (from the west, for they had repeated their tactics at Nibeiwa and the Tummars), the Guards Brigade were in reserve to the south, 4th Armoured were manoeuvring to the north-east, while a semicircle of armoured cars screened them all from the north and west and the Jock Columns extended the screen eastwards along the line of the Escarpment.

Below them the screens could watch the Ariete and Neumann-Sylkow's force pouring back along the Trig Capuzzo under gun-fire from the Jock Columns, then swinging south-west outside the armoured car screens and down towards El Adem – while beyond them the 90th Light held the northern lines of their passage against attempts to interfere by the Tobruk garrison. Afrika Korps orders were to concentrate west of El Adem together with all the remaining German and Italian artillery, and be ready either to beat off a strong British attack or, if none developed, to drive south-east and relieve the Italian positions around El Gubi.

It seemed, therefore, that December 5th would see yet another massed conflict – and most probably the one which would prove conclusive. If the Axis forces there were destroyed or even badly mauled, then the way would be open for the Allies as far as El Agheila and perhaps even to Tripoli; if 4th Armoured Brigade suffered the fate which had befallen both the 7th and the 22nd, then only dispersed infantry would bar Rommel's route to Cairo.

But as it happened, 4th Armoured were not even to be allowed to wait and see. Ritchie had become anxious about the reports still coming in of Rommel's second 'Dash to the Wire' and after a slightly acrimonious exchange of signals with Norrie who pointed out that his forces could be better employed carrying out Ritchie's original purpose than reacting over-sensitively to Rommel's,

Ritchie rather irritably ordered that the 'centre of gravity of 7th Armoured Division should be moved back to where it was'. During the night of December 4th/5th, the Honeys therefore drove back to Bir Berraneb, leaving the two infantry brigades around El Gubi to face the combined armour of the Afrika Korps when daylight came. Like the gains of the first 'Dash to the Wire', those for the second had been reaped after it was all over.

The Afrika Korps did not get under way until late afternoon on the 5th, as Rommel was waiting both for the Ariete to close up, and for signs of movement from the British; and when the blow did fall, its recipients were the Mahrattas near Point 182. Just as darkness was falling, twenty-five panzers followed by lorried infantry swept down upon them, and during the confused and bitter fighting which followed, the Indian anti-tank guns were all knocked out and both A and C Companies overrun, though many members of C Company managed to slip away individually to fall back on the Camerons to the rear. From there, somewhat incredulously, they watched the German formations milling around their newly won positions in a state of obvious indecision, then retiring westwards into the desert in a manner distinctly reminiscent of British armoured tactics. They did not even carry out their retirement efficiently, the panzer columns floundering about in the dark, losing one another and often their sense of direction, with the result that some units back-tracked and the survivors of the 11th Indian Brigade spent much of the night emulating mice in the middle of enemy dispositions.

There was thus no overwhelming victory on December 5th, and it seemed at last that sheer exhaustion was blunting the edge of German efficiency, so perhaps Allied victory was within reach.

In fact, it was – but for very different reasons. Out of sight and out of mind, the Royal Navy and the Royal Air Force had been doing just as much at and over the sea to defeat Panzergruppe Afrika as Eighth Army had been doing on land; and in their tasks had been receiving increasingly valuable help from Ultra intelligence, which could now often give them the destination and route of Axis convoys before they left Italy. The results had been spectacular, as Rommel was about to learn.

He had spent an extremely worrying day. Not only had the figures of German losses presented to him on the 4th depressed him considerably, but certain unpleasant aspects of the supply situation were being forced to his attention in a manner which he could no longer ignore.

He had cabled Mussolini on December 2nd to the effect that the fighting efficiency of Panzergruppe Afrika depended upon a continuous stream of reinforcements, fuel, ammunition, and replacement armour and artillery, and the reply, that sea traffic between Italy and Libya was becoming increasingly dangerous, and that warships were the only vessels capable of getting through – and then with only limited cargoes of fuel and ammunition – had been dismissed by him as just another example of Italian obstructiveness.

His own Q branch had then warned him that stocks of practically everything from shells for the guns to boots for the infantry were down to an alarming level, but his somewhat cavalier attitude to such matters, combined with faith in his Staff's capabilities in emergency and also in his own luck, allowed him to brush these aside.

But on the evening of the 5th, an Italian Staff officer arrived from the Operations Branch of Comando Supremo, Tenente-Colonello Montezemolo, and proceeded to paint so gloomy a view of Rommel's supply position that even he was forced to reconsider his prospects.

The most revelatory fact of Montezemolo's résumé – and the one he produced at the outset of his argument – was that, of the 22 ships of over 500 tons dispatched from Italian ports to North Africa during November, 14 had been sent to the bottom of the sea taking with them 62 per cent – nearly 60,000 tons – of Rommel's supplies. Tankers had been particularly badly hit and only 2,500 tons of aviation or motor spirit had arrived; but it was the loss in Italian shipping which was proving most significant. It had now reached such a level that although Comando Supremo would do everything possible to send such essential supplies as rations, medical equipment and perhaps ammunition, Rommel must understand that shipping of reinforcements in anything but derisory numbers was totally out of the question, at least until the end of December. By that time the German Luftflotte 2 would be operating from Sicily and air protection over convoys would be possible – but until then, he must expect no more men, no more tanks, no more aircraft, much less ammunition – and he would be lucky to get enough fuel to retreat, let alone to advance even further from his bases.

This was a stunning blow and one to which Rommel's reaction was, for the moment, low-keyed. He pointed out that his present position was, to say the least, grave, that of the 250 panzers with which he had begun the battle fewer than 40 were left, and that existing stocks of ammunition were totally inadequate to fight another battle of consequence. Did the Italian Command realise that Panzergruppe Afrika could not hold the positions in which the forces were disposed at that moment, and must either advance to the lines held when the battle began, or retreat? And if they retreated under present conditions there could be no question of holding Cyrenaica, in view of the probability of a British outflanking movement south of the Jebel Akhdar? They would have to go back to Agedabia at least, and probably to El Agheila and into Tripolitania.

Whether in Rommel's mind the questions were rhetorical or not, the effects upon the Italian Comandante Superiore when they were put to him were pronounced. Generale Bastico proclaimed himself 'dumbfounded' at the news of the losses suffered by the joint forces under his command, and of the difficulties revealed by his German subordinate. For the moment, he agreed that the defences around Agedabia must be strengthened, and suggested also that a force be sent to recover the Jalo Oasis; after which he returned to his own headquarters near Tmimi to consider the situation further. Left alone, Rommel endeavoured to find out where his main forces were and what they were up to.

According to the Afrika Korps War Diary for December 6th, this was no easy task. The involved movements of the previous few days and the confusions of the night had left British, Indian, German and Italian units thoroughly mixed up, and the dirt and dust of two weeks' battle combined with the interchange of vehicles which had taken place (for quite a number of Axis vehicles had also found employment in British and Commonwealth formations) made it quite difficult for the combatants themselves, let alone their commanders or their staff, to know who was who. The results were sometimes startling, and often ludicrous.

During December 6th and the day which followed, there was a great deal of shelling but very little mobility, but on one occasion the commander of an armoured car stopped all artillery action on both sides in his immediate neighbourhood by waving his beret – dust-covered and totally unrecognisable. On another, a column of Italian vehicles jerked to a halt when one of the 11th Hussars' armoured cars, driving somewhat unconcernedly alongside, hoisted a blue flag on its radio antenna, and on yet another, one of the 11th's armoured cars fled for protection into what was quickly demonstrated to be a German lorry column, from what later proved to be a troop of King's Dragoon Guards.

Perhaps the best illustration of both the difficulties of identification and the exhaustion to which everyone had been reduced occurred during the afternoon of December 7th, when the adjutant of one of Rommel's reconnaissance battalions, looking for his commander, found himself driving parallel to a column which at first he regarded with deep suspicion. He then saw, towards the rear, one of his own unit's eight-wheeled armoured cars, so driving close in, he approached the leading vehicle to challenge in German and, receiving no answer, in Italian. There followed a moment's conversational hiatus, broken eventually when the driver, dust-

covered and naked to the waist, looked down and shouted irritably:
'Oh, piss off, mate . . . for Christ's sake!'

And he did.

But by this time, Rommel had made up his mind. That morning at Afrika Korps Headquarters he had declared that if the British were not beaten that day, he would abandon the Tobruk front and go back to the defensive positions south of Gazala, to which he had already directed the heavy artillery and some of the Italian divisions, and to which he now sent 90th Light and his own headquarters. As the day wore on it became evident that neither side was engaging closely, that the British artillery fire was growing heavier all the time, and that in the late afternoon the 4th Armoured was attempting – not very aggressively – an outflanking movement to the south.

Accepting the inevitable, Rommel issued the necessary instructions, and after dark the remnants of the two panzer divisions with their accompanying guns and infantry drew back from Bir el Gubi, their retirement covered at first by yet another of their spectacular Brock's Benefits. The cover was not enough, however, to save elements of the Pavia Division just to the north, for Comando Supremo in Rome had signalled that after all everything possible was to be done to hold Cyrenaica, whatever Rommel might feel, and Gambara as Bastico's Chief of Staff had cancelled one of Rommel's orders for their withdrawal. As a result, some of the luckless Italians around El Adem were caught, the Brescia and Trento Divisions holding the western end of the Tobruk perimeter were roughly handled before they were eventually forced to disengage, and bitterness between Italian and German staffs increased.

Rommel's personal bitterness was increased, too. Not only had the decision meant the abandonment of the frontier positions and the gallant Major Bach, but on the previous evening, the argumentative but faithful Neumann-Sylkow – capable, attractive and half-Scots – had been severely wounded by a shell which landed beside his command vehicle. He had been rushed back to a Derna hospital but no one had any illusions about his condition and he was to die two days later.

The bitterness showed. On the morning of December 8th, Bastico came to see him at his new headquarters just behind Ain el Gazala and Rommel kept him waiting for fifteen minutes before admitting him to his Mammoth. He then treated him to an explosion of Teutonic wrath in which he not only blamed the Italians for the failure to beat the British, but announced that in view of the unsatisfactory nature of the co-operation he had received, he intended to take his divisions not only back into Tripolitania, but on and into Tunisia where he would give himself up to the French and be interned!

It took some time and great deal of soothing gesture to cool the atmosphere, but Rommel – who was quite capable of staging fits of temper solely in order to aid the winning of arguments – established the point that, once the consequences of Gambara's 'insubordination' and 'interference' had been overcome and the Italian divisions safely withdrawn behind the Gazala defences, the retirement should be continued and Cyrenaica abandoned to British hands. The argument flared up again a few days later, but when Cavallero arrived from Rome to adjudicate, neither Bastico nor Gambara could produce viable alternative strategies and spent most of their time with their Chief of Staff complaining about Rommel's rudeness. This, they were told, they must grin and bear – and in the meantime they had better comply with their overbearing but efficient ally's suggestions.

It cannot be said that Eighth Army pressed very hard on Afrika Korps's heels during the second British advance through Cyrenaica. There were, of course, inevitable logistic problems as the lines of communication and supply lengthened (one of Rommel's arguments for a long Axis withdrawal had been this resultant disadvantage for the Allies) but the fact remains that by the end of *Operation Crusader* the high confidence and optimism with which the British troops had entered the battle had been largely replaced by a cynical wariness which tended to keep them back from German rearguard screens, formed and manned, as now they knew they would be, by soldiers of high professional competence.

An attempt by XIII Corps (which had taken over the pursuit through Cyrenaica while XXX Corps dealt with the frontier garrisons) to outflank the Gazala positions was efficiently beaten back by 15th Panzer at Alam Hamza on December 15th, whereupon plans were laid for an advance by Gatehouse's armour (which had been attached to Godwin-Austen's force for the operation) towards Mechili, and by 4th Indian Division to Lamluda west of Derna. Oasis Force was directed up from Jalo to Agedabia while 22nd Guards Brigade was to be held like an arrow in a bow for a lunge straight through the Jebel, to take Benghasi by a *coup de main* at the critical moment. It was all to begin on December 19th.

Then, during the night of December 16th/17th, Rommel, with consummate timing, slipped away himself sending Afrika Korps and the Italian armour straight down along the edge of the desert, first to Mechili and then to Msus, and the Italian infantry off around the coast roads. Caught off balance, the British armour scrambled after Afrika Korps but petrol shortages and bad going, exacerbated by hastily improvised supply, slowed them badly and it was not until the morning of December 23rd that their spearheads reached Antelat, where they hoped to repeat the successes of Beda Fomm by cutting off the bulk of the enemy still to the north.

They were too late. Facing them was the whole of the Afrika Korps, reinforced, to Rommel's mingled relief and annoyance, by twenty-two new panzers which despite Montezemolo's forecast had arrived two days previously at Benghasi. (Twenty-three more had been delivered to Tripoli, though two ships carrying a further forty-five between them had been sunk en route from Brindisi.) The result was a bloody nose for 3rd R.T.R. and the hurried dispatch forward from Mechili of a reconstituted 22nd Armoured Brigade with eighty cruisers and thirty Honeys – which ran out of petrol at Saunnu and remained stuck there for twenty-four hours.

In the meantime, King's Dragoon Guards and a column from the Support Group had entered Benghasi in time for their Christmas dinner, to find that Brescia Division's rearguard had just moved out, the inhabitants were not quite so enthusiastic in their welcome as they had been a year before (possibly due to the ever-increasing damage being wreaked upon their once pleasant and prosperous town by the R.A.F.) and several chalked messages from the last Germans to leave, suggesting an early return engagement.

By December 27th, 22nd Guards Brigade were moving down on the Afrika Korps positions around Agedabia and the 22nd Armoured driving out wide to the south to outflank them. With an air almost of *déjà vu*, Cruewell – thoroughly appreciating the over-extension in space of the forces attacking him – struck powerfully at Scott-Cockburn's new force on December 28th and reduced it sharply by thirty-seven tanks before returning to base to confront the Guards. Wisely, Marriott held his infantry brigade back and on the penultimate day of the year, Cruewell sallied forth again, knocked out another twenty-three of Scott-Cockburn's tanks and then, with an almost studied insouciance, retired in rain, mist and depressingly cold winds to Rommel's chosen stopping place at El Agheila.

Operation Crusader was over, fizzling out in bad weather and worse temper in the desolate sands from which, nine months before, Rommel had launched the first spectacular advance of the Afrika Korps. He had good reason for anger. His army had been defeated, and he knew it, not by superior military conception, training or even prowess – but by logistic inadequacy on the part of his own government and their allies. He had undoubtedly himself made mistakes (and a more expert adversary might well have taken advantage of them to his own irretrievable undoing) but after his destruction of the New Zealanders, only the inadequacies of his logistic support (he felt) robbed him of victory. He would pay more attention himself to that side of affairs in future, for it was obviously courting disaster to leave such matters in other hands than his own.

As for the British, although Auchinleck and Ritchie had good cause for satisfaction, the troops themselves were aggrieved and disgruntled. The promises made to them by Churchill, by their own press and by many of their senior commanders regarding the superiority of their arms and equipment and the pre-eminence of their leaders had proved empty; and they had developed a dangerous admiration for the leadership of the Afrika Korps and an envy, much of it unfounded, for the enemy's weapons. Though they had been provided with nothing to equal the 88mm., their tanks were not so greatly inferior in power or armour to the panzers, and the British and Commonwealth troops had, in fact, done rather better than many of them realised.

On November 18th, the Allied forces in the operation had numbered 118,000 and the total Axis forces 119,000; and at the end of the month in which the enemy had vacated the field, the British losses had amounted to 17,700 (15 per cent) and the Axis losses to 24,500 (20 per cent), though the British losses in killed and wounded had been the greater. Moreover, when the Axis frontier garrisons surrendered during January, another 13,800 were to be added to the Axis 'missing', and the final casualty figures can be seen in Table 1.

Table 1

	Killed	Wounded	Missing*	Total
British	2,900	7,300	7,500	17,700
German	1,200	3,300	10,100	14,600
Italian	1,100	2,800	19,800	23,700
Axis totals	2,300	6,100	29,900†	38,300

* Generally prisoners of war
† 13,800 taken at Bardia and Halfaya

The British losses in equipment during the land battles were, of course, much greater than the Axis losses, to some extent because they had much more to lose, and also because none of their armoured fighting vehicles could stand up to the 88mm. But if the desert behind them was littered with the debris of smashed British armour, the sea-bed between Sicily and North Africa was dotted with torn ships vomiting panzers and unused Axis artillery through the gaps in their plates; and if the Royal Navy, the Royal Air Force and the diverse elements which made up the Army could ever learn that they were all fighting the same war, they would together constitute a formidable fighting team. As it was, they had all learned from their experience of the last few weeks something of the grim business of war, and no longer regarded it quite so much as an adventurous game for gifted amateurs.

It had been a soldier's battle with even the best generalship – Rommel's – at a second-best level. If Auchinleck's handling of the battle when he had taken charge had temporarily improved the quality of direction, it had still been his choice of Army Commander which had caused the rot which he had had himself to stop; and only the courage and endurance of the fighting men (aided on the German side by the moral courage and competence of Westphal and his staff) had saved commanders on several occasions from the results of their own folly.

This was reflected in many ways, and principally in the fellow feeling shown between the opposing soldiers – in the respect accorded Major Bach and the garrison at Halfaya when, hungry, thirsty, bombed, shelled and short of ammunition they eventually surrendered on January 17th; in the many quite amicable discussions on recent events and tactics between German and British officers at many levels in the various prison-camps which now dotted the North African coasts, and in the general treatment of prisoners and of wounded by both sides.

One event on the British side especially underlined it – the award of the Victoria Cross to Jock Campbell. It was almost unheard-of for so senior an officer to win the Cross, but when the news reached the men who had fought at Sidi Rezegh it was universally applauded through the ranks, from private soldier to general.

No man so epitomised the uncaring, stubborn, slogging resolution of the men who had fought – on both sides – during the closing weeks of 1941.

4 · Embattled Spring

On January 1st, 1942 the United Nations Declaration was signed in Washington, by which twenty-six nations agreed that only by defeat of the Axis Powers – Germany, Italy and Japan – could life, liberty, independence, religious freedom, justice and ordinary human rights be preserved, and in pursuance of this cause the signatory nations pledged themselves to devote their full military and economic resources to defeat of the Axis, and to the agreement that none of them would entertain a separate armistice or make a separate peace with the enemy.

But the drawing up and signing of this declaration was attended by none of the pomp that such an event might be expected to provoke – indeed only four signatories were present at its first inscription, the remainder being canvassed in their own embassies by comparatively junior officials from the State Department who in some cases had carefully to explain the contents of the declaration to the respective ambassadors, and to argue its merits.

It was thus not surprising that the occasion hardly justified the description 'momentous', and indeed of the signing countries, nine – Costa Rica, Cuba, the Dominican Republic, El Salvador, Guatemala, Haiti, Honduras, Nicaragua and Panama – were not deeply or irretrievably concerned in the defeat of the Axis Powers and were never to become so, while eight – Belgium, Czechoslovakia, Greece, Luxembourg, the Netherlands, Norway, Poland and Yugoslavia – although deeply concerned could in the circumstances contribute but little to the Allied cause, for they were all occupied by Axis forces, their attempts at resistance severely limited by the varying degrees of brutality the S.S. and Gestapo were prepared to use in its suppression.

Of the remaining signatories, Russia and China were both defending themselves desperately from deep invasions into their own heartlands, India was watching with considerable anxiety her own eastern border and the behaviour of the millions of supporters of Mahatma Gandhi who were apparently quite willing to accept Japanese domination if it rid them of the British, while Britain herself and the countries of the Commonwealth, having spent the eighteen months since the Fall of France fighting German, Italian and now Japanese

forces with varying degrees of success, were wondering when the tide
of war would turn in their favour, and if it would do so before
exhaustion weakened them beyond recovery.

Although the Royal Air Force had in 1940 beaten back the
attempts of the Luftwaffe to secure command of the air over the
British Isles, thus defeating Hitler's plans for an invasion of Britain
herself, their own bombing campaign over Germany since then
seemed to be scoring little but propaganda successes, while at sea the
U-boat campaign was still gravely threatening the island's very source
of life, let alone her ability to wage war. And America's recent entry
into the conflict, however welcome, seemed for the moment only to
add victims to the U-boat tally, for the sinkings off the eastern
seaboard between Miami and Cape Hatteras were already assuming
alarming proportions.

There were also several other causes of concern for Britain and the
Commonwealth, one of which was the general attitude of the people
of the United States to the war, which bore understandable but
alarming resemblances to that in Britain during the 'Phoney War'
period of late 1939. This had been typified by the then Prime Minister
Chamberlain's announcement to his family – just before that first
war-time Christmas – that he had 'a hunch that the war will be over
next spring . . . [not] by defeat in the field but by German realisation
that they *can't* win and it isn't worth their while to go on . . . '

This was a prophecy which looked peculiarly unfounded on New
Year's Day, 1942, yet it now seemed to be undergoing revivification,
for a large proportion of the American people apparently believed
that the defeat of Germany and Japan would be achieved quite soon
and with but the minimal disturbance of ordinary life. President
Roosevelt's New Year message might promise an abundance of war
materials undreamed of before in Allied circles – a target for
American industry in 1942 of eight million tons of shipping, 45,000
aircraft, 45,000 tanks and half a million machine-guns – but this
production on its own would not win the war and its sudden necessity
was in itself an admission of grave weakness. Even Field Marshal Sir
John Dill, recently sent to Washington to establish close liaison
between British and American staffs (and who by the end of the war
was to become so beloved and admired by Americans that upon his
death a statue to him was erected in Arlington Cemetery), was
shaken by the attitude there, to such effect that he wrote that day to
the Chief of the Imperial General Staff in London, 'Never have I seen
a country so unprepared for war, or so soft.' If his judgment was
perhaps a little hasty, it nevertheless gave justifiable warning of the
time which must elapse before American military strength could
come to the relief of the British and Commonwealth forces already in
the field.

And since the Japanese attack on Pearl Harbor and the associated assaults of that epochal day, these had been stretched to – and indeed well beyond – their limits. Within days of the crippling of the United States Pacific Fleet, the Royal Navy was reeling under the losses of the battleship *Prince of Wales* and the battle-cruiser *Repulse* off the Malayan coast, while the British military command in Malaya watched helplessly as Japanese invasion forces poured ashore into Thailand and then into Malaya itself, pushing aside the single Indian brigade holding the northern airfield at Kota Bahru and beginning their swift and seemingly irresistible advance down the peninsula. By the end of 1941 Singapore was under threat and Japanese forces massing in Thailand were obviously about to debouch into Burma, while Borneo, Sarawak, the Dutch East Indies and the Philippines had all been invaded and, worst of all from the point of view of British prestige, Hong Kong had surrendered to the Japanese on Christmas Day after a defence lasting less than two weeks.

Only on the one front in North Africa was there any sign of success for the forces of the Allied Powers – and in view of the exploits of the Afrika Korps during those wet and depressing days at the very end of 1941, even here there was room only for the most cautious optimism. Obviously, in order to push Panzergruppe Afrika back further, Eighth Army would now need time to regroup, to recoup its losses of recent weeks, to rest its exhausted men and replace their battered arms and equipment, and to increase their striking force with fresh reinforcements.

But where would they come from? For in the face of the Japanese onslaught taking place further east, all uncommitted troops and material must be sent there. So even for the one currently victorious force at the disposal of the newly formed United Nations, the prospects as 1942 opened looked bleak, and in the area itself memories stirred of the previous arrival of the British there, when their successes had been negated and their victories thrown away by the decision to send aid to Greece.

Not that higher authority at any level intended to repeat those mistakes. The lessons of that early débâcle were declared properly learned and this time no vital military strength in men or material was to be stripped away from the crucial area in order to bolster inadequate defences elsewhere, however deserving or even critical. Tripoli was still to be the main objective for Eighth Army; plans for the advance through Tripolitania, code-named *Acrobat*, already existed and there were plans for a complementary invasion, code-named *Gymnast* and intended to put an army ashore in Morocco and Algeria, which would open up the back door and help sweep the Axis forces from North Africa once and for all. This plan received support and was indeed extended within days of America's entry into the war, when Mr Churchill visited Washington in order to co-ordinate American and British war efforts, and so interested the American Chiefs of Staff that they agreed to examine the possibilities of expanding *Gymnast* to *Super-Gymnast* by the inclusion of American divisions.

But although nothing should be done to *decrease* Eighth Army strength, in these new circumstances little or nothing could be done immediately to *increase* it, and the Commanders-in-Chief, Middle East, would appreciate that divisions and equipment en route to them must, alas, now be diverted to the Far East. Anti-tank and anti-aircraft regiments, several fighter and some light bomber squadrons, and the entire 18th Division at that moment rounding the Cape must be diverted to India, while the 17th Indian Division which had been intended for duty in Iraq would now remain at home; and in fact, although the intention was that nothing vital should be taken from Auchinleck's strength, could he please release some of his light tanks? – a request to which he had generously reacted by allowing the despatch to Burma of a reconstituted armoured brigade with Stuart light tanks, a 25-pounder battery and an anti-tank battery.

Such had been the pace of events immediately after Pearl Harbor that most of these decisions had been made before the Afrika Korps had retired behind El Agheila – before, indeed, they had so robustly handled 22nd Armoured Brigade as to cause Auchinleck to wonder if he had been wise in his generosity. It was then far too late for him to reconsider his position or to withdraw his offer, and as a result he found himself in early January 1942 examining the condition of his forces facing Rommel's across the Tripolitanian border with some anxiety.

To a letter from Ritchie, still commanding Eighth Army, reporting that last brush between German and British armour, he replied on January 1st, saying amongst other things:

> I agree that our tanks are outgunned by the German tanks, but surely superiority in numbers should counter-balance this to some extent, and the number of German tanks with the heavier gun in them cannot be so great?
>
> I agree too, about the cruiser being too complicated, and delicate a machine for the rough conditions of the Near and Middle East, and that the American M3s [Stuarts], though mechanically excellent, are not comparable to our cruisers or the German medium tanks as fighting vehicles. Still we have got to make do with what we have got, and the Boche has got to be beaten! . . . If we add to our inferiority in material an apparent inferiority in leadership, then we shall be in a bad way and will not deserve to win . . . I have a most uncomfortable feeling that the Germans outwit and outmanoeuvre us as well as outshooting us . . .
>
> If it is true, then we must find new leaders at once . . . No personal

considerations must be allowed to stand in the way. Commanders who consistently have their brigades shot away from under them, even against a numerically inferior enemy, are expensive luxuries, much too expensive in present circumstances.[1]

This opinion was also held by at least one other commander in the area.

Lieutenant-General A. R. Godwin-Austen who had commanded XIII Corps during *Crusader* (XXX Corps had been added to make up Eighth Army and had contained most of the armour) now commanded the troops in Cyrenaica and already considered the 22nd Armoured Brigade unfit for further action. He therefore replaced it at the frontier by the Support Group from the 7th Armoured Division, with orders to hold the line with the Guards Brigade on their right and use their experience to continue harassing Rommel; but the Support Group had been in almost continuous action since mid-November, its men were tired and its vehicles and artillery badly worn.

Thus, despite the intentions in both Whitehall and the Cairo Headquarters, the formations expected to hold the lately won gains were quickly in some disarray, on this occasion because of the need to reorganise fighting units for the next leap forward, and, just as importantly, to accumulate supplies to support it. Moreover, Auchinleck was deeply concerned about the northern flank of his huge command area (which stretched now from Tripolitania to Afghanistan) and the ever-present threat of a German advance down through the Caucasus and on through Turkey or Persia towards the vital oilfields at the head of the Persian Gulf, so he had ordered that once the 7th Armoured Division had recovered from its *Crusader* losses, it should be given a change of scene in Palestine and Syria. The newly arrived 1st Armoured Division should take its place – but even in this substitution, there were extra complications.

The commander of the 1st Armoured Division, Major-General Herbert Lumsden, had been wounded in an air attack within a few days of the completion of *Crusader*, and his place was taken by Major-General Frank Messervy who now found himself with a division which for nearly a year had suffered frustration and fragmentation, and was in a highly unsatisfactory state as a result.

It had been reorganised after Dunkirk, re-equipped with a positively bizarre assortment of tanks of which the most modern had been almost immediately stripped away to make up numbers in the convoy for *Battleaxe*, after which it had again been re-equipped, this time entirely with Crusaders. The division had then been ordered to the Middle East, but as a result of complaints about the mechanical state of tanks arriving in the Delta, the Crusaders had been withdrawn for the necessary modifications to be carried out in England – so little if any training had been done on them. Shortly after that, the 22nd Armoured Brigade was removed and despatched for immediate attachment to 7th Armoured Division as *Crusader* began, and in mid-September the remaining brigade – the 2nd – and the division's Support Group, had set out on the long haul around the Cape.

The experiences and condition of 22nd Brigade around Antelat at the beginning of 1942 have already been described, and it must be said that those of 2nd Armoured Brigade were unlikely to render it much more effective. It was sent forward into Cyrenaica at first as a brigade group, with an infantry battalion, a Royal Horse Artillery regiment and an anti-tank regiment from its own Support Group incorporated and training en route with it, but as soon as it arrived in the area it lost these units, which rejoined the division's Support Group as this took the place of 7th Support Group at the frontier. Moreover, 2nd Brigade's tanks had made the journey from the Delta by rail only as far as Mersa Matruh, and had driven the remaining 450 miles on their own tracks – which as a result were already in need of replacement; though not quite immediately, as the brigade had used all its petrol allocation on the way up and for some days there was no more with which even to drive to the frontier positions, let alone carry out advanced training there.

By mid-January, therefore, Godwin-Austen's XIII Corps, occupying Cyrenaica and facing Panzergruppe Afrika (about to be re-christened Panzerarmee Afrika), consisted of two brigades of the 4th Indian Division at Benghasi and Barce respectively (the third was still back at Tobruk where it had been joined by the remnants of 22nd Armoured), the 2nd Armoured Brigade hastily training around Antelat, and the Guards Brigade at Mersa Brega with the 1st Support Group to their left in the ground leading down to the Wadi Faregh – the last-named also endeavouring to gain experience, but in ground so broken and hummocky that wheeled vehicles were slower than tracked ones, and suffered so much from burst tyres and broken axles as to be almost useless.

It was extremely fortunate, in Auchinleck's view, that Rommel's forces could still be considered far too weak and disorganised to be able even to consider taking the offensive. This opinion – shared by Ritchie – he communicated to Churchill in a letter dated January 12th:

> I do not think it can be said that the bulk of the enemy divisions have evaded us. It is true that he still speaks in terms of divisions but they are divisions only in name. For instance, we know that the strength of the 90th German Light Division originally 9,000, now 3,500, and has only one field gun left.
>
> . . . These are much disorganised, short of senior officers, short of material and due to our continuous pressure are tired and certainly not as

strong as their total strength of 35,000 might be thought to indicate.

I have reason to believe that six ships recently reached Tripoli averaging 7,200 tons.

I am convinced that we should press forward . . . in view of the heartening news from the Russian front I feel that we should do all we can to maintain the pressure in Libya. We have very full and interesting records of daily conversations between our prisoners Generals von Ravenstein and Schmidt [taken at Bardia]. Making all allowances for mental depression natural in prisoners of war there is no doubt that German morale is beginning to feel the strain not only in Libya but in Germany. They speak freely also of great losses in the recent fighting, mismanagement and disorganisation and above all of dissatisfaction with Rommel's leadership. I am convinced the enemy is hard-pressed more than we dared think perhaps.[2]

It was unfortunate for Auchinleck that his intelligence staff had not been able to listen to conversations between other German officers. Even while Auchinleck was writing his letter, Rommel's chief of intelligence, Major F. W. von Mellenthin, was predicting that at least for the next two weeks, Panzergruppe forces in the area would be more powerful and much better supplied – that is, in much better shape for battle – than the British forces facing them, and that now would be the best time to attack. What is very strange about the situation is that von Mellenthin had little more information at his disposal than had Auchinleck.

Rommel's fortunes had improved remarkably during the four weeks following the diatribe delivered to him by Montezemolo, as a result of several disparate but converging factors. Perhaps the most important was the recovery in energy and morale of the Afrika Korps, which had carried out one of the most difficult of military manoeuvres – retreat in the face of the enemy – without losing cohesion, without losing vast quantities of stores such as the British had abandoned in their retreats, without showing the slightest signs of panic, moving always at their own pace, and with such confidence that at the end they could still turn and deliver those two numbing blows upon the pursuing British armour. They had every justification for regarding themselves as a first-class fighting force still capable of giving an excellent account of themselves.

A second and more immediately apparent factor could be seen on the map – the shortening of Axis supply lines and the consequent easing of their logistic problems. Moreover, not only had the distance from their main supply port – Tripoli – to the front lessened, but the difficulties of the sea passage had eased immensely of late, as had been demonstrated by the arrival of the ships bearing panzers at Benghasi and Tripoli just before Christmas and of the even larger and more important convoy, to which Auchinleck referred, on January 5th.

This had brought Rommel a further fifty-five panzers, twenty armoured cars and a large consignment of fuel and was, as the Chief of Staff to the Afrika Korps, Oberst Fritz Bayerlein, remarked, 'as good as a victory in battle'; but its real significance lay simply in its safe arrival. Montezemolo's predictions, though not entirely inaccurate with regard to timing, had been too pessimistic in tone, for the onset of the Russian winter had released enough German aircraft for Kesselring's Luftflotte 2 to begin operations, and to make an immediate impact.

Moreover, Rommel's forces were for the time being secure from the more serious attentions of the Royal Navy, for whom the closing months of 1941 had proved one of the most disastrous periods in their long history. Of the five capital ships in the Mediterranean at the beginning of November, only one was still afloat at the end of the year, the aircraft-carrier *Ark Royal* and the battleship *Barham* having been torpedoed by U-boats (the latter blowing up with enormous loss of life) and two more battleships, *Valiant* and *Queen Elizabeth*, falling victim to Italian 'human torpedo' crews in Alexandria harbour.

In addition, two cruisers had been sunk by torpedo, two badly damaged in minefields and one withdrawn by the Australian Government for service nearer home. As a result, command of the waters of the mid-Mediterranean and, even more importantly, of the air above had passed into Axis hands. Panzergruppe Afrika was the most immediate beneficiary, and von Mellenthin's prognosis only too accurate.

Rommel struck early on the morning of January 21st – just sixteen days after the last of his rearguards, cautiously pursued by patrols from the Guards Brigade, had retired to El Agheila. He had deliberately omitted to inform both his own High Command and his allies of his intentions, and was thus not very surprised when angry messages arrived from Bastico, or when the Italian Chief of Staff, Generale Cavallero, arrived on January 23rd in a state of high excitement to order that the advance must be nothing more than a sortie to be recalled at the earliest opportunity.

But it had already gone too far for that, and Rommel was glimpsing victory again. To Cavallero's expostulations he replied that only the Führer could order a retirement as it was mainly German troops who were so far engaged, and when his own immediate superior, Generalfeldmarschall Kesselring, voiced opinions which could have been interpreted as backing for Cavallero, Rommel went so far as to hint that Kesselring's expertise as an airman was not totally relevant at

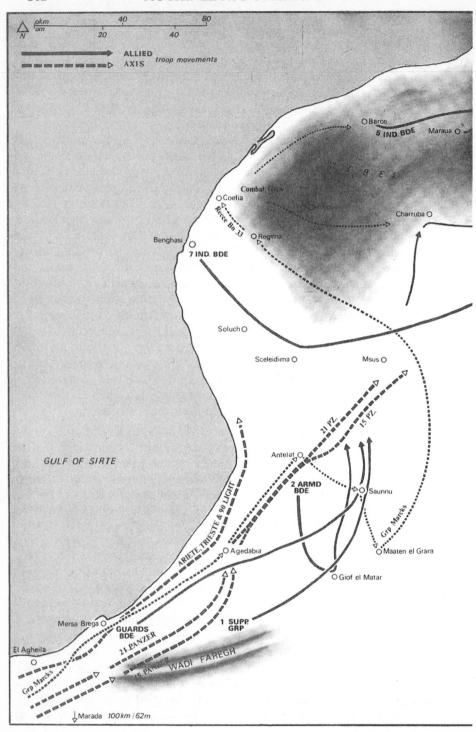

okm 40 80
om
20 40
N

ALLIED
AXIS troop movements

Barce
5 IND. BDE Maraua

Coefia
Combat Grp

Benghasi
7 IND. BDE

Regima

Charruba

Soluch

Sceleidima Msus

21 PZ. 15 PZ.

Antelat

GULF OF SIRTE

2 ARMD
BDE
Saunnu

Grp Marcks

Agedabia

Maaten el Grara

Giof el Matar

Mersa Brega

GUARDS
BDE

1 SUPP.
GRP

El Agheila

21 PANZER

15 PANZER WADI FAREGH

Grp Marcks

Marada 100km / 62m

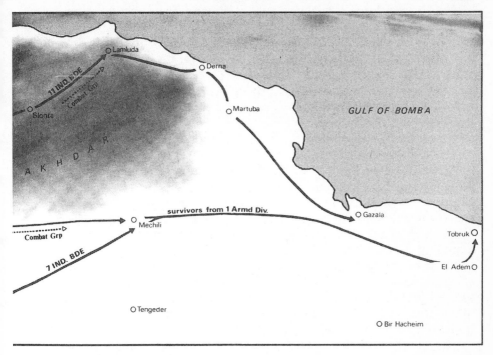

Map 10   Rommel's riposte, January 21st–February 4th

that moment and invited him to look at the map.

Already, it revealed a remarkable picture.

Bad going had held up the advance during the first day, for 15th Panzer on the right flank had become bogged in the dunes at the mouth of the Wadi Faregh, and on the left the combined Ariete and Trieste were content to keep pace; but the bad going which held up the panzers also bedevilled the British 1st Support Group, who by the end of the day had left behind sixteen of their 25-pounders, a number of their lorries and nearly a hundred of their soldiers. And as the main road back to Agedabia and the line of the Wadi Faregh diverged, there was by the evening a gap between the Guards Brigade and the Support Group.

Into this gap, Rommel quite reasonably assumed, the British would send what they could of the 2nd Armoured Brigade in the belief that he would lunge for it at dawn the next day – so with a dislocating shift of weight to his left he instead sent two lorried infantry battalions from 21st Panzer and 90th Light, augmented by German and Italian artillery and under command of a first-class tactician, Oberst Werner Marcks, straight up through the Italian divisions on the main road to push aside the right flank of the Guards Brigade and reach Agedabia by 1100 on second day (January 22nd,

1942), then to forge straight on to Antelat and swing east to Saunnu.

General Messervy had acted almost as Rommel had foreseen (although not exactly, for he had directed 2nd Armoured Brigade down to Giof el Matar, behind the 1st Support Group, and not into the gap), so, by the evening of January 22nd, Marcks Group and the Italians held the line of the road from Agedabia up to Antelat and across to Saunnu, with all Messervy's command contained in the hook and cut off from its main supplies at Msus. Meanwhile, to the south of the British, the Afrika Korps armour had crossed their front to reach Agedabia and follow the main advance.

Rommel's idea for January 23rd was for a further extension of the hook by Marcks Group down to Maaten el Grara, the strengthening of the main shaft as the panzer regiments came up towards Antelat, from which position they should be able to block the British armour's attempt to reach their stores, and perhaps even drive them southwards into the desert. From the anxious inquiries his intercept services were overhearing from British tank commanders desperately short of petrol, it seemed likely they would never reach Tengeder, let alone Mechili – and in any case, the Luftwaffe dominated the air above the battlefield this time as the R.A.F. was too busy evacuating its forward airfields, and was itself short of fuel.

This, then, was the picture with which Rommel faced Cavallero and Kesselring, and it is easy to see why, at the end of the argument, the former went off growling doubtfully, the latter silent and thoughtful. And except for two slight misjudgments, it might all have come off.

The first misjudgment was the move forward by the Marcks Group from Saunnu to Maaten el Grara which took place too early, with the result that when one of the tank regiments of 2nd Armoured Brigade, ordered back to guard the approaches to Msus, arrived at Saunnu they found the place empty, and the second was that a direction to 21st Panzer to get across to Saunnu to take Marcks's place was delayed so the gap in the net remained open. Through it, after a day of confused actions fought out in the barren country south of the Antelat–Saunnu track, most of 2nd Armoured Brigade, the whole of the Guards Brigade and the survivors of 1st Support Group made their uncertain way, congregating at dawn on January 24th about ten miles north of Antelat in positions from which, in theory, they should be able successfully to block Rommel's route to the stores dump at Msus.

They were even given extra time in which to prepare for this, for Rommel had not realised the facts of their escape and Afrika Korps spent most of that day (24th) sweeping south-east and finding nothing but abandoned tanks and lorries (many of which their recovery units were to put back into service); but early on the 25th, the combined panzer divisions moved north on to Messervy's division and literally drove it from the field. According to von Mellenthin who watched the first onslaught and amassed the details of the battle at the end of the day:

On the right flank, 21st Panzer Division met little opposition, but six miles north-west of Saunnu 15th Panzer ran into very superior tank forces. These were overwhelmed by Panzer Regiment 8, closely supported by anti-tank guns and artillery; it soon became apparent that the British tank units had no battle experience and they were completely demoralised by the onslaught of 15th Panzer. At times the pursuit attained a speed of fifteen miles an hour, and the British columns fled madly over the desert in one of the most extraordinary routs in the war. After covering fifty miles in under four hours 15th Panzer reached Msus airfield at 1100, overwhelming numerous supply columns, and capturing twelve aircraft ready to take off. Further exploitation was impossible as the division was out of fuel, but 96 tanks, 38 guns, and 190 lorries were the booty of the day.[3]

As 2nd Armoured Brigade had already lost nearly seventy of its tanks between January 21st and 23rd, it had thus been effectively eliminated as a fighting force within ninety-six hours of its first contact with the Afrika Korps, which now occupied the road junction at Msus and was happily filling its lockers with English food, drink and cigarettes. Rommel, however, was not so happy as he had hoped to be, for there was very little fuel found there, and he could certainly not achieve his greatest immediate ambition of driving straight to Mechili and then to Derna, thus cutting off the entire British force in Cyrenaica.

In his appreciation of this one fact, General Ritchie was right for the first time since Rommel's advance had begun. He had been in Cairo on January 21st, but arrived in the area the following afternoon (by which time Marcks was driving up to Antelat) announcing among other things that Rommel's latest exploit provided a 'God-sent opportunity to hit him really hard when he puts out his neck, as it seems possible that he may be already doing.'

This was, as the *Official History* points out, a robust reading of the situation, but not an accurate one, for if anyone's neck was stuck out, it was the Eighth Army's.

Not all British opinion in the area was so mistaken, however, for Godwin-Austen's opinion of the fighting ability of the 2nd Armoured Brigade had been conditioned by that demonstrated by the 22nd, and within thirty-six hours he was pointing out that the defences of Benghasi consisted of but one infantry brigade, to which the British armour could hardly come to the rescue if it was also expected to defend Msus as well as 'cover the eastern flank' – which were Ritchie's latest orders. In the circumstances, he requested permission to order a general withdrawal from Benghasi and eastern Cyrenaica as far as Mechili at least, with administrative units going back to Gazala – a request at which Ritchie baulked on the grounds that Rommel must by now be near the end of his resources and that very soon would come the opportunity to turn and strike him. In this Ritchie was supported by both Auchinleck and Air Marshal Tedder, both of whom had come forward to Ritchie's headquarters.

But by the evening of the 25th, what little remained of 1st Armoured Division was back at Charruba, and so far as Godwin-Austen could see there was nothing to prevent Afrika Korps driving on to Benghasi and capturing at least one Indian brigade, plus the ships, port installations and accumulated supplies there. He saw no reason to believe that the resistance so far offered to Rommel's advance would have done much to blunt its edge, and in the circumstances he thought it right to use his own discretionary powers to order total evacuation – of the Indians to Derna, of the shipping to Alexandria, and of the remnants of 1st Armoured Division to Mechili. He was thus somewhat incensed to learn that Ritchie, divining correctly that Rommel was short of petrol but also leaping over-eagerly to the conclusion that the Afrika Korps must now be at the limits of its strength, cancelled the move, instructing 7th Indian Brigade instead to send raiding columns down to attack Rommel's communications south of Antelat, and 1st Armoured Division to stand and defend Charruba and the approaches to El Abiar. Ritchie also took 4th Indian Division under his own direct command, which, in view of the fact that Godwin-Austen had held the rank of acting Lieutenant-General rather longer than he had himself, was tactless, even though the Commander-in-Chief was present at the time and made no attempt to countermand the move.

There now followed almost two days of military hiatus, while the divisional commanders endeavoured to deploy their forces in accordance with Ritchie's instructions, and then, in the face of military reality, to try to persuade him that they were impractical – and all the time, Rommel was reading the intercept reports of the squabbling between his opponents while he scavenged the field for booty, gradually accumulated supplies and decided what he would do next.

As severe sandstorms blanketed the area during January 26th, nobody there was much concerned by the general immobility, least of all the troops themselves among whom were the 1st Armoured newcomers, 'getting their knees brown', as the saying went, and learning the bitter truth about the desert in which they were to fight their war.

The sandstorms that day had not been dense enough however to prevent two reconnaissance aircraft of the 250th South African Squadron from spotting a move by some panzers south-eastwards

from Msus and reporting them to Ritchie, who delightedly interpreted it as a splitting of Rommel's forces – one half moving on
Mechili and the other on Benghasi. He promptly ordered 1st
Armoured Division to move south and fall on the rear of the reported
panzers, and 7th Indian Brigade down to block frontally whatever
forces Rommel was sending up towards Benghasi, encouraging them
with the statement that 'The enemy has divided his forces, and is
weaker than we are in both areas. The keyword is offensive action
everywhere.'

But the movement of the panzers had been a feint (and only
Rommel's luck had put the South African aircraft over it at the
crucial moment) and, hearing that the main British moves were
planned for the 29th, he ordered the Marcks Group out on the 28th to
sweep up around to the north of Benghasi while the Italian divisions
and the 90th Light came up from the south. The panzer regiments,
after decoying the British armour out into the desert, would remain
in the Msus–Charruba area as flank guard to the attack.

In pouring rain he led the Marcks Group himself across the broken
country towards Regima, and by dark his Reconnaissance Battalion
33 were blocking the raised causeway at Coefia along which 7th
Indian Brigade were endeavouring to escape to join their brother
brigade at Barce. There was a frantic confusion of reversing and
overturning lorries, a retreat by the Indians back into Benghasi and a
well-judged decision by the brigade commander that their best way
out of a fast-closing trap would be across the front of the Italians
approaching from the south, through Sceleidima and flat out for the
Trig el Abd and Mechili. Aided by appalling weather and a great deal
of luck, the three columns got through with but few encounters with
enemy forces – or at any rate enemy forces willing to prove obstruc-
tive – but they had perforce to jettison a great deal of equipment and
to travel light. They all reached Mechili where they found the
remains of 1st Armoured Division and then went back further, first to
El Adem and then into Tobruk, while to the north of them 5th Indian
Brigade and 11th (which had been rushed up from Tobruk to Maraua
when danger first threatened) made their joint way back along the
northern roads through Slonta, Lamluda, Derna and Martuba. They
were all back into or behind the Gazala defences by February 4th,
though during the last sprint home a number of 11th Brigade guns
and vehicles blew up on the mines left on one of the *Crusader* battlefields where XIII Corps's attempt to cut off the Afrika Korps retreat
had been roughly handled only seven weeks before.

For many reasons, Afrika Korps did not follow up the British
retreat much more closely than they had themselves been followed on
their way back to El Agheila. First there was the chronic shortage of
petrol, then there was the riveting attraction of the enormous bulk of

supplies captured when they entered Benghasi, enough to distract the attention of the most ascetic warrior. The last action of one of the British quartermasters had been to put a match to seven million cigarettes and to organise the evacuation of twelve lorry-loads of rum – but the fire went out and some of the lorries broke down long before they were clear of the hills.

And there were always the constraints of higher command. Mussolini's permission to advance and occupy Benghasi with a small mobile force 'if the British saw fit to withdraw voluntarily' arrived shortly after Rommel's headquarters had actually taken up residence there, but both Il Duce and Bastico insisted that the forward positions for Panzerarmee Afrika could be no further east than Maraua, in front of which only small mobile forces were to operate; and although Rommel briefly considered incorporating Ariete, Trieste, 90th Light and 15th and 21st Panzer Divisions into what he was quite prepared to announce was just such 'a small mobile force' in order to drive the British even further back, he reluctantly concluded that there was not enough petrol to make the project feasible.

None the less, his reconnaissance units, some anti-tank batteries and enough infantry to form them into two combat groups had followed on the heels of the British retreat and were watching the formation of the Gazala positions as the last fugitives slipped into them, and soon afterwards the bulk of Afrika Korps and 90th Light were close behind in the Jebel. Italian divisions stayed in Benghasi and around Antelat while a blocking force came out again from Tripoli to hold the border positions from Mersa Brega down to Marada.

Weary, weatherworn, thirsty but triumphant, Panzerarmee Afrika under their remarkable leader were well back into Marmarica, with Tobruk – for so long their apparently unobtainable objective – again only thirty-five miles beyond their grasp.

On February 2nd, when it was evident that the situation had stabilised, Lieutenant-General A. R. Godwin-Austen formally requested that he be relieved of his command in view of the lack of confidence shown in him by the Eighth Army commander, demonstrated by the abrupt reversal of his decision to evacuate Cyrenaica on the evening of January 25th, and by Ritchie's assumption of direct command of one of his divisions at the same time. General Auchinleck saw fit to accede to this request and, according to the *Official History*, 'this, in the circumstances, was understandable.'

But as the *History* then goes on to admit that Godwin-Austen's reading of the situation during the retreat had been on the whole

more realistic than Ritchie's, the question arises as to *how* Auchinleck's agreement had been 'understandable'. Godwin-Austen had
been senior to Ritchie at the time of the changeover of commander
during *Crusader* – and although the substance of that changeover had
been acceptable in the circumstances which prevailed at the time,
every account written since stresses the fact that Ritchie's appointment was to be subject to review when the operation ended, and
some justification demonstrated for the continuation of Ritchie's
command if it were not to be transferred to another, more senior
corps commander.

And what justification was there? Ritchie's performance as Eighth
Army commander during the second half of *Crusader* had certainly
not been as much at fault as Cunningham's, but on the other hand it
had not been so outstanding as to obscure Godwin-Austen's right to
consideration for the higher post, especially as it had been New
Zealanders from Godwin-Austen's corps who had made the junction
with the Tobruk garrison during *Crusader*, Indians from his corps
who had masked the frontier garrisons, and it had certainly not been
Godwin-Austen's fault that the British armour had been so severely
handled.

Presumably the immediate justification at the end of *Crusader* was
that the Eighth Army under Ritchie's command had won a demon-
strable victory, and certainly between the arrival at Mersa Brega and
Rommel's riposte there had been little enough time for a cool and
just review of the situation; but the lull when the Gazala Line was
reached should have provided one – and in view of the validity of
Godwin-Austen's prognosis compared with the lack of realism in some
of Ritchie's pronouncements, one would have thought the outcome
foregone. But perhaps Auchinleck was prompted by one of those
qualities which made him so admirable a person – loyalty to his
friends and to his personal staff – in which case, he should have
omitted that phrase in his letter to Ritchie of January 1st, regarding
'personal considerations'. Perhaps, also, he felt some responsibility
for Ritchie's decisions taken during those crucial days when he
himself had been present.

Needless to say, the disappointment felt throughout Eighth Army at
the sudden reverse was echoed in the British Isles, and cables from 10
Downing Street alternated astonishment with reproof, sympathy with
regret. In his replies, Auchinleck made some crucial aspects of the
war in the Middle East abundantly clear to Mr Churchill – the
2-pounder gun and the cruiser tanks were both of inferior quality to
those in the enemy's service, he claimed, and went on to observe
sombrely that these defects were causing Royal Armoured Corps
personnel to lose confidence in their equipment.

He did not, however, add that they were also losing confidence in their leadership – perhaps because he was not aware of it; but the fact remains that the troops were beginning to look askance at their officers at many levels and were assessing their abilities with growing scepticism. Cunningham had promised Eighth Army a speedy and complete victory at the beginning of *Crusader*; if Ritchie had not promised them anything it could have been because he had been too busy to visit any formation lower than Corps Headquarters, but as a result the troops felt that not only did they not know him, but he did not know them either. Unfortunately, this set of conditions applied equally to the Commander-in-Chief, who had also not found time to make himself known to a very high proportion of the men under his command. It is difficult for men to believe that the authority under which they serve cares much for them if it remains shrouded in Olympian mystery, especially if its promises prove empty and its directives impracticable.

Their admiration was therefore being increasingly given to the enemy commander, Rommel, who not only won victories but did so by leading from the front where his men could see him – a fact which quickly became well known throughout North Africa. The fact that he led an army with better guns was obvious, that it had better tanks was believed – and it was becoming generally accepted that it was also better trained and operated on a more realistic doctrine. In this the men of Eighth Army were undoubtedly correct, for German appreciation of the interdependence of all arms was fundamental; but the Afrika Korps had another advantage which was not yet evident to all.

The Eighth Army was being enlarged by the arrival from Britain of new formations – the intention was to send out whole divisions but as had happened in *Crusader* sometimes just brigades came out, and these went into action as such, and on occasion found themselves alone. As a result, although the officers and men may have known each other well through training together, when they went into action they were all equally inexperienced, at least in local conditions, and in 1942 often in any form of battle at all.

But Rommel's reinforcements at this time arrived invariably as individual soldiers for his existing formations and were fed into them piecemeal – and when they went into action they were accompanied and most often led by men who had just come out of it. When the inexperienced men of the 1st Support Group retired in front of the first probes of 15th and 21st Panzer Division on January 21st, they were pursued by formations each with a core of battle-hardened veterans who could not only shrug off the discomforts of desert fighting with accustomed ease, but recognise danger immediately it appeared, ignore empty sound and irrelevant fury in concentration on the purpose in hand – and thus teach the newcomers to do the same.

Panzerarmee Afrika Headquarters sent reports on the battles to Berlin, and these contained cool and realistic appraisals of their enemy's performance. As far as *Crusader* was concerned, they had praised the general preparation and the manner in which the approach to battle had been concealed, but they were highly critical of the fragmentation of force and the inability ever to concentrate it all at one decisive point. They also praised the steadiness and reliability of the troops, especially the N.C.O.s. But one paragraph directed a criticism which – if the British public could have brought itself to accept it – would have come as a devastating shock:

> British troops fought well on the whole, though they never attained the same impetus as the Germans when attacking. Officers were courageous and self-sacrificing, *but rather timid if they had to act on their own initiative.*[4] (author's italics)

Too many of those who had spent months in the ranks could still hear ringing in their ears, from their days as raw recruits, the British drill sergeant's basic precept: 'In the army, you're not paid to think, you're paid to DO AS YOU'RE BLOODY WELL TOLD!' – and at first when there was no one to tell them, many of them were lost.

But not all; some of those whose individuality was strong enough to withstand the onslaught of clumsy training (it had improved throughout 1941) began to look for spheres in which their energies and enthusiasms might be more profitably used.

There had grown up in the desert a number of what had become known as 'Private Armies', and in the early days a few of them – notably the Jock Columns formed first to harass the Italians – had been spectacularly effective. However, during the latter days of Wavell's command and the beginning of Auchinleck's too many of them had been conceived and often commanded by men with imagination, but not enough realism and very little professionalism, and many of the quite bizarre adventures upon which these had set out had ended in ludicrous failure. As a result a large number of brave but rather amateur soldiers were now passing their days in German prison-camps wondering what had gone wrong, but their very failure had brought home to those groups which had not suffered disaster the necessity for hard training, and considerable success was now attending some of their efforts. And after the grim disappointments of the early months of 1942, the ranks of these Private Armies were swelled by men who, although they were prepared to risk and even give their lives for their country, were not prepared to have them thrown away by incompetence at the top.

The Long Range Desert Group was by far the most professional of these Private Armies, operating a 'taxi-run' between Cairo and the Jebel Akhdar or points even further west, keeping a regular watch on the roadways along the Gulf of Sirte or in the Jebel itself, and, during the closing stages of *Crusader*, shooting up German and Italian convoys at night and wrecking Axis communications.

Lately, they had been operating from Jalo, but with the Eighth Army withdrawal to Gazala they too came back to set up a forward headquarters at Siwa. This was a much more congenial spot, where Cleopatra was reputed to have bathed in 'Cleopatra's Pool'; now a mixed bag of British, Rhodesians, New Zealanders and Free French disported themselves after their journeys across the desert in the same pool, in the 'Island Pool', the 'Sheikh's Pool', the 'Figure of Eight' and the 'Bubbly Pool' where warm, clear, sparkling artesian water bubbled up from a twenty-foot-deep spring to their infinite refreshment.

Siwa is the nearest approach to the story-book oasis between the Red Sea and Tunisia, and in the early months of 1942 it became a veritable traffic centre through which all who had business behind Axis lines must pass, for all of them had to use the L.R.D.G. service. Every day the patrols went out – taking Arabs to spy on the garrisons at Jalo or Agedabia, taking agents of various nationalities to live with their wireless sets and circle of contacts in the wadis of the Jebel, sending off their survey section under Captain Lazarus to plot yet another piece of unmapped desert; and occasionally aircraft would come in to bear away to hospital the men shot up on the patrols and fortunate enough to get back, aircrew picked up after a crash during one of the Benghasi 'milk run' raids, or escaped prisoners suffering from exhaustion and dehydration after a heroic struggle first against the prison-camp organisations, then against the often crueller forces of nature.

The agents who went up into the Jebel were an extraordinary breed of men – men, as one authority describes them, 'with that cold, two-o'clock-in-the-morning courage' – though rarely of professional agent status and most often of early middle age and retiring nature. One was a marine engineer who had made a great success of his hobby, Egyptology, in the pre-war years, and was now using his knowledge of the dialects of the region to collect particulars of garrison strengths from Benghasi to Derna; another had been a schoolmaster in Cairo where his wife and three children still lived while he organised a circle of Arab agents whose friends and relations worked for the Germans and the Italians and reported the gossip in the messes and canteens to him for onward transmission to Cairo.

One of the most remarkable was the Russo-Belgian Vladimir Peniakoff, who had fought through the First World War as a private

1 The Cunninghams – Andrew and Alan

2 Major-General Freyberg and General Auchinleck

3 Brigadier Jock Campbell and Major-General Strafer Gott

4 Infantry waiting along the Sidi Rezegh ridge

5–6 The Corps Commanders: Lieutenant-General Godwin-Austen and
Lieutenant-General Willoughby Norrie

7 Brigadier Armstrong, whose 5th South African Brigade were destroyed on *Totensonntag*, talking to Field Marshal Smuts

8 Brigadier Pienaar, whose 1st South African Brigade could do nothing but stand by and watch

9 The Tobruk Corridor formed – 'for whatever it was worth'. The link-up at El Duda.

10–11 The heroic figures of *Crusader*. *Above*, Major the Reverend Wilhelm Bach upon his surrender. *Below*, Major-General Jock Campbell talks to Auchinleck after receiving the Victoria Cross.

12-13 The commanders:
right, General der
Panzertruppe Erwin
Rommel issues orders,
with von Mellenthin on
the right and Luftwaffe-
General Hoffmann von
Waldau in the centre;
below, General Sir
Claude Auchinleck and
Lieutenant-General Neil
Ritchie

14-15 Birth of a legend: *above*, Captain David Stirling
(left) plans a raid with Lieutenant 'Jock' Lewes;
right, Lieutenant 'Paddy' Mayne waits
to carry it out

16 Generalleutnant Walter K. Nehring and his staff

17 One of the Grant tanks which seriously worried Rommel at the start of the Battle of Gazala

18 Ritchie confers with his corps commanders, Willoughby Norrie (left) and 'Strafer' Gott

19 Major-General Bernard Freyberg, V.C., who brought his New Zealanders safely back to El Alamein

20 Auchinleck takes over; behind him his newly appointed Chief of Staff, Major-General 'Chink' Dorman-Smith

in the French Army, between the wars had worked as an engineer in an Egyptian sugar-factory and in 1940 obtained for himself a commission in the British Army. Middle-aged officers on the General List are normally employed at headquarters, but Peniakoff had spent most of his time since enrolling with a battalion of Libyan Arabs raised for patrol and garrison duties, though during the recent retreat he had seen some action with the 4th Indian Division.

By the end of March 1942, he had managed to disengage himself from this service, recruit a small body of Arabs with a deep-seated dislike of the Italians who had driven them from their homeland, and a young British subaltern whom he had known as a schoolboy in Egypt. He then had himself and his diminutive command transported by the L.R.D.G. to the eastern part of the Jebel, in order to 'spread alarm and despondency' – a phrase just coming into fashion.

The first few weeks had perforce been spent assuring the sheikhs of the Obeidat in whose tribal district he wished to operate that the recent reverse suffered by the British was purely temporary, and arranging for them to receive supplies of food, arms and equipment in order that they would be able to play some part in the return of the Eighth Army which, he hoped to convince them, was inevitable.

But once he had gained their confidence and established a rightful presence in the area, his party could commence more destructive operations. These were not spectacular at first – sugar poured into the petrol tanks of unguarded lorries, sand down the oil-intake; an Italian despatch-rider caught at night by a rope across the track, a German sentry knifed. But one evening an Arab came into the camp with a story of a cache of petrol-drums which calculation later revealed to hold 100,000 gallons.

The detailed story of its destruction has been told many times – in fact and in fiction – but the account of the party's retreat from the scene, and of that curious mixture of triumph and reaction, of the dull, stupefied exhaustion of mind and body which typifies such withdrawals, is best told in Peniakoff's own words.

They had spent the day in a nearby cistern, been fed by the brother of the man who was to be their guide in the evening, left their refuge soon after dark and by nine o'clock were at the dump. At one end, three Italian lorries were being loaded with petrol, and the glare from their headlights was a help to the party as they began laying their charges at the other. By eleven o'clock, all charges had been laid, enough prepared evidence left lying around to give the impression that the operation had been carried out by British Commandos (thus providing helpful alibis for the local Arabs, who would undoubtedly be taken in for questioning the following day) and the party had arrived back at the cistern to collect their kit for the long march to safety.

An hour after they had started out, a dull boom behind revealed the premature explosion of one of the charges and as there was no immediate repeat, Peniakoff became convinced that the operation had failed – especially when the scheduled time for the charges to go off came and went. An hour of sweating despair followed as the party toiled on over the scrubby hills, wondering what could have gone wrong, *how* it could have gone wrong, and what could be said to the Arabs who had helped them at so much danger to themselves?

At five minutes to two the skyline behind us exploded. A broad curtain of yellow flame lifted to the sky and stayed there, lighting the bare land-scape around us. Rumbling thunderous explosions followed one another, throwing up more flames. Drums of petrol, projected upwards, burst in mid-air, blazing globes of fire that floated slowly down. A moment later a rolling wall of heavy, billowing smoke, lit to a fierce red by the fires burn-ing on the ground, had taken possession of half the horizon and reached to the sky. It seemed incredible that the petty manipulations we had done so quietly in the dark could result in such a glorious catastrophe. It was more than we expected; our reward was ten times what had been promised. Such a munificence made us wonder; we felt slightly awed and very powerful.

For a whole hour the blaze increased in intensity. Our men kept falling out to gaze back at the wonder and then caught up again at a trot. The glare of the burning dump lit our way and made the going easier. Then, as we increased our distance and intervening hills threw longer shadows, I found myself once more stumbling in the dark and hard put to it to keep up with our indefatigable guide. On we walked. Overcome with ex-haustion, I renounced my self-respect and asked Mohammed el Obeidi how far we were now from Kaf el Kefra. 'Not far,' he replied laconically and we plodded on.

The first light of dawn came. The fire behind us shone with un-diminished fierceness. We plodded on. The sun rose: we were in a barren wilderness of sandy hills and scrub. My head swam with fatigue; to keep awake I tried working out a sum: *The Germans have 200 tanks – they do five miles to the gallon – in battle they run fifty miles a day. How many days' supply are 100,000 gallons of petrol?* I kept losing the thread of my argument and starting again from the beginning – then I got a surprising answer – *sixty-two days*. This was too good; it couldn't be correct.

Patiently I began again. This time the answer came: *a third of a day, eight hours*. As a period as short as that was rather disappointing, back I went to my premises. Mohammed el Obeidi came up to me and said: 'Kaf el Kefra is now near.' We were all well tired out by now, but we went on under the warmer sun. I worked once more on my problem and got as an answer *twelve days*. It seemed satisfactory and I lost interest. We walked . . . Our guide said 'Beyond that hill is Kaf el Kefra.' I laughed out aloud because of a joke of ours: 'When you start on a trip the guide says the objective is *far* – after four hours' walk he says it is *not far* – four hours later he says it is near – four hours' walk again and he says it is *beyond that hill* – then you walk another four hours before getting there.' With dragging feet and an aching body I tramped along for another eternity, then I looked up again: the sun was hardly higher in the sky, which was surprising. Someone said in Arabic: 'There comes Musa riding a camel.' And indeed I saw a rider approaching across the yellow plain – one of our own men, mounted on one of our camels. We had arrived. Musa slid off his camel and shook my hand with fervour – he patted me on the shoulder and pointed to the eastern horizon, where a solid black cloud of smoke stretched from north to south.[5]

If the logistic facts upon which Peniakoff's mind had been working had been correct, his answer to his sum would have been fifty days – but panzers in desert conditions rarely averaged two miles to the gallon, and in battle conditions could easily use up twenty gallons in a morning. With all the back-up and supply vehicles necessary to keep it in action, the Afrika Korps needed a minimum of 150,000 gallons a day – so Peniakoff's second answer was the nearest to the truth. But a battle could easily be lost for want of eight hours' petrol.

It was the partnership between the Long Range Desert Group and the fast-growing Special Air Service which was showing most promise and attaining some unexpectedly good results.

After an initial catastrophe at the onset of *Crusader*, the founder of the organisation Captain David Stirling and his chief aide Lieutenant 'Paddy' Mayne, ably assisted by two other young officers who had realised the necessity of military professionalism, Lieutenants Lewes and Fraser, worked out a system of hard and realistic training which quickly weeded out those volunteers whose motivation in joining had been either search for glamour or escape from discipline, and moulded those who remained into tightly knit units of self-reliant and expert raiders of extremely high morale. Early successes increased that morale, the occasional and inevitable failure did little to dampen it.

As the first parachute drop to be attempted had proved pro-hibitively expensive in men – and as the R.A.F. were in any case loth to use their machines for such purposes when they thought they could be better used bombing Benghasi – Stirling approached the L.R.D.G. with a proposition: first, the L.R.D.G. should take them to their objectives and collect them after they had carried out their missions; secondly, the L.R.D.G. should train S.A.S. men in the techniques of desert driving and navigation so that in due course their 'taxi-service' would not be required. The response was enthusiastic and a most profitable partnership began.

Four parties had set off from Jalo while *Crusader* was still at its height, and on the night of December 14th they attacked airfields at Tamit, Sirte, El Agheila and Agedabia, and of the four, only one proved unfruitful. Mayne's party at Tamit destroyed a petrol dump and twenty-four planes in fifteen minutes of concentrated action, then broke into a building in which it was evident that some sort of party was being held and sprayed the unfortunate celebrators with Tommy-gun fire. This raid was distinguished by Paddy Mayne's extraordinary feat of destroying one of the planes with his bare hands – tearing out the instrument panel and all the equipment behind it, as, he afterwards claimed, a souvenir. He had, before the war, played Rugby football for Ireland, and his physical strength had always been remarkable.

At Sirte, David Stirling's party was disappointed to watch the planes which had been their objective take off while they were hiding close by, and at El Agheila Lewes's party also found the airfield empty – but they then broke into a transport park and left their 'sticky bombs' on a large collection of transport, and on their way out shot up a roadhouse where Italian drivers were eating.

Fraser's party at Agedabia met with the greatest success, breaking through a well-lit perimeter fence, eluding all the guards and destroying altogether thirty-seven aircraft, then getting clear away in the confusion which flared as soon as their bombs began exploding. It was a notable 'bag' for only four men – and indeed the total strength of the S.A.S. party to leave Jalo had been only thirteen (four officers and nine N.C.O.s and privates) and between them they destroyed sixty-one aircraft and an unknown but considerable number of vehicles, in addition to killing and wounding a number of enemy soldiers.

Another raid was organised almost as soon as the party had returned to base, but this time Fortune did not favour them so highly, for Lewes was killed and Fraser and his party missed the pick-up rendezvous and eventually added to the growing legend of desert marches by walking home – two hundred miles in eight days on half a pint of water each per day.

Reports of some of the early operations, as dictated shortly after they had taken place by the laconic Lieutenant Mayne, make fascinating reading.

5th Operation
Objective: Tamit aerodrome
Method: LRDG S Patrol
Date: 24 December 1941

Operation: Party consisting of Lieutenant Mayne, Sgt McDonald, Ptes Bennet, White, Chesworth and Hawkins. Left Jalo with Sirte party and broke off at Wadi Timet. Motored to within 3 miles of drome and then walked in. Destroyed 27 aircraft but were fired on by MGs etc. and had to run for it. Sergeant McDonald and Private White were cut off but were picked up later. Contacted patrol and returned to Jalo. Both parties celebrated Xmas on the way back. Plenty of beer, Xmas pudding, gazelle etc.

10th Operation
Objective: Derna Aerodrome
Method: LRDG
8 March 1942

Operation: Party consisting of Captain Mayne, Bennet, Rose, and Burns. Walked in to drome 30 miles and arrived at 0400 hours. Walked round drome and split up. Captain Mayne and Pte Bennet destroyed 15 planes. Cpl Rose and Burns destroyed 15 torpedo bombs, petrol and equipment. On subsequent walk back Burns fell out. We met but failed to find rendezvous but were picked up next day. Searched for Burns but without success. Whole party returned to Siwa and subsequently to Kabrit.[6]

One of the perpetual hazards of such operations was the prospect of being left behind, lost, exhausted or wounded, and another was of being shot up by your own aircraft; but as one of the survivors was to remark many years later, it was a better bet than taking part in a bayonet charge.

By this time, the S.A.S. had won recognition and support from the High Command, and had been given permission to increase their strength by another six officers and forty men – though as most regular units were understandably reluctant to release men good enough to meet Stirling's requirements, this increase was only met by the incorporation of fifty Free French parachutists who had come down from Syria. The S.A.S. had also adopted its own cap-badge and motto, 'Who Dares, Wins', and designed and had produced its own parachute emblem based upon a symbolic Ibis with outstretched wings, which the men could wear on their right shoulders when they had qualified as parachutists, and above their left tunic-pocket if and when Stirling considered that they had done well enough on operations. This latter was to become a highly-prized distinction.

On January 17th, 1942, a joint L.R.D.G. and S.A.S. operation was mounted against a different type of objective – the port installations at Buerat – for which purpose a canvas canoe was included, with crew from what was already known as the Special Boat Section; but the expedition was shot up on the way in and lost their wireless truck, the canoe did not stand up to the rigours of desert travel and the shipping in the harbour thus remained unscathed. However the local radio station was blown up (by the S.B.S. crew), bombs were left on several of the port installations and eighteen petrol carriers were destroyed; and a sandstorm protected them all from aerial attack during their journey home.

There then followed a series of unsuccessful attempts to reach Benghasi and attack shipping in the harbour there, but although S.A.S. parties wandered around the port during several nights, bad luck attended these operations and they achieved little. In one of them Randolph Churchill took part, but even his presence was not enough to excite violence, though the party was very nearly discovered by an Italian sailor – too drunk, however, to realise the importance of the occasion. On the way back, fortunately after they had reached their own lines, their car, which was being driven with great élan but rather less skill by David Stirling, overturned – and Churchill's back was so badly injured that he had to be invalided home. It is interesting to reflect upon the opposing emotions which would have been raised throughout Europe and the Mediterranean basin, had it become known at the time how closely the son of the British Prime Minister had escaped capture – and indeed, death.

During May, it became obvious that Malta was in danger of starvation and possible collapse as a result of the blockade which the Luftwaffe and the Italian Navy had been able to mount of late, and that somehow a supply convoy must succeed in getting through. In order to assist such a convoy, it was decided to attempt to weaken the air attack which might be mounted against it by a series of co-ordinated raids against airfields in both Cyrenaica and Crete.

For these raids the entire strength of the S.A.S. was mobilised, including the Free French who had by now completed their specialist training. Eight five-men patrols were briefed, three for Benghasi, three for Derna, one for Barce and one for Heraklion on the north coast of Crete. The raids in Cyrenaica met with varying success; Stirling's personal attack wreaked extraordinary damage but the one made by fifteen Free French ran into total disaster, for in order to help them through an area believed to be swarming with German troops, they had taken with them members of the group known as S.I.G. – Special Interrogation Group – composed of Germans with strong anti-Nazi opinions. Many of the group were Jewish refugees from Nazi Germany, whose courage in undertaking such a mission was extraordinary, but on this occasion they also included two German prisoners-of-war who had persuasively professed sympathy with their views, but who in fact broke away at the first opportunity and reported the presence of the party to their own side. In the resultant battle, fourteen of the Frenchmen were killed or taken prisoner.

But it was the raid on Heraklion in Crete which won the greatest success.

Under command of the Free French Commandant Bergé, the party consisted of three Free French privates, a Greek guide, Lieutenant Costi, and as second-in-command, Captain the Earl Jellicoe, son of the admiral who had commanded the British Grand Fleet at the Battle of Jutland.

After a voyage of four days aboard H.M. Submarine *Triton* the party paddled ashore in rubber boats to land some miles east of Heraklion, whereupon, after unloading, Jellicoe swam back out to sea towing the boats behind him and sank them, for the party was to be picked up from the island's southern shore. They then faced a long and arduous approach march, for the country was very broken, and their confidence was not improved by the fact that the Cretans they encountered on the way invariably greeted them in fractured but enthusiastic English.

They sheltered the first night in a convenient cave, and from nearby spent the next day observing their target, Heraklion airfield, upon which at one time they counted over sixty aircraft, mostly Junkers 88s. Attempts during the next day to move closer in order to mount the attack that night were foiled by the number and depth of defence positions, but by the following evening, after a third cold night and a fourth hungry and thirsty day, the party was close enough for Jellicoe and two of the men to work their way along the side of a German barrack block and reach the inner defences. It was satisfactorily dark, but as the others closed up and Jellicoe moved in to cut his way through the inner perimeter wire, a German patrol came along and the torch carried by one of them illuminated Jellicoe's large and curly head. Incipient disaster was only avoided by quick thinking on the part of one of the Free French privates, who emitted a drunken and ghastly snore which resulted in the patrol moving away with rather Puritan disgust, and by the time they had thought the episode over and returned for closer examination, the raiding party had cut their way through and were concealed in a bomb dump.

As it happened, the effects of the revelation of the gap in the wire were lost in the confusion occasioned by the landing of a flight of eight Junkers 88s, followed immediately by an enterprising R.A.F. Blenheim, which zoomed in at low level and dropped a string of bombs along the edge of the field. Within minutes, the S.A.S. party were running into the darkness which fringed the airfield and laying charges on the aircraft dispersed there in the bomb-proof shelters. They then worked their way back towards the entrance to the camp, still laying charges on any aircraft they came across, and as they reached the area of the main gate they saw in front of them a party being assembled, obviously in order to move out and patrol the roads.

They followed this party through the gates, laid the remainder of their charges on various lorries just outside, and escaped into the darkness; and three days later, having climbed two mountain ranges and walked 120 miles, they were waiting near the rendezvous to be picked up. Unfortunately, their hiding place was accidentally discovered by some Cretans who most uncharacteristically gave them away to the Germans, and after a brisk battle Commandant Bergé and two of the Frenchmen were taken prisoner and the other Frenchman killed.

Jellicoe and the Greek guide Costi, however, had been away reconnoitring a nearby village at the time and so escaped – and they were picked up that night by a caique manned by Royal Naval personnel, which also evacuated a number of Greek refugees and some New Zealanders who had escaped capture when the island fell.

The S.A.S. raid was undoubtedly a success and the idea of co-ordinated operations seemed to promise well for the future. Although the convoy for which the raids had been intended as support still lost fifteen of its seventeen ships, the other two might also have been hit by one or more of the forty-odd aircraft destroyed in those raids. As it was, the stores they carried proved just enough to sustain Malta until the next convoy arrived.

But all such operations were only peripheral to the main conflict. They might occasionally affect its course, but the decisive battles would still have to be fought out by massed armies, such as those which by the end of May had formed in the country to the south of Gazala inlet – poised for yet another clash of arms in which both sides hoped to decide who would dominate the North African theatre and the vital sea-lanes to the north of it.

5 · No Drums, No Trumpets

During the period between the end of Rommel's counterstroke in February and the beginning of the next great desert battle at the end of May, the strategic significance and plight of the island of Malta dominated discussions in both the Axis and the Allied camps.

Malta was, as one authority put it, 'the windlass of the Allied tourniquet' on Rommel's supply lines, its continued existence as a base for submarine and aerial attacks on Axis convoys an ever-present hazard to all his plans, its elimination a boon for which he had frequently clamoured. But for many months, Hitler and the German High Command had turned a deaf ear to all such entreaties, for their attention was fixed on the Russian front and Hitler at least, ever suspicious of naval arguments, was still smarting at the cost to the Wehrmacht of the airborne assault on that other pestiferous Mediterranean island, Crete. So far as the High Command of the German Army were concerned, the entire Italian theatre of war was a 'sideshow' in which victories were unsolicited gifts from heaven but which no one was prepared to take seriously – certainly not if added interest was likely to increase the overblown attentions already paid to the upstart Rommel, who was extremely unpopular with most of them, especially with Oberstgeneral Franz Halder, the Chief of Staff.

Until February 13th, 1942.

Upon that date, Grossadmiral Erich Raeder in his capacity of Commander-in-Chief of the Kriegsmarine had an audience with Hitler during which he pointed out to an unusually receptive Führer that Britain's purpose in waging war in Libya and Egypt had little to do with colonial ambitions, but was to protect her main oil supplies in the Middle East. If these could be captured, then not only might Britain be knocked out of the war, but German and Japanese hands might link on the shores of the Indian Ocean.

This was by no means the first occasion when Hitler's mind had dwelt upon that strategic interpretation of affairs, but now it made a deeper impression than before and he ordered Raeder to examine the possibilities of what later became briefly known as 'The Great Plan' – the strategic nightmare which had haunted both Wavell and Auchinleck, of an advance down from the Caucasus into Persia meeting a greatly reinforced drive by the Afrika Korps across the Nile and into Palestine.

Obviously, supplies to Rommel would loom large in any such examination, and as a result the reduction of Malta as the principal block to such supplies quickly assumed a high priority. But as responsibility for operations in the Mediterranean still lay with the Comando Supremo in Rome, Generale Cavallero soon became embroiled in the discussions, and an interesting circle of argument was revealed. No drive to the Nile could be launched until a sizeable reserve of supplies had been built up in Tripoli and Panzerarmee Afrika itself considerably strengthened; no supplies or reinforcements could reach Tripoli in the required numbers or at the necessary rate while Malta remained active as a British submarine base or 'unsinkable aircraft carrier'; no major assault could be launched against Malta until R.A.F. bases from which counter-attacks could be delivered had been pushed much further east than those now lying behind the Gazala positions.

This hardly presented an unbreakable impasse, but the solutions to the problems involved served to focus attention in Berlin on the Mediterranean to an unusual extent. Two plans were evolved – *Operation Herkules* for the invasion of Malta for which Cavallero obtained the promise of a German parachute division, and *Operation Aida* for the drive to the Nile; and in the meantime, in order to soften up the Malta defences, Kesselring was ordered to use his Luftflotte 2 to carry out a series of heavy attacks on the island. As this direction was hardly in conflict with the original instructions to Luftflotte 2 to safeguard convoys to North Africa it was carried out with formidable determination, and during April alone Malta suffered two hundred raids – an average of six per day. Some 6,700 tons of bombs fell on the island that month and over 11,000 buildings were destroyed, though fortunately the shelters built in the rock of which the island consisted saved all but 1,000 lives.

This fierce bombardment had two immediate effects. It enabled a much higher percentage of Rommel's supplies to reach him, and it so affected Churchill that he insisted upon an Eighth Army offensive at an early date – and when it became obvious to Rommel that that offensive was due, he easily obtained Hitler's agreement that the Afrika Korps should strike first.

On May 1st, a meeting took place at Berchtesgaden between Führer and Duce and the decisions were made: the first half of *Operation Aida* would begin at the end of May to forestall the British offensive and would consist of the defeat of the Eighth Army in the Gazala Line, the capture of Tobruk and possibly the clearance of the desert as far forward as the Egyptian border. There the Afrika Korps would stand while *Operation Herkules* took place during the second half of July. And with Malta eliminated and Benghasi and Tobruk open as supply ports, fuel, ammunition and reinforcements could be rushed forward during August for the drive to the Delta, where quite possibly enough loot would be captured to enable immediate further penetration beyond the Nile. By December 1942, therefore, British power in the Middle East could be at an end.

To Rommel, the prospects opened to him were entrancing and the situation novel. Not only were supplies reaching him at an unprecedented rate, but he was being positively encouraged instead of flatly forbidden to develop and carry out his plans. For this attack he need fear no anxious eyes peering over his shoulder, no curbing hand at his elbow, and although he had no intention of revealing all his intentions to anyone but his own personal staff, at least he was not obliged to throw a heavy cloak of secrecy over even the decision to move forward.

As for the enemy opposite, recent experiences and the present euphoric atmosphere of aid and encouragement combined to give him a feeling almost of contempt for them. There had apparently been no change in the command structure which had so signally failed to organise effective resistance to his latest offensive, and as far as enemy troops were concerned, those who in the past had proved the

Map 11   Rommel's view of Gazala defences

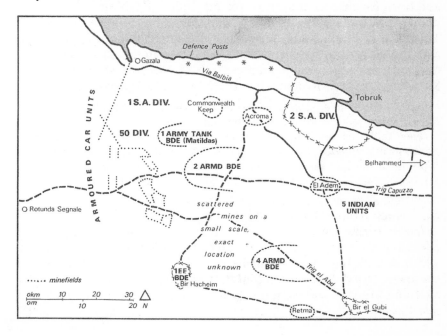

most obdurate – the Australians and the New Zealanders – were conspicuously absent. South Africans held the 'bastion' at the northern end by the coast, a new British division – the 50th, brought across from Cyprus and entirely inexperienced in desert warfare – held the stretch of the line down to just north of the Trig Capuzzo, while well away to the south a Free French brigade held a heavily fortified position at Bir Hacheim.

Undoubtedly, the fortifications themselves were deeply dug and stoutly constructed, the minefields surrounding and connecting them being laid so thickly and in such wide belts as to merit in places the description of 'mine-marsh' – but to Rommel the entire concept of a strongly held line was wrong:

> The basic British plan for the defence of the Marmarica was shaped by a desire to impose on the attacker a form of warfare more to the liking of their own command than manoeuvring in the open desert. The technical execution of the plan was first-rate.
>
> But the premises from which they approached the problem were false. In any North African desert position with an open southern flank, a rigid system of defence is bound to lead to disaster. The defence must be conducted offensively for it to be successful. Naturally, fortified lines can be of great value in preventing the enemy from undertaking particular operational moves. But the manning of such lines must not, under any circumstances, be at the expense of the forces required for the mobile defence.[1]

Even behind the main line, the British seemed wedded to a policy of static defence. Strongpoints, or 'boxes' as they came to be called, had been formed from units of the 5th Indian Division at Point 209, known as Commonwealth Keep, at Acroma on the western flank of Tobruk and at El Adem guarding the port's southern approaches; and there were apparently other, smaller defence posts along the northern coast as a natural precaution against a sea-borne attack – for which, indeed, Rommel had plans. Later he was to write:

> All these fortified points were provided with powerful artillery, infantry and armoured car units, and abundant supplies. The entire line was remarkable for the extraordinary degree of technical skill which had gone into its construction. All defence positions and strongpoints conformed to the most modern requirements of warfare. Countless numbers of mines had been laid – over a million in the Marmarica positions.[2]

But as far as mobile defences were concerned – the armoured units with which Rommel associated the only chances for victory in either defence or offence in the desert – these, as usual, seemed to have been split up into penny packets and distributed about the area, more with the idea that they would be available to go to the help of the static infantry defences than that they might be concentrated to form a striking force of sufficient power to cause a serious check to his own intentions.

According to information reaching him, there was a brigade of heavy infantry Matilda tanks up behind the junction of the South African and 50th Divisions, a brigade identified as 2nd Armoured from 1st Armoured Division lying just west of the junction of the Acroma–Bir Hacheim track with the Trig Capuzzo, and another – 4th Armoured Brigade – well away to the south, level with Bir Hacheim but nearly ten miles east of the fortress and lying across the Trig el Abd. There had, Rommel knew, been some reorganisation inside the British armoured divisions, the Support Groups having been dropped and replaced by what were called Motor Brigades, each consisting of three motorised infantry battalions and a regiment of field and anti-tank guns. One of these – the 7th (presumably part of the 7th Armoured Division) – was loose even further to the south and east, though this unit too appeared irretrievably bound to yet another defence box at a remote location known as Retma.

There had been talk of the British re-arming with a more powerful tank, but Rommel had taken little notice of this as he was of the ever-strengthening opinion that even the best weapons were valueless in the hands of troops not properly trained to use them, especially when the troops themselves were commanded by men who had little understanding of the basic doctrines of armoured, mobile warfare. This was undoubtedly a tenable theory, and his attitude to other information to the effect that heavier anti-tank guns were now arriving in the enemy front line area was conditioned by the same reasoning. In the end, he felt, it would be the experience and training of the men behind the guns which would count.

The only orthodox Allied formations which still commanded Rommel's respect were the armoured car units holding his own reconnaissance battalions well away from the main British and South African positions and, he was well aware, keeping a close eye on every movement of the forces under his command. The highly experienced 11th Hussars were unaccountably absent, but the 4th and the 6th South African Armoured Car units, the King's Dragoon Guards and the 12th Lancers seemed to have inherited some of the 11th's expertise, and certainly did not lack their daring.

However, so far as concealment of intent was concerned, Rommel had a few tricks of his own which might baffle even the shrewd observation of these men when the crucial moment came and his great offensive got under way.

His plans for the opening moves were simple, and herein, he felt, lay their great virtue. He would close up to the South African and 50th Division positions in the north with four Italian divisions – Sabratha, Trento, Brescia and Pavia – strengthened by two regimental groups from 90th Light along the coast, while Group Hecker, consisting of a battalion of Italian marines strengthened by German gunners and engineers, demonstrated at sea and thus drew all enemy attention to the north. In order to add to this deception, two panzer regiments, one from Ariete and one from Afrika Korps, would accompany the first daylight moves towards the enemy in the north, making as much dust as possible to exaggerate their size and to add an extra verisimilitude to the pretence that here lay the axis of the main attack.

But as soon as darkness fell, these panzers would return to their parent formations concentrated around the Rotunda Segnale, for the main thrust. This was to be a hook around the southern end of the Gazala Line, delivered by his massed armour – Ariete Armoured and Trieste Motorised Divisions on the left, 21st and 15th Panzer in the centre, while the bulk of 90th Light, their apparent hitting power augmented by aero-engines mounted in lorries which would churn up so much dust that the appearance of yet another panzer division would be created, would swing even wider out to the right, well down past Bir Hacheim.

Bir Hacheim itself, Rommel considered, would be virtually stamped into the ground in less than an hour by the combined weight of 21st and 15th Panzer Divisions, after which the main panzer force would stream on northwards, defeat the British armour as it came against it in its spread-eagled, isolated positions, smash through the Acroma box and reach the sea. Meanwhile, 90th Light on the outer rim of the wheel would have driven north-east, either by-passed or eliminated the box at El Adem and gone on to reach the edge of the main British supply dump laid out to the east of Belhammed.

All this should happen within the first twenty-four hours, after which the panzer divisions aided by the Italian armour (if they had kept up) would turn *west* and attack the South Africans and 50th Division from the rear, and as these would now be neatly sandwiched between the original Italian attacking force and his own armour, they would probably be eliminated quite quickly despite the strength of their defences. The combined Axis forces then would turn their attention to the final reduction of Tobruk, in which endeavour they would be sustained by the food, water, fuel and ammunition from that enormous British supply dump east of Belhammed, which 90th Light would have captured. In the light of this virtually guaranteed windfall, Panzerarmee Afrika would need to organise re-supply for only three days and fuel for 300 miles, to be brought up behind them by fast convoy.

Euphoria would seem to have been affecting judgment.

As a student of Napoleon's maxims, Rommel was a great – and indeed sustained – believer in the doctrine that, in war, it is not the men who count; it is the *man*. Well, he would, of course, lead Afrika Korps himself; but even with far better communications than the great

Corsican ever had at his command, it was necessary for him to be certain of other important men. Gambara – lately Italian Chief of Staff and commander of XX Corps – had gone; he had been heard to remark, perhaps in pique as a result of his astringent treatment during *Crusader* or possibly even because of more deeply felt emotions, that he hoped 'to live twenty years longer in order to command an army which will then fight the Germans' – and an association which had been abrasive for some time was abruptly terminated.

His place had been taken by Generale Count Emilio Barbasetti, a soldier whose name is engraved but lightly on the pages of military history.

Afrika Korps was no longer commanded by General Cruewell, for he had been overdue for leave and during the latter stages of *Crusader* had suffered acutely from jaundice – a complaint rife among both armies in the desert, generally as a result of drinking inadequately treated water drawn from old, native wells. However, Cruewell returned to Africa just before the offensive began and took command of the infantry movements in the north.

His place as Afrika Korps commander was taken by General-leutnant Walther Nehring, a soldier of cool judgment, quiet wit and great administrative competence, and for the situation in hand he was probably the perfect choice. If *Operation Aida* developed as planned he would never move far out from under Rommel's shadow.

All three German divisions had new commanders – General-leutnant Georg von Bismarck took over 21st Panzer Division from Böttcher, Generalleutnant Gustav von Vaerst replaced Neumann-Sylkow as 15th Panzer commander and Generalleutnant Ulrich Kleeman took von Sümmermann's place in command of 90th Light; and although only von Bismarck was at all well known to Rommel, the homogeneity of training throughout the German Army was enough to ensure that the newcomers would still understand the orders they received, and be well aware of the manner in which Rommel expected them to be obeyed.

Despite Rommel's belief to the contrary, there had also been changes at the top in Auchinleck's command, as a result of his acceptance of Godwin-Austen's request for relief. One of the great figures of the desert fighting, 'Strafer' Gott, who had commanded the Support Group during the O'Connor offensive and the 7th Armoured Division since then, was now promoted lieutenant-general and given command of XIII Corps which contained the infantry divisions, while Willoughby Norrie retained command of the armour of XXX Corps which he had held throughout *Crusader*. Within Norrie's XXX Corps, Major-General Lumsden had recovered from his wounds and resumed command of 1st Armoured Division, so Major-General Messervy took Gott's old appointment commanding 7th Armoured Division.

There were other aspects in which Rommel's information was at fault, too, for there were *three* divisions in Gott's XIII Corps, though Rommel's belief that only two were in the front line was correct. The 1st South African Division held the bastion at the northern end of the Gazala Line, its three brigade groups manning the fifteen miles running down from the coast in descending numerical order – 3rd, 2nd, 1st. Its original commander, General Brink, had returned to the Union after the end of *Crusader*, and in his place had been promoted the commander of the 1st Brigade, Dan Pienaar. This had not been a popular promotion among other troops serving in Eighth Army, especially the New Zealanders who believed with some reason that their ordeal below Belhammed during *Crusader* could have been alleviated had 1st South African Brigade shown a little more willingness to come to their aid; but by May 1942 the South Africans had been in position for four months and, as they were already thoroughly experienced in fortification work, their defences were deep indeed, each brigade group almost boxed in with minefields.

Behind them, garrisoning Tobruk, were the two remaining brigades of 2nd South African Division (one had been totally destroyed during *Crusader*), their divisional strength made up by 9th Indian Infantry Brigade Group from 5th Indian Division, whose two other brigades were held in reserve back in Egypt. This 2nd South African Division and the ancillary troops in the Tobruk garrison were commanded by Major-General H. B. Klopper.

The 50th (Tyne and Tees) Division which had been brought over from Cyprus was commanded by Major-General W. H. C. Ramsden and two of its three brigade groups were where Rommel expected them to be – continuing the line southwards from Pienaar's brigades towards the Trig Capuzzo; but the South African Armoured Car units had been particularly successful in masking the middle part of the line from Axis eyes and the third brigade group – 150th – was well dug in behind minefields south of the Trig Capuzzo, filling the gap between it and the Trig el Abd where it in turn crossed the defence line. Thirteen miles of thickly sewn mine-marsh separated the Trig el Abd position from the Free French brigade at Bir Hacheim, commanded by Brigadier-General Pierre Koenig and united in its determination to re-establish their country's military reputation after the sorry events at home and in the Middle East of the last months. As they too had been in position for some time and had laboured long and hard at their defences, it seemed likely that Rommel's estimate of an hour's possible resistance from them would prove inaccurate.

It was certainly inaccurate with regard to the amount of armour dispersed behind the Gazala Line to meet his own in the drive north. There were, for instance, *two* Army Tank Brigades – the 1st and the 32nd – instead of the one of which he knew, lying up behind the infantry divisions in the north, and between them they could put 116 Valentines and 110 Matildas into the field against him. There was also an extra Armoured Brigade Group (22nd, under a new commander, Brigadier W. H. Carr), the 29th Indian Brigade Group back at Bir el Gubi, and by the time the battle opened another Motor Brigade Group just south of Bir Hacheim – of all of which he knew nothing. Even more important from both offensive and defensive points of view, the Guards Brigade had now been motorised (and renumbered 201st) and stationed in yet another defensive box at the junction of the Trig Capuzzo and the Acroma–Bir Hacheim tracks, quickly and appropriately known to all as 'Knightsbridge'. The Household Brigade always does its best to feel at home.

There were thus five more brigade groups facing Rommel than he was bargaining for – one infantry, two motorised, two armoured – and he had placed one infantry brigade group in the wrong position. Where he was right, however, was in his belief that the men of the army facing him were inadequately trained to meet the kind of assault which the Afrika Korps could mount, and that the co-ordination of all arms which was the key to his own success was still lacking in the Eighth Army.

This condition was exacerbated by differences of opinion at the topmost command level, and disagreement of principle at levels only just below which showed itself on occasion in downright personal antagonism.

There is no doubt that by this time Ritchie's position had become so awkward as to be invidious. Auchinleck's confidence in him had declined since the retreat from El Agheila and the C.-in-C. later told one of his staff, Brigadier Dorman-Smith, that he had had 'to hold his [Ritchie's] hand' the entire time. It seems that he was determined to continue holding it now, especially as there was a fundamental difference of opinion between them as to probable future developments.

The highly secret source of intelligence in England – the Ultra Organisation which by enormous intellectual activity and use of reconstructed Enigma encyphering machines was by now reading Wehrmacht cables almost as soon as the intended recipients – had been able to warn Auchinleck of Rommel's intentions to attack, and to give an accurate forecast of the date. What Ultra had not been able to do, however, was to give him any idea of Rommel's tactical plans for the battle (for these had obviously not been the subject of cables between Tripoli and Berlin) and Auchinleck's personal opinion was that the main attack would come as a smashing blow in the north – at the junction of the South African Division and 50th Division – with an auxiliary attack in the south against Bir Hacheim which, though doubtless serious for the defenders, would still be in the nature of a feint.

On May 20th, therefore, Auchinleck wrote a long letter to Ritchie, setting out the situation as he saw it and urging him to keep the two armoured divisions of XXX Corps together and within supporting distance. After suggesting that 'both your armoured divisions complete should be positioned astride the Trig Capuzzo' he went on:

> I consider it to be of the highest importance that you should not break up the organisation of either of the armoured divisions. They have been trained to fight as divisions, I hope, and fight as divisions they should. Norrie must handle them as a corps commander, and thus be able to take advantage of the flexibility which the fact of having two formations gives him. Moreover, you will be getting the 1st Armoured Brigade before long, and it should join the 7th Armd. Div. . . . [3]

But Ritchie strongly believed that Rommel's main thrust would come around the south of the line – either around or through Bir Hacheim – and replied three days later with a long letter which included the following paragraph:

> I still feel that if his maintenance makes this possible he will try to go round our southern flank. In any case there will be a diversion there and this will probably be the Italian Mobile Corps . . . Anyhow whatever course he may adopt, our main strength is the counter with our armour to destroy him. We are ready for this . . . the ground carefully studied, and I feel confident that our armed forces are prepared to operate either to the south or to the north-west.[4]

However, whether from an excess of politeness or from a feeling of subordination to higher authority, the whole tone of the rest of the letter glossed over this important, indeed fundamental difference of opinion between them, and such was the note of accord struck that Auchinleck replied the same day, saying, among other encouraging phrases, 'I am quite happy about the positioning of the armoured divisions, and I am glad we are thinking on the same lines; this is always comforting!'

It seems likely, however, that had a comparison been made between the battle maps at Ritchie's and Auchinleck's headquarters it would have become evident that they were *not* thinking on quite the same lines. Ritchie had *not* positioned both armoured divisions 'astride the Trig Capuzzo', but deployed 1st Armoured Division to the south of it, and 7th Armoured Division even further south with its armour – as Rommel had divined – more disposed to go to the

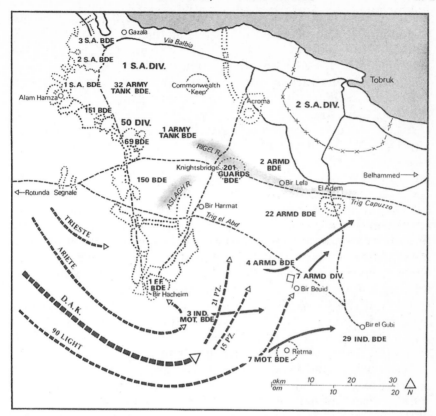

Map 12   May 27th, dawn

support of the isolated infantry boxes than to coalesce with 1st
Armoured Division into a massive armoured force.

Ironically, Auchinleck himself contributed even more to this
potential wide dispersion of the armour when, right at the last
moment, he sent up the two further infantry brigades to hold static
positions along the southern flank of the battle area – 29th Indian
Brigade to Bir el Gubi and the 3rd Indian Motor Brigade to a position
just a few miles south-east of Bir Hacheim. Had they only to act as
blocks to a feint operation (and had the Motor Brigade near Bir
Hacheim been given rather more time to prepare defences) it is
possible that they would have amply fulfilled their purpose, but in the
face of Ritchie's belief that they might lie in the path of Rommel's
main offensive, they acted instead in Ritchie's mind as magnets for
more armoured protection.

Auchinleck was also greatly responsible for the constitution of the
forces holding these isolated positions.

'It was not only the enemy', says the *Official History*, encouragingly, 'who had noticed that the British armour, artillery and infantry had often been unsuccessful in concerting their action on the battle-field.' When some of the lessons of *Crusader* had been studied, Auchinleck had issued directives intended to bring about a closer integration of the various arms essential to any modern battlegroup, and one of the immediate results was the emergence of the concept of the 'Brigade Group'.

Instead of divisions consisting of brigades composed entirely of armour or of infantry, with 'divisional' anti-tank, anti-aircraft, field artillery, engineers and administrative units held separately, these latter units would now be incorporated into each brigade so that, for instance, an infantry brigade group would consist of its three infantry battalions *plus* a regiment of field and anti-tank guns and its own anti-aircraft and engineer units, all trained together. An armoured brigade group would contain three tank regiments, a motor battalion (vehicle-borne infantry) and a regiment of field and anti-tank guns, while a motor brigade group would consist of three motorised infantry battalions and a similar allocation of artillery and engineers. Infantry divisions would consist of three infantry brigade groups, armoured divisions eventually of one armoured brigade group and one motorised brigade group – though for the coming battle both armoured divisions would be stronger than that.

One obvious and beneficial effect of this integration of all arms within a brigade would be to give it a degree of independence which could prove extremely useful should it become isolated; but on the other hand that very independence, unless carefully controlled, could weaken cohesion inside a division. Ironically, this divisive factor was perhaps exacerbated by the fact that the brigades were also being substantially strengthened as new weapons arrived in the Delta – a point to which Rommel might have been advised to give rather closer attention, despite the justification of his attitude to their use or misuse by untrained troops.

Over a hundred new 6-pounder anti-tank guns had arrived in the Delta to begin the replacement of the unpopular 2-pounders, and nearly 250 General Grant tanks had also arrived from America. These, in addition to the reliability of engine and general robustness which had so endeared the American Stuarts to their crews, carried a 75mm. gun firing both anti-tank and high explosive shells together with a 37mm. high velocity turret gun similar to the main armament of the Stuarts. The arrival of these tanks, with more Stuarts (known to their British crews as Honeys) from America and more Crusaders from Britain had not only given Auchinleck a substantial reserve stock (though not the third armoured division which he had stated was necessary) but also the material with which to carry out the 'brigade group' reorganisation.

Obviously, it would take time for the physical side of such reorganisation and re-equipment to take place; how long it would take for the philosophical acceptance of a doctrine which tended to break down the age-old barriers between cavalry and infantry, and to a lesser extent between both of these and the gunners and engineers, remained to be seen. But one extra disrupting factor was already in evidence which made it unlikely that that co-ordination which Auchinleck so rightly desired would be achieved.

Ritchie's problems did not all come from above. As has been related, Godwin-Austen's place had been taken by Strafer Gott – promoted from command of the 7th Armoured Division – and although this meant that at least one of the corps commanders was junior in appointment to Ritchie, the fact remained that Gott had been serving in the desert for longer, and his prestige throughout the entire desert theatre was far higher. He was, moreover, a close personal friend of the other corps commander, Norrie, who consulted him on frequent occasions – hardly an unreasonable course of action, but one which sometimes appeared to exclude the Army Commander from discussions in which he should have played the dominant role.

Further down the scale matters were, if anything, worse. The South African commander, Major-General Dan Pienaar, had already gained for himself a reputation for what has been described as 'sheer bloodymindedness' and his relations with Gott were already strained. As for those between the armoured divisional commanders in XXX Corps, Lumsden and Messervy, since the retreat from El Agheila these had deteriorated to such an extent that they hardly spoke to one another. Herbert Lumsden was a man who combined an intense loyalty to those who served with – and especially under – him, with a hasty temper and a somewhat unforgiving nature, and during the period after he had been wounded, command of his 1st Armoured Division had been given to Messervy, whom – rightly or wrongly – Lumsden blamed for the disasters which followed. Never again, he felt, should any of his own beloved units be entrusted to such inexpert hands, and he made little attempt to disguise his conviction that Messervy was unfit to command armour of any description.

The conferences held by Ritchie before the battle, therefore, were by no means congenial occasions, and little attempt was made by any of those present to adjust their preconceived views. And one of the views held by at least three of them was that if their revered Commander-in-Chief, General Auchinleck, felt that the enemy would attack in the centre or the north, that was where the attack should be expected – whatever the opinions of this comparative newcomer to desert fighting, the Eighth Army Commander.

However, in the face of Ritchie's continued insistence that Rommel *might* come around the south of the line, Norrie did agree in

principle that, in that event, the main armour of 7th Armoured
Division – the 4th Armoured Brigade – should move to protect those
isolated infantry boxes out in the blue, and that 22nd Armoured
Brigade should go to their support despite the icy disfavour with
which their divisional commander received this suggestion.

Not, Norrie thought, that the situation was particularly likely to
arise.

Incredibly – and all the irony of history is reflected here – there was
now a combination of circumstances by which Britain might, in
theory, have benefited from that discrepancy between Ritchie's
apparent agreement with Auchinleck, and his deployment of forces
in the field.

Although the Ultra Organisation was undoubtedly the greatest
intelligence coup of the Second World War, the Axis Powers were
not without their own triumphs in the field, and one of these was the
breaking of the American State Department cypher by which its
military agents communicated with Washington. Since early 1941, an
American 'observer', Colonel Bonner Fellers, had been in Cairo, and
such had been his interest and sympathy with the British cause that he
had been attached to Eighth Army during the whole of the *Crusader*
operation and been given, moreover, a free hand to roam the
battlefield. After the attack on Pearl Harbor, his credentials and
standing were of course greatly increased, and he was invited to
attend General Auchinleck's conferences with the chief British staff
officers and their naval and air force colleagues which, as the time for
the battle at Gazala came nearer, were held every day.

And every night, Colonel Fellers cabled Washington with their
details, and busy interceptors in Bari recorded them, busier in-
terpreters translated them more or less efficiently into Italian and
German army jargon, and their superiors then forwarded what
information they considered desirable (for like intelligence experts
the world over, they felt that it was necessary to guard their sources
and often that short-term military advantage was not necessarily the
right price to pay for loss of their own long-term omniscience) to
Rommel.

So in the last hours before the opening moves of the Battle of
Gazala, the German Commander-in-Chief of Panzerarmee Afrika
learned – more or less – what the British Commander-in-Chief,
Middle East, believed that he and his commander in the field had
decided was the best deployment of the Eighth Army troops behind
the Gazala Line; and Rommel was to be just as surprised as Auchinleck when he discovered that Auchinleck's intentions and Ritchie's
reality were some way apart.

To Rommel, all the auguries on May 26th seemed to beckon him on to swift and convincing victory. A stifling *khamsin* blanketed the area during the afternoon, effectively cloaking both the first stage of the movement of the Cruewell Group towards the enemy defence lines and also the first concentration of armour around Segnale. In the northern half of the line heavy Stuka attacks on the South African and 50th Division positions, followed immediately by concentrated artillery bombardments (and the Italian gunners had lost none of their skill or enterprise) must undoubtedly be focusing enemy attention there, and in the early evening the dust and cloud died away just enough for the armoured feint eastward from Segnale to be seen – and seen to be seen – by South African reconnaissance air-craft.

By the time dusk had fallen the *khamsin* had died and the massed armour of Panzerarmee Afrika could move away to the south-east – and with Rommel in the lead, the first exhilarating stage of the march into Egypt began:

> At 2030 I ordered Operation 'Venezia' and the 10,000 vehicles of the striking force began to move. My staff and I, in our place in the Afrika Korps column, drove through the moonlit night towards the great armoured battle. Occasional flares lit up the sky far in the distance – probably the Luftwaffe trying to locate Bir Hakeim. I was tense and keyed up, impatiently awaiting the coming day. What would the enemy do? What had he already done? These questions pounded my brain, and only morning would bring the answers. Our formations rolled forward without a halt.[5]

One late amendment to his orders had been made, for within the last few hours details of the unexpected density and width of the mine-marsh south of the Trig el Abd and down to Bir Hacheim had come in, and as a result the whole axis of the advance had been side-stepped to the right. It would now be the Ariete Division who would roll over Bir Hacheim on the drive to the north, with Trieste on their left, 21st Panzer on their right and 15th Panzer and 90th Light Division even further out on the rim of the wheel. As the night wore on, the Luftwaffe found Bir Hacheim, bombed it briefly and then pin-pointed the turning-point for Rommel's force out in the desert to the south.

Onward clanked and rolled the vast force – well on schedule – and having executed with admirable competence the massive wheel through over one hundred and twenty degrees, it refuelled and settled down to await the morning. By daybreak 332 panzers (practi-cally all with additional armour at the front) and the 228 Italian M13s and 14s were poised – breakfasted and rested – for the lunge up behind the enemy lines. So far as Rommel could tell, their move had been entirely unobserved, and his optimism was sufficient to dispel any doubts that so gigantic a movement could escape the attention of the vigilant enemy armoured cars. The only apparent check to his plans was the mysterious disappearance of the entire Trieste Motorised Division, unaccountably absent from their position on the left of Ariete.

But there was no time to spare for search or even questioning, for the sky was a clear translucent blue and enemy aircraft must be expected soon to rob him of that vital element of surprise. Orders were shouted, the panzer engines roared and the whole vast cavalcade rumbled forward, creating a huge trident of dust as the three prongs of the advance separated out.

Ariete were first into action, against Indian infantry and gunners of the 3rd Indian Motor Brigade of whose presence they had had no warning but whom they wiped out in half an hour of intense action, overrunning the flimsy infantry positions and the hastily dug-in guns, killing or taking prisoner nearly four hundred and fifty officers and men, and chasing the survivors away to the east. By the end of this short action the Italian tank crews realised that this was not their main objective – the Free French at Bir Hacheim – but that first taste of battle increased their morale and they forged ahead towards the fort now visible on the horizon. Already, Stukas were flying in towards it from the west. It was not quite 0700 on May 27th.

Ten miles away to the east, the artillery and motorised infantry of 90th Light were enjoying a similar success. They had bumped into patrols of the 7th Motor Brigade, pursued them as far as the Retma box and isolated them there, after which they proceeded methodically to break into the defences. These had obviously been hastily prepared and were quickly destroyed – sangars crushed, rifle and machine-gun pits overrun, a few thin-skinned lorries shot up or overturned – and it was only a matter of minutes before the bulk of the defenders were seen streaming off to the east, presumably seeking the shelter of whatever force held Bir el Gubi.

By 0900 the Retma box had been eliminated and 90th Light Division were plunging onwards, to arrive at Bir Beuid where they rounded up a group of astonished British officers and administrative personnel who proved upon investigation to be none other than the Advanced Headquarters of 7th Armoured Division! (In their excitement the captors failed to attach any importance to the greying hair of one of the privates, with the result that General Messervy and two of his senior staff officers, who had taken the precaution of removing their badges of rank as soon as danger threatened, managed later to escape; but 7th Armoured Division were without a command structure and were to remain so for many vital hours.)

But it was in the centre that the most significant successes were scored. The panzer divisions caught the Grants and Crusaders of 4th

Figure 3   Cruiser tank Mark VI (Crusader): weight 14 tons; armour 7mm.–39mm.;
engine 340 h.p.; maximum speed 30 m.p.h.; armament one 2-pdr, two 7·92mm.
Besa machine-guns; crew 4

Armoured Brigade not only still on their way towards their battle
positions (they had completed a leisurely breakfast before moving)
but in two separate halves. This enabled 15th Panzer to destroy 8th
Hussars as a fighting unit in half an hour of swift but violent action,
then to crash on into two squadrons of 3rd Royal Tank Regiment
which they quickly reduced to ten tanks (out of ammunition by this
time, and three of them with smashed guns) and these they chased off
to the east – where they were promptly seen by the exuberant men of
90th Light, who picked up the scent and drove the quarry away past
El Adem and on towards Belhammed.

All this constituted a spectacular morning's work and behind the
spearheads the desert was already littered with wrecked tanks
belching flame and towering clouds of black smoke, smashed lorries
and trucks, groups of dejected prisoners searching through wreckage,
helping the ambulance crews as the wounded were tended and
moving out towards the periphery of the action in the hope of getting
away. But it had not been achieved without loss, and Rommel,
annoyed by some unnecessary risks run by his over-enthusiastic
assault troops, was already concerned by the cost of the battle so far.

Unfortunately our panzer units attacked without support, although I
had constantly been at pains to impress them not to do so until our
artillery had opened fire. There was also a British surprise awaiting us
here, one which was not to our advantage – the new Grant tank, which

was used in this battle for the first time on African soil. Tank after tank, German and British, was shattered in the fire of the tank-guns. Finally, we succeeded in throwing the British back to the Trig el Abd, although at the cost of heavy casualties.[6]

Ariete had by this time lost over forty M13s (for Bir Hacheim was proving a much tougher nut to crack than anyone on the Axis side had thought probable) and 15th and 21st between them as many panzers, though these of course still lay in the desert behind the advance where the excellent German recovery service was already at work. Nevertheless, at a cost of but one-seventh of their strength, Afrika Korps had already scattered two British motor brigade groups and one armoured brigade group, decapitated 7th Armoured Division and seemed likely to have proved Rommel's assertion that the British armoured command had still to learn the basic arts of their profession.

That this was so was to be demonstrated yet again, some ten miles north of the scene of the destruction of 4th Armoured Brigade Group, when 22nd Armoured Brigade Group moved slowly into view, alone and well out of range of support from its sister brigade group in 1st Armoured Division – the 2nd, then sitting immobile away to the east of the Guards Brigade at Knightsbridge. The resulting slaughter was this time carried out by 21st Panzer Division and within half an hour 22nd Brigade survivors were limping disconsolately back towards the 2nd positions, leaving behind them among the indifferent clumps of camel-thorn the smoking wrecks of thirty of their Grants and Stuarts together with several of their field and anti-tank guns.

But now, the pace of the advance began to slacken. Both panzer divisions had been emptying their ammunition racks and fuel tanks at an alarming rate, and the very success and speed of their victories had dispersed their forward elements even more than had been allowed for in Rommel's original plan. Where Trieste were no one knew, Ariete were still back at Bir Hacheim, the two panzer divisions were more or less together south of Knightsbridge, but 90th Light were away to the east driving up towards El Adem; and between the prongs of the advance was occurring that phenomenon of battles with the British – remarked upon by many frustrated commanders through the ages – the ability of junior ranks from battalion commanders down to troopers to improvise effective action and extricate themselves from the perils in which their generals had left them. Random groups of tank crews, infantry and gunners were coalescing and, out of touch with and thus untrammelled by orders from their superiors, were beginning to fight back effectively. The first intimation of this came to Rommel when he tried to go in search of 90th Light (radio contact had broken down) and found his column blocked by tanks and artillery from the remnants of 4th Armoured Brigade, and some time later he learned that the urgently needed supply columns endeavouring to follow in the wake of the panzer divisions were being fiercely attacked and often completely destroyed by raiding columns of British infantry and artillery from the dispersed motor brigades, materialising apparently out of nowhere.

Moreover, Ariete were suffering ever-mounting losses at the hands of the stubborn French at Bir Hacheim, and in their endeavour to obey orders to 'roll over' the isolated garrison, had already emptied their own ammunition racks and were thus commandeering every shell and every drop of fuel coming up, even when these were brought up by German supply columns trying to get through to their own panzer divisions along the shortest route around the end of the minefields. It was obvious that a crisis was approaching and that if the morning had given Rommel's forces victories with a lavish hand, the afternoon promised nothing but hard fighting.

It began about 1430 as the leading columns of both 15th and 21st Panzer Divisions probed northward towards the area between Acroma and Commonwealth Keep, when they found themselves attacked from the east by ever-increasing forces from the 2nd Armoured Brigade now strengthened by the remnants of 22nd, and then – to their consternation and to Rommel's surprise when he heard about it (he had become separated from his main armour by more of these mysterious small groups) – from the west by Matildas from 1st Army Tank Brigade. It looked as though the British armour was concentrating at last.

Fire and black smoke welled up from the lorries and panzers dotted about the scrub-covered desert, and the battle degenerated into a hundred small but bitter actions fought out on one side by German panzer crews who were still tending to charge forward out of the protective range of their anti-tank guns, and British tank crews finding themselves in action for the first time in toughly armoured vehicles that did not break down, firing guns which could hit their enemies hard at a satisfactory range. Figures for panzer casualties mounted inexorably, and then another near-disaster for the Afrika Korps occurred.

When the combined 2nd and 22nd Armoured Brigades had hit the right flank of the advancing panzer divisions, the tank squadrons on the left had in fact missed the tail of the German armour and found themselves amid the rear echelons and divisional soft-skinned transport where they wreaked considerable havoc, remaining on the field afterwards in order to collect and evaluate some of their booty.

Unknowingly, in so doing they effectively cut off Rommel and his staff from his main striking force, isolating them just north of Bir el Harmat where they were later joined by the harassed and dis-

comfited remains of Ariete, moving north to leave the unquench-
able Frenchmen to at least a few more days and nights of undisputed
possession of their fortress. Rommel was very angry (but also quite
relieved) when nightfall at last brought an end to an astounding day,
during which at one moment he had believed the battle won and the
British armour destroyed, but which now presented him with a
completely different picture.

By the time darkness had fallen, his panzer divisions were 'hedge-
hogged' in an area south of the Rigel Ridge not very far west of the
intact Guards Brigade, while 90th Light, still out of direct touch, were
also hedgehogged just south of El Adem and under attack from
recuperated and re-supplied tank formations from 4th Armoured
Brigade Group. No supplies were getting through, 15th Panzer were
out of fuel and very nearly out of ammunition, and although the
recovery teams would undoubtedly have improved the position by
the morning, 15th had only twenty-nine 'runners' left. Even 21st
Panzer had only eighty runners immediately available, and petrol for
only a few more hours of battle.

> I will not deny that I was seriously worried that evening. Our heavy tank
> losses were no good beginning to the battle (far more than a third of the
> German tanks had been lost in this one day.) The 90th Light Division
> under General Kleeman had become separated from the Afrika Korps and
> was now in a very dangerous position. British motorised groups were
> streaming through the open gap and hunting down the transport columns
> which had lost touch with the main body. And on these columns the life of
> my army depended.[7]

There was, however, one aspect of the situation from which so
confirmed an optimist as Rommel could draw comfort while he
planned and issued his orders for the morrow. Despite the recent
simultaneous attacks on the head of his panzer columns by units from
three identifiable armoured brigades – 2nd, 22nd and 1st Army Tank
Brigade – Rommel still believed that the British command was
fumbling, still lacking both the will to concentrate and co-ordinate,
and the technical ability to do so. The overrunning and dispersal of so
many separate units during the morning convinced him of this, and he
felt that the events of the afternoon had been more coincidental than
planned.

In this he was justified, for the reversal of fortunes during the
afternoon had been brought about far more by the independent
action of British brigade, battalion, company and even platoon
commanders than by any co-ordinating action at divisional, corps or
army command level, which on May 27th ushered in a period
generally agreed to represent the nadir of British generalship during
the desert campaign.

From the moment the Afrika Korps had left the Rotunda Segnale the previous afternoon, they had in fact been under close observation by the British and South African Armoured Car units. During the night, one of the South African squadrons had moved so close to the outside flank of the 90th Light that a German motor-cyclist had raced away through their columns, and all the time their signallers were sending out messages giving the movements and locations of Rommel's armoured divisions. These were all picked up by 7th Motor Brigade close to Retma and relayed to 7th Armoured Division on their forward net, and during the hours of darkness alone 7th Motor Brigade H.Q. logged thirteen messages sent out.

They were dismissed at 7th Armoured Division H.Q. as the panic-stricken imaginings of men retiring at night in front of a larger but nevertheless token force, for the majority opinion at that and higher levels was still that Rommel's main assault was coming in the north.

One alert mind at corps level, however, was following the reported movements of Rommel's spearheads with interest and growing anxiety. Major R. M. P. Carver, G.S.O.2 at XXX Corps, was listening in to all these signals, and at 0100 he was sufficiently concerned to telephone the G.S.O.1 at 7th Armoured Division to ask him what he was doing about it all – to be rebuked first for listening in to 7th Armoured Division forward net which the G.S.O.1 regarded somewhat in the light of his own private telephone line, and then for waking him up. The G.S.O.1 certainly had no intention of waking General Messervy on the strength either of the signals which had come in, or of Major Carver's worries – which he suggested could be put to better use in the service of his own formation.

Half an hour later, Carver took the bull by the horns and woke up his own superior, General Norrie, told him of the reports coming in and suggested that he rang Messervy direct – which, somewhat reluctantly, Norrie did. It was, however, to no effect, as Messervy agreed with his own G.S.O.1 that the reports were more likely to be inaccurate than not, and although undoubtedly some force was coming south it was more probably the expected Italian feint than the main German thrust. With this Norrie agreed, and so refused Carver's next suggestion, that he ring Lumsden and order him to put 22nd Armoured Brigade on notice to move south to join 7th Armoured Division some eight miles away. So far as Norrie was concerned, Auchinleck had said the enemy attack would come in the centre or the north, and that was where it should still be expected!

Carver's next move was to ring Lumsden's G.S.O.1 and give him all the information so far to hand and his own interpretation of it – to receive in reply the opinion that even if Carver's information and prediction proved accurate, Lumsden would use every argument he could think of to avoid parting again with 22nd Armoured Brigade, especially to Messervy.

There matters remained while Rommel's armour moved implacably towards their turning-point south of Bir Hacheim, the reports from the armoured cars came in regularly and Major Carver became increasingly worried. At 0400 he felt that he could wait no longer, spoke again to the sceptical and now irritated G.S.O.1 of 7th Armoured Division and, realising that little good was coming of that conversation, woke General Norrie again.

At his instigation, Norrie rang Messervy and suggested that he order his main armour – 4th Armoured Brigade – to battle positions east of Bir Hacheim (to which Messervy eventually agreed) and then rang Lumsden to give him a warning order that 22nd Armoured Brigade should make ready to move south to join Messervy's force. But in the resultant conversation, which went on for some time, Lumsden proved the more passionate advocate, his argument for the moment being that as his tank squadrons were composed mostly in the proportion of one squadron of Grants to two of Crusaders whereas Messervy's regiments were made up of two Grant squadrons to one of Honeys, surely Messervy should come to his aid and not the other way round? What relevance this argument had to the developing tactical situation is now somewhat obscure, but it seems at the time to have convinced Norrie who, to Carver's concern, refrained from giving Lumsden the direct warning order.

Even with Messervy's acceptance of his order, it was nevertheless nearly 0630 before much life was injected into 7th Armoured Division headquarters, and this happened as a result of the startled announcement on the part of the commander of the 3rd Indian Motor Brigade south of Bir Hacheim, Brigadier Filose, that he had 'a whole bloody German armoured division' in front of him; but cool thought on the part of the recipients, despite the conversations between Norrie and Messervy, reasoned that this could not be so (and, indeed, they were right for it was the Ariete) and the brigadier's alarm was adjudged the result of the late arrival of his brigade at the front, as it had only come up the previous day and was still missing many of its anti-tank gunners and support units. Auchinleck's opinion at divisional level at 0645 on the morning of May 27th was still sacrosanct.

It was not to remain so for much longer. Shortly afterwards a report arrived at XXX Corps from an air reconnaissance which Carver had requested, which confirmed all his fears – over four hundred enemy panzers were refuelling south of Bir Hacheim and there was now no doubt as to where Rommel's main attack was aimed. At last all was clear and certain, and it should now be just a matter of following agreed plans and moving brigades to their allotted battle stations, none of the movements across more than twelve miles of known ground, none taking more than half or at most three-quarters of an hour. All should be well.

But it was not to be as easy as that. Messervy when rung a second time by Norrie agreed that 7th Armoured Division had issued a warning order at 0430 as instructed, that 4th Armoured Brigade had 'stood to' at 0545 – and Messervy would now order them to battle positions as soon as possible; but an account written later by the commander of one of 4th Armoured Brigade's tank regiments, Lieutenant-Colonel 'Pip' Roberts, casts an illuminating light on the degree of urgency with which events and orders were at that moment being regarded.

> 'Stand-to' at about 0545 hrs passed off without incident, so we repaired to breakfast. At about 0700 hrs, Brigade HQ, having been disturbed for some hours and now apparently without much on hand, rang up to request that we should furnish a full report as to why tanks numbered so-and-so and so-and-so were returned to Ordnance in a dirty condition.[8]

Colonel Roberts managed only the first two or three sentences on this crucial matter before the phone rang again, and his tanks were on the move by 0720 – by which time Norrie was again deep in argument with Lumsden, endeavouring to persuade him that now it really was time for 22nd Armoured Brigade to go to the support of 4th Armoured Brigade as had been agreed if Rommel's attack came around the south – and again listening to the arguments and pleas which Lumsden had employed before to shield his precious formations from Messervy's control. Surely it was still not 100 per cent certain that the attack was coming around the south? Surely if Auchinleck had said it would come in the centre, more weight should be given to his opinion than to the perhaps muddled and hurried reconnaissance reports of less experienced soldiers? Anyway, as Lumsden had said before, 22nd Brigade regiments had only one squadron of Grants, etc., etc., etc. . . . and when Norrie proved impervious to argument and insisted upon obedience, Lumsden rather sulkily agreed but pointed out that 22nd Armoured Brigade would be unable to move until 0830 at the earliest because, as Norrie would remember, they had not as yet received even a warning order!

By the time 22nd did move, of course, 4th Armoured Brigade had been overrun, two of its regiments annihilated, 7th Armoured Division Advanced H.Q. captured – and within an hour 22nd Armoured Brigade would themselves be facing the weight and ferocity of a triumphant 21st Panzer Division on their own. It was certainly a bad morning for the British, yet the recovery during the afternoon combined with the lack of communications with 7th Armoured Division (Norrie was sure this was purely a technical matter) seems to have given everyone great confidence and according to the battle reports Auchinleck received that evening, to quote from the *Official History*, 'the day ended with the British higher command more satisfied with the day's fighting than was General Rommel.'

On the face of it, there was good reason for this. Except for the 3rd Indian Motor Brigade which had been very roughly handled, the other brigades of 7th Armoured seemed merely to have been scattered, and as both XXX Corps and Eighth Army were still refusing to believe that Messervy and his staff had been captured, no news from them was assumed to be good news. Lumsden's armour had certainly taken a knock and O'Carroll's 1st Army Tank Brigade had lost eighteen Matildas – but the smoking hulks of innumerable panzers dotting the desert demonstrated the effectiveness of the Grants' main armament, and the evening situation maps revealed Rommel's mobile forces apparently contained in an area bounded on the west by the South African, British and Free French positions and minefields, to the north and north-east by the 1st Army Tank Brigade and the brigades of 1st Armoured Division respectively, and in the area along and below the Trig el Abd by the recuperating armour and motorised infantry of the 7th Armoured Division.

Moreover, the vast dump of materials east of Belhammed was still inviolate and even unthreatened, and the reserve 1st Armoured Brigade still unused – though it had lost a few of its Grants (to the fury of the crews) to make up losses in 4th Armoured Brigade Group. Assuredly, there was room for some satisfaction in the Allied camp on the evening of May 27th.

Unfortunately for the British, satisfaction in the evening would seem to have bred inaction in the morning, for during the 28th, Lumsden's armour did little but watch 15th Panzer lying west of Knightsbridge awaiting petrol, while 4th Armoured half-heartedly chivvied 90th Light back towards Bir el Harmat (to which place Rommel had already ordered them) and the British and Indian motorised infantry in the south, still without any firm controlling hand, grouped together and occasionally raided any supply columns they saw. On one occasion they did this to such effect that the unfortunate Oberleutnant in charge burst into tears and declared that Germany had lost North Africa, so perhaps they felt that they were all doing rather well.

But in the meantime, Rommel was busily gathering information, visiting his formations with a total disregard for his own personal safety, and preparing to reassert his dominance of the battlefield. He had ordered a continuation of the drive of the panzer divisions northwards towards the Via Balbia before fully appreciating the state of 15th Panzer, so 21st Panzer went on alone. They reached the edge of the escarpment and shelled movements below, but then could not get down themselves so they turned and attacked Commonwealth Keep, where a mixed garrison of less than a hundred and fifty South African and Yorkshire infantrymen put up a redoubtable resistance with nothing but their small-arms, six old Italian 47mm. guns and some mortars, before they were overwhelmed.

By this time Rommel had found a way through from the south to 15th Panzer positions, ordered 90th Light back towards Bir el Harmat and Ariete to close up, and thus set in train a concentration of his armour in the centre of the Allied positions. Moreover, the mystery of the disappearance of Trieste had been solved, to his unexpected advantage; they had not received the late amendment to his orders and so instead of sweeping to the south of Bir Hacheim, had hit the mine-marsh half-way between the Trig el Abd and the Free French – and as it was undefended, had spent the intervening time 'gapping' a way through it. Not only, therefore, were Rommel's forces now receiving some additional strength as Trieste came through, but a safer and shorter way had been found, albeit tenuous for the moment, along which urgently needed supplies could be brought.

Of course, not everything had gone quite so smoothly for him. Ariete had been attacked first from the west by Matildas of 1st Army Tank Brigade and suffered some losses in M13s, and then by Crusaders of 22nd Armoured Brigade – but these they had fought off with the 88mms which Rommel had given them with instructions to form an anti-tank screen, and which they handled very adeptly. Rommel himself came under what he called 'a wild fire' from an Italian column, and when he eventually returned to Bir el Harmat after his visit to 15th Panzer, he found that his own headquarters had been overrun by British armour and dispersed over the desert.

But the following day, May 29th, started in splendid form for the Afrika Korps, with what was to become a famous piece of *Rommelei*. He had found the head of a large supply column fumbling its way up to the east of Bir el Harmat and personally led it up to 15th Panzer Division positions through an area thickly infested with British tanks, artillery and mobile infantry, at times under heavy fire and all the way in considerable personal danger. Having refuelled 15th Panzer and given them fresh orders, he then took the rest of the convoy across towards the concentration area he had chosen, between the Trig Capuzzo and the Trig el Abd, and to which he had already ordered 21st Panzer to return. Soon all his armour would be together, with full fuel tanks and ammunition racks.

As one of the fiercest tank battles of the desert campaign was about to be fought, this was as well for the Afrika Korps.

Early that morning (May 29th) 90th Light had moved off westward to make the rest of their way back to Bir el Harmat (undisturbed, as

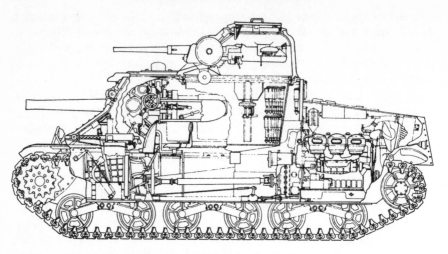

Figure 4   Medium tank M3 (General Grant): weight 28·5 tons: armour 35mm.–55mm.; engine 370 h.p.; maximum speed 26 m.p.h.; armament one 75mm., one 37mm., three ·30 in. machine-guns; crew 6

4th Armoured had just been ordered back to El Adem in reserve), and Ariete moved north from Bir el Harmat to join the two panzer divisions. Just before 1100, Ariete saw in front of them the Grant squadrons of 2nd Armoured Brigade, followed by the Crusader squadrons, advancing westwards from Knightsbridge against the last known positions of 15th Panzer. There was a brisk exchange of fire but the Grants ploughed stolidly forward until they caught up with the retiring 15th Panzer, who immediately turned and gave battle – protected at first by their invariable anti-tank rearguard screen and then reinforced, to their own surprise and 2nd Armoured's discomfort, by the leading columns of 21st Panzer as these came back down from the north.

For a short time, 2nd Armoured were thus fighting by themselves on three fronts, and it was midday before 22nd Armoured – sent off in the morning on their own to attack Bir el Harmat – returned to the aid of their sister brigade, by which time the battle was reaching its crisis-point. The Grant crews shot accurately and confidently but suffered losses because their main armament – their 75mm. guns – were housed in side sponsons and were thus too low for the crews to adopt 'hull down' positions; but the Crusaders brewed up with dreadful regularity, slewing aside with tracks ripped off to litter the desert like sloughed crocodile skins, their crews burning to agonised deaths or scurrying desperately among the gouts of sand and the smoking hulls. The panzers were being hit harder than ever before, too, and at longer range, and their crews were learning some of the more bitter lessons of armoured warfare; but for them there was at least the comforting crack of their 88mms, the bark of the newly arrived captured Russian 76mm. and the sight of their anti-tank screens implacably holding off the British attacks.

And all the time the battle was fought out in the excruciating conditions of a hot and blinding dust-storm which drifted choking clouds across the field with infuriating inconsequence to blind the gunners, to confuse the drivers, to add to the suffocation of the black, oily smoke which plumed out from smitten tanks and flaming ammunition boxes.

'Tanks and lorries', wrote one observer, 'huddled together like sheep: men cowered behind their vehicles panting for breath while the scorching wind swept around them.'⁹

Heat was killing men in that cauldron as surely as shell or bullet, and scorched and blistered flesh was a more frequent cause of agony than open wound or broken limb. At one moment a light tank was holed and set alight while moving up, but its engine had escaped damage and for some time it waltzed around in the dust of no-man's-land, belching smoke from its turret, a mobile crematorium.

> All day long the battle raged and by evening nothing had been won. As the sun sank, blood-orange and huge behind the minuscule silhouettes of the Panzer Divisions, the firing began to die down, and soon in the twilight the last rounds of the day traced like comets across the battlefield and bounced, high above the haze, into a sky of darkening purple.¹⁰

The British drew back eastwards towards Knightsbridge, the Germans and Italians closer together in their chosen area. During the night the wind died and the dust filtered back to the desert floor; but the fires still burned, the gutted steel hulls glowed with fearful promise for the morrow, and the stench of oil, of death, of anguish lay over the whole area.

This had not been the only battle to be fought on May 29th. On the previous day, Oberstleutnant Westphal, the Operations Chief at Panzerarmee Headquarters, found himself in a situation with which he had become all too familiar during *Operation Crusader* or The Winter Battle as the Germans called it. With Rommel both absent and out of touch, he was forced to act as *de facto* commander of Panzerarmee and, trusting that Rommel would eventually approve, he requested Cruewell to bring heavier pressure to bear on the South African and British infantry in the northern sector, possibly to break through them, but at least to ensure that they could not interfere in the crucial battles being fought to the south. This had had results which would have been ludicrous had they not held the element of tragedy. An officer of the Transvaal Scottish, in the line just north of Alam Hamza, described what happened to the Italian soldiers on the morning of the 29th:

In the dawn a great murmur of talking and shouting arose from the enemy positions, which in the dim light were revealed as within 400 yards of our own. We were aghast at such folly. Transport and gun limbers stood well dispersed between the Battalion and the Cape Town Highlanders. The red scars of freshly turned earth and the white blur of rocks in regular lines marked the enemy positions up the entire length of the depression.

A mortar opened fire. The bomb burst under the nose of a troop carrier. Then as one man, hundreds of Italians rose to their feet and, clear and obvious in the morning sun, began to advance down the valley. Through my glasses I watched them approach us and saw the sun flash on their steel. The ground in front and around them began to flick up in clouds of dust; the rattle of machine-guns broke the amazed silence in which we stood. The artillery and mortars opened fire. Gaps appeared in the ranks but still they came on. Of a sudden the ranks wavered and broke, weapons were dropped and the valley was filled with panic-stricken men running for their lives. Hundreds of them wheeled in ragged formation and made up the hillside towards the Cape Town Highlanders, where they halted and broke again before withering fire. Those in front came towards us, racing like hares between the shell bursts, weaving and dodging, running and falling; then in blind panic turning away and fleeing towards the western mouth of the depression, where furious shelling between them and safety turned them back towards us again.

The whole depression shook and echoed to the crash of high explosive and smoke drifted in thick clouds over the face of the battlefield. It was fascinating to watch the enemy rushing in mad fear up and down, too crazed to know where to run. Scores of them running uphill would disappear into the smoke of previous salvos and appear again through the smoke only to run into the yellow dust and black clouds of fresh explosions. The action could not have lasted more than a quarter of an hour before the order was given to cease fire. Scores of men in their yellowish Italian khaki came towards us waving scraps of white cloth and holding their hands high above their heads . . . [11]

Over 400 men and 13 Italian officers were taken prisoner, and one of the officers had with him their operational map – a sketch of the country between Tmimi and Tobruk with hardly a sign of the Gazala positions anywhere. Their feelings of bewilderment and surprise must have been akin to those of the British and South African 2nd Echelon troops caught in Rommel's first Dash to the Wire during the *Crusader* battles, but at least these had had lorries and trucks to take them away from the danger area.

But not all of Group Cruewell's efforts had been so ill-fated, and although none of the South African or 50th Division defences had been breached, Italian engineers had managed to gap quite deeply into the minefields along the line of the Trig Capuzzo, and so by the evening of the 29th, Rommel had two narrow paths through which supplies could be brought for his concentrating armour and of which, because

of the battle they had fought that afternoon, they were already again
in need.

By this time he had of course abandoned the first *Venezia* objective of reaching the coast and then turning to obliterate the enemy
infantry in their defence lines. Despite its dispersion the British
armour had proved too strong for this to be achieved, so for the
moment he intended to mass all his strength in the middle of the
enemy positions with its back to the enemy minefields, and to
complete the iron ring around it with an impenetrable anti-tank
screen along its northern, eastern and southern flanks, using the
massed artillery and anti-tank guns of all his armoured and motorised
divisions. He would then employ his infantry and engineers to open
wide gaps in the minefields immediately to the west, around Got el
Ualeb, and through these gaps he could order forward the fuel,
ammunition, food and water for the next stage of his offensive which,
with his armour rested and reorganised, would be a break-out either
to the north to deal with the enemy infantry in the defence lines or to
the south to deal with the Free French at Bir Hacheim. After which,
the main thrust would be mounted – due east to shoulder aside the
British armour and break into Tobruk.

During the night of May 29th/30th, therefore, the orders were
drafted, the men briefed, the remaining petrol and ammunition
allocated in accordance with immediate needs, and at dawn the
formations began the final moves towards their operational positions;
and it was during this process that Rommel learned for the first time

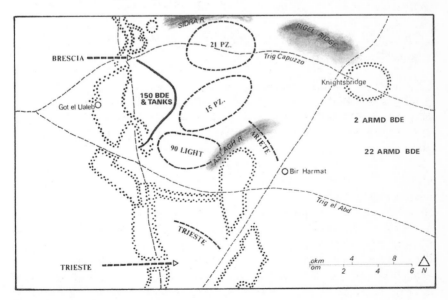

Map 13   May 29th, evening

of the existence of the 150th Brigade Group box between the Trig Capuzzo and the Trig el Abd, reinforced by thirty infantry tanks from 1st Army Tank Brigade, sitting solidly across his proposed supply route and presenting an immovable obstruction to any attempts to reach the minefield or break through to the west.

As it happened, Cruewell had found out about the 150th Brigade on the previous afternoon. Flying across the area in a Storch in an attempt to find Rommel, he had been shot down and taken prisoner. Early summer 1942 had been a bad time for him; his young wife had died while he had been on leave and his last memory of his homeland for many years would be her funeral.

Brigadier C. W. Haydon, commanding 150th Brigade, had been aware of the potential danger in which his command lay ever since the arrival of the German panzers in the area just behind him, and since the evening of May 28th, he had watched that danger develop. He had therefore drawn back the battalion holding the southern section of the position during that evening (it had been harassing the Trieste engineers working in the minefield) and set his entire force to work on slit-trenches and gun-pits from which they could defend themselves from the coming storm. Fortunately, the brigade's regiment of Field Artillery – the 72nd – had recently become adept at resiting its 25-pounders and new 6-pounder anti-tank guns at short notice (for it had been obvious from the start that all-round defence would be needed) and as 150th Brigade consisted almost entirely of men from the mining and ship-building towns of the Tyne and Tees, the digging was done quickly and efficiently and the defences would be manned with a spirit of dogged determination unlikely to waver whatever the odds.

But of course, no infantry brigade armed as they then were could be expected to hold static positions for long against a heavy armoured attack – especially when the main minefield defences were behind instead of in front – and it was evident that Haydon's men could not stem the onslaught alone; reinforcements must be sent in and diversionary attacks mounted against Rommel's armour from the flank or rear as soon as possible. One earnest of the first was the welcome arrival of the Matildas of 44th R.T.R. the following afternoon (29th), though the expected return to the brigade of a store of 25-pounder ammunition – removed from them by a censorious Tobruk quartermaster before the battle on the grounds that they had accumulated more than their allocation – did not materialise. The ration per gun thus remained at twenty-five rounds per day.

As for the second – the diversionary attacks – General Lumsden sent in words of encouragement and even announced to his staff that with Rommel's armour penned against the 150th Brigade box, Eighth

Army 'had him boiled' – and indeed it was obvious that if continuous and concentric attacks could now be mounted against the Afrika Korps, its fate would be sealed as soon as its fuel and ammunition ran out. With this in mind the officers and men of 4th East Yorkshire Battalion and the 4th and 5th Green Howards of 150th Brigade settled down to what they knew would be a tough fight, but one in which they were sure that the High Command would see that they were adequately supported.

The first probing attacks against them began during the morning of May 30th as Afrika Korps engineers moved up and began lifting the hastily sewn mines. There was a brisk skirmish between the opposing groups of sappers followed by a rush by German infantry, and then the rest of the morning was occupied by a battle between the Matildas and the German artillery, as the former tried to regain the ground lost. It was only partially successful, but all positions were held during the afternoon against growing but sporadic pressure, and as soon as darkness fell aggressive patrolling began in order to prevent night-time intrusion by the Afrika Korps across the new minefields.

General Ritchie's evening message of 'Well done!' was received impassively by the troops, who had begun to wonder if he knew they were there. So far as they could see, there had been little sign of further reinforcement that day, or of diversionary activity to take the pressure off their hard-pressed front.

In this they were uncharitable. Under the personal direction of General Lumsden, the 9th Lancers had attacked the Afrika Korps positions along the Bir Aslagh Ridge in both morning and afternoon, and in the later attack they had been supported by a squadron of the 3rd County of London Yeomanry and a heavy artillery bombardment by nearly sixty guns, including a number of 25-pounders. Unfortunately, after the first attack the Lancers had only eleven Grants and four cruisers left and the C.L.Y. squadron was not up to strength – so the total armoured strength flung against Rommel's anti-tank screen could hardly be called massive; and the artillery shoot for the second attack had been mistimed, the guns running out of smoke before the tanks reached the ridge from which their close assault was due to be launched, and as a result they were shot to pieces long before they closed. As they were facing an anti-tank screen consisting of ninety guns and including several 88mms the result was hardly surprising; but according to their regimental history, General Lumsden, who had been present for most of the time, thought they had done jolly well.

As for the rest of XXX Corps armour, one regiment of 4th Armoured Brigade Group spent the day attacking unidentified enemy units in the Bir Harmat area, while the rest went down towards Bir Hacheim where thirty panzers and a German repair workshop had been reported. They found neither, but during that day and the next rounded up nearly sixty vehicles and two hundred prisoners from supply columns still down in the area and presumably lost. Doubtless Eighth Army would be glad to receive the extra transport, but the energy used in capturing it was doing little to relieve the plight of 150th Brigade.

But they were not forgotten elsewhere. About 2045 that evening, a column left the Knightsbridge box consisting of a battery of R.H.A., a company of infantry and two troops of 6-pounder anti-tank guns – with what specific object it is difficult to ascertain at this remove – and drove westwards along the Trig Capuzzo until they bumped into the section of the anti-tank screen held by 21st Panzer Division. The survivors returned to Knightsbridge in the early hours, leaving behind them 157 of their companions, five 25-pounders and seven 6-pounders; but at least some of the Green Howards in the northern section of the pocket must have heard the noise of battle and had their hopes lifted, however briefly.

As for activity on their behalf at command level, Ritchie had spent many hours that day consulting with his corps commanders in order to arrive at the best decision, and had almost come to the conclusion that the right course to follow would be a break-out south-westwards by infantry from Gott's XIII Corps in conjunction with a drive around Bir Hacheim by the mobile elements of Norrie's XXX Corps, to put them all astride Rommel's communications and also in an excellent position from which to exploit towards Benghasi and Tripoli once the Afrika Korps had been liquidated. Of course, most of XXX Corps's armour would also have to stay east of the 'Cauldron' for the moment, just in case Rommel broke out towards Tobruk.

But by the evening of May 30th the extent of the casualties suffered by his armour during the day had convinced Lumsden that the only hope of mounting a worthwhile attack on the Afrika Korps by XXX Corps armour lay in infantry attacks against the anti-tank screens followed by mine-lifting by the engineers, after which the tanks could go through. With this analysis both Norrie and Ritchie agreed, and it was felt that such an attack should take place during the next night – that of May 31st/June 1st – by infantry from 69th Brigade attacking Sidra Ridge from the north where they had been lying in the line next to 150th Brigade, and by 10th Indian Infantry Brigade (held so far in Eighth Army reserve) from the east, heading for the Aslagh Ridge and the scene of 9th Lancers' recent set-back. Briefings and movement orders should be prepared as early as possibly the next morning, and issued to the formations concerned before noon. What might be happening to the men of 150th Brigade in the meantime seems hardly to have been mentioned.

Dawn on May 31st had in fact brought them stand-to in their rifle and machine-gun pits, then, astonishingly, a formal summons to surrender from Rommel which was equally formally rejected by Brigadier Haydon. There followed a sharp but heavy artillery bombardment and an attack by 90th Light infantry who had moved up under the barrage to just within bombing range. The next hour was one of tough small-arms fighting which never reached actual hand-to-hand combat as the attackers were held back from the line of skilfully camouflaged slit-trenches, and at about 0800 the two sides briefly drew apart and watched each other for the next moves.

These came an hour later with mixed German infantry and panzer attacks which finally lost momentum in the face of fire from the new 6-pounders and some Bofors anti-aircraft guns, but not until they had overrun some of the forward positions held by the East Yorkshire companies; and from then on the fighting never really stopped until darkness came and the two sides fell away from each other in sheer exhaustion.

By this time the East Yorkshire positions had all gone and the survivors were back in the two main defence lines held by the Green Howard battalions, some of the 25-pounders and Bofors had been captured or put out of action, and those left were desperately short of ammunition. There was no message from Ritchie that evening, perhaps because he felt that the only real news he had for the troops was that the projected night infantry attack on the Sidra and Aslagh Ridges had had to be postponed yet a further twenty-four hours, as neither of the corps commanders felt capable of mounting and following up such a radical departure from previous plans in so short a time.

But if Ritchie felt unable to do more about the situation in which 150th Brigade now found themselves, Rommel was about to take very drastic action. During the afternoon he had been approached by one of Afrika Korps's prisoners, Major Archer-Shee of 10th Hussars, with the complaint that the water-ration for those captured so far had been half a cup per day, and Rommel replied that this was all anybody in the Cauldron – German, Italian or British – was getting. 'But', he added, 'I quite agree that we cannot go on like this. If we don't get a convoy through tonight I shall have to ask General Ritchie for terms. You can take a letter to him for me . . .'[12]

But some supplies did get through along the narrow passages, and Rommel knew that June 1st would be the decisive day. He ordered the mounting at first light of the heaviest possible Stuka attack on the 150th Brigade positions followed immediately by massed panzer and infantry onslaughts, and at one crucial moment took personal command of the leading infantry platoon – possibly the first time a military formation of so small a size was taken into action by so high-ranking an officer.

'The encircled enemy,' says the Battle Report of the Panzerarmee, 'supported by numerous infantry tanks, resisted stubbornly . . . Each separate point within the fortress-like, strengthened defences had to be fought for. The positions had to be taken in a hand-to-hand fight for each individual bunker . . . The enemy suffered extraordinarily heavy bloody losses.'[13]

So did the Afrika Korps, and even Rommel's personal staff, for both his Chief of Staff Generalleutnant Gause and his Operations Chief Oberst Westphal were wounded that morning, as had been the new 15th Panzer Division commander, General von Vaerst. *Operation Venezia* was proving almost as expensive of senior officers in its early stages as *Crusader* had towards its conclusion. But the end of 150th Brigade was inevitable in the face of the force thrown against them, and shortly after 1400 the weary gunners fired their last remaining rounds, the infantry smashed their rifles, and three thousand survivors of the brigade group climbed bitterly out of their shelters and raised their hands into the air.

Rommel, still close behind his assault troops, went forward quickly to find and congratulate Brigadier Haydon upon the fight he and his men had put up, but alas, the brigadier was dead, killed by a shell-burst during the morning; and Rommel's sincere regret was only equalled by the scorn he expressed for an organisation which could place brave men in such a position, and then do so little to help them. The fact that it could nevertheless spare time and thought to evacuate Cruewell from the area before the battle developed, did nothing to change his opinion.

But in fact Ritchie had not been idle and was expecting the full burgeoning of his plans that very night. With the brigade group from XIII Corps attacking the northern Sidra Ridge and the one from 5th Indian Division attacking the eastern Aslagh Ridge, a concentric attack on Rommel's forces in the Cauldron could begin about midnight, to which 150th Brigade's contribution should be a break-out to the east – and as it was not until the following morning that he became aware of the flaws in his planning, he was able to spend the rest of June 1st exuding an air of calm confidence.

'Ritchie', according to General Messervy writing at a later date and perhaps with some of the inestimable benefits of hindsight, 'was rather stupidly optimistic in remarks and demeanour, though uncertain beneath it all. He was always saying "Ah, now we've got him!" when it was quite clear we hadn't.'[14]

On the afternoon of June 1st Ritchie was unaware not only of the destruction of 150th Brigade, but also that it had been decided at divisional level that 69th Brigade would not after all supply the force for the northern assault; that would come instead from 151st **Brigade**

Group further to the north, who in the event could only supply one battalion for the operation, instead of the brigade which Ritchie expected. As for the attack on Aslagh Ridge, the allotted Indian brigade left Tobruk so late that they could not concentrate in time so General Messervy cancelled that part of the scheme, only informing Norrie after he had done it, a significant indication of the lack of firm control – or even good communications – which existed now in the higher echelons of Eighth Army command.

The single battalion which went into action on the night of June 1st/2nd failed, not surprisingly, to reach even its first objectives.

But General Ritchie gave no sign of being much cast down by these developments, and spent the morning of June 2nd, after the reports had come in, making yet more plans for the destruction of the Afrika Korps, still to his mind penned against the British minefields by the massed guns and armour of XXX Corps, with XIII Corps's infantry poised to the north awaiting the signal from him to sweep down to the south-west and wreck Rommel's entire supply and communications system. Nevertheless, the loss of 150th Brigade could obviously not pass without comment.

'I am much distressed over the loss of 150th Brigade after so gallant a fight,' he assured Auchinleck that afternoon, 'but still consider the situation favourable to us and getting better daily.'[15]

As Auchinleck could see that the situation had now changed dramatically from one in which Eighth Army was surrounding an enemy force in its midst and was strangling it, to one in which it had a wedge driven into its guts by that same enemy force now with open access to its supplies, he was not happy about Ritchie's appreciation and his reply expressed misgiving. He gave Ritchie the benefit of some doubt by suggesting that he must have information not then available to the Commander-in-Chief, but warned his commander in the field against the danger of losing the initiative; and it is some indication of the quality of information reaching Cairo that Auchinleck believed that Ritchie was still in a position to exercise very much.

Ritchie's method of doing so during the days which followed was to hold a long series of committee meetings with his corps and divisional commanders, soliciting their advice and then endeavouring to get them to act upon it before they changed their minds. Dan Pienaar's reception of his idea of an advance south-westward out of their bastion by the South Africans had been, not altogether surprisingly, so irredeemably negative that, on the morning of June 3rd, the commander of the reserve 5th Indian Division, Major-General Briggs, was called forward and asked if he could carry out the attack instead at short notice, through the South African positions.

'My answer was in shape of an alternative,' wrote Briggs later. 'I suggested a desert move around the south of Bir Hacheim on to Tmimi and Rommel's L. of C. . . . This was agreed to by both Ritchie and Gott.'[16]

So Briggs went away to draw up the necessary orders, but while he was away the logistic difficulties of the idea became apparent and when he came back the whole plan had been changed, on Messervy's suggestion, to a frontal attack on Rommel's positions in the Cauldron on the assumption that, with more time available for planning and preparation, the original scheme of pincer attacks from Sidra and Aslagh Ridges was more feasible. As this solution had the advantage of not leaving Tobruk uncovered, Ritchie preferred it – but Gott considered it too reminiscent of the catastrophic infantry advances of the First World War and actually refused to participate; and such was the atmosphere now reigning at Eighth Army Headquarters that Ritchie accepted Gott's refusal and handed responsibility for the operation to Norrie – who in turn passed it on to Briggs and Messervy, only one of whom had any faith at all in the plan.

It is thus hardly surprising that *Operation Aberdeen*, launched during the night of June 4th/5th, 1942, proved one of the more lamentable fiascos to attend British arms during the North African Campaign – a campaign which between the end of the O'Connor offensive and the Second Battle of Alamein was hardly distinguished by any high, or even acceptable, degree of generalship.

The opening artillery bombardment intended to clear the way for the first stage of the infantry advance towards the Aslagh Ridge crashed down on empty ground as, to quote the *Official History*, 'the enemy's defensive positions lay further to the west than had been thought,' with the result that when the Grants, Stuarts and Crusaders of 22nd Armoured Brigade moved up through the advancing infantry, they ran into the concentrated fire of the waiting (and watching, for no attempt at deception or surprise had been made) German artillery and anti-tank screen, which exacted its usual toll of casualties and caused the survivors to sheer off to the north. A German panzer assault then struck up towards Bir et Tamar, and having shouldered the armour aside went on to attack dispersed infantry positions beyond, and the armour – *believing themselves to have been absolved by divisional orders from all responsibility for the infantry* – made no attempt to help. Needless to say, the infantry positions were lost and those men not killed or captured retired in disarray behind the start lines. Meanwhile, in the northern attack down towards Sidra, 32nd Army Tank Brigade had run on to an unexpected minefield under the guns of the anti-tank screen along the ridge, losing fifty of its seventy Matildas before extricating itself. In the words of von Mellenthin who watched it, 'From the tactical point of view this was one of the most ridiculous attacks of the campaign.'

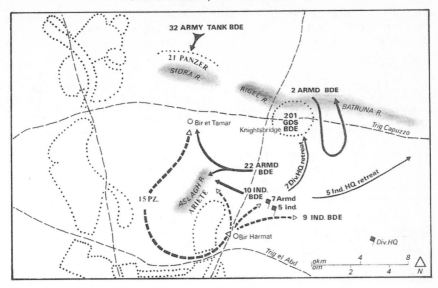

Map 14 June 5th

The situation resulting from all this is cogently epitomised in **the** *Official History*:

> The unpleasant turn taken by the battle was soon realised at the Tactical Headquarters of the 7th Armoured and the 5th Indian Divisions, but each was occupied by its own problems and there was nobody in sole command to concert their actions.[17]

So much for Auchinleck's directive that co-ordination should be assured at all levels. Even the concept of the 'brigade group' had gone by the board now, as old habits and attitudes surfaced under pressures of a battle fought without firm control at any level, and confusion at the top.

At this point, Rommel took a hand. He led 15th Panzer Division down through a gap in the minefields south-west of Bir Harmat, hooked up to the north, scattered two battalions of the 9th Indian Brigade which were being held in reserve together with those members of 10th Indian Brigade who had managed to extricate themselves from the Cauldron, then overran the headquarters of both brigades and the Tactical Headquarters of 7th Armoured and 5th Indian Divisions, driving Messervy into the Knightsbridge box and Briggs back to El Adem. Still trapped inside the Cauldron were three Indian battalions and four artillery regiments, who with dwindling hope settled down to one of those 'last round, last man' battles now fast becoming an accepted hazard of desert fighting for Eighth Army infantry.

And all the time the Grants and Stuarts of 2nd Armoured Brigade were assembled east of Knightsbridge, moving backwards and forwards in response to a number of orders which eventually cancelled each other out:

> No help reached the doomed units in the Cauldron, for although the 2nd and 4th Armoured Brigades had been placed under General Messervy, who was now in sole command, he was unable in the prevailing confusion to bring them to action.[18]

Beneath this chilly pronouncement by the Official Historian lies another unavoidable conclusion. In the hollow aridity of command at the higher levels of Eighth Army during the opening days of June 1942, even men of the calibre of Gott and Norrie were being emasculated, and losing not only their determination but also confidence in themselves.

This was to have highly significant effects everywhere. One young Hussar officer who had been partly responsible for the accidental death of Brigadier 'Jock' Campbell, one of the heroes of the early desert fighting, was now endeavouring to get himself killed in order to expiate his misfortune (he failed, but in doing so won for himself as a junior officer the Distinguished Service Order, three Military Crosses, the French Croix de Guerre and the American Legion of Merit) and was commanding a small composite force during *Aberdeen*. Many years later, he wrote of those days:

> Then began certain miscalculations by the Generals, which turned victory into defeat. I do not know what other facts have come to light, but no soldier who fought in that battle can ever excuse those highranking officers who at the time were damned but have since been resurrected.[19]

If a regular officer of a famous cavalry regiment could feel like this, the effect of the uncertainty of command upon the ranks of enrolled civilians, unaffected by bonds of professional loyalty and sceptical anyway of military competence at any level, was likely to be profound. And lack of confidence in June was unlikely to be cured in July or in August; and would be very difficult to restore even by November.

Needless to say, one person who was not losing confidence was Rommel, who, with his centre now free, was concentrating on clearing the French from his southern flank:

> As I had foreseen, the British command had decided against committing any major force from the two divisions in the Gazala line to form a second point of pressure on the 21st Panzer Division. Nor had any units of the 2nd South African Division been committed. In a moment so decisive they should have thrown in all the strength they could muster. What is the use

of having overall superiority if one allows one's formations to be smashed piece by piece by an enemy who, in each separate action, is able to concentrate superior strength at the decisive point?

After this British defeat we no longer expected any major relieving attack on our forces around Bir Hacheim, and hoped to get on with our assault undisturbed.[20]

His hopes were justified. Except for columns raiding his supplies up in the north (where Sergeant Quentin Smythe won South Africa's first Victoria Cross of the Second World War), and harassing tactics by the recovered 7th Motor Brigade Group down in the south, the only efforts made by Eighth Army to hinder Rommel's attacks on the besieged Frenchmen were to be the organisation of some supplies (which 7th Motor Brigade took in) and a stream of exhortatory messages sent from Ritchie to Koenig.

Since June 2nd, Bir Hacheim had been subjected to increasingly heavy Stuka attacks, though these had at least been fought off to good effect by the R.A.F., presented at last with an area in which friendly positions were clearly demarcated from those of the enemy, and in which they could thus attack ground forces as well. Moreover, so deeply and skilfully had the French worked on their defences that they were at first almost invulnerable to Stuka bombing, for the ground was so hard that anything but a direct hit on a slit-trench or dug-in position wasted its energy on the desert air.

But at daybreak on June 3rd, it became evident that both Italian and German forces (Trieste and 90th Light) were closing in and shelling began from German 105mm. guns which the French could not reach with their 75mms. Shortly afterwards a message was brought from Rommel by two English soldiers who had been taken prisoner, requesting the surrender of the fort in order to save blood, and pointing out the fate of 150th Brigade; but Koenig refrained from answering this, instead warning his men that their time of ordeal was approaching and reminding them that the eyes of the world were on them – as, indeed, they were.

The event had a fitting sequel. Early on the morning of June 5th after forty-eight hours of heavy and continuous bombardment, a German truck drove up under a white flag to one of the outposts held by the 2nd Battalion of the Foreign Legion, and the officer demanded a parley. As luck would have it, the sentry he approached was a German himself, and was thus able to express the garrison's opinion of the suggestion with considerable force; at which the officer drove off in high dudgeon, only to have his vehicle blown up on a mine within a few yards. To derisive shouts from the onlookers, he and his driver leapt clear of their blazing truck and retired rapidly on foot, and for a few more days the garrison was subjected only to more bombing and shelling.

But the ring around Bir Hacheim was now closing, and with *Operation Aberdeen* so clearly a German victory Rommel could move heavier forces down to deal with this thorn in his southern flank. Elements from 15th Panzer came down, together with the whole of the Hecker Group which had been intended to carry out the sea-borne attack behind Pienaar's positions but had never been used. Through the thick fog which blanketed the area at dawn on June 8th, the French could hear the rattle of tank tracks and the shouts of infantry moving up for attack.

It came at 0800 with German heavy artillery – still well outside the range of any counterbattery fire the French could bring to bear – putting down a heavy concentration on one sector in the north-west, while Stukas screamed in overhead and Me 109s swept in at low level, machine-gunning batteries and observation posts. Then just before 1000, a combined panzer and infantry attack drove in upon the dazed and shaken defenders, aiming for one of the low rises along the perimeter from which, in such uniform surroundings, they would hold a dominant position.

All through the midday period under the scorching June sun, the battle was fought out between the German panzers and the infantry from Chad and the Congo of the Bataillon de marche de l'Oubanghi, with the French Colonial losses mounting all the time, although just behind them the Bren carriers of the Legion waited to rush reinforcements forward if the line broke. Sixty Stukas delivered another concentrated attack in the early afternoon, Kleeman's infantry rushing forward before the last plane had gone or the dust settled; and by now the whole of the northern front was under attack, a dense cloud shrouding the entire fort, and as the signal lines had been ripped apart, Koenig was unable either to communicate with his forward positions or even to see them. Many of the anti-tank guns were hit or captured, at least one 25-pounder had been smashed to shapeless metal and its crew killed, and then a chance German shell landed on an ammunition dump and the resulting flash and roar obliterated all other impressions for several vital minutes. By the time night fell, the line, though not broken, had been pushed back and was badly bent.

By now, medical services were breaking down as the casualties mounted and supplies of everything from drugs and anaesthetics to water for washing the wounds ran out; and an attempt by the R.A.F. to drop supplies was unsuccessful as the parachute failed to open and the precious contents of the pack smashed to pieces on the rock-hard ground.

Yet the morale of the garrison remained high – perhaps because of the severity of their ordeal, and because of the fame they knew their efforts were garnering. London, Berlin, New York and Paris –

especially Paris – were watching this epic in the desert, which had become far more than just a fight for the junction of a few meandering desert tracks. A nation whose military tradition had been the main bulwark of her self-esteem was praying for a miracle which would refurbish her badly tarnished reputation.

Tuesday, June 9th, was another day of scorching sun and mounting thirst. Throughout the previous night the attacking forces had kept up the chatter of machine-guns, the thump of mortar fire and the wide, white glare of Very lights and parachute flares; the defenders were now very tired. Red-rimmed eyes peered from sunken eye-sockets over lined and unshaven cheeks, watching for the assault which would come, almost automatically, as soon as the light grew and the mist thinned.

High explosive first – bomb and shell to blast the gun-pits, to cut again the communication lines, to bury the infantry in choking dust; and then the clanking panzers with the racing, dodging, chunky figures of panzergrenadiers close behind. By midday the line was bending again, more 75mms and another 25-pounder had been smashed, and the Bofors guns manned by British gunners were almost out of ammunition. In one particularly vicious bout of hand-to-hand fighting, the attackers were shot down only yards from a battery.

In the southern sector, too, the pressure was growing all the while as more 90th Light infantry moved around after relief by 15th Panzer; and Rommel was himself on the scene now, urging his troops forward, watching for signs of weakness – but not finding any.

> Continuously exposed to the fire of the French, who fought grimly to the end, our storming parties suffered grievous casualties. However, by eight o'clock that night they worked their way forward to within about 220 yards of the Ridotta Bir Hacheim. During the day, Ritchie made a weak diversionary attack against the 90th Light Division's covering units south of Bir Hacheim . . . We had no difficulty in beating it off.[21]

As night fell, a massive Stuka attack came in, hitting the main dressing station and killing some of the wounded, setting fire to a bunch of lorries and destroying practically all the remaining rations. It was obvious that time for the Free French at Bir Hacheim was running out, and the only decision to be made was whether the end was to be total annihilation or an attempt to save something from the holocaust to fight another day.

That afternoon, in contradiction to Ritchie's continual exhortations to hold out, Messervy had signalled asking if Koenig did not now deem it advisable to pull out – to which Koenig replied that if transport could be brought close enough to evacuate his wounded, he was in favour of withdrawal that night – so much in favour, indeed, that that evening he handed over command of the garrison to the colonel of the Foreign Legion detachment, Colonel Amilakvari – and had himself driven out in his staff car by his British girl driver, presumably to press his arguments more closely.

Unfortunately, Messervy could not organise so complicated a manoeuvre in less than twenty-four hours, and the ordeal of the Frenchmen, Poles, Russians, Germans, Africans – and British – thus continued throughout June 10th, with, in Rommel's own words, 'the French desperately defending every single nest of resistance and suffering terrible casualties as a result.' A break-in along the hard-pressed northern sector was contained again by the Legionnaires, in the early afternoon the heaviest air attack of the siege dropped 130 tons of bombs upon the shrunken circle of the fortress, and by evening the last rounds of mortar-bombs had been fired off, the last issue of shells made, and men were going from body to body collecting all that remained of the garrison's small-arms ammunition.

As darkness closed in, a small group of French engineers worked their way out towards the western minefield and began clearing a narrow passage on this, the most unlikely side for a break-out to be attempted. All equipment which could not be moved was prepared for destruction, the most important and secret papers collected into a briefcase and taken in charge by a senior officer who knew exactly what to do to them if danger threatened their capture; and two companies of infantry were detailed to remain behind to maintain the appearance and noise of defence while the rest of the garrison crept away.

As always, there were difficulties and mistakes. With the men so exhausted, it took longer than expected to load up, and in the dark trucks went astray and at least one gun and limber fell into a trench and had to be left. But at 2030, the head of the procession – the ambulances and trucks full of wounded, with walking wounded staggering along between them – felt its way through the narrow lane, and turned south to where the guns, trucks and additional ambulances brought up by the faithful 7th Motor Brigade were waiting. Behind them German artillery had set fire to other trucks, and the flames lit the arid desert scene with garish light.

Then things began to go wrong. The besiegers realised what was happening and machine-gun fire chattered on all sides; heavy artillery opened up and shells crashed on the abandoned defences while parachute flares floated down to add whiteness to the nightmare scene.

The guide for the headquarter column missed his way and was blown up three times on unexpected minefields (and lived to tell the tale!) and when Amilakvari eventually caught up with the main body he found it held up by a strong group of 90th Light infantry. As there was nothing for it now but to smash a way through, he gave the necessary orders and two promising officers, Capitaine de Lamaze and Lieutenant Dewey, led and were killed during the desperate foray which ensued.

But they won through. By 0500, the wounded were well on their way, first to Bir el Gubi and then to Gasr el Arid, and by 0700 on June 11th, 1,500 of the garrison had been brought to safety – a number considered disappointing at the time, especially as Koenig himself was unaccountably absent. But by nightfall he had arrived and so had another thousand of his men, and they were still coming in. In the end even some members of the two companies left in the fortress managed to escape and walk back to British lines, and the final count came to nearly 2,700 of the 3,600 who had fought off the first attack by the Ariete on the morning of May 27th, though a large proportion of them were wounded and many would never fight again.

They had left behind them a great deal of equipment – Rommel later claimed the capture of twenty-five guns and several hundred vehicles – and also a reputation. As von Mellenthin put it, 'In the whole course of the desert war, we never encountered a more heroic and well-sustained defence.'

France's honour, so bedraggled after the events of 1940 in the homeland and in 1941 in Syria, had begun its long slow march towards redemption.

It has been said that the French stand at Bir Hacheim 'won valuable time for Ritchie'.

It cannot be claimed that he put it to much use. He had spent a great deal of time visiting and talking to his corps commanders, and on June 4th had written a long memorandum to Auchinleck setting out his appreciation of the situation and his plans for the future, but despite the fact that by then three days had elapsed since the destruction of 150th Brigade opened the wide gap through which Rommel's supplies and reinforcements were pouring, he could still write, 'We must regard the Gazala–Hacheim line as our "Frontier Defences" – the firm base for all future operations until Cyrenaica is secured.'[22]

The fact that Auchinleck replied to it in all seriousness on June 9th (by which time *Operation Aberdeen* had been seen by those on the spot for the fiasco it was and Bir Hacheim was under strong siege) again reveals the quality of information being retailed to Cairo – all of it, even when accurate, first filtered through Ritchie's mind – still so irredeemably optimistic that after Bir Hacheim had fallen he claimed 'our withdrawal from Hacheim releases enemy forces but I think it releases more of ours.'

It was, of course, true that Eighth Army strength in men and armour on June 11th was still, on paper, greater than Rommel's. Of the seven infantry brigades in the line when the battle had opened, five had hardly been engaged, two South African brigades in Tobruk were still intact and two new Indian infantry brigades – the 11th from 4th Indian Division in Egypt, and the 20th from 10th Indian Division in Iraq – had moved up into the battle area. As for armoured strength, Ritchie's estimate of what was left to him was high, but nevertheless Lumsden and Messervy between them did still command 185 cruiser tanks including quite a large number of Grants, and Willison's 32nd Army Tank Brigade still disposed of 63 Matildas and Valentines. Rommel after Bir Hacheim had just over 200 panzers, but of these 85 were either Italian M13s or Panzer 1Is, and it is evident that in Grants and infantry tanks Eighth Army equalled or outnumbered their battlefield equivalents – the Panzer Marks III and IV – and in Crusaders and Stuarts well outnumbered the Axis light tanks.

Endeavours made by Ritchie, however, to urge XXX Corps into more offensive action foundered amid the doubts and dislikes which plagued the armoured command, and all that had been accomplished while the Fighting French were enduring their martyrdom was the disposal of Allied strength in more defensive boxes and lines in which to await Rommel's next attack whenever he cared to make it. The comparison with a flock of sheep awaiting their fate at the fangs of marauding wolves is unavoidable, despite the protestations of aggressive intentions at high levels.

Gott, whose relations with Pienaar had by this time deteriorated to a level below even those between Lumsden and Messervy, had nevertheless been able to prise away from the South Africans two companies of infantry to form a strongpoint at Point 154, east of the 69th Brigade and on the line leading back towards Acroma, and another force to hold Elwet et Tamar three miles further east. The positions held by 69th Brigade itself had also been extended eastwards to Bir Heleisi, while a battalion of British infantry (1st Worcesters) held Point 187 just south-west of Acroma. The Guards Brigade Group still held Knightsbridge but had detached 2nd Scots Guards to the north to hold the pass down the Rigel Ridge, while fifteen miles away to the east lay 29th Indian Brigade Group at El Adem, also with one battalion detached to the north, in this case to guard the pass down the Batruna Escarpment where the Tobruk by-pass crossed it.

The gap between Knightsbridge and El Adem was to be guarded by 22nd and 2nd Armoured Brigades under Lumsden and 4th Armoured Brigade under Messervy, all grouped for the moment around Knightsbridge. Their strength and condition is best described in the *Official History*:

On 10th June General Ritchie estimated that he had about 250 cruiser and 80 'I' tanks fit to fight, though an analysis of unit records suggests that the true figures were: in the three armoured brigades 77 Grants, 52 Crusaders and 56 Stuarts, and in the 32nd Army Tank Brigade 63 'I' Tanks. Attempts to bring the armour up to strength had been most complicated and not very successful, the basic cause being the differences between the three sorts of cruiser tanks. To get the required tank with a suitable crew to the unit that wanted it was not easy. It led to sub-units being combined, or sometimes lent to other units. Even single tanks and crews had to be sent here and there. Regimental organization was disrupted, and the 1st Armoured Brigade, much to its disgust, had been used as a pool of immediate requirements. In fact expediency ruled, and any fairly well-filled till was raided for the benefit of empty ones. Units disliked this policy intensely. They complained also of many defects in their replacement tanks – of missing wireless equipment and of guns arriving rusted or in grease.[23]

The men complained of other matters, too, and very bitterly. Perhaps because of some realisation of the inadequacy of previous methods of replacing strength lost during the battle, some of the survivors of smashed or brewed-up tanks were now gathered together and formed into crews, then sent to 1st Armoured Brigade, where they were ordered back into action with Grants, Stuarts or Crusaders taken from the Greys, whose crews had manned and cared for them for many months during training and who now regarded them with proprietorial affection.

This system ingeniously combined the worst aspects of any method of replacement. The survivors were often suffering from battle shock, needing rest and hoping for escape from a battle in which they had already experienced set-back and were now sensing ultimate defeat. Now they were to go back in, leaving to the comparative safety and ease of the rear areas entire tank crews who were fresh and unscathed. These in their turn were infuriated to see their own tanks upon which they had often lavished great care being driven off to battle by others, with so evident a reflection upon either their own courage or their own ability.

'Why the hell can't you take your own bloody tanks up yourselves?' was a bitter question being asked by exhausted men of angry ones who had just asked their officers the same question but with more personal pronouns – and as their officers could not answer and felt the same way, the anger which men feel in defeat against authority grew rapidly into hatred and contempt.

There was indeed nothing to be said in favour of this system, for in addition to the fury it aroused it did little to solve the main problem of getting inexperienced men into battle under cool and experienced leadership.

Rommel wasted little time at Bir Hacheim. He and Bayerlein spent the early morning of June 11th examining with some interest and admiration the defence system, and issuing instructions for the disposal of the prisoners and all the captured material. They then planned and put into operation the next moves for the advance to the frontier.

These bore strong resemblances to the original *Operation Venezia*, for 90th Light and the Reconnaissance Battalions were ordered east to pass south of El Adem and make for the Escarpment at Ed Duda and the stores dump beyond at Belhammed, while 15th Panzer with Trieste on their left flank were to move north-east through the gap, making for the airfield just to the north of El Adem. Meanwhile, 21st Panzer, who had remained along the Sidra Ridge on the northern flank of the Cauldron, were to demonstrate against the new line of defences in order to nail the Allied infantry firmly into their positions, while Ariete remained on the eastern flank of the Cauldron, guarding the main Axis supply route and facing the Guards Brigade and the British armour concentrated around Knightsbridge.

These moves began in the middle of the afternoon, and by evening had been reported to Norrie by the R.A.F., who had been over the area covering the last stages of the Free French withdrawal. By this time, the 7th Motor Brigade and two columns of Indian infantry were attempting harassing tactics on the outside flank of 90th Light, and 4th Armoured Brigade were moving rather ponderously south-east from Knightsbridge upon an interception course which, however, ended on high ground in an area known as Naduret el Ghesceuasc. It was a location well known to 4th Armoured, and its commander, Brigadier Richards, felt that it gave him a certain dominance over his old opponents of 15th Panzer, who by nightfall had formed a hedgehog a few miles to the south-east, just within long-range shelling distance.

By the following morning, Norrie had studied the maps and, adding up the estimated armoured strengths available to each side, had come to the conclusion that if the 17 Grants and 28 light tanks of 2nd Armoured Brigade from Lumsden's division were added to the 39 Grants and 56 Stuarts from Messervy's division with Richards at Ghesceuasc, they should be able to inflict considerable damage upon the 64 mixed Panzers III and IV reported opposite them, especially if they attacked in flank and from higher ground. The 27 Grants and 39 light tanks with 22nd Armoured Brigade, reinforced by Willison's 63 mixed Matildas and Valentines, should be ample to keep 21st Panzer and Ariete in check.

This not unreasonable plan was defeated by the ever-present personal antagonisms at the top, and by something akin to churlish disobedience at lower levels, which had of course been affected by

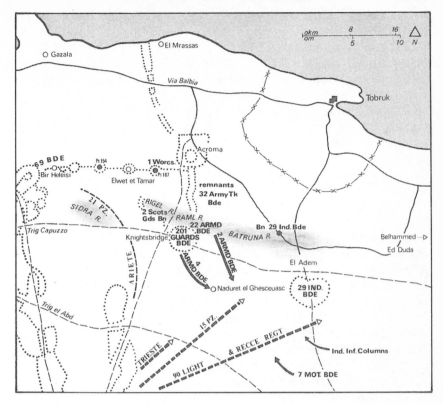

Map 15   June 11th, evening

the attitudes of the divisional commanders. Lumsden as usual was loth to hand over one of his brigades to Messervy, who in turn wished to concentrate his division – now split in half by Rommel's move – by sending 4th Armoured Brigade around behind 15th Panzer, 'regaining the open desert' and joining 7th Motor Brigade well away to the south, from which position they could harry any further advances towards the frontier. But neither the commander of his own brigade nor the one commanding the brigade reluctantly released to him by Lumsden were in agreement with this, the first because he had no wish to leave the Ghesceuasc area for which he seems to have formed a strong attachment, and the second because he wished to return to 1st Armoured command; so after a certain amount of acrimony, Messervy left to find Norrie and discuss the whole matter further.

En route he was nearly caught by flank patrols of one of Rommel's reconnaissance battalions, and was forced to spend the rest of the day hiding in a disused well while both 2nd and 4th Armoured Brigade commanders waited in chilly disagreement for further orders.

But not for long. At least one person concerned had broadcast details of the developing row, either in clear or in so ingenuous a code that it could quite easily be broken, and Rommel's intercept service had reported that '4th Armoured Brigade has refused to carry out an attack to the south-east' early enough for him to plan accordingly. Just before noon, 15th Panzer faced north and moved towards the waiting British tanks – but so hesitantly (for fatigue was affecting the German panzer crews and neither Rommel nor Nehring was present) that the attack was held off by the Grants of both 2nd and 4th Armoured, who then remained on their eminence gloomily watching the enemy manoeuvring below and still awaiting orders from either Messervy or Norrie.

These came at noon, by which time Norrie had realised that Messervy was again missing and had placed all the armour in the area under Lumsden. He now ordered 22nd Armoured Brigade down from Knightsbridge to join the others and thus for the first time concentrate all the cruiser tanks in XXX Corps together, but unfortunately for the British, both Rommel and Nehring had moved fast to correct the enervation in the Afrika Korps. With both men driving hard, 21st Panzer came across from the west to hit 4th Armoured in the flank at about the same time that Lumsden was ordering 22nd down from Knightsbridge, and Rommel himself galvanised 15th Panzer into delivering a devastating attack northwards against both 4th and 2nd Armoured.

According to the *Official History*, it is difficult to establish exactly what happened then, as 'The scanty and conflicting records make it impossible to disentangle the details of the ensuing fighting.' But this is surely an official gloss over a lamentable episode in the history of British arms.

Everybody, from the most junior members of the latest tank crews to join 2nd or 4th Armoured Brigades to the brigade commanders themselves, was affected by the atmosphere and situation in which they found themselves. Those of the tank crews who had fought in the battle beforehand were already cynical about the competence of the men directing it, and their unease was quickly transmitted to newcomers; and however ardently the regimental officers might attempt to stem the tide of disillusion, they were themselves only too well aware of the antagonisms and disagreements at brigade and divisional levels, and of the creeping paralysis caused by lack of confidence up in the more exalted spheres of division, corps and army. Sour discontent seethed throughout the two formations and boiled up into hatred, only a portion of which was directed against the enemy.

This was no frame of mind in which to win a battle against or even withstand attack from troops who, however tired they might be, had lately won two tactical victories and whose morale was high. When von

Bismarck's 21st Panzer crashed into 4th Armoured's right flank they knocked out twenty cruisers in less than half that number of minutes, while 15th Panzer's attack from the south met a line of British tanks whose commanders were watching over their shoulders for the moment when those behind might begin falling back, probably without bothering to inform them beforehand.

At first there was not much chance of this, for both brigades soon found themselves surrounded by panzers and – more dangerous still – by their accompanying anti-tank guns, and as no one fights more fiercely than the trapped, the Ghesceuasc area for over an hour was the scene of desperation, flame and fury in which men performed deeds of enormous bravery under the spur of even greater fear. But when Lumsden at last brought 22nd Armoured down from the north these drew off elements of 21st Panzer, thus opening a gap through which the remains of 4th Armoured promptly fled, leaving a large number of their tanks smouldering on the field, and eventually abandoning even the ones in tow. They drove headlong down the steep Raml Escarpment and did not halt until they reached the Tobruk by-pass not far short of the perimeter, by which time they had been reduced to fifteen runners, medium and light.

Meanwhile, both 2nd and 22nd Brigades had also suffered severely, but were at least back together again and under their own commander, Lumsden. He now drew them close and anchored the right flank of 22nd on Knightsbridge, extending the defence line for both brigades back north-east to reach the Raml Ridge, thus forming a shield parallel to the Knightsbridge–Acroma track along which the inhabitants of the box could escape – for it was evident to all that the Guards now held a salient which might easily be flanked on both sides and then pinched out.

Moreover, although it was impossible then to obtain an exact figure for the day's losses, it was evident by nightfall on June 12th that the balance of forces engaged in the Gazala battles had changed irrevocably. Not only would the British and South Africans continue the battle with lowered morale and an ever-decreasing confidence in their leadership at all except the lowest levels, but from now on they would fight with a numerical inferiority in both armour and artillery. Only in infantry would they possess superior numbers, and as five brigades of these were still penned in fixed positions thirty miles to the west and in obvious danger of being cut off, even this advantage might in the end prove an embarrassment.

One final episode on the evening of June 12th pin-pointed the main cause of the British inadequacy. Auchinleck had become increasingly disquieted by apparent contradictions in some of Ritchie's reports, and so had travelled up to Eighth Army Headquarters that day to investigate them. He found the atmosphere there, however, detached and tranquil, and no hint of disaster or even undue emergency reached him during the whole of that traumatic day; reassured, he flew back to Cairo, but before doing so signalled London, in all sincerity and innocence, saying, 'Atmosphere here good. No undue optimism and realities of situation are being faced calmly and resolutely. Morale of troops appears excellent.'[24]

But within a few hours he was facing the possibility of Eighth Army being thrown back to the Egyptian frontier.

On the morning of June 13th, both the British and German forces in and around Knightsbridge were desperately tired. Although the Guards Brigade had not been so fiercely engaged as the British armour, their position had been the focus of a battle which had swirled about them for nearly seventeen days, they had spent the previous night listening to 21st Panzer move back westwards across their southern flank in order to face up towards Rigel Ridge on the west, and they knew that 15th Panzer were already closed up to their north-east on Raml Ridge. Unless the Scots Guards at the Rigel Pass and the remains of Lumsden's and Willison's armour could hold the narrow corridor up to Acroma, the Guards would therefore very soon be facing exactly the same situation as had faced both 150th Brigade and the Free French, and might share the same fate.

An even greater strain, of course, was imposed on those holding the sides of the corridor, and although the first moves by 15th Panzer were those of men just as exhausted as those who watched them, they were unnerving just the same. One of the watchers was an artillery officer who later wrote:

> About a mile away a column was breaking leaguer. As we watched we saw about thirty tanks open out and begin to move towards us, behind them a long column of guns and lorries stretched down to the Trig Capuzzo. It was a horrible sight to see on an empty stomach at such an early hour.[25]

This attack and the first moves by 21st Panzer towards Rigel Ridge were both held off, but in the afternoon the attacks were pressed home more fiercely (as a result, though the men facing them did not know this, of the presence of both Rommel and Nehring). The Scots Guards supported by South African artillery fought grimly to hold the western flank – so grimly indeed that when the last South African gun had been silenced and the survivors taken prisoner, 'The German commander admonished Major Newman for continuing the fight so long, as needless loss of life had been involved' – which was a compliment in itself. On the eastern wing the battle was so severe that by the end of the day 32nd Army Tank Brigade had been reduced to twenty Matildas and Valentines, while the estimated cruiser strength in the three armoured brigades was now down to fewer than fifty; and Lieutenant-Colonel H. R. B. Foote had won the Victoria Cross for continually leading tank charges against heavy odds in a manner reminiscent of Jock Campbell at Sidi Rezegh.

But the end was inevitable, and during the night of June 13th/14th, Knightsbridge was evacuated and the Guards retired to Acroma, an event which gave rise to an unexpected comment by Rommel much later. Although the battle had raged around Knightsbridge for so long, the box had not been directly attacked except during the last twenty-four hours, yet despite this Rommel was to write: 'This brigade was almost the living embodiment of the virtues and faults of the British soldier – tremendous courage and tenacity combined with a rigid lack of mobility.'[26]

Either something had impressed him of which no detailed record was made at the time, or his later experiences with Guards formations coloured his memory.

With the removal of the Knightsbridge salient and the subsequent closing up by the Panzerarmee to the new defence line to the north, it was evident that the infantry still in the Gazala Line must get out – and as the Via Balbia was already within shelling distance of Rommel's guns, the move must be made quickly. As such a withdrawal would signal the beginning of retreat for the Eighth Army, the decision had suddenly to be faced as to where the retreat should stop – a decision within which was bound inextricably the fate of Tobruk.

This was not a matter which had received of late a great deal of thought, though it had received attention and study some time previously. Four and a half months before, Auchinleck had issued to Ritchie as his commander in the field a detailed survey of the overall situation in the area west of the Nile. In the shape of Operational Instruction No. 110, this began with the words, 'My present intention is to continue the offensive in Libya and the objective remains Tripoli' but in its final passages quite rightly considered the course of action to be followed should Rommel prove able to launch a large-scale and subsequently successful offensive.

In the preparation of this section Auchinleck had consulted both Air Marshal Tedder, who felt that his aircraft would be better used over a battlefield than as an umbrella for a besieged port, and Admiral Cunningham, who had stated categorically that with his greatly reduced forces in the eastern Mediterranean, a repetition of the supply problems of Tobruk under another siege would prove so grave an embarrassment for the Royal Navy that the situation might become untenable. As a result two paragraphs in that directive were now about to become highly relevant:

(6) It is not my intention to try to hold permanently Tobruk or any other locality west of the Frontier.

(10) Work will be continued in accordance with the original plans on the El Alamein position as opportunity offers, until it is completed.[27]

Although a copy of this directive went, as a matter of course, to the C.I.G.S. in Whitehall, it seems unlikely that it came to Mr Churchill's attention at that time, for after the nine-month siege of the port in 1941, Tobruk had assumed a symbolic importance in his mind which would have produced violent reaction at any suggestion of future abandonment.

And it should be borne in mind that, whatever the military realities of the local situation, Mr Churchill was not alone in his attitude. The British public at home felt much the same way as their Prime Minister, and so did much larger publics in both Europe and America. Tobruk's fame after 1941 ranked with that of Troy, Gibraltar, the Pekin Legation and Mafeking in the past, and was Britain's pledge to Leningrad in the present. Its defence was irretrievably linked in the public mind with defiance and ultimate Allied victory, and its fall would strike the cracked note of disaster ominously enough to raise a spectre of final defeat.

The fact that its fall was also not seriously considered even on the spot is borne out – paradoxically – by the state of its defences; in June 1942 it was in no condition to withstand a resolute attack. On the eastern side, where O'Connor's original attack had gone in, the anti-tank ditch had been allowed to fill, and many thousands of the mines now sewn in the Gazala defences had originally been buried along the Tobruk perimeter – and removed from that perimeter in the confidence that Tobruk would never again be threatened.

Now, suddenly, the impossibility became a probability, especially in the mind of the commander in the field, buoyantly confident of victory until evidence of heavy defeat stared him in the face, and then – no matter what temporary resurgences of hope might come as the result of conference with his corps commanders – rapidly becoming convinced of the necessity of retreat back into Egypt.

As early as the afternoon of June 13th, Ritchie was suggesting the withdrawal of all the infantry in the Gazala Line, which in turn, in his view, would entail the withdrawal of the whole of Eighth Army to the frontier; but to this, Auchinleck, still with the picture of overall success gathered during his visit to headquarters in his mind, would not agree, instructing him instead to hold the defence positions as they stood – Gazala Line facing westward against the Italian divisions, Alam Hamza to Acroma line facing south against Rommel's armoured divisions, with Norrie's remaining armour shielding the Tobruk south-western perimeter around to El Adem and armoured car units and 29th Indian Infantry Brigade continuing the line down to Bir el Gubi. With the information at Auchinleck's disposal, this was not an entirely untenable position, and having instructed Ritchie to adopt it, he cabled the Prime Minister telling him of the decision – a message to which Mr Churchill replied, 'Your decision to fight it out to the end most cordially endorsed. We shall sustain you whatever the result. Retreat would be fatal. This is a business not only of armour but of will-power. God bless you all.'[28]

There are many accounts of what took place during the following days, mostly written from an objective point of view in which the outlooks from Whitehall, Cairo and the battlefront are all presented, generally at the same time. It is an illuminating exercise to follow the events solely from one point of view, that of the battlefront.

Despite Auchinleck's specific instruction to hold on to all present positions, at 0700 on June 14th Ritchie decided to withdraw the South Africans and 50th Division right back to the Egyptian frontier and told Gott to put the matter in train. At 0900, Ritchie telephoned Auchinleck from Tobruk and during a conversation which the South African historians describe as 'guarded and obscure' told him that the state of the army was such that the Gazala Line could no longer be held – an announcement which Auchinleck again countered by urging him to hang on if humanly possible, saying that he would send one of his staff up immediately to review the situation and report back to him that afternoon.

Nevertheless, at 1020 Ritchie issued not only formal orders to Gott to evacuate the infantry from the Gazala Line, but also to Lumsden to take his own headquarters and the remains of 2nd Armoured and 22nd Armoured Brigades back to the frontier after XIII Corps had withdrawn. He then sent a memorandum to Auchinleck, stating that he had ordered Gott to withdraw the forward infantry 'into Army Reserve' (but not stating where he considered this to be located) and that it was his intention to occupy frontier positions and at the same time build up a strong armoured and infantry force in the desert west of the frontier. He hoped, he said, to hold a line from the western perimeter of Tobruk through El Adem to Belhammed and would rely upon the mobile forces to the south to hold back Rommel's armour, thus keeping open lines of communication to Tobruk. As far as Tobruk itself was concerned, he said that the port had supplies for a month, that he was clearing out inessential services and that he might either have to accept temporary investment of the port or, alternatively, he could 'go the whole hog, give up Tobruk and withdraw to the Frontier. But surely investment would be the better alternative?'

Ritchie then went forward and visited both Gott and Norrie to discuss with them the details for the withdrawals to take place that night, and when he returned to his headquarters at 1600, found a long message from Auchinleck giving him at least one specific and incontrovertible order:

General Auchinleck to General Ritchie　　　　　　　　14th June 1942
　　　　　　　　　　　　　　　　　　　　　　　　　　　　11.30 hrs

1. If in your opinion situation has so deteriorated that you can no longer leave 1st S.A. and 50th Divs in main Gazala positions without certain risk of their being cut off and isolated, then I agree to their withdrawal, undesirable though this is in view of tactical advantage this bastion gives us.
2. While I realise that our armoured forces have been defeated and are now weaker in quantity as well as in quality than those of the enemy, I must stress in my opinion that the enemy, who so far has won all his successes with two German armd and one German motor divs, helped to some extent by one Italian motor div., cannot really be in position to carry out large-scale offensive operations for indefinite period at pace he is doing. He must, I feel, have lost heavily, and we know his ammunition is short. Moreover, we are definitely superior to him in the air.
3. This being so, Tobruk must be held and the enemy must not be allowed to invest it. This means that Eighth Army must hold the line Acroma–El Adem and southwards and all enemy attempts to pass it. Having reduced your front by evacuating Gazala and reorganized your forces, this should be feasible and I order you to do it.
4. If you feel you cannot accept responsibility of holding this position you must say so.[29]

It was perhaps this last paragraph which caused Ritchie the most embarrassment, for having as a result of his past confidence inspired in his superior far too bland a view of the progress of the battle, he was now finding it impossible to bring home the gravity of the situation as he now saw it. Auchinleck's directive to keep Rommel away to the west and south of Tobruk was all very well – but Ritchie had already ordered five infantry brigades and the remnants of two armoured brigades back to the frontier, and he doubted the possibility of altering those orders without engendering the chaos that order and counter-order so often bring about; and he would seem to have been somewhat reluctant about admitting to Auchinleck what he had done.

In this impasse, he reacted in his normal fashion and sought advice from his more experienced subordinates, in this case Gott – and Gott's advice in this instance was coloured by two, and perhaps three, unfortunate disadvantages. First, he was unaware of the deterioration of Tobruk's defences along the south-eastern and eastern flanks of the perimeter and thus still considered it possible for the port to withstand a siege; and secondly, his mind was fully engaged with the problems of extricating the two divisions of his corps from the Gazala Line and getting them back to the Egyptian frontier in accordance with the orders he had been given some ten hours before. Thirdly –

although this is a matter which must remain in the realms of pure conjecture – it is possible that Ritchie did not make it clear to Gott that the Commander-in-Chief was expecting the withdrawal of XIII Corps to stop at Tobruk, so that the two infantry divisions, plus the whole of the remaining XXX Corps armour, would thenceforth be available to hold Rommel's advance along the Acroma–Bir el Gubi line.

Gott's advice was therefore that with the bulk of XIII and XXX Corps back on the frontier, Tobruk's investment was inevitable – but that there was no reason why it should not withstand a siege for at least one and possibly two months. During this time Eighth Army could be thoroughly reorganised in the frontier area with, undoubtedly, considerable reinforcement from such formations as the New Zealand and Australian Divisions, 4th, 5th and 10th Indian Divisions, and 10th Armoured Division now training in the Delta. There was, in Gott's opinion, not the slightest reason to abandon all the permanent installations in Tobruk, or even to set about withdrawing or destroying the huge dumps of supplies stockpiled there for the advance into Cyrenaica. Another siege of Tobruk was inevitable – but the certainty of its successful defence was equally undisputable.

Ritchie's confidence now revived by such forthright encouragement, he returned to his own headquarters and endeavoured to telephone Auchinleck again to obtain permission to allow Tobruk to be invested, but could only speak to one of the Commander-in-Chief's staff officers with whom he left his request. Auchinleck, however, remained adamant, and during the night which followed Ritchie received another directive ordering him to hold the Acroma–El Gubi line and containing this sentence: 'The defences of Tobruk and other strong places will be used as pivots of manoeuvre but on NO account will any part of Eighth Army be allowed to be surrounded in Tobruk and invested there.' It then went on to assure Ritchie that strong reserve forces were being accumulated for him in the Sollum–Maddalena area, and concluded:

> To sum up:
> (a) The general line Acroma–El Adem–El Gubi is to be denied to the enemy.
> (b) Our forces will NOT be invested in Tobruk and your army is to remain a mobile field army.
> (c) The enemy's forces are to be attacked and destroyed as soon as we have collected adequate forces for an offensive.[30]

It would be interesting to know how General Ritchie spent the remainder of the night after receipt of this signal, for he had done nothing to change his original orders to XIII Corps and 1st Armoured Division to withdraw to the frontier, and he did nothing now.

6 · 'A progression of avoidable disasters'

In their superb history of the Sidi Rezegh battles, the South African historians J. A. I. Agar-Hamilton and L. C. F. Turner say about the commander of the 1st South African Brigade at that time, 'It was not Brigadier Pienaar's habit to allow the orders of any superior to pass without thorough examination and discussion . . .'[1] and it was now evident that the recent promotion to major-general had done nothing to modify Dan Pienaar's attitude in such matters. The detailed orders from Eighth Army Headquarters regarding the evacuation of the South African Division from what had been a bastion but had now become an exposed salient were examined – and immediately rejected; and it comes as no surprise to discover that the rejection was thoroughly justified.

According to the staff officer who telephoned General Pienaar early on June 14th (just as coffee was being served to the general and his G.S.O.I.) Ramsden's 50th Division would begin leaving the Gazala Line that evening with a break-out *westwards* through the Italian lines opposite them, while his own South Africans waited throughout the night to lend support as and if 50th Division might need it. Pienaar's men would then evacuate their positions at first light the following morning, June 15th – withdrawing in broad daylight along the narrow coastal strip (indeed, for most of its transport, along the black ribbon of the Via Balbia) unprotected from enemy attack until they reached the Tobruk perimeter twenty-nine miles to the east.

As the events of the night would have warned Rommel that evacuation was in progress, it needed little imagination to foresee the activities of the Luftwaffe and the Afrika Korps (already within shelling distance of the Via Balbia) once the first South African movements had been reported; and if Gott's and Ritchie's staff officers seemed to lack that imagination, Pienaar's own made up for it. Within a very short time the orders were changed and permission given for the South Africans to pull out at the same time as their

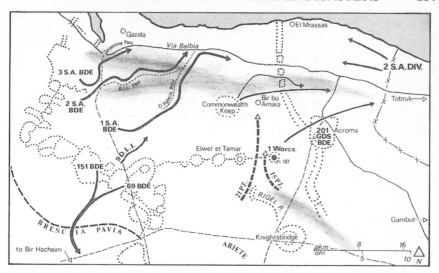

Map 16   Retreat from Gazala, June 14th–15th

neighbours – and so complete was the change of mind at corps headquarters that Pienaar was then instructed that 1st South African's tail must be through the entrance to Tobruk by 0700 the following morning. Moreover, units from 2nd South African Division, assisted by the remnants of 1st Armoured Division, would come out towards them and hold the line of minefields from Mrassas to Acroma, thus covering them for at least the last ten miles of their journey.

Pienaar and his staff wasted no time. From 0930 onwards on June 14th a stream of non-essential vehicles made their way down through the three escarpment passes just behind them – Serpentine Pass, Bill's Pass and El Agheila West Pass – and in the salient itself the dispiriting tasks of destruction began.

> It was heartbreaking to see men picking holes in invaluable 2-gallon water tins, sticking bayonets through tins of bully-beef, cheese and canned fruits, and throwing them down the wadis. Two things, however, the men were determined to take – the Fortress ration of milk and sugar – which stood them in good stead later on. They hurried to where the Fortress reserve of water was kept and filled waterbottles and every available container and then as the sun sank, the Commanding Officer gave the word. The guard peppered the 44-gallon drums with bursts of tommy-gun fire, and the water, that most precious liquid of the desert, ran out over the sand . . . [2]

Speed was obviously essential, but equally obvious was the logistic impossibility of moving the transport of three infantry brigades twenty-nine miles in single file along a narrow road, at regulation speed and with the specified intervals between each vehicle, in the time between sunset on June 14th and 0700 the next day. 1st South African Brigade therefore started moving out early that afternoon, but even so traffic blocks built up at such bottlenecks as the top of Agheila West Pass, and when drivers reached the open road below they tended to stamp on their accelerators and race off in bunches towards their destination. It was not long before enemy eyes were watching the developing chaos and taking steps to increase it.

> Some of the Battalion are down the pass, others still jammed in the bottleneck at the top, when the first Stukas arrive. The trucks at the foot of the pass stop. The men run for cover. At the top, the men fling themselves down beside their trucks. The Stukas scream down . . . into the path of the Bofors fire, up and off. The gun at the foot follows their flight through the murk of explosive smoke. The gun at the top ceases to chatter: dead men hang over it and lie among torn sandbags . . .
> The column jerks forward . . . Stragglers from other units cut in among the Battalion transport and force the pace. As the Battalion vehicles try to regain their places, convoy discipline begins to go; a panicking few are breaking up the disciplined many: each small group of trucks is becoming an isolated unit. On the Tobruk road a continuous stream of traffic heads for the fortress or is directed around it at the junction of the Tobruk and Acroma roads. This road from Gazala to the Acroma Monument is relentlessly machine-gunned and bombed. Trucks blaze. Men run: ambulances howl towards the hospital in Tobruk: dead men lie in blood and oil and broken glass.[3]

East of the passes, Rommel had spent June 14th spurring on the exhausted men of his two panzer divisions in a heroic effort to reach and cut the Via Balbia and thus add the destruction of more South African brigades to his tally of victories. From late morning the panzers and their attached grenadiers had been probing northwards from the Rigel Ridge trying to break through between the South Africans holding Elwet et Tamar and the Worcestershire Regiment at Point 187 and finding themselves held back at first by unexpected and deep minefields and then, as they tried to lift them, by heavy and concentrated shell-fire.

In this they were unfortunate, for the highly effective system of defence they now encountered was only provided in view of the weakness of British armour in the area; had 1st Armoured Division not suffered such heavy losses during the previous few days, they would have been thrown into the battle in a 'tank versus panzer' action and doubtless brushed aside by Rommel's properly co-ordinated armour and artillery – in which case Dan Pienaar's entire division might well have found themselves in dire circumstances. As it happened, in the absence of strong tank formations all the artillery in the area, including that of the Guards Brigade still concentrated around Acroma, was rushed forward and for many hours held the bulk of both 15th and 21st Panzer Divisions back south of the minefield.

During the morning battles the panzers thus made very little headway, but when news of the start of the Gazala evacuation in the afternoon reached Rommel and Nehring, the two began again to flog the Afrika Korps into yet greater efforts, and 21st Panzer were bleakly ordered by Nehring to take the position at Elwet et Tamar by nightfall in such terms that both divisional and regimental commanders knew that their future careers were at stake. Five miles to the east, 15th Panzer had broken into the Worcestershire positions by 1500 but were still being held by the British infantry and their supporting anti-tank guns when the essential weakness of the British position suddenly became evident.

The Worcestershires were under command of 2nd South African Division in Tobruk, the defenders of Elwet et Tamar under Dan Pienaar at Gazala, the Guards artillery were still under their own brigade commander, and what armour there was in the area (and by evening it had been reduced to two Grants and eight Crusaders) was under Lumsden, who, however, had no means of communication with either of the infantry strongpoints. A decision had in fact been taken shortly after noon that the commander of 2nd Armoured Brigade should take charge of all troops in the area, but no one affected by the order learned of it until days afterwards, and it is not surprising therefore that eventually a critical error was made.

Shortly after 1630 a message arrived at the Worcestershire's headquarters which seemed plain enough, though it was, in fact, corrupt. As there was no overriding authority to which to refer, the battalion began a withdrawal in accordance with its apparent instructions, but under such difficult conditions that they lost over two hundred killed, wounded and missing and it was twenty-four hours before the remnants managed to make their way into Tobruk; and in the meantime, 15th Panzer had overrun Point 187 and pushed on towards Acroma, while on their left 21st Panzer were coming through the gap and aiming for the main objective for the day – Commonwealth Keep.

By nightfall, they were at Bir bu Amaia on the Escarpment just to the east of the Keep, the entire British and South African defence line had been outflanked, the Via Balbia was just below and well within sight and striking distance, and the escape of Pienaar's division and all other troops still between Gazala and the Afrika Korps apparently cut off.

But even Afrika Korps flesh and blood could only stand so much.

That night the exhausted crews of the Panzer Divisions lay in the desert outside Acroma, with nothing between them and the crowded Via Balbia, but they did not stir for all the urgent signals of their Commander-in-Chief, who saw clearly enough that the prize of the Gazala garrison was slipping out of his grasp. When the little force at Commonwealth Keep (Point 209) scrambled down the escarpment in retreat their transport had perforce to make for Acroma direct and trundled past a mass of sleeping Germans on the way. The South Africans politely refrained from disturbing the strangers and were allowed to pass without even a challenge.[4]

While the Afrika Korps slept, XIII Corps escaped. Ramsden had instructed the commanders of his two remaining 50th Division brigades to begin the break-out to the west as soon as darkness allowed, and by 2000 one battalion from each brigade supported by artillery and engineers had gone forward to open the passages through the minefields opposite them, and then through any fixed positions the Italians might decide to hold against them. The actions fought that night by 5th Battalion East Yorks and by the 8th Durham Light Infantry, cloaked at first by dust-storms and then by nightfall, were brisk, violent, and entirely successful – and through the gaps they tore in lines held mainly by the Brescia Division, the bulk of 151st and 69th Brigades then poured and were through the Italian positions and driving down towards Bir Hacheim well before dawn. During the next two days they fought sporadic actions with some of Rommel's supply trains, but as they had had to abandon much of their heavy equipment at Gazala, they were so short of essentials such as wireless sets, anti-tank guns and water-carriers when they reached the Egyptian border on June 16th that they could not be regarded as battleworthy or fit to play much further part for the moment in the defence of the Delta.

They were also under strength, for the third battalion of 151st Brigade – 9th Durham Light Infantry – had been delegated as the last formation to leave the defence line, and when they did so they found the Italian opposition so thoroughly awakened and aware of their plans that their commander, Lieutenant-Colonel J. E. S. Percy, decided that their safest course would be to turn back. They therefore followed the trail of 1st South African Brigade, who by midnight were down El Agheila West and making their way through Tobruk and on towards Gambut and Egypt. Unfortunately, 2nd South African Brigade had missed the top of Bill's Pass and were not down on the Via Balbia in bulk until nearly 0600 on the 15th, and by this time 3rd South African were only just clearing Serpentine Pass even further west. There was thus a very great deal of fast-moving traffic racing along the road towards Tobruk as dawn broke, and as a result, Percy's battalion and the South African rearguards found themselves in increasing danger as the Afrika Korps awoke – to a new day and an infuriated Commander-in-Chief.

By 0800 15th Panzer were on top of the Escarpment shelling the traffic below them, and by noon – by which time only Percy's Durhams and the South African rearguards were still west of Tobruk – they had put one battalion from Rifle Regiment 115 across the road, supported by half a dozen Panzer Mark IIIs and a captured 25-pounder. It looked briefly as though 50th Division would after all pay a heavy price for their escape, but Percy and his dour Geordies had no intention of giving up so near to Tobruk and a semblance of safety. They collected what random guns they could find in the neighbourhood, some South African carriers and armoured cars and smashed their way through the enemy screen during the afternoon. Unfortunately, few of the South African rearguards elected to follow them and the remainder were taken prisoner during that afternoon.

By nightfall on June 15th there were no Allied formations west of Tobruk or the Acroma–Bir el Gubi line, and Rommel could write that evening in his daily letter to his wife, 'The battle has been won and the enemy is breaking up. We're now mopping up the encircled remnants of their army.' Even Rommel's habitual optimism was hardly exaggerating the situation now, and those two sentences were very close indeed to the truth.

Not that Rommel had exhibited much optimism earlier in the day.

Some time later he was to remark to one of his aides, 'It's a great thing to be a Field Marshal and still remember how to talk to them like a sergeant-major!' and when that morning he had discovered that Afrika Korps had slept while the South Africans had escaped, his anger had been intense and his language violent, picturesque and to the point.

But the outburst was brief, and having vented his feelings in a manner which reminded all present of their days of recruit training, he switched off his anger and began issuing his orders for the day. For the moment, 15th Panzer must stay on the western edge of the Tobruk perimeter and clear up the position there, but 21st Panzer were to undertake the first stage of the encirclement of Tobruk and would move immediately to Bir Lefa. Away to the south, Ariete and the three reconnaissance battalions would form a screen to keep at bay the 7th Motor Brigade and any raiding columns which Eighth Army might send up towards the crucial areas, while closer in 90th Light would again attack 29th Indian Brigade at El Adem.

'*Es kommt darauf an,*' Rommel announced, '*den Kessel um Tobruk zuzumachen,*'[5] which can be roughly translated as, 'the time has come to put the lid on Tobruk!'

There were, as he saw it, three 'cornerstones' outside the main defences of Tobruk – the box at El Adem, the one between Ed Duda and Sidi Rezegh, and the main position at Belhammed – and these

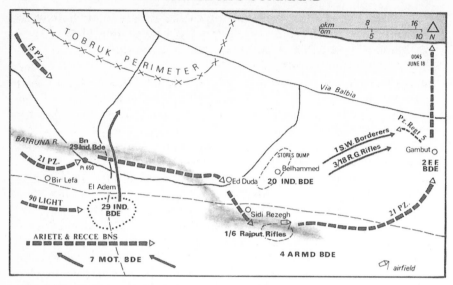

Map 17   Investment of Tobruk, June 16th–18th

must be knocked away before the main assault on the fortress began. By noon he was at the first one south of El Adem watching 90th Light mount yet another attack in the face of heavy and well co-ordinated Indian artillery, and waiting for the bulk of 21st Panzer to arrive just to the north-west – and as they came up he sent them on further. One of 29th Indian Brigade's battalions had been detached and was holding Point 650 at the top of the pass leading down the Batruna Escarpment, and 21st Panzer were told to obliterate them and then carry on towards Ed Duda – aiming at Gambut as their final objective for the day.

Speed, speed and more speed was the criterion and Rommel's driving urgency vitalised everyone; though the Indians at El Adem threw back this latest assault by 90th Light, Rifle Regiment 115 backed up by extra artillery and some of Panzer Regiment 5's Mark IIIs smashed into the hapless 3rd/12th Frontier Force Rifles at Point 650, and in three hours of fierce action wiped them out taking some seven hundred prisoners, many of them wounded – and 21st Panzer were then free to roll on towards Ed Duda where they arrived soon after midnight to find the place practically unoccupied.

The first day of the sweep around Tobruk had therefore gone well, and early the following morning Rommel went back to the Via Balbia at the western end of the perimeter to urge 15th Panzer after 21st. He found them still rounding up prisoners and collecting booty:

> Another six thousand British troops had found their way into our prison camps. Evidence of the British defeat could be seen all along the road and

verges. Vast quantities of material lay on all sides, burnt-out vehicles stood black and empty in the sand. Whole convoys of undamaged British lorries had fallen into our hands . . . [6]

They were very quickly put to use, and as the leading units of the Italian infantry divisions were arriving from Gazala, Rommel sent 15th Panzer off to follow 21st around the perimeter. Then he was himself again at El Adem, urging 90th Light to renew their assault, hurrying up more artillery to help them against the apparently immovable Indians. Overhead the Luftwaffe were occasionally engaged by Bostons and Kittyhawks, but R.A.F. energies for the moment were engaged on ground support for the army in the intervals between evacuating their own landing-strips.

By noon, the news had come to Rommel that Ed Duda was occupied by 21st Panzer and that they were forming up for an attack up the well-remembered slope to the Sidi Rezegh box, now held by more Indian troops (1st/6th Rajputana Rifles). But here the R.A.F. were attacking in force with fighter-bombers and some new tank-destroying Hurricanes, and the division was suffering losses and delay; moreover, isolated groups of British tanks were appearing to the south of the box, apparently from a reorganised 4th Armoured Brigade.

But nothing was to stand in the way of Rommel's determination, and by 1600 the 21st Panzer were grinding up the slope towards the box with one detached anti-tank screen fanning away towards the British tanks – and as darkness fell these dropped back south towards their leaguer area, leaving the Rajputana Rifles to their fate. This was sealed when their artillery ran out of ammunition and by 2030 21st Panzer had taken the airfield, most of the defenders were captured, a small remnant dropping back towards Belhammed.

And half an hour before, Rommel had been told by 90th Light that all the signs pointed to the evacuation of El Adem by the remaining battalions of 29th Indian Brigade, after a resistance which the Afrika Korps War Diary described as 'extraordinarily stubborn'. Tuesday, June 16th, had been a day of significant accomplishment and even Rommel slept a few hours that night. The War Diary entry for that night reads:

> Our next task is to clean up the outlying area of Tobruk and to carry through the encirclement of the Fortress while preventing interference from the south and from the east . . . Army intends to thrust with D.A.K. in the afternoon of 17.6 first to the south-east, then, wheeling to the north, to Gambut and the Via Balbia north of it. Thereby the enemy in Tobruk, and to the east of it, is to be locked in. The encircling ring will be narrowed in the days following so as to create the requirements for the attack on Tobruk itself. [7]

Now there seemed only two obstacles to the encirclement of Tobruk – the remains of the 20th Indian Brigade at Belhammed (it had been one of their battalions that was lost at Sidi Rezegh the previous afternoon), and the apparently recuperated 4th Armoured Brigade – and there was no doubt in Rommel's mind which had to be dealt with first. Not only was the mobile armour the greater threat, but a move towards it would create an impression he required – that he was more interested in sweeping on towards the frontier than in capturing Tobruk.

But in view of the recent expert use by the British of their artillery south of Elwet et Tamar, it would be as well to proceed carefully. Some time was therefore spent regrouping and a few provocative feints were made, but it was not until 1114 (on June 17th) that Rommel received the news he wanted – the British tanks were massing for an advance towards Sidi Rezegh, apparently unaware that the place was already in Rommel's hands. Panzer Regiment 5 moved off to the right wing and waited, the anti-tank screens moved out cautiously and watched for the opening moves.

They came at 1550, in conditions which could hardly have been more advantageous for the panzers – the British tanks advancing slowly and somewhat raggedly straight into the sun, which effectively blinded the gunners, most of whom had had no opportunity beforehand even to fire their new weapons, let alone correct or adjust their sights. Such a dire improvisation of machines and manpower had in fact been necessary to put this force together that even though the tank strength of 4th Armoured Brigade had been raised to ninety, in at least two cases the crews consisted entirely of officers; and – as so often in the past – the three composite regiments which now came into action did so separately.

Yet the two panzer divisions had quite a stiff battle. At one time 21st Panzer was calling for extra artillery support and then somewhat indignantly complaining that much of it was dropping on themselves instead of their opponents – but in the end training and co-ordination paid. By dark the panzers commanded the field of battle upon which the broken, smoking carcasses of yet another thirty-two British tanks remained, while the battered remnants of 4th Armoured Brigade (in truth, the remnants of the two armoured divisions which had faced Rommel when he first attacked the Gazala Line three weeks before) limped away to the south and then back behind the frontier. As a battleworthy formation, XXX Corps had ceased to exist.

But in Rommel's mind this was no time to pursue the vision of a local victory of annihilation, for his most earnestly desired prizes waited to the north. At 1930, he swung 21st Panzer around to face up towards the Via Balbia and the coast, and with his own *Kampfstaffel* some two miles in the lead, drove straight for the area between

Belhammed and the airfield at Gambut, still in use by the R.A.F.

They overran a small but spiteful defence post just south of Gambut and took some Free French prisoners, then ran into extensive minefields which, however, Rommel and his advanced units were able to skirt – and by 2200 they were driving on to the airfield, capturing as they did so fifteen serviceable aircraft and considerable quantities of oil and petrol; and now, stretching away to the west as far as Belhammed, lay the vast stores dump which Auchinleck and Ritchie had accumulated for what they had thought would be their own advance into the Jebel Akhdar and beyond.

Half an hour after midnight came the news that the Via Balbia had been cut to the east of Tobruk, and within another fifteen minutes German troops were on the coast. Tobruk was invested again, the area to the immediate south was clear for the regrouping which would be necessary before the attack on the perimeter could begin, and already reports were coming in from the delighted and revitalised Afrika Korps troops of the enormous haul of loot which had fallen into their hands. And not only loot; two battalions of 20th Indian Brigade – 1st South Wales Borderers and the 3rd/18th Royal Garwhal Rifles – had been ordered by Norrie to break out eastwards from Belhammed during the night and, making uncoordinated attempts to run the gauntlet just before dawn, had run into Panzer Regiment 5 and been captured almost to a man.

The rest of Thursday, June 18th, was spent by Rommel's troops clearing out the remaining pockets of resistance outside the perimeter. One extraordinary defence was encountered at Acroma Keep dominating the Axis By-pass just to the north of the old Acroma box positions, put up by a single company of Transvaal Scottish who had sited and learned to use a captured German 88mm. and four Italian 47mm. guns, all without their proper sights. The position was only eliminated that night after a curt written instruction had been issued by Rommel to the Italian XXI Corps commander, and even then all but one of the valiant South Africans retired successfully into Tobruk.

Meanwhile, Panzerarmee Headquarters were revising plans and issuing orders for the forthcoming assault of the port, while the quartermasters were resupplying units from the Aladdin's Cave which had fallen into their hands. Enormous quantities of food, water and fuel were available for the troops and their equally voracious vehicles, together with clothing to replace tattered uniforms – 'beautiful English leather boots' for the troops and, to their astonishment, 'soft, elegant suede shoes with thick rubber soles' for those officers who did not consider them too effeminate. Ammunition was there in abundance, too, and one of Rommel's chief worries was eliminated when huge stocks of 25-pounder shells were found for the captured British guns which now made up quite a sizeable proportion of his artillery – but this beneficence was rendered almost unnecessary when an astonished but excited gunner officer came in with the news that their own artillery and ammunition dumps, laid down eight months before in preparation for the November attack (which *Crusader* had upset) had just been discovered exactly where they had been left, undisturbed and intact. As Rommel intended to use the same plan of attack as had been drawn up for that occasion – a powerful thrust on a narrow frontage – it seemed that everything was working out in his favour.

Certainly he would have the fullest co-operation for the assault from all his allies and supporting arms. Kesselring, mindful especially of the timetable by which, once Tobruk had fallen, his air fleets would be switched westward for the *Herkules* attack on Malta (after which they would be free to rejoin the massive struggle in Russia), promised the greatest concentration he could organise, and was preparing to bring over every available bomber from Greece and Crete to add to those already in Africa. The Italians were just as enthusiastic, Pavia and Trieste Divisions of XX Corps anxious to play their part on the left flank of the attack, Ariete as eager as the men of the panzer divisions to take part in the armoured breakthrough.

Never before had Rommel been supported by such enthusiasm at every level of the Axis Command in Africa, never before had he directed so eager, so well-equipped, and so experienced a force as that which was now grouped together along the Tobruk perimeter. Already they were staging diversionary attacks on the western flanks to distract the attention of the besieged, but the main force was concentrating to the south-east. The only areas of disappointment were to the south of El Adem where the newly arrived Littorio Armoured Division was spread in a wide fan to guard against any attempt to interfere by the remnants of 7th Motor Brigade, reputed still to be away to the south, and to the east where the men of 90th Light Division were deployed south of the Trig Capuzzo between Gambut and Bardia – which they entered and occupied on the afternoon of June 19th. Their shielding role would undoubtedly be important, but was likely to be neither so spectacular nor so profitable as those of the assault troops.

By dusk on June 19th, all was ready. During the morning patrols had ventured as near to the Tobruk perimeter as they dared and on two occasions skirmished briefly with Indian and South African troops holding the bunker line; during the afternoon armoured cars had driven along the outer perimeter exchanging machine-gun fire with static posts. As darkness fell, the panzers left the positions around Gambut and moved up to start lines less than six kilometres from the anti-tank ditch, and among the troops from 15th Panzer

Division was the battalion commanded by Oberleutnant Schmidt:

> Groups of crouching figures huddled in woollen blankets in a little wadi
> at Ed Duda. There was almost no conversation, and that in whispers, as
> though the enemy, who was, perhaps, miles away, might hear us. What
> chatter there was seemed flippant and irrelevant: it was characteristic of
> talk before a battle.
>
> Next to each group – combat engineers and infantry storm-troops – lay
> the arms and other paraphernalia gathered during the day: explosives,
> grenades, mine-detectors, wire-cutters, flamethrowers, smoke-screen
> candles, machine-guns, ammunition.
>
> A few minutes to zero hour.
>
> A few minutes for thought – especially for those of us who had taken
> part, during April and May of the year before, in the futile assaults on
> this almost hated fortress.[8]

But like so many of the attacking troops as they waited that night,
Schmidt could console himself with one thought; at least he knew the
terrain over which he and his men would advance, and had many
times during 1941 watched skirmishes being fought there between his
own men and the Australians. He had thus accumulated a great deal
of valuable local knowledge – far more, for instance, than the Indian
troops opposite, similarly gazing out over the darkened waste,
similarly whispering between themselves, similarly waiting in concealed trepidation for what the dawn would bring.

It brought the most concentrated bombardment the Western Desert
had ever seen. Rommel and von Mellenthin were standing together
outside the battle headquarters on the escarpment north-east of El
Adem and the latter described what happened:

> Promptly at 0520 [on June 20th] the Stukas flew over. Kesselring had
> been as good as his word and sent hundreds of bombers in dense for-
> mations; they dived on to the perimeter in one of the most spectacular
> attacks I have ever seen. A great cloud of smoke and dust arose from the
> sector under attack, and while our bombs crashed on to the defences, the
> entire German and Italian army artillery joined in with a tremendous and
> well co-ordinated fire. The combined weight of the artillery and bombing
> was terrific.[9]

Schmidt was now waiting with his assault group only a hundred
yards back from the edge of the first minefield, and in front of them
lay engineers, some of whom had already lifted a few mines and even
reached the wire fence and cut some small gaps.

But the main destruction was still to come, and one duty unexpectedly allocated to the Stukas was to blast through the minefields; flight after flight plunged down just in front of the waiting men,

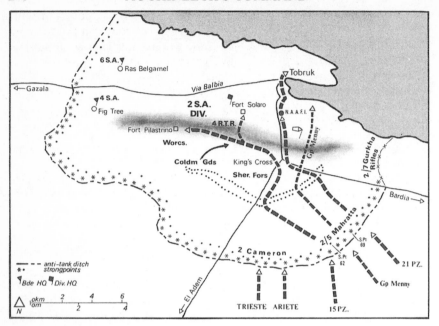

Map 18   Tobruk, June 20th

and the crash of one bomb would be followed by another as the first
mine went off, and then more and more in a series, 'like some atomic
fission continuing on beyond the first explosive shock'. Then the
Stukas would turn and whine back over their heads to El Adem and
be back over again within minutes with another bomb load.

As the bombardment started, Schmidt had seen a few isolated
defenders race back from the wire and disappear into the ground, but
after that little human movement was visible through the fog and
murk of the explosions – just the flash of bomb-blast, the gouts of
dust and smoke, and once, dimly seen, the hoped-for spectacle of
metal uprights trailing strands of wire entanglement whirling high in
the air. Every nerve tense, the group waited in their small wadi for
the next phase of the attack; a brief pause, a shout and engineers in
front rose and raced forward under covering fire from chattering
machine-guns on each side. More explosions, wide yellow flashes low
to the ground, a few coloured Very lights soaring inexplicably into
the air and then suddenly, from points spaced equidistantly along the
assault fronts, jets of thick orange smoke which joined together and
blanked off the entire scene.

At this, the gunfire ceased abruptly, the assault teams raced
forward into the fog, and as they jumped, stumbled, tripped, fell,
rose and raced onwards again, choking in the acrid, tarnish-flavoured

reek, they heard more shells scream over as the guns opened fire on a new range. Then they were clear of the fog and through the torn and flattened wire, to see in front of them the first of the defenders' trenches – empty and only partly blown-in. As they tumbled down into safety, they heard the sounds of Spandaus opening up on each side and knew that their neighbouring teams were level and their own flanks secure. Somewhere in front British artillery was coming into action, firing over their heads, presumably in search of the lorried infantry and armour still behind.

More assault teams came racing up from the rear, machine-gun fire increased everywhere, men were working along the trench line and grouping for the next overland rush towards the nearest strongpoint. Already a few stunned and totally bewildered Mahrattas were being winkled out from the solidly constructed Italian underground posts – which had certainly helped to save their lives but had also concealed from them everything that had been happening on the surface.

Less than an hour after the bombardment had opened, Strongpoint 69 was taken; by 0630 those on each side had fallen, others were coming under attack and as more and more of the defenders – deafened and shocked by the violence of the assault and blinded by their retreat into spurious safety – gave themselves up, the gap widened while behind it the ubiquitous support engineers were rapidly clamping into position the prefabricated bridges across the anti-tank ditch, or levelling up where silting had taken place. By 0745, ten strongpoints had been taken, the leading infantry were two miles inside the perimeter, the centre company of the defending 2nd/5th Mahrattas had ceased to exist (happily, most of them were prisoners) and to the rear, the leading Mark IIIs of 21st Panzer were arriving at their crossing-points.

By 0830, 21st Panzer's leading squadrons were across and into the bridgehead and 15th Panzer were coming through on the left flank, the first led into action by their divisional commander von Bismarck (in a motor-cycle side-car careering between his files of panzers), the second by General Nehring taking the place of the wounded von Vaerst, all urged onwards towards the vital position of King's Cross at the junction of the El Adem and Bardia roads by the chunky, excited, inspiring figure of their Commander-in-Chief, who had personally supervised the first crossings of the anti-tank ditch in order to ensure smooth passage, and was inside the bridgehead by 0800. Only occasionally did anyone in the bridgehead have time to wonder why the British artillery was so sparse and ineffective, or why there was so little sign of anything which could be interpreted as a well-organised counter-attack – though carrier-borne Gurkha infantry did appear briefly on the right flank, and pin down some of the assault troops there until driven off by panzers. On the left flank of the breakthrough a hard battle was being fought as Ariete tried but failed to smash their way through positions held by the 2nd Camerons, who had not been subjected to so violent a bombardment as had crashed down on the Mahrattas.

Just before 0900 heavy calibre shells began to rumble overhead as South African batteries beyond Pilastrino came into action, but as the bulk of the panzers were through the gap now (over a hundred of them) the fire would not affect the momentum of attack. Just before 1000, 15th Panzer met two British tanks which scuttled rapidly away once the crews saw the mass against them – and on the right 21st Panzer came up against one of the inner minefields which held them up briefly until von Bismarck in his motor-cycle side-car threaded a way through and, with some trepidation, his panzers followed. By 1030, with Nehring and von Bismarck leading one on each flank and Rommel amid the bulk of his armour in the centre, the whole superbly co-ordinated mass of asault troops and artillery, panzers and support infantry, drove inexorably northwards, rolling over defence posts in their path, machine-gunning batteries which tried to harass them on either flank, or sending assault infantry and engineer groups out to obliterate them. Nothing could stop them now.

By 1100 they were approaching the main inner minefield which they knew protected King's Cross, and here they met for the first time something like a serious attempt to check them – by Matildas which came out through gaps in the minefield to try to get within range with their puny 2-pounders; but the anti-tank screen soon stopped them and when the leading Mark IIIs opened up as well, the Matilda crews could be seen jumping from their turrets and racing back towards some form of safety. By 1145, the panzers were at the edge of the inner minefield and the engineers were out in front with their mine-detectors – and a lull fell across the main battlefield. Behind them on the left the panzer crews and assault infantry could hear Ariete still battling in vain with the 2nd Camerons, in front Stukas were howling down on to some unfortunate objective just out of sight while further off flights of bombers cruised unmolested over the port and harbour, their bombs falling away in apparent slow motion, their explosions muted by the escarpment in front, and the cliffs.

Then the engineers signalled clear passage, 21st Panzer struck slightly away to the right and reached the Bardia road to turn westwards along it, 15th Panzer's left flank hit the El Adem road and turned due north, while in the centre a group of over forty mixed Mark IIIs and IVs drove straight over the gapped minefield towards the vital road junction. Here, almost for the first time, they encountered serious opposition – nearly thirty 25-pounders and a few anti-tank guns deployed in a wide fan against them, their crews still working frantically to give themselves some shelter in the form of sangar or sandbag wall. It was obvious that most of them had only just arrived.

The panzers slowed and where necessary reloaded with high explosive instead of anti-tank ammunition; the protective artillery screens moved forward, the infantry dropped from their vehicles and, as machine-gunners began covering fire, moved up to attack. Soon each British or South African troop and battery position was pock-marked with exploding shell and streams of tracer laced above and between the advancing German infantry, each bead of light with seven unseen bullets behind it – while in front the British 25-pounders barked, coughing their heavy shells overhead towards the jostling panzers behind. As the infantry teams closed with each gun, fire concentrated upon it for a few more vital seconds, then lifted abruptly on to the next until, one by one, they all fell silent, smoking and impotent, their crews sprawled bleeding, unconscious or dead behind the riddled screens, around the disordered heaps of empty cartridge cases or unused shells. In the distance, some towing vehicles were limping away, carrying a few lucky wounded to hospital.

By 1230 the gun-line had been destroyed or chased away (one troop from 12th/25th Battery escaped westwards across the El Adem road and 15th Panzer let them go) and the massed strength of D.A.K. moved forward again, to be briefly hindered on the left flank by a brave but ineffectual attack by some Valentines – baulked and the tanks destroyed by the anti-tank screen. And by about 1330, the leading squadrons of both divisions had passed King's Cross, 21st driving on northwards towards the airfield and the port beyond, 15th Panzer veering westwards along the line of the Pilastrino Ridge towards Fort Solaro.

By 1400, Rommel was at King's Cross, standing up in the turret of his command truck to look down at the port and harbour which had been so long denied him. Along each side of his vehicle trudged the dejected, bewildered files of prisoners, few of them – if any – realising who he was.

They had certainly never seen any of their own senior commanders as close to the battle as this.

The main reason for the lack of serious reaction by General Klopper to the events of the morning was that both he and his brigadiers had long assumed that Rommel's attack when it came (and none of them had expected it quite so soon) would be directed against the south-western flank of the perimeter instead of the south-eastern, and as a result the whole of the 2nd South African Division plus the reconstituted Guards Brigade, all the tanks in the fortress and most of the artillery, were deployed west of the El Adem road and the road leading from King's Cross down to the port, while only the 11th

Indian Brigade with a derisory artillery support occupied the eastern half of the garrison area.

Despite the tremendous din of the opening bombardment, Klopper and his senior advisers at H.Q. were united in their belief that the attack on the Indians was nothing but a feint, and that their main attention must be focused on the arc of the perimeter sweeping westwards from El Adem. In this they were sustained by early optimism on the part of Brigadier Anderson commanding 11th Indian Brigade whose first reports had been quite reassuring as only his Mahratta battalion had been penetrated, and as the morning wore on by the dearth of further information on events in the south-east sector. This they chose to interpret as good news; in fact, it was due to a basically inadequate communications system which had totally broken down under the first shock of battle. But behind all the early complacency was the unshakeable conviction that the perimeter defences were still just as strong as when the Australians had held the fortress, despite the fact that not one of Klopper's H.Q. staff had ever bothered to go out and investigate the situation for himself.

The atmosphere in Fortress Headquarters can best be sensed in the Situation Reports (sitreps) sent out at regular intervals to Ritchie at Army Headquarters. The first was sent at 0810 recording 'shelling at 0645 and dive-bombing at 0700', plus a few details of the patrols carried out along the western perimeter during the night. At 0915 a second sitrep reported two enemy companies held and counter-attacked near Strongpoint 67, and a third at 1000 admitted enemy penetration of one mile, this penetration also being counter-attacked.

At 1033, 'Main. S.A. Div.' sent out a sitrep announcing the presence of '20 tanks outside R 48. 15 tanks and infantry in vehicles coming through Gap at 418 420 [*between R 63 and R 65*]. 7 tanks advancing on R 72. 40 tanks and battalion of infantry coming through R 62.'

This situation was at last enough to cause Fortress H.Q. 'some uneasiness' and half an hour later General Klopper admitted that he was 'completely in the dark about what was happening' and proposed to go over himself to King's Cross to investigate. He was, however, persuaded by his staff that his duty was to remain where he was and bear the obscurity with fortitude. Another sitrep was despatched about noon which reported withdrawal by British tanks from a position which it is extremely doubtful that they ever reached, but the signal which most devastatingly depicts the dream world in which the Tobruk Command were living was sent off at 1345 – by which time Rommel was about to arrive at King's Cross and both his panzer divisions were fanning out towards even more vital objectives. '40 tanks now inside perimeter,' it stated, adding that the information was three hours in arrears, but not suggesting that much import should be attached to this condition.

But now at least some awareness of danger began to penetrate the honey haze in the 'Pink Palace' (as the headquarters building west of Fort Solaro had been dubbed) and at about 1400 General Klopper issued orders to the Guards Brigade to face about eastwards and take up positions which would deny the Pilastrino Ridge to the enemy. Then Brigadier Willison rang up and announced that 4th Royal Tank Regiment would seem to have been destroyed in a scrappy and thoroughly ill-organised attempt at counter-attack, and just before 1500 a sitrep was sent out to Eighth Army revealing that panzers were through the last line of defences before King's Cross – information then only an hour out of date.

From then on, news of ever-growing disaster flooded in to Klopper's H.Q. Willison rang in to say that his entire command had now been destroyed, Anderson himself arrived at the Pink Palace with details of the destruction of the Mahrattas, pointing out also the isolation of the Gurkhas east of them and the increasing risk of the destruction of the Camerons; and it was at about this time that someone poring over a map realised that the lorry park in which had been accumulated transport for use in any putative break-out was to the east of the King's Cross–Tobruk road, and that if Rommel drove for the port he would effectively cut the garrison off from their means of escape and win himself a handsome bonus in the process.

Rommel, of course, was intent on doing just that. By 1445, 21st Panzer were down the escarpment to the east of King's Cross, aiming for the N.A.A.F.I. stores building and the eastern airfield – itself given over to supply and transport services, covered with dumps and guarded only by administrative personnel. Further out to the east, 21st Panzer's infantry component, known for the moment as 'Group Menny', were marching almost unhindered for the cliffs overlooking Tobruk harbour.

Driving a covey of British lorries in front of them, the panzers manoeuvred with ever-growing efficiency and confidence. When South African artillery was encountered near the N.A.A.F.I. building, the leading files split into two, adopted hull-down positions and opened up with their machine-guns on the gun crews, whose 25-pounders were unable to wreak much damage on concealed panzers at so short a range. Soon one gun was out of action, and after half an hour's firing ammunition was running low for the others because the main artillery dumps were away to the west behind the South African defences. The battery commander therefore withdrew behind a smoke-screen – and the panzers were free to drive on down towards the airfield and Tobruk beyond.

At 1600, 21st Panzer reported possession of the airfield, and suggested that if 15th Panzer would protect their left flank they could push on down the last escarpment – from the top of which Group Menny were already looking down on small craft attempting to escape from the harbour. However, both 15th and 21st Panzer now ran into unexpected trouble.

The British had long been in possession of a gun which at least equalled the German 88mm. – the 3.7-inch anti-aircraft gun – but unfortunately all suggestions put forward to higher command that a leaf be taken out of the enemy's book and this gun used to administer the kind of punishment to the panzers that the armoured brigades had suffered ever since the arrival of the Afrika Korps, had fallen on deaf ears. The suggestions had in fact been rejected upon grounds which seem to have been based solely upon theory and principle, by staff officers who had never had to face the reality. Field Marshal Lord Carver has recounted one early attempt to use the gun in an anti-tank role in the Knightsbridge box, dubbed a failure by one of the staff officers present because it stood so high off the ground, was provided with inadequate sights and blew a pillar of sand high into the air whenever it was fired. 'One wonders', he commented sadly, 'if German gunners made the same sort of complaints, when the first 88-mms were used as anti-tank guns.'[10]

But now there were three 3.7-inch guns at Fort Solaro and no staff officers present – in fact no officers at all above the rank of captain – and the crews could set to work with enthusiasm and efficiency to offer a resistance which Rommel later described as of 'extraordinary stubbornness'. They had already dug their guns into emplacements, and although they had no specific anti-tank ammunition to fire through their now horizontal barrels, the range was short enough for

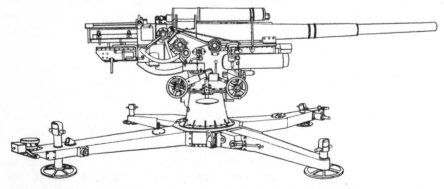

Figure 5   88mm. Flak 18: overall length 25 ft; weight in action 5 tons; horizontal range 16,200 yards; weight of projectile H.E. 20 lbs, A.P. 21 lbs; rate of fire 15/20 per min.; crew 6

them to wreck two panzers with their anti-aircraft shells and stop three more. They caused severe casualties among the panzer crews, replied with 'hellish fire' to a demand for surrender, and in the end were only put out of action by a storming party led with enormous gallantry by Rommel's own driver, which stole up under cover and then rushed the emplacements amid a shower of hand grenades. A single platoon of protective British infantry there might have made history.

But with this last serious obstacle removed, Rommel could order 21st Panzer forward from the airfield and down into Tobruk. There was a brief flurry of signals when it seemed that Group Menny would have to advance into the artillery bombardment which was crashing down on to the port, and then the final thrust was under way. Lumbering forward with self-propelled guns in close attendance, the Mark IIIs and IVs crashed through hastily erected roadblocks or swept them aside, machine-gunned strongpoints into surrender or shelled them into obliteration, reached the road leading down to the port and turned along it. From all sides came the sounds of explosions as the garrison troops strove valiantly to destroy huge dumps of rations, ammunition, fuel and general stores, while from the harbour itself came intermittent fire from ships attempting to hold off for a little longer the moment when they must either abandon the rest of the refugees flooding down in hope of escape, or accept the strong possibility of capture or sinking themselves.

The headquarters of the area administration was overrun by 1720, its commander Brigadier Thompson taken prisoner firing a machine-gun from the roof of a nearby house, as were several naval ratings gamely endeavouring to hold the panzers back from Navy House with rifles issued to them but minutes before. By 1800, a hail of fire was pouring down into the harbour area, the few vessels still there were casting off and manoeuvring to reach and pass through the narrow exit under a ragged smoke-screen; on one of the last to leave, the Naval Officer in Charge, Tobruk, Captain Frank Montem Smith, D.S.O., was killed by a shell fired from the quayside.

And above the port a huge black cloud from the demolitions, from the shell-fire, from the crushed rubble of the buildings, from the flaming petrol tanks rose and wavered in the light breeze – the funeral pyre of all the hopes which had been pinned, justifiably or not, on the British defence of Tobruk since it had first been occupied seventeen months before. Twenty miles away to the south the men of a raiding column which Ritchie had somewhat belatedly sent out to help the defenders saw the evidence and knew, almost without the necessity of discussion, what it meant.

But there were still the main bulk of the 2nd South African Division in their positions in the western half of the area, the majority of whom had so far been untouched by the land battle, however much they may have been harassed from the air; though not all infantry formations were still intact.

The Guards Brigade had by now been forced to surrender to 15th Panzer, for when Klopper had ordered them to face about eastwards and move to protect the Pilastrino Ridge from the east, they had found themselves suddenly stripped of all prepared positions, in open ground so rock-hard that it was impossible to dig even fox-holes without explosive. Their only defence against the panzer line which by 1530 was moving against them now rested with twelve 6-pounder anti-tank guns, standing on their portées in the open desert, and these did not last long. Blinded by a heat-haze which cut visibility to less than half a mile, the crews were suddenly confronted by about forty panzers lurching towards them with both main armament and machine-guns blazing; one 6-pounder and its portée were hit immediately and simply disintegrated in an explosion of steel, ammunition and torn bodies, and the others were hardly into action before the panzers were among them, machine-gunning the crews and in two cases simply barging the guns and overturning them.

The panzers ignored the infantrymen, who were totally powerless against them; indeed, such was their impotence that during the whole of their stay in Tobruk, losses for the Coldstream Guards amounted only to six killed and three wounded – but most of them were to spend the remainder of the war in prison-camps, for when the panzers moved on, German armoured cars and lorried infantry arrived and rounded them up. Some of the Sherwood Foresters holding positions south of the ridge were by-passed by the main panzer thrust, but when their commander made contact with Brigade Headquarters just before 1900, he was told that resistance was to cease and that the brigade had surrendered – so hopeless was the position considered.

It is pleasant to be able to record that some at least were not prepared to accept the situation. Major H. M. Sainthill and his reserve company of Coldstream Guards withdrew westwards along the ridge and at some time during the débâcle which ensued, assembled their transport and broke out to the south, made contact with South African armoured cars and escaped across the frontier to fight again. But such feats were the exception, for Klopper had by now lost all control of the situation. In the bickering and argument which occupied the command levels for the next few hours no firm guidance was available to the troops – who were more than willing to fight if given the chance – except orders to stay where they were and not bother their betters.

Klopper's position was now invidious and had, in fact, never been anything but unfortunate. He had been promoted major-general only a month previously and although he had commanded a brigade for the previous four months, his only operational experience had been as Chief of Staff to the commander of 2nd South African Division when they took Bardia six months before. He thus had several brigadiers serving under him in Tobruk who were senior to him in years and in service, and were considerably more experienced, though it cannot be said that advice received from them during the vital hours was of great value or prescience.

As for advice and direction from above, General Gott's views of the defence potentialities in Tobruk have already been outlined, and some flavour of the guidance Klopper was receiving from Eighth Army is indicated by an order received from Ritchie the previous morning, instructing him to relieve the box formed at Point 650 on the Batruna Ridge by the battalion from 29th Indian Brigade. 'If necessary,' the order read, 'you must stage an operation to achieve this.' Such were the relations between the two staffs that Klopper's G.2, in the words of the South African official history, was 'perhaps too polite to point out to the Army Commander that the place had been in enemy hands for four days'.[11] Ritchie's habit of sheltering his superior from grim reality had proved infectious and was now hoisting him with his own petard.

This morning there had come to Klopper from Ritchie a long signal labelled MOST SECRET but which in its wording was so convoluted as to make it almost incomprehensible and its label thus redundant; but from one part of it Klopper gained the impression that a large striking force comprising twelve separate columns with 116 guns and 66 tanks was already poised to fall upon the rear of Afrika Korps immediately it attacked his perimeter. The columns had in fact never even been formed, let alone despatched, but as the long day wore on it seemed to Klopper that any hour must bring this promised relief.

After the series of events which had caused him (at about 1400) to order the redeployment of the Guards Brigade, disasters crowded in upon him at such a rate that a far more experienced man could be forgiven for losing touch with reality. And out of touch with reality was what he and many headquarter and administrative units undoubtedly were! The South African history tells of the annoyance of the staff of one South African brigade when a heavy bomb fell but failed to explode near their mess tent, so their lunch was delayed until sappers could be fetched to destroy it – this at a time when Rommel was already at King's Cross! – and of the officers of a supply company who were taken prisoner by infantrymen from Group Menny while enjoying their post-prandial nap!

But by 1550, Klopper at least was sufficiently alarmed to signal

Ritchie news – only two hours out of date – to the effect that sixty enemy tanks were at King's Cross, and it was a pity that neither Ritchie nor his Chief of Staff, Brigadier Whiteley, were at Eighth Army Headquarters to receive it; not that by now there was much they could have done to help. Then at 1600 (and it is possible to pin-point the time because one of Klopper's staff officers was cele-brating his birthday, and the kettle had just been put on for tea) enemy tanks were seen approaching the headquarters area, shell-fire upon it increased rapidly, a flood of refugees streamed past, and with danger apparently so near and immediate Klopper gave the orders for the destruction of all documents, codes, ciphers and even orderly room files – an instruction carried out with such enthusiasm that in the holocaust which followed the telephone exchange and several wireless sets were also put out of action, so from that moment all communication between Fortress Headquarters and the remainder of the Tobruk Garrison ceased. Some signal vans remained to keep Eighth Army in dubious contact with events, but for the next several hours there was no way in which Klopper could have redeployed the still considerable military force under his command, even had he conceived some practical objective for them.

Almost as soon as the destruction of these vital communication systems was complete it became obvious that the exercise had been, for the moment at least, unnecessary. The panzers observed ap-proaching the area had been from 21st Panzer and these now veered north towards Tobruk, while 15th Panzer were still busy dealing with the Guards Brigade and unaware of the proximity of the garrison command – which as a result was now to remain undisturbed for some time to come. Klopper used this period for further discussions with his staff, but finally concluded that he must move from the area anyway, deciding at first to join 4th South African Brigade H.Q. at a location known as Fig Tree, just to the south of the Via Balbia as it approached the western perimeter. At 1700 he sent off a message to Ritchie reading, 'Holding the line El Adem Road. Perimeter almost intact but eastern sector badly mauled. Can you give any information re columns?'[12] but he received no reply to this, perhaps because there was no one at Eighth Army H.Q. sufficiently aware of the situation to concoct a useful answer. In fact Eighth Army's silence was not to be broken until Ritchie returned from his day's peregrinations at 1815 – by which time the last Royal Naval units were endeavouring to escape from Tobruk harbour – when he despatched a personal signal to Klopper. It began, 'Well done, Acroma Keep has made history,' and after some abstruse but optimistic comment, went on:

You are having a very tough fight today and I see this afternoon some enemy tanks have got through the outer perimeter. But I feel quite confident of your ability to put them out after destroying as many as possible . . . All good fortune to you personally and the whole of your grand command.[13]

But by the time Ritchie had delivered himself of this piece of cheerful banality, Klopper had left the Pink Palace and was in the process of re-establishing his headquarters elsewhere. His original choice of Fig Tree had been changed by a rumour of threats to 4th Brigade H.Q. by panzer attack, so he went instead to Ras Belgamel, the H.Q. of 6th South African Brigade to the north of the Via Balbia, though it was perhaps unfortunate that the decision to change destination was only revealed to a part of his staff, and operations and intelligence sections still went to Fig Tree.

It was dusk before Klopper and the last of the signallers left the Pink Palace, and on the road they were caught by the last heavy Stuka attack of the day, fortunately suffering no casualties; but on the journey Klopper decided that the position of the troops in Tobruk had become hopeless and that brigade commanders should now prepare their troops for a mass break-out, to be launched as soon as possible and with 2200 as the zero hour to be aimed for. After a nightmare journey across a westward flood of refugees – angry, disorientated, often wounded and battle-shocked, without arms, rations, water or any idea but to escape from the chaos and danger they had just experienced – he was greeted with considerable surprise at Ras Belgamel, as 6th South African Brigade had been out of touch for some time and had no warning of his arrival. But to its commander he quickly gave the orders for the break-out, instructing him to pass them on to the other brigadiers.

He then embarked upon a frustrating attempt to communicate his decision to Ritchie, which eventually culminated in a reply from Whiteley (as Ritchie was out of touch again) reading 'BGS to GOC. Come out tomorrow night preferably if not tonight Centre Line Meduuar–Knightsbridge–Maddalena. I will keep open gap Harmat–El Adem. Inform me time selected and route. Tomorrow night preferred. Destruction petrol vital.'[14]

Here at least was some note of agreement and signs of possible outside co-operation, though the preference for a delay of twenty-four hours was obviously unacceptable; but as Klopper and the 6th Brigade commander planned the launching of the break-out, the 4th Brigade commander and his staff arrived from Fig Tree, announcing unanimously that it would be quite impossible for 4th Brigade to get out of Tobruk 'on their flat feet!' The whole South African Division was used to being transported by vehicle wherever they went, and Brigadier Hayton and his staff saw no way in which the habit could be broken, even in these circumstances. It was, after all, a hell of a long way back to Egypt and safety, and a formation of brigade or larger size could hardly expect to escape notice while marching across the desert in broad daylight – even if such a feat were practicable – from an enemy of Afrika Korps's efficiency and sense of purpose. Caught on the march by Rommel's armour, the South African infantry would undoubtedly be annihilated – and a far better solution to all their problems would be to form a defensive line running parallel to the western face of the perimeter and facing eastwards, organise the considerable force now concentrated behind it and fight it out until Eighth Army sent in relief.

The best description of the atmosphere at Ras Belgamel as the rest of the night wore on is given, as usual, by J. A. I. Agar-Hamilton and L. C. F. Turner:

> Other officers objected to 4th Brigade plan, chief among them the C.R.A. arguing that the position in Tobruk was hopeless; the guns could fire only until they had exhausted the ammunition in their limbers, and the infantry had no defence against attack from within the perimeter. They recommended that the artillery and such troops as were mobile should be got out at once to strengthen the Eighth Army. Some officers actually worked out a plan by which the two or three surviving tanks would lead a break-out, followed by the armoured cars and the artillery. Another officer is reported to have pleaded tearfully and emphatically for immediate surrender, urging on the General that his was the responsibility for preserving 'the cream of South African manhood.'
>
> There followed what has sometimes been described as a Conference, but which was in fact a series of desultory and disconnected conversations during which the arguments for and against breaking out were wearily traversed again and again. Suggestions were thrown out, as for collecting the ammunition for the field-guns from the Supply Depot at the cross-roads, or for attacking the German leaguers, or for laying an additional minefield to cover a 'western box', but they were no more than suggestions, not pressed home. Officers drifted in and out. Someone called in Lieut-Colonel Chadwick, the A. and Q., who was asked about the ammunition supply, but Colonel Bastin, who alone knew the details, was well on his way back to Egypt by sea and Lieut-Colonel Chadwick could not help. Brigadier Anderson, who was anxious to get back to the Camerons at the perimeter, sat dourly outside with a Staff Officer, awaiting instructions.[15]

It was not an atmosphere in which major decisions were likely to be made, or, if made, carried through with much resolution.

Klopper, however, did arrive at one conclusion. Just before 0200 on June 21st he signalled to Eighth Army, 'Am sending mobile troops out tonight. Not possible to hold tomorrow. Mobile troops nearly nought. Enemy captured vehicles. Will resist to last man and last round,'[16] and then he despatched his brigadiers back to their head-quarters with the first firm directive they had been given since noon. It was unfortunate, but perhaps predictable, that during their journeys any resolution which Klopper had managed to infuse into his subordinate commanders evaporated, and by the time they arrived back at their various headquarters there were already dark mutterings about 'the size of the butcher's bill'. At 4th Brigade H.Q., according to the brigade major, when Brigadier Hayton told his battalion commanders that the C.R.A. could only guarantee ammunition for two hours, they all expressed the opinion that wholly useless slaughter would result from further resistance, and it was not long before Hayton was on the line to Klopper, drearily repeating all the arguments which had already been well rehearsed.

Yet all this time, the bulk of the men of the South African Division were waiting with some eagerness for orders for action, coping with the floods of refugees and bullying them back into some degree of confidence, and in a large number of cases working hard for tomorrow's battle (or tonight's if the orders came in time). Without any direction at all from above, gunners had resited their batteries and dug them in, support infantry had already begun digging defence positions facing eastwards, the Worcestershires and the remainder of the Coldstreams had dug in around Pilastrino and a Crusader tank had been sited and dug in as a pillbox up in the northern sector of the line, where a battalion formed from South African police had abjured their proscriptive duties and were preparing to fight like more ordinary men. One company of 2nd Transvaal Scottish had armed itself with all the sticky bombs they could lay their hands on and were impatiently awaiting permission to raid forward into the Afrika Korps leaguers and blow the panzers to smithereens.

As the panzer crews were by this time sleeping that same sleep of exhaustion which had overcome them six nights before on the ridge outside Acroma (to such an extent that one South African party visited a nearby supply depot and drove away a truckload of mines while two other parties made their way westward out of Tobruk port, all picking their route between the forms of German soldiers sleeping so profoundly that they could not be woken) it is tempting to wonder what would have happened had the junior officers and men of the garrison – and there were some 20,000 of them at least – been roughly organised and told to fight their way eastwards, destroying as many of the enemy as they could as they went. It is not inconceivable that they would have so seriously weakened the Afrika Korps that many subsequent battles need not have been fought.

But the garrison's fate was not in their own hands, and as the night wore on the hands in which it did rest became more and more uncertain. The arguments continued, every order passed down from Command was disputed, not even a token gesture of obedience was offered and false information of impending panzer attacks was even fed to Klopper, though perhaps by mistake. His dejected figure was seen, dimly shadowed in the blackness before dawn, alone, weighed down by his responsibilities and deserted by those from whom he should have been given, especially at such a time, unqualified support. He had had one more exchange of signals with Eighth Army, this time with Ritchie himself, which revealed only too clearly the weak grasp of the realities of the situation held at headquarters.

> Ritchie [in answer to Klopper's 0200 signal]: Noted about mobile elements. In respect remainder every day and hour of resistance materially assists our cause. I cannot tell tactical situation and must therefore leave you to act on your own judgement regarding capitulation. Report if you can extent to which destruction P.O.L. effected.

> Klopper: Situation shambles. Terrible casualties would result. Am doing the worst. Petrol destroyed.

> Ritchie: Whole of Eighth Army has watched with admiration your gallant fight. You are an example to us all and I know South Africa will be proud of you. God bless you and may fortune favour your efforts wherever you be . . . [17]

What Klopper meant by his announcement, 'Am doing the worst,' remains something of an enigma, for shortly after the above exchange was concluded, he sent out emissaries to the German forces lying nearest to him with an offer to surrender. A huge white flag was hoisted above 6th Brigade headquarters by some native drivers, and as it flapped open in the first morning breeze, a great moan of disappointment, anguish and misery welled up from all over the western half of the garrison area.

Defeat is bitter in any circumstances, but now in the minds of thousands who were experiencing it, it was compounded by disgrace.

An expression which, albeit colloquial, accurately portrays the feeling throughout the Afrika Korps on the morning of June 21st, 1942, is 'cock-a-hoop'. Certainly there was still some clearing up to be done for in the eastern sector of the fortress the Camerons were still keeping Ariete and Pavia Divisions at bay, while the Gurkhas across the road to Bardia were showing not the slightest signs of surrender, holding as they did no belief in the validity of such a course of action; in any case they were still largely unaware of what had been happening further westward. But to the men of 21st and 15th Panzer Divisions, the proclamation the previous evening of the 'proud victory' of the capture of Tobruk, supplemented within the hour by the news that 15th Panzer had occupied both Fort Solaro and Pilastrino, had been followed for the majority of them by a comparatively uninterrupted night's sleep, and at dawn on the 21st they were well-rested, satisfactorily breakfasted (largely upon captured rations) and eager to consolidate and enjoy their success.

Evidence of the solidity of the victory surrounded them on all sides. Large assemblies of downcast British and South African prisoners were collecting, while from the as yet untaken areas came the sights and sounds of destruction as guns, fuel and ammunition dumps were blown up with a grim efficiency which was itself an expression of the frustration felt by the bulk of the garrison. Lorries were burning on all sides (to the regret and added fury of those who later found that in the chaos of mass surrender they might have escaped had they held on to some form of transport), armoured cars were being pushed over the cliffs into the sea, and infantrymen were smashing their rifles – often with a strange reluctance, considering how violently most of them had cursed the things previously. Major Sainthill, already organising his company's break-out – by far the most successful of those attempted – watched the scene from the high ground west of Pilastrino: 'To the north-west, west, and south, a hundred fires – soon to become a thousand – dotted the landscape: burning guns and vehicles glaring like beacons in the half-light of early morning.'[18]

But few of the panzer crews or their gunner or infantry comrades were much concerned with this destruction; they had their eyes firmly fixed on the huge stores dumps and warehouses wherein their quartermasters were already taking inventories, and the early-comers were already replenishing their stocks of food and comforts:

> There were stacks of tinned beer; huts bursting with pure white flour, cigarettes, tobacco and jam; gallons of whisky; priceless tinned food of all kinds; and tons of khaki clothing – that magnificent clothing, which looked so heavy and was so light and cool to wear.[19]

In addition to travelling for the most part in British vehicles, the Afrika Korps would soon be doing so in British uniforms.

Such bounty and such a feeling of triumph engendered a spirit of euphoria which showed in the Afrika Korps treatment of their new prisoners – already regarded with a degree of fellow-feeling because of the known and shared experiences of desert life. One of the British infantrymen remarked upon it in his account of being captured:

> We scrambled out of our trenches and were soon marched off after being allowed hurriedly to collect a few things together. However, the Germans – Rommel's Afrika Korps – treated us with reasonable consideration and I saw several signs of compassion and nothing of the snarling Nazi we had been led to expect – let's hope it stays that way. As we marched by, a German officer, smiling triumphantly, leant down from the turret of his tank and said to me 'For you, the war is finish. Thank God you have got away alive!'[20]

On another occasion, some South Africans were giving themselves up under the protection of a somewhat bedraggled white towel, when they were horrified by a burst of machine-gun fire directed from behind them on the panzers to whom they were surrendering. In a number of previous instances such an episode had been interpreted (on both sides) as a deliberate violation of the White Flag and indiscriminate slaughter had ensued, but on this occasion the panzers merely returned the machine-gun fire, one of the crew waved the South Africans into cover and later came back to take them prisoner. Occasionally a captor would relieve his captive of a few cigarettes, but generally they were not only allowed to keep any comforts they had with them, but positively encouraged to find themselves some more.

There was, however, one dissident from this mood of happy triumph in which Afrika Korps bathed, and unfortunately for almost everyone inside the fortress area, irrespective of nationality, this exception was Rommel himself. Despite the fact that he was greeted wherever he went by his officers and men as the hero of the hour; that congratulations were pouring in from every headquarter organisation from Tobruk back to Tripoli and would assuredly continue to do so for many hours, from ever more remote but ever more puissant areas of command – and that Tobruk was at last firmly in his hands – Rommel on the morning of June 21st was almost beside himself with fury. His men might view the burning lorries with some indifference, but their Commander-in-Chief's eyes were already fixed on horizons further to the east (despite what may or may not have been agreed before the onslaught on the Gazala Line) and he knew that the destruction which surrounded him was well devised to thwart his plans. Clean shirts and whisky would not take him or his men a kilometre closer to the Nile; what he needed was more transport, a secure source of water (and the Navy had wrecked the water supply and both the refrigeration and distillation plants by the harbour) and, most important of all, petrol; a perpetual goad to his anger during the hours he spent in Tobruk was the towering black cloud drifting back across the fortress from the flaming fuel tanks.

One early result of his exasperation was a violent and uncharacteristic outburst at his meeting with General Klopper at 0940 when, to the astonishment of his captives and the embarrassment of his own staff, he indulged in a spasm of fury which robbed him of all the dignity which might have been expected at such a triumphant hour; and another, even more uncharacteristic, was his proclamation that the prisoners would be made to rue their own destructive activity. Many of those who had added to his difficulties by wrecking subsidiary fuel tanks and in so doing soaked their boots and lower garments in petrol so that they rotted, were not allowed to replace them, and everyone was very thirsty until Rommel himself had moved up to the frontier and less irate tempers were controlling their destinies.

Perhaps fortunately for the prisoners, Rommel wasted no time. Five minutes after the conclusion of the stormy interview with Klopper, he issued an order to Afrika Korps which cut short many a developing celebration by ending, 'All units will reassemble and prepare for further advance,' and by the afternoon, 21st Panzer were making their way with some reluctance eastwards towards Gambut, while 15th Panzer were closing down on the Camerons and marshalling almost the entire heavy artillery under Rommel's command in order to obliterate the recalcitrant Scots if they continued to behave so unreasonably.

In the event, an agreement was reached under a white flag that the Camerons would surrender the next morning – having now held out twenty-four hours longer than the rest of the fortress – and that they would be allowed the honours of war, marching out under arms and headed by their pipers. Lieutenant-Colonel Duncan, the Camerons' commanding officer, also took advantage of the occasion to deliver a sharp lecture to the German officer who came to accept the surrender upon the latter's untidy, unkempt and generally unsoldierly appearance, after which Duncan then drew his revolver and flung it at the astonished man's feet.

On the far side of the break-in gap, the Gurkhas had been dispersed into the precipitous wadis by an onslaught from the rear by Rommel's own *Kampfstaffel*, followed by a hunting-down operation carried out by the whole of the Italian X Corps which occupied them for several days. The last Gurkhas were eventually rounded up between Bardia and Sollum, having walked along the coast, occasionally wading across wadi-mouths and around enemy bathing or search parties, and across the Egyptian frontier.

The frontier, of course, was Rommel's next immediate target, with 90th Light already at Bardia and 21st on their way to join them. But there was always the matter of that agreed timetable by which Afrika Korps would stand on the frontier while the Luftwaffe, a considerable force from the Italian Fleet, and one Italian and one German parachute division with sea-landing brigades in attendance would all descend upon Malta and remove that island once and for all from the chessboard of Mediterranean strategy. And it was to further the implementation of those arrangements that Kesselring arrived at Tobruk that afternoon, determined – after offering his sincere congratulations to his brilliant associate – to begin the withdrawal of Luftwaffe units from North Africa to Sicily.

He found himself faced by no associate, but by an adversary buoyed up with victory, stimulated by anger, and totally committed to a new policy of ruthless pursuit of a beaten enemy however far he might retire, regardless of any agreements entered into with allies or

even with the commanders of supporting arms who had recently
given him such close and ardent co-operation; and any use of superior
rank which Kesselring might have considered bringing to bear was
negated by the news that evening that an enthusiastic Führer had
rewarded his favourite general by promotion to Generalfeldmarschall!

Even this news was scarcely enough to cause a moment's distraction from Rommel's now dominant purpose. The Eighth Army
was for the moment in a state of such all-embracing disarray that it
must be caught and finally broken; Afrika Korps had now enough
captured transport, enough fuel, enough vehicles, arms and ammunition to take them to Cairo – and a delay of a few weeks, perhaps
even only a few days, might allow Auchinleck time to regroup and
augment the forces between the frontier and the Nile and perhaps
thereby to block Afrika Korps once and for all. This must not be
allowed to happen.

To Kesselring's remonstrances that Malta was recovering from the
Luftwaffe onslaught of April and early May and would soon be
throttling Rommel's supply lines again, Rommel replied that with
Benghasi already out of range of British aircraft from Egypt and
Tobruk soon in the same happy condition as a result of his own
intended rapid advance, the supply problems could be overcome –
though this would, of course, make demands upon the gentlemen of
the administrative departments in Rome and Sicily almost as great
as those given freely every day by the tank crews and infantrymen of
the Afrika Korps!

At this, the discussion became, in von Mellenthin's words (he was
present all the time) 'exceedingly lively' and ended when Kesselring
left, proclaiming his intention to withdraw all his Luftwaffe units to
Sicily – a move countered by Rommel who promptly sent off a liaison
officer to Hitler's headquarters to argue his case, and a cable to von
Rintelen in Rome, which read:

> The first objective of the Panzerarmee Afrika viz. to defeat the enemy
> field army and to take Tobruk has been attained. Elements of the enemy
> are still holding out at Sollum–Halfaya–Sidi Omar. The intention is to
> destroy this enemy, thus opening the road into the heart of Egypt. The
> state and morale of the troops, the present supply situation thanks to
> captured dumps, and the present weakness of the enemy, permit our
> pursuing him into the depths of the Egyptian area. I request you therefore,
> to induce the Duce to lift the present restrictions on freedom of movement
> and to put all the troops at present under my command at my disposal so
> that I can continue the battle.[21]

Needless to say, he had not the slightest intention of awaiting
reaction to either of these strokes, and, pausing only to issue an
Order of the Day to his troops which though it paid full tribute to

their recent achievements, exhorted them to even greater effort, he took a few brief hours of rest and at dawn next morning went forward to Bardia. From here he and his staff organised the closing up of the 15th Panzer Division and the Ariete to the frontier, received with some relief the news that 90th Light had seized yet another huge supply dump at Capuzzo which contained 'particularly large quantities of fuel', and prepared to do verbal battle with the Italian commanders who now came racing up to register their protests.

To Generale Count Barbasetti Rommel announced that he intended to go straight through the Delta, across the Nile, the Canal and the Sinai Desert, not pausing until he reached the Persian Gulf; and Generale Bastico's orders to halt where he was he brushed aside as 'unacceptable advice', adding undoubtedly intentional irritation to this cavalier treatment of someone who was still his chief with an invitation to dine with him in Cairo! As both Italian generals had now learned by bitter experience that Rommel was more likely to get his own way than not, they merely registered their disapproval and did not insist very hard upon obedience.

In this they were wise. Rommel's message to von Rintelen had by this time arrived in Berlin, von Rintelen having felt that so important a change in plan should go straight to the real focus of decision, without unnecessary delays at interim and ineffective stations; and to the surprise of a number of people, Rommel's suggestions received the immediate and unqualified support of Oberstgeneral Alfred Jodl, Operations Chief of the Supreme Command. There were protests from Raeder and the naval staff in Berlin but Jodl was well aware of Hitler's reluctance to engage upon maritime adventures, especially after the costly assault on Crete, and guessed how the decision would go. During June 22nd, the Führer cabled the Duce to the effect that 'it is only once in a lifetime that the Goddess of Victory smiles,' and such was the inspiring effect of this Delphic inducement that that night Mussolini sent his full approval to Rommel for the pursuit into Egypt. The following day he replied to Hitler that he fully agreed ' . . . that the historic moment has now come to conquer Egypt' and energetically set about the really important aspects of so momentous an event.

Cavallero was despatched to North Africa to discover how soon Rommel expected to be in Alexandria and Cairo, and once Mussolini received this vital piece of information (June 30th) he issued further orders to the new Generalfeldmarschall to press on immediately to Suez and there to block the Canal. Il Duce himself would take over command in the Delta, to which end he flew to Derna on June 29th, piloting his own aircraft, accompanied by a large transport plane carrying all the necessary equipment for his triumphant entry into Cairo, including a white charger.

It is not known whether he intended Auchinleck and Ritchie to drag a carriage full of wreaths behind him.

But much happened on the battlefield during the eight days between the time Il Duce agreed to Rommel's advance, and his own journey to North Africa.

By the evening of June 23rd, Afrika Korps spearheads were crossing the frontier some forty-five miles south of the Sidi Omar box and skirting around the other defensive positions in which Ritchie had reposed the safety of Egypt, prettily named 'The Stables', 'The Kennels', 'The Nursery' and 'The Playground', with the passes down the Escarpment protected by positions known as 'Lovers' Lane', 'The Pub', and 'The Cradle'. However, as there was now no worthwhile armoured force to give support to the unfortunate infantry held in these boxes ('The Kennels' was designed, stocked and equipped to accommodate a complete division for three months, and indeed Pienaar's 1st South African occupied it for four days) Ritchie had decided as early as June 21st that these defensive positions were after all untenable and that 'we can only gain time with distance, repeat distance'. In other words he intended for the moment to put as much space between the Eighth Army and Rommel's forces as possible.

Map 19   Into Egypt, June 24th–25th

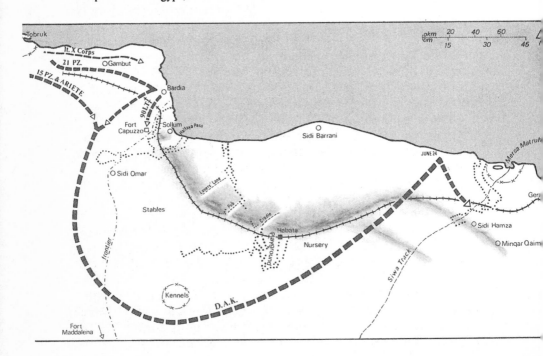

As a result, the triumphant German forces surged almost un-opposed into Egypt and by the evening of the following day (June 24th) had made an astonishing advance of well over a hundred miles to reach the coast nearly fifty miles east of Sidi Barrani – and this with only forty-four panzers, the others having broken down as a result of the wear and tear of the battles fought over the last twenty-seven days and two hundred miles. By the following evening both panzer divisions were deploying south-west of Mersa Matruh, their Commander-in-Chief well aware of Fortune's favour which had given him yet another timely windfall of petrol at the railroad at Habata, salvaged from a store which had been inefficiently set ablaze. According to what intelligence reports his staff could draw up from extremely meagre sources, the British and South African forces were intending to stand on the Mersa Matruh–Siwa line, and if he were to maintain the momentum of the advance, Afrika Korps must break that line tomorrow.

All that day (25th) they had been subject to increasingly heavy air attacks, and they now knew that they would have to do the job on their own for Ariete and Trieste had been reduced by battle and exhaustion to fourteen M13s, thirty guns and less than two thousand infantrymen between them! These, however, were factors which would not affect by one whit the morale of Rommel's men, for by now they felt themselves to be invincible.

This was not an opinion – remarkably enough – shared by the men opposite. These were tired and disorganised – one observer who watched them coming back remarked that in the entire flood of men he did not see one single formed fighting unit of infantry, armour or artillery – and they were very angry; and this anger bolstered their morale. They were not in any way angry at their opponents – to whom, in fact, they gave little thought – but they were furious with those who had sent them into battle with what they believed were inferior weapons, with what they knew to be inferior training and techniques – and, most important of all, under leaders who quite obviously were incapable of discharging their responsibilities.

Their morale therefore received an added fillip that night when news filtered through their ranks that the 'Auk' had at last relieved Ritchie and taken command himself. Perhaps matters might improve now, they thought, exhibiting yet again the propensity of troubled humanity to find a single source for all their ills, a single scapegoat to carry all their communal sins.

Luck plays an enormous part in every phase of life, of course, and in the military profession, especially in its higher reaches, perhaps an even more significant part than in most. There is no doubt that

Ritchie had been extremely unfortunate. His promotion from major-general on Auchinleck's staff to lieutenant-general commanding the Eighth Army in the field – on the face of it a God-sent opportunity – was in fact a trap from which only the high regard in which he was held in important places allowed him eventually to escape.

Command of an army in 1942 would seem to have been above his ceiling, even had the army been already well trained with corps and divisional commanders working in harmony. As it was, those very qualities which caused the Chief of Staff of the Army, General Sir Alan Brooke, to write of him, 'I am devoted to Neil,' and everybody who knew him to refer to him as 'an awfully nice chap', acted to his own – and the Eighth Army's – undoing. What was needed to command the Allied forces after the retreat from El Agheila in 1942 was ruthlessness not charm, leadership not chairmanship of a committee – especially of a committee whose members did not particularly care whether their decisions were unanimous as each was determined to go his own way anyway.

Sandwiched as he was between Auchinleck's determination to 'hold his hand' at almost every stage of the operation, and indifference to his opinion by his corps commanders and almost contempt for them from lower levels, it is not surprising that Ritchie's grip on the battle as it developed was at first weak and in the end non-existent. In the circumstances he is probably to be admired for his sustained optimism, despite its emptiness, for in similar conditions seven months before his predecessor, Cunningham, had lost heart and recommended total abandonment of gains already won.

Ultimate responsibility for the disasters of Gazala and the following weeks lies, not only formally but also actually, with the Commander-in-Chief, General Auchinleck. He appointed Ritchie, and then retained him there despite evidence that his nominee had as yet neither the experience nor the toughness of character or intellect to bear such heavy responsibilities.

Even now, Auchinleck was not relieving Ritchie because of past errors, but for what he rightly perceived to be an even more dangerous mistake that he was about to make. Having first intended to stand on the frontier in positions which could easily be outflanked on the south and only blocked there by the Kennels position (described caustically by one observer as 'like its infamous counterpart Bir Hacheim, it protected nothing but sand and it too hung like a rather less ripe pear on a rather longer stalk'),[22] Ritchie, having at last perceived his danger, proposed to stand instead at the Matruh positions – which without an adequate armoured force were equally indefensible tactically, and as the defence lines had been allowed to deteriorate to the same extent and for the same reasons as those at Tobruk, indefensible even as a static position.

The overall theory for the conduct of the next stage of the defence of Egypt had been that X Corps under Lieutenant-General W. G. Holmes (who had been rushed forward from Syria) should occupy and hold Mersa Matruh, XIII Corps under Gott the area to the south around Sidi Hamza, while Norrie back at El Alamein organised the defences there and held them with XXX Corps. This looked very well on paper, but examination revealed that between them the three corps held hardly enough complete formations to form three divisions.

General Holmes's corps consisted of the remains of 10th Indian Division (which had been flung piecemeal into the battles of the last few days and been knocked about and thoroughly disorganised as a result) inside Matruh, the two remaining brigades of 50th Division, still without replacements for much of the equipment they had left behind in the Gazala Line, some ten miles back at Gerawla and, briefly, two brigades of the 2nd New Zealand Division. General Freyberg, however, had taken one look at the Matruh defences, uttered a few brusquely condemnatory remarks about the chaos in which he and his men were now expected to operate, and roundly declared that he would not allow them to be locked up and almost certainly extinguished as a fighting force in so palpable a trap. He and his command were promptly transferred to XIII Corps and ordered to move out to take position on the southern escarpment around Minqar Qaim.

Needless to say, Freyberg's expostulation had been equalled and even exceeded in caustic criticism by Dan Pienaar's, and when he had at last been given permission to withdraw his division from the Kennels, he had taken them right back to El Alamein and XXX Corps.

As for Gott's XIII Corps, circumstances had combined to rob it of all semblance of cohesion and it consisted of a number of isolated units scattered about the desert. Its only infantry, apart from Freyberg's New Zealanders, were the 29th Indian Brigade after their escape from El Adem and the loss of one battalion at Point 650, and its remaining two battalions had been split into six small groups, of which two – named Gleecol and Leathercol, each consisting of one battery of field artillery and one of anti-tank guns with two infantry platoons in support – covered the entire nine-mile gap between the two escarpments. The others lined the southern escarpment west of the New Zealanders.

The armour was deployed further to the south – 99 assorted Crusaders, Stuarts and Valentines and 60 Grants in the two brigades of 1st Armoured Division (4th and 22nd), while the 7th Motor Brigade, the 3rd Indian Motor Brigade and the armoured cars of 4th South Africans and the Royals, making up the entire remaining complement of 7th Armoured Division, were deployed further to the west along and beyond the Siwa track as outpost and shield.

The intention behind this deployment of tatterdemalion formations was that Afrika Korps should be held in front of Matruh and Sidi Hamza by the infantry stationed there, but if the Germans broke through either between the escarpments or around to the south, they should be struck in flank by Gott's armour. There was enough of it, properly handled, to annihilate every formation in Rommel's command at the moment – though this of course was not known at the time.

But as Auchinleck flew up to Maaten Baggush to relieve Ritchie in the early evening of June 25th, he had already decided that this plan was unacceptable. He had taken with him Eric Dorman-Smith (lately promoted major-general), informing Whitehall that he intended to use him as 'my Chief of Staff' and thereby instigating an academic and occasionally vitriolic argument which was to rage for many a year, as such an appointment was not officially recognised in the British Army. The two men analysed the situation with which they expected to be faced, and planned in accordance with three basic principles which Auchinleck was to stress time and time again during the weeks that followed.

All troops were to be kept mobile and armour was not to be committed except on very favourable terms:

> At all costs and even if ground has to be given up, I intend to keep Eighth Army in being and to give no hostage to fortune in the shape of immobile troops holding localities which can easily be isolated.[23]

This was, of course, rather easier said than done in the existing circumstances, but Auchinleck and Dorman-Smith were encouraged by the thought that Ritchie had at least promised to put space between himself and his antagonists, thereby gaining time; and they had not yet discovered that this last suggestion of the recent Eighth Army commander was as unfulfilled as many of his previous ones had been. On the trip up, they therefore decided that immobile infantry were not to be retained at the front, and that only men for whom transport existed in the form of carriers, limbers, tanks or other vehicles *integral to their units* would stay, the remainder being sent back immediately either to the El Alamein positions or even further back to help man the Delta defences.

This design, when propounded that evening to the various divisional and brigade commanders, gave many present the impression that the era of the independent Jock Column had come again, for in practice at that moment it meant that every infantry brigade would be split into battlegroups, the number and size of which would be dictated solely by the amount of artillery available, further restricted by the amount of transport to hand for protective infantry. This was the only interpretation which those immediate circumstances would allow –

and it served to disguise for a long time that Auchinleck and Dorman-Smith were, ironically, both devoted to the principle that battles are best fought by divisions fighting as divisions or, better still, corps fighting as corps; but *mobile* divisions and corps.

But on the night of June 25th, it brought immediately from Freyberg a declaration that he would appeal over Auchinleck's head to his own Government against the splitting up of the New Zealanders into penny packets, and an air of some uncertainty throughout both X and XIII Corps which was to have unfortunate results in the immediate future.

Additionally, for the moment time was working against Auchinleck. To quote the South African historians again, during the twenty-four hours following his assumption of command:

> 10th Indian Division and 50th Division were trying to establish them-
> selves in the static defences of Matruh and simultaneously to 'make
> themselves mobile' in the new style, and all this was being done under the
> threat, implemented forthwith, of an enemy attack. It came perilously
> near to changing horses in mid-stream.[24]

The New Zealanders began their move to Minqar Qaim that night but suffered some irritating delays, and the bulk did not reach their destination until the following afternoon – by which time XIII Corps in an endeavour to create some sort of cohesion in their ranks had discovered that their entire signals and communications network was – to put it mildly – a shambles; and Rommel had ordered Afrika Korps forward to battle!

His plan for the reduction of Matruh was indistinguishable from that against Tobruk; the panzer divisions were to push the British armour away to the south-east, 90th Light were to encircle the port and reach the coast to the east, the Italians to attract all attention to the west and south; and in the words of von Mellenthin's later account, 'Our advance began on the afternoon of the 26th, and purely by chance it struck the British at their weakest point.'

Massed for a battle against strong armoured and infantry forces which Rommel expected to find concentrated south of Matruh, 21st Panzer and 90th Light advanced due east between the two escarpments, tore aside the thin defences behind the minefield as though they were paper, annihilated both Gleecol and Leathercol and took four hundred prisoners, then leaguered for the night thankful that the attention of the R.A.F., who had been bombing and strafing them all day with powerful effect, had at last ceased.

This move produced a truly ironic situation. Good fortune may have given Rommel access to the heart of the British positions but further advance would, on paper, sandwich the essential striking force of 90th Light and 21st Panzer – together less than one full

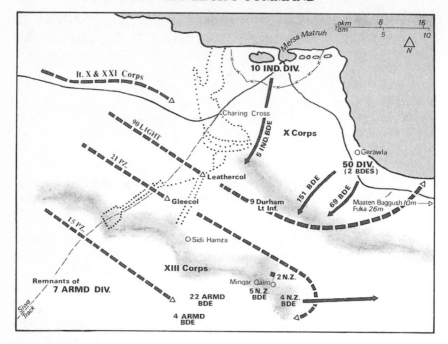

Map 20   Mersa Matruh, June 25th–28th

division in strength and with only sixteen Mark IIIs to face sixty
Grants – between two British corps, of which the one containing the
most coherent division, the New Zealanders, occupied a ridge
overlooking their proposed route.

Meanwhile 15th Panzer had reached the Siwa track above the
southern escarpment, and on the northern flank of the advance the
remains of the Italian X and XXI Corps were limping up along the
coast road to the western defences of the objective.

It all added up in theory to a recipe for disaster; but not in practice.
The destruction of Leathercol and Gleecol had been enough to cause
the hurried despatch that night of parts of two of 29th Indian
Brigade's other formations 'out of danger' into reserve, thus reducing
Gott's infantry even further, followed by a report to Auchinleck that
the gap below had been penetrated by a force of 'over a hundred'
panzers. Already too many people were looking over their shoulders.

Even when daylight on the 27th brought the possibilities of a
clearer view, early misfortune thickened the haze of fear and distrust
through which the British and New Zealand commanders were
peering. During the night Percy's gallant 9th Durhams had moved
out from Gerawla into the gap behind Leathercol, found the rock
almost impossible to dig and with no mines allocated to give them
some kind of protection, found themselves directly in the path of 90th

Light when these moved off at dawn. In the resulting catastrophe 9th Durham Light Infantry were totally destroyed; only three hundred men of the four thousand who had stood in the Gazala Line survived to march off into the prison-camps, the only small consolation for the British being that the noise of their resistance had brought such a storm of artillery fire down on to the area from north-east, north-west and south that their captors were forced away to the east and lay immobile for the rest of the morning until 21st Panzer came up on their right.

But when this happened it caused thoroughly unjustified alarm, among the New Zealanders of all people, even the commander of 5th Brigade Howard Kippenberger describing the scene as containing 'a huge column of transport . . . shimmering in the haze and headed by a group of fifteen tanks. It moved slowly, growing in width and depth.' It also – with the luck of the winners – caused critical damage; in the first artillery exchanges with the New Zealanders a shell landed amid a group of senior staff officers at Divisional Head-quarters, and in the early afternoon a shell splinter tore a deep and ragged gash in Freyberg's neck – the thirtieth scar, according to Winston Churchill, that he bore from war wounds, though of course as Freyberg had explained, 'You nearly always get two wounds for every bullet or splinter, because mostly they have to come out as well as go in.'

By this time, 21st Panzer had become only too aware of the enemy presence on the Minqar Qaim Ridge, and with quite notable initiative curved south around its eastern extremity, thus giving the paper impression that it had cut off the retreat of the entire division, if not of the entire XIII Corps. Unfortunately for the New Zealanders, this move did result in the scattering of their transport echelons which had been parked to the rear for 'safety' – and even more unfortunately for British fortunes as a whole, the move was seen by Gott, charac-teristically patrolling the battlefield alone but for his driver, and interpreted by him as the overrunning of the entire division.

There is no doubt that Gott was very tired by now. He had been fighting in the desert since 1940 with ever-increasing responsibilities, and although his promotions had been well received throughout the Eighth Army – for he was brave, attractive in appearance and manner, and friendly to everybody he met irrespective of rank – it is possible that he was now being asked to act above his ceiling of competence. He was not an intellectual soldier; he had probably been happiest commanding the 7th Armoured's Support Group and un-doubtedly his brief command of that famous division had given him great satisfaction. But he seems to have been overburdened by command of XIII Corps – especially during Ritchie's reign over Eighth Army when he had had to act as a mentor to his chief – and his interpretation of what was happening around him on June 26th shows signs of nerviness and exhaustion.

He had been with the New Zealanders during the first artillery exchange shortly after 0900 and been forced to conduct his conversations with Freyberg in a slit-trench; he knew of the losses among the New Zealand staff and, concerned about 29th Indian Brigade's account of 'over a hundred panzers, had told Freyberg that he 'should side-step if necessary' and not regard the ground around Minqar Qaim as inviolable.

He had then received, just before noon, a signal from Auchinleck to the effect that if withdrawal became necessary, the two corps should fall back into a defensive area south of Fuka upon receipt of the codeword 'Pike' – which was in fact a perfectly normal administrative arrangement for Auchinleck to have made, but perhaps on Gott's overwrought mind left an impression that withdrawal was already being seriously contemplated. He had managed to put Lumsden (whose 1st Armoured Division had been holding 15th Panzer back quite successfully all morning) into touch with Freyberg, and Lumsden had detached one tank regiment to go to Freyberg's aid – and was just contemplating moving his headquarters back closer to Freyberg's in order to give further co-operation, when he received a message from Gott himself saying, 'It's all over. The New Zealand Division doesn't exist.'[25]

At 1655 XIII Corps commanders received directives from Gott to withdraw, and to Freyberg's intense fury (although his head and neck were swathed in bandages and Brigadier Inglis had taken over formal command of the division, Freyberg was still dominant) just as it seemed that he had sufficient armoured support to deal with the panzers to the east, it withdrew and left him and his men to fend for themselves. It was all too reminiscent of Sidi Rezegh, and the New Zealanders' position was made even more critical – though they did not know it at the time – by another action of Gott's. Still out in the desert to the south by himself, he had intercepted a New Zealand supply column bringing up ammunition and water, and deeming its arrival too late, had sent it back to Fuka.

In the meantime, General Holmes's troops in Matruh itself had not been greatly concerned with events so far, their main problem stemming from the appalling quality of communications throughout the entire army. But by mid-afternoon Holmes had gathered that all was not well with XIII Corps, and he was organising attacks southward across the escarpments in order to aid them. In the west, 5th Indian Brigade would drive across the gap towards Sidi Hamza, while further east the two 50th Division brigades would drive down parallel towards Minqar Qaim and the New Zealanders.

By nightfall, therefore, a highly complicated situation existed. The whole of Afrika Korps was strung out between the coast (which 90th Light had reached some ten miles east of Gerawla about 2000) and a point on the Siwa track sixty miles away to the south-west, with 90th Light wedged up in a corner east of Matruh, 21st Panzer isolated fifteen miles to the south with the two New Zealand brigades just to the west, cutting them off from 15th Panzer, who were themselves pressing on the heels of 1st Armoured and being harried by the Motor Brigades of 7th Armoured.

To Auchinleck, who at dusk had no idea that Gott had ordered XIII Corps to withdraw, the situation appeared satisfactory – for even accepting reports which put Afrika Korps strength at between 100 and 150 panzers, the maps showed that the panzer divisions were both isolated and cut off from each other. He was therefore disappointed when during the night he received Gott's interpretation of the situation but, accepting his corps commander's appreciation he duly issued the code-word 'Pike' by which he intended X and XIII Corps to withdraw *in co-ordination* to the Fuka positions – probably beginning the following morning.

But there was no co-ordination, for XIII Corps were already streaming back – not only independently of X Corps, but with their own internal formations acting independently of each other. As in Gott's opinion the New Zealand brigades had ceased to exist no one made any attempt to co-ordinate with them, and the brigades of 1st Armoured Division apparently considered the Motor Brigades of 7th Armoured quite capable of looking after themselves (correctly, as it happened) and left them to do so. No one had actually uttered the words '*sauve qui peut*' but the atmosphere south of the escarpment during those hours was distinctly flavoured with the attitude 'I'm all right, Jack.' It was perhaps appropriate that most were retiring towards positions around a place named Fuka.

But not the New Zealanders. Their break-out from Minqar Qaim has won an epic place in the annals of desert warfare, for with their trucks and carriers scattered and out of touch (one of the officers had left the charging sets with the transport so the signals batteries with the fighting troops quickly ran down) it was decided that the 4th Brigade should cut a way through the enemy force to the east with bayonet and bomb. The 5th Brigade and a Reserve Group, packed on to whatever transport they had with them, would then follow them through the gap:

All vehicles, including guns, were to form up after dark, head to tail in nine columns ten yards apart, with 5 Brigade in the rear. Zero hour for the attack was 10.30 p.m. and we would move on the success signal from 4 Brigade.

The trucks were packed to the limit and the hundreds of men whom they could not carry were crammed on to the fighting vehicles. Men were hanging on wherever there was standing room, squeezed inside the gun quads, on the guns themselves, on carriers and anti-tank portées, everywhere imaginable.[26]

The bayonet attack by 4th Brigade was entirely successful and practically eliminated the first battalion of Rifle Regiment 104; unfortunately it would seem that German wounded were also killed in the close, fierce, unrelenting violence which encompasses this most searing of all types of battle. But it was soon over and the massed transport behind moved off, picking up speed as it did so.

This was not, however, the end of the action for the leading vehicles veered slightly south and bumped into what General Kippenberger described as 'a laager of about a dozen tanks lying so closely that there was no room to break through between them'. As 21st Panzer had approximately that number left, it looks as though 5th Brigade had run headlong into the entire enemy armoured force between themselves and freedom, and a small but spectacular battle resulted, with tank and anti-tank shells raining down on them, liberally laced with machine-gun fire containing tracer. In the middle of the charge down upon the panzers, Freyberg's head, swathed in bandages until it resembled a football, was seen emerging from the front of his truck as he stood up, and his rather high voice was heard floating back over the mass of vehicles remarking 'By God! Another Balaclava!'

For a few moments we ran on amid pandemonium, overtaking and being overtaken by other frantic vehicles, dodging slit-trenches, passing or crashing into running men, amid an uproar of shouts and screams. I recognised the men as Germans, pulled out my revolver and was eagerly looking for a target when suddenly there was silence and we were out running smoothly on level desert. We were through.[27]

Although Auchinleck's plans had been for the first stage of retreat from Matruh to end around Fuka, there seems to have been yet another misinterpretation of orders at corps level and the New Zealanders went right back to the neighbourhood of Bab el Qattara to join their 6th Brigade south of Alamein where, not unnaturally, they spent the next few days sorting themselves out and counting heads as the rearguards and stragglers came in.

As 1st Armoured Division and the Motor Brigades of 7th Armoured were still withdrawing eastwards in the open desert to the south, and the remains of 29th Indian Brigade were limping into the positions along the Fuka Escarpment, it can be seen that when X Corps received the code-word 'Pike' at 0430 on June 28th (X Corps communications were no better than anyone else's), the possibilities of co-ordination with XIII Corps were by that time minimal. The plan for withdrawal had entailed XIII Corps holding the crests of the escarpments, especially at Fuka, while X Corps columns passed through below, so the hazards which General Holmes and his men had been left to face as a result of General Gott's misreading of the situation were hardly inconsiderable. They were in no way lessened by the fact that neither Auchinleck nor Holmes was aware of XIII Corps's withdrawal until much later the following day (June 28th) – by which time yet another infantry divison were bitterly asking themselves whether any trust should ever be placed in armoured formations.

Ten weeks later, the findings of a board of inquiry set up to examine the causes of the collapse at Matruh were quite clear, and were laconically summed up in the remark by the chairman, 'XIII Corps just disappeared and left X Corps up the pole.'

Ironically enough, of course, during that first stage of XIII Corps's retreat to the east on the evening of June 27th, three brigades from X Corps had been driving south to bring them aid! On the western flank, the assault group from 5th Indian Brigade attempted to cross the Afrika Korps's entry gap, and one company of 1st/4th Essex actually reached Sidi Hamza to find no one there and be heavily shelled before withdrawing the following morning; and further east, 69th Brigade bumped into a part of 90th Light and retired after a brisk action, while 151st Brigade 'hit air' in their search for the New Zealanders, and also returned to their positions east of Matruh. An account by one of the gunner officers who took part reflects the caustic attitude increasingly adopted by the troops to such unprofitable enterprises.

> We marched due south in Brigade groups, exposing our soft skins to every machine-gun and A/Tk gun that cared to fire at us across the moonlit flats. The whole desert seemed to be full of criss-crossing tracer through which we had to march. And then before the moon was down we had to march back through the hole we had punched so that the enemy, now thoroughly aroused, could have more practice.[28]

By the time they had all returned to their positions, General Holmes had received the 'Pike' order, but as what inadequate signals system had been available earlier had by now disintegrated entirely, the general and his chief staff officer had perforce to set out themselves in different directions to find and inform the unit commanders of the plans for break-out. As daylight had come before this chore was completed, it was evident that the men in Matruh would have to remain where they were for at least one more day – by which time (though neither Holmes nor Auchinleck would be aware of it)

XIII Corps would have disappeared totally from the scene, the New Zealanders having arrived back at the Bab el Qattara defences and the armoured and motor brigades to positions some fifteen miles south of Fuka from which it would seem they later refused point-blank to move. Even the battered remains of the 29th Indian Infantry columns – the only troops to find their way to their designated objectives on the Fuka Escarpment – were no longer there by the evening of the break-out, for they had been swept away by the spear-heads of 21st Panzer who, under Rommel's insistent spur, had forced themselves further eastward during the afternoon of the 28th, reached the escarpment, overrun the Indians capturing 20 officers and about 200 other ranks, cut the coast road below, occupied the airfield and captured more transport and general stores. By the evening of June 28th, Matruh was well and truly cut off.

In the event, it is surprising that so large a proportion of X Corps managed to get through, though this is possibly due to the fact that, as one recent writer so cogently put it, 'During 29th June the desert between Matruh and El Alamein was covered with small columns of British and Axis vehicles all moving eastwards, trying to avoid each other'[29] – a problem rendered more complex by the fact that so much of the Axis transport was British in origin, and when collisions took place and their cargoes spilled out on to the ground to join action, they appeared in the moonlight all to be dressed in the same uniforms.

Holmes's break-out plan was simple and on a Homeric scale. All the brigade groups, leaving at 2100, were to drive southwards for twenty miles, then to turn east and make for the Fuka Rendezvous along the level ground between the two escarpments. Unfortunately, this plan was somewhat upset by Rommel's intention to attack Mersa Matruh at the same time, but commencing a little earlier, at 1700.

As a result, the Italians on the west found themselves being unexpectedly overrun by the retreating British, although these wasted little time looking for prisoners but pressed on leaving the Italians to enter Matruh as they pleased – while to the east there developed some fierce fighting in the tangled wadis leading up the first escarpment, with German infantry trying to get down and into Matruh and Gerawla and British and Indian infantry trying to get up and out.

This phase occupied most of the time up to midnight, but when the top of the escarpment was reached by the British and Indians, many Axis headquarters found themselves suddenly caught up, unex-pectedly and violently, in a battle. One such headquarters was that of Colonel Menton, commanding one of the 90th Light Division's battlegroups, and in the frantic mêlée which followed staff officers found themselves fighting with pistols in hand-to-hand conflict; and when the Corps column eventually shook itself free it left behind one brigadier, 20 junior officers and 450 other ranks with the somewhat shaken Colonel Menton.

Even Rommel himself became involved in action far too close for a Commander-in-Chief, even of his ardent temperament. He was under the impression that his attackers were the New Zealanders whom he still believed to be in Matruh, but his account presents an otherwise vivid and colourful picture of the night's action:

> A wild mêlée ensued, in which my own headquarters, which lay south of the fortress, became involved. *Kampfstaffel* Kiehl and units of the Littorio joined in the fighting. The firing between my forces and the New Zealanders (*sic*) grew to an extraordinary pitch of violence and my headquarters was soon ringed by burning vehicles, making it a target for continuous enemy fire. I soon had enough of this and ordered the headquarters and the staff to withdraw to the south-east. One can scarcely conceive the confusion which reigned that night. It was pitch dark and impossible to see one's hand before one's eyes. The R.A.F. bombed their own troops, and, with tracer flying in all directions, German units fired on each other.[30]

One of Rommel's staff who received the order to retire with considerable relief was von Mellenthin, who at one time had found himself firing a sub-machine gun against a 'British column . . . unkind enough to choose a route through Panzerarmee battle headquarters.'

Against this account should be read that of the British gunner officer who had taken part the night before in the abortive raid south of Matruh:

> I gave the signal and went forward at carrier pace, compass set at 180° in one hand, revolver in the other and shouting blue murder at the top of my voice. At once we seemed to be among them. Tracer flew in all directions from a score of flashes of light, AP rushed past our ears or kicked up the sand, the Brens from the carriers on either side clattered and flashed. Boche rose from the ground and scattered from our path. We ran them down – and over. I took pot-shots at Huns; my driver ducked to dashboard level; I glanced at my compass and over the open truck back to my guns. Bullets seemed to pour through the quads or bounce at angles from the wheels. One was fired; it blazed and men jumped on to the next one; the mass came on. The carriers creaked steadily forward firing burst after burst and magazine after magazine. I was never so excited in my life.
>
> We ran our two miles and pulled up in the first clear space while the others came in. Our order of march was gone. We recced round our area, found a Boche column in leaguer on our flank, raked it with fire and withdrew to our bridgehead. Slowly our nerves relaxed; we began to laugh. We were alive again.[31]

So felt many members of those columns as they broke through the encircling 90th Light formations that night, and they pressed on with eager hearts to Fuka where, they had been assured, the armour and infantry of XIII Corps were awaiting them – only to find, as they drew up in the early morning mist alongside British three-tonners and trucks waiting at the rendezvous, that these were occupied by Afrika Korps troops, who at the beginning were just as surprised as they were at the encounter.

But Rommel's men soon appreciated the position in which they found themselves and extracted considerable amusement from the events of the next few hours. Their final count of prisoners delivered so easily into their hands amounted to 60 officers and 1,522 other ranks, together with a large haul of lorries, carriers and trucks and quite a few more guns to add to their now extensive collection of British artillery.

Nevertheless, General Holmes and his headquarters got through after some close shaves; at one time during the night, according to the South African historians,

> They had picked their way through hostile forces, across desert sand in which the deep tracks of enemy armour showed black in the moonlight, escorted for some time by unwitting German armoured cars, past a furnace fire where the clink of beating hammers told that fitters were hard at work on a German tank, standing back politely to allow an unidentified motorised column to pass, which in turn politely refrained from vulgar curiosity, and so into the mist an hour before dawn.[32]

Fellow-feeling makes us wondrous kind, and no doubt many of that 60 per cent of X Corps who, in General Holmes's opinion, reached the haven of the El Alamein defences, did so because at some time German observers thought it best not to enquire too deeply into the identity of those passing in the night. Their thoughts as they watched or listened to the rumbling columns probably echoed those of the British driver during *Operation Crusader*, who found himself approached by the adjutant of Rommel's reconnaissance battalion.[33]

Rommel had three of these reconnaissance battalions now (though like all other formations which had been fighting since May 28th they were by this time well under strength): 580th Battalion were with 90th Light, engaged on the morning of the 29th in penetrating and occupying Matruh and rounding up more prisoners and assessing the loot, while the 3rd and 33rd Battalions were with the Panzer divisions; but it cannot be said that they were providing him with much accurate information about enemy defences in front, for obvious reasons. Their Commander-in-Chief was pressing the advance so fast that not even the British commander knew where all his own forces were, and in any case, there had been no time for Axis reconnaissance in any depth – and now they were both operating and probing forward into areas of which no one, however long they had been with the Afrika Korps, had the slightest experience.

On the morning of June 29th, therefore, as Rommel hustled his exhausted men on again without rest – without even, as 90th Light War Diary sorrowfully records, 'a swim in the sea' or a chance 'to sleep its fill after the heavy fighting for Mersa Matruh and all the hardships of the previous days' – his staff were unable to supply him with a very accurate picture of what lay ahead in the El Alamein defences. To fill this lacuna in his armoury, it seems that Rommel might have fallen into the trap of 'making pictures'.

It was well known that defences had been built around the railway station of El Alamein, making it, in effect, a half-sized Tobruk – and presumably into this must be flooding the survivors of X Corps, perhaps now grouped into one division, say 50th Division. He had received intelligence to the effect that a fresh Indian brigade had been brought up from the rear, and it would seem that they were constructing a defensive box in one of the shallow depressions lying about ten miles south-west of El Alamein station, probably the outer one, Deir el Abyad; away to the south occupying the inland half of the defensive line would be the New Zealanders who had escaped his clutches at Matruh.

British dispositions at El Alamein therefore looked to Rommel remarkably similar to those at Matruh, and it was not unreasonable to suppose that whatever was left of the British armour when it reached the El Alamein positions (for on the 29th it was still strewn over the desert to the south of Fuka) would take up the same position relative to the New Zealanders as it had occupied there, that is, just to the west. In short, in Rommel's opinion, X Corps held the northern sector of the line, XIII Corps the southern sector, and a repeat of his favourite 'bomb-burst manoeuvre' – break in along the junction-line between the corps, fan out north and south behind them – should again be enough to spread panic throughout Eighth Army and cause them to stream off eastwards yet again, not stopping this time until the whole of the Delta lay between them and his pursuing hordes.

Not that the forces under his command really justified the term 'hordes' any longer – or, come to that, even 'horde' – but what they lacked in numbers they must make up in energy and enthusiasm despite their exhaustion. He looked forward to the time when he would be able to give them their well-deserved rest and reward, but that time was still ahead; perhaps in Cairo or in Alexandria. But until then they must keep on the move.

The morning of June 29th he therefore spent chivvying 90th Light out of Matruh and along the coast road towards El Daba and beyond, with the Italian XXI Corps and Littorio wearily dragging themselves along after. The panzer divisions, once they had been relieved of the prisoners who had fallen into their hands at Fuka, were diverted south-eastwards across the desert towards El Quseir, some twenty-five miles south of Daba, the diversion intended to catch some of the stray British groups, columns or isolated vehicles still littering that irregular patch of desert stretching from between Fuka and El Daba on the coast, down to the edge of the Qattara Depression.

Having set them on their way, he then had time to assess the strength at his command, and to plan to utilise it to its best advantage within his overall scheme.

As a result of heroic efforts by recovery teams, it seemed that the panzer divisions would by the following morning have 55 panzers between them, of which 15 were Mark IV Specials with the new long 75mm. gun; in artillery, his own German troops would have over 300 guns of various calibres, of which 29 would be the invaluable 88mms and 39 were captured British 25-pounders – in their own way, almost as effective when used correctly. Even the Italian artillery included eleven 88mms and five 25-pounders among their 200-odd pieces, and they also had 30 of their own 'mobile coffins' as the M13s were by now universally called, for what they were worth.

The problem was manpower, for although the panzer and gun crews were enough to handle their weapons, there was a woeful lack of infantry. There could hardly be 500 grenadiers left to the panzer divisions, or many more than 1,000 infantry to 90th Light – while the total strength in the three Italian Corps – X, XX and XXI – came to but 5,500 rifles. Quality must make up for quantity. It had happened before.

Map 21   Towards El Alamein, June 29th, morning

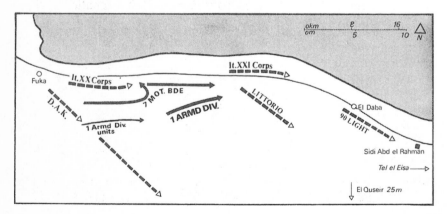

29 June 1942

Dearest Lu,

Now the battle of Mersa Matruh has been won and our leading units are only 125 miles from Alexandria. There'll be a few more battles to fight before we reach our goal, but I think the worst is well behind us. I'm fine.

Some actions make demands on one's strength to the point of bodily exhaustion, but there are quieter periods when one gets a chance to recover. We're already 300 miles east of Tobruk.[34]

The evening reports were mixed. The panzer divisions had struck appalling terrain on the journey to the south-east, which had taken toll of the vehicles and used up a disproportionate amount of fuel; and in the late afternoon they had had a brush with British armour intent on forcing a way through from the rear, probably units of 1st Armoured on their way back to the Alamein positions. On the other hand, 90th Light had not only reached El Daba, but had pushed some South African rearguards out through a cluster of burning supply dumps, and then gone on further to hedgehog for the night about five miles west of a spot marked on the map as Sidi Abd el Rahman. Tomorrow would be the day for briefing and deployment.

Dawn on June 30th brought another series of half-desperate, half-ludicrous confrontations between groups awakening to find their neighbours enemies instead of friends; the panzer crews at El Quseir watched armoured cars just behind them draw rather casually away to the south before racing eastwards at full speed, and breakfast-time at Panzerarmee Headquarters was suddenly disturbed by frantic calls for help from XX Italian Corps, still well to the rear, who had found themselves unexpectedly attacked from behind by 7th Motor Brigade. These, with sublime impertinence, having overrun the Italian corps headquarters and the major part of one division, then halted, about-faced and prepared to hold XX Corps in place until further notice, and the ensuing complaints and calls for help from XX Corps resulted in an outburst of anger from Rommel who signalled back, 'I demand that your Corps should carry out the attack, destroy the enemy and reach its objective. The enemy is under orders to withdraw.' An hour later he added somewhat gratuitous insult to this by signalling, 'Trust your Corps will now find itself able to cope with so contemptible an enemy' – an epithet which history might have warned him was ill-starred.

By 1000, 90th Light were on their way, closing up along the coast road and probing to find the first hint of solid resistance, but they were seriously hampered during the morning by heavy bombing attacks by S.A.A.F. Bostons which caught them in the open and destroyed a number of vehicles, besides dispersing them into the soft sand by the road. By noon they were at Tel el Eisa, and under artillery fire which increased whenever they showed signs of further advance; but so far, so good.

The hapless Italians, however, lacking sufficient transport, equipped with inadequate armour and with their only effective arm, the artillery, on the move, were soon in trouble again. XX Corps managed at last to push the 7th Motor Brigade out of their way, but these indomitable infantrymen then caught up with the bulk of 1st Armoured Division still rumbling back towards the Alamein positions, and both fell upon the rear of the Littorio Division and its accompanying infantry, en route to fill the gap between 90th Light and the panzer divisions. There was a brisk action as the British armour ploughed its way through, and although no attempt was made by 1st Armoured to annihilate its unexpected prey, Littorio later reported that all its tanks had been hit and two-thirds of them were wrecked. Moreover, their artillery was down to six guns, and a hundred men had been killed.

While this had been going on, Rommel was briefing his commanders. His plan was simple, and would on past experience promise the highest chances of success that men in battle could expect. Late that afternoon the panzer divisions at El Quseir would move southwards, making as much dust and noise as possible, thus attracting enemy attention and giving them the impression that they were contemplating a hook around the El Alamein Line – for this was how Rommel insisted on referring to the British position, despite its actual structure of four defensive boxes with minefields scattered between. After dark, they would double back and concentrate around Tel el Aqqaqir in the north, at the western end of the derisory slope known as Miteiriya Ridge and immediately on the right of the 90th Light positions. The Italians would provide flank cover to this concentration of striking power, and during the movements would manoeuvre to the east, thus providing a screen.

At 0300 the next morning (July 1st) the German forces would breach the enemy defences along the line of the Miteiriya Ridge, 90th Light passing along its northern edge, driving through the gap and skirting around the El Alamein box until they reached the coast road and the sea, probably near the place named on the map Alam el Dakar. The panzer divisions on the right would drive along the southern edge of the ridge, passing north of the Indian brigade at Deir el Abyad and leaving them to be masked by one of the Italian XX Corps divisions. The panzers would then swing south, cut down through the British lines of communication and supply until they were behind the New Zealanders and the remnants of the 5th Indian Division next to the Qattara Depression, when they would face west and endeavour to stem the retreat which would undoubtedly follow.

In the meantime, Italian XXI Corps would attack the western face of the El Alamein box and thus hold the attention of 50th Division inside, XX Corps (Ariete and Trieste) would accompany the panzer divisions and attack the New Zealanders from the north, while Littorio, their artillery augmented by two batteries of 88mms, would hold 1st Armoured Division in their place immediately west of the New Zealanders until such time as confusion and chaos had over-taken the Colonials, and the British armour began their retreat through them to the Delta.

It should all be over in a matter of days, if not hours, for there was no reason to expect the task to be any more difficult than that at Matruh, and Rommel wished to be in Alexandria by the weekend – and it was now Tuesday. Although the news that Mussolini and his entourage had arrived at Derna the previous day left Rommel singularly unmoved, the timetable was nevertheless running a little late, and the utmost efforts must be made to correct this; and such was the atmosphere of cool confidence at the briefings that not even the most experienced staff officers seem to have expressed doubts as to whether the tired and understrength panzer divisions could be expected to carry out, at night, a march of thirty-five miles through enemy lines and across unknown country, probably having to over-come at least some opposition on the way.

As a token of which, at about 1600 the panzer divisions, who had spent the day resting (though severely tried by the stifling heat) were suddenly shocked into action as the tail of the British armour swung through them; but their attempts to bring them to decisive battle

Map 22   Rommel's plan for July 1st

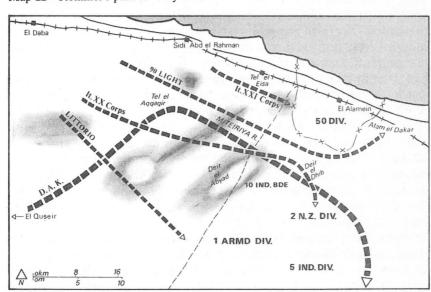

were foiled by the sudden thickening of the sandstorm which had been threatening all day, and the British tanks drew off and disappeared sluggishly eastwards into the choking yellow murk.

Soon it was time to move off. It was late afternoon on June 30th, 1942.

The diversionary move to the south was made by only one panzer division so as to save fuel, but after darkness fell and the two divisions had combined again, something very near to chaos descended upon them both. The going up towards Tel el Aqqaqir proved appallingly rough, an escarpment had to be descended and only one way down was found with the result that 15th Panzer drove straight through 21st and collected one of the latter's rifle battalions by mistake while doing so; and in an attempt to shed (literally) some light on the confusion, both divisions put up such a Brock's Benefit of flares and Very lights that even the Korps War Diary commented on it. 'German Afrika Korps betrays its advance by an uninterrupted pyrotechnic display,' it notes dourly, yet despite the illumination, by 0130 it was evident that they would all be late at their assembly point. Nehring therefore signalled Rommel to the effect that the armoured assault on the El Alamein Line would be delayed by at least three hours, and in the resultant atmosphere of disapproval D.A.K. floundered unhappily northwards.

Their condition was not improved by the sight, as dawn broke, of thirty British tanks congregated exactly on their assembly point at Tel el Aqqaqir (they were 4th Armoured Brigade in their last leaguer before reaching their battle positions) but these moved off as the German panzers arrived. Exhaustion, confusion and delay had depressed everyone present, and, as one of them is reported to have mentioned, it only needed a heavy bombing raid to make their misery complete. This was delivered at 0615 by eighteen Wellingtons, and had the paradoxical effect of getting the armour moving rather quicker than it would otherwise have attempted, for it was soon evident that in mobility lay their only safety.

In the meantime, 90th Light had moved off at 0300 on its task 'to shatter the front line of the enemy, reach the sea in an outflanking attack and thus cause the fall of the enemy's northern Strong Point'.[35] Rommel was there to see them off and all seemed to be going well (but slowly, for no reconnaissance had been possible) when, just after dawn, the leading files saw some British tanks leading away in front and were drawn after them.

These were, in fact, the 4th Armoured Brigade vacating Tel el Aqqaqir and, making too far north, the British tanks bumped into the western face of the El Alamein box and were lightly shelled by South African artillery as a result. Attached armoured cars managed to persuade the box defenders that they were firing at friends instead of enemies but the defenders were now wide awake and when they saw 90th Light coming into view on the heels of 4th Armoured, they poured into them such a concentration of machine-gun, anti-tank and artillery fire that, for the moment, the northern flank of Rommel's advance was brought to an abrupt halt.

To the south, however, beyond the Miteiriya Ridge, it seemed at first as though the panzer divisions were going to have as easy a ride as 21st had had at Matruh, for when they reached the area to the north of Deir el Abyad, it became quite obvious that the position was empty. They could therefore begin their swing to the south as soon as they liked, and it was during the first stage of this manoeuvre that they realised that their information had been at fault. The Indian brigade that should have been at Deir el Abyad was found three miles to the east – at Deir el Shein at the western end of Ruweisat Ridge – and when 21st Panzer circled around to the north in an attempt to by-pass it and then cross Ruweisat itself in their drive to the south,

Map 23   First Battle of Alamein, July 1st

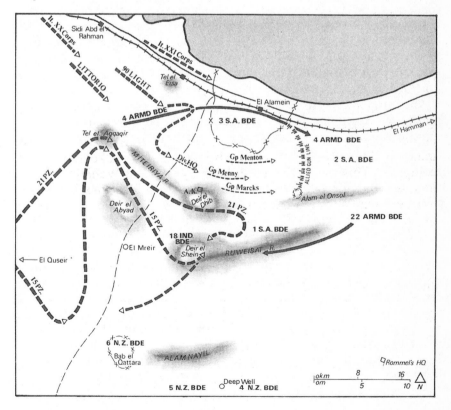

they ran into another strong defence at the base of the northern slope.

At this point, Nehring decided that the Indians at Deir el Shein must be eliminated and a halt was called for reconnaissance and refuelling. During it, both panzer divisions received further unwelcome attentions from the Desert Air Force, together with shelling from the strongpoint and the ridge behind, and it was noon before they were ready to move again – noon on a day made more atrocious than ever by an appalling *khamsin* which produced a fierce, oven-like wind and a thickening sandstorm.

But the sandstorm at least allowed 90th Light to the north to get moving again. Pinned down by the Alamein box artillery for the whole of the morning but conscious of their Commander-in-Chief's presence close behind, they then managed to draw back as visibility worsened and were by 1300 feeling their way carefully along the northern side of Miteiriya – to Rommel's relief and delight. Such was his enthusiasm as he saw the columns disappearing eastwards, that he signalled the Italian XXI Corps to the effect that the breakthrough was almost complete, that they and 90th Light could expect very soon to be able to clean up the Alamein box entirely and reach the coast road, and that XX Corps and Littorio should be ready to move in two hours, straight through the gap opened by the leaders on and past El Hamman towards a point on the coast road only twenty kilometres from Alexandria, named Amiriya! He was not to know that one realistic Italian colonel pencilled on the signal form 'Littorio has fuel for 20 km. To Alexandria – 150 km.'

The attack on Deir el Shein began just before noon with a bombardment under which 21st Panzer's 104 Rifle Regiment worked their way through the sandstorm up to the wire on the north-east corner. Machine-gun fire swept the approaches, some of their vehicles blew up on newly laid minefields, shells and mortar bombs crashed and thumped down on them from every direction, in particular from the ridge behind.

But they reached the wire, slid their Bangalore torpedoes under it and just before 1300 they blew them – and through the gap thus torn the panzers could begin their slow, inexorable creep forward. They were not to have an easy victory, however, for they soon came within close range of 25-pounders whose crews had refrained from wasting their ammunition by firing blind into the murk of the sandstorm, and who now made good practice. One by one the first panzers slewed out of line or brewed up, and only the second wave seemed to be making much progress towards the centre of the box – when suddenly out of the still dense fog they saw the unmistakable outlines of nine British Matildas.

It was fortunate for the panzers that their attendant anti-tank batteries, including three 88mms, had escorted them closely, for the next stage of the battle was intense though not long prolonged. But when it was over, the smoking wrecks of a dozen panzers lay alongside the equally shattered hulls of the nine Matildas, and 21st Panzer Division's striking power had been reduced by nearly a third.

By 1730 the Deir el Shein box was in their hands amid scenes of spectacular desolation. In the break-in section, the bodies of almost an entire British battalion – the 2nd/5th Essex whose first experience of battle this had been – littered the ground and slumped in the rifle-pits, only a dozen survivors remaining. Sikh and Gurkha prisoners watched every move of the panzer crews with impassive, unfriendly gaze, flickering into interest only when the victors, to their enormous relief, came across a bountiful supply of canned beer and could slake their ravening thirst. And when the Germans turned from this engrossing pursuit, they found the ranks of their prisoners considerably thinned as nearly a thousand of them had taken advantage of their preoccupation and slipped away to fight again.

On the south-east sector of the box, 15th Panzer had failed to break in, but as they waited for the final resistance beyond the wire to fade (and this was slackening mostly because of lack of ammunition) they were suddenly threatened by Stuarts and Grants (of 22nd Armoured Brigade), come somewhat laggardly along the Ruweisat Ridge to the rescue of the Indian brigade. In the face of obviously superior force, 15th Panzer retired westwards, but then found themselves under fire from the New Zealanders in the south . . . but dusk was thickening, the British armour were following their normal course and retiring from the scene of action, the shelling ceased, and D.A.K. hedge-hogged for the night where they were, hopeful of peace and quiet – but still fifteen miles short of their objective. They wondered what their Commander-in-Chief would feel about this.

In fact, Rommel was less displeased with the day's fighting than might have been expected, perhaps because he had had such a thoroughly uncomfortable day himself that he recognised that he was lucky still to be alive.

Once the plans for the attack on Deir el Shein had been laid, Rommel had established his Battle Headquarters at Deir el Dhib at the eastern end of Miteiriya Ridge in order more closely to follow the fortunes of 90th Light – but this proved by no means easy for wherever his headquarters moved during this crucial day, the Desert Air Force seemed inevitably to find them and subject them to concentrated attack. His *Kampfstaffel* lost many men and several vehicles, and Gause, his Chief of Staff, had been blown off his feet so many times that eventually he had to be evacuated with severe concussion.

But on the afternoon of July 1st, it was not Rommel's personal entourage which suffered the heaviest concentration of fire but the unfortunate 90th Light infantrymen attempting to encircle the El Alamein box.

After they had disentangled themselves from the western face, they had split into four battlegroups – Groups Menton and Marcks leading on the left and right respectively, Group Menny immediately behind with Divisional Headquarters at the rear – and in this formation they had worked their way slowly eastwards for nearly five miles until they were just short of Alam el Onsol.

And here they ran into a storm of fire from a crescent of gun positions extending from Alam el Onsol just in front around to the north where it reached the edge of the El Alamein box itself. Nothing was missing from it – heavy guns, howitzers, light and medium field guns, mortars, anti-tank guns, all contributing to a *Trommelfeuer* which shook even Rommel, who came hurrying up in an armoured car immediately the extent of the opposition to 90th Light's advance became obvious.

> Furious fire again struck into our ranks. British shells came screaming in from three directions, north, east and south; anti-aircraft tracer streaked through our force. Under this tremendous weight of fire, our attack came to a standstill. Hastily we scattered our vehicles and took cover, as shell after shell crashed into the area we were holding. For two hours Bayerlein and I had to lie out in the open. Suddenly, to add to our troubles, a powerful British bomber force came flying up towards us.[36]

But in his account, Rommel does not mention the most significant fact of all. For the first time in any account of the battles of the Afrika Korps, the word 'panic' appears – in the War Diary of the 90th Light itself.

> A panic breaks out in the Division which is stopped just in time by the energetic action of the Divisional Commander and the Chief of Staff. Supply columns and even parts of fighting units rush back under the ever-increasing enemy artillery fire. The Commanders of Battle Groups, however, succeed in keeping the majority of their units facing the enemy and bring back the troops which have taken to flight.[37]

A rout was in fact prevented and 90th Light dug in along the lines it had reached; but notice was being served that even flesh and blood formed in the Prussian mould can stand only so much.

But gradually, as the German infantrymen dug desperately into the rocky ground to give themselves some form of shelter, the encircling fire slackened and as light began to fade from the sky it ceased altogether – though there was again cause for alarm just before dusk when German fighters swooped above trailing lilac flares – the signal of imminent tank attack, which, however, did not develop. With relief, the exhausted and shaken infantrymen settled down praying for a quiet night despite the fact that they had received an order from Rommel to continue their advance in the moonlight. Nothing, it seemed, would blunt their taskmaster's determination.

Despite the set-backs during the day, Rommel was still confident that victory was at hand. His communiqué that night stated that Panzerarmee had broken through the enemy's defensive front south of El Alamein and that operations were still continuing – an announcement which was translated by the German Supreme Command into the stirring *Sondermeldung*, 'In Egypt, German and Italian divisions supported by strong formations of dive-bombers have broken through the El Alamein positions after bitter fighting. They are now pursuing the beaten British forces which are retreating towards the Nile Delta.'[38]

Shortly afterwards Rommel heard that the British Fleet had evacuated Alexandria and sailed away to the Canal Zone and beyond, and this did nothing to dampen his optimism and helped reconcile him to the flamboyant interpretation of his report in Berlin; but he had nevertheless to think deeply and to make some fundamental adjustments to his plans, for it was now quite evident that the premises upon which he had based them had been far from accurate.

For instance, the defenders in the El Alamein box had proved to be South Africans, not the battered remnants of 50th Division (which had, in fact, gone back to the Delta). Moreover, the formations holding the base of the Ruweisat Ridge were also South Africans, and so were those holding the position at Alam el Onsol – and fresh and rested men at that, thus proving that XXX Corps was holding the northern end of the line and not X Corps as he had believed. Moreover, whether or not there was British armour where he had presumed it to be, west of the New Zealanders, there was certainly a large force of it north of Ruweisat Ridge – including several of the redoubtable Grants – and if these were still exhibiting their habitual distaste for engaging themselves in infantry battles, this did not affect the fact of their presence or the power of their armament if ever it was brought into effective action.

In which respect, that night brought another piece of information to Rommel which gave him pause, and also explained a degree of skill behind the British defence which had already struck him as unusual. Ritchie had gone, and Auchinleck had taken over. He had a new opponent; he must certainly rethink his plans.

But until he had made his final decisions the battle must continue along the agreed lines and 90th Light must press forward, however exhausted they might be, taking advantage of the moonlight and the fact that the men opposite them would be just as tired as themselves, and not quite so experienced. So at 0400 on July 2nd, having enjoyed

a 'completely quiet night', the faithful German infantry gathered
themselves together, their anti-tank guns and artillery moved to their
allotted places, and the whole cavalcade of over six hundred vehicles
formed up and began once more their drive to reach the coast; and
within fifteen minutes of moving off and less than half a mile of
progress, they ran into exactly the same unending, concentrated
bombardment that had stopped them in their tracks the previous day.
However rapidly the South Africans may have retired from Gazala,
they were certainly prepared to stand and fight now.

In the face of such stubborn resistance, Rommel brought new ideas
quickly into play. Concentration of force against determined defence
must be the keyword, the 'bomb-burst manoeuvre' must for the
moment be abandoned, and the panzer divisions go to the aid of 90th
Light and take part in the drive to the coast themselves. By 1000
General Nehring had been told that the axis of his advance was to be
completely changed, and that XXX Corps and not XIII Corps were to
be his opponents; as soon as the panzer divisions had been redeployed, they were to advance eastward abreast of the Ruweisat
Ridge, 21st Panzer on the northern slope and 15th on the southern,
crush the South Africans and any other opposition in their path,
swing around to the east of Alam el Onsol and then drive up to the
coast. On their left, 90th Light would be conforming to their own
advance.

As for the southern portion of the attack against XIII Corps, the
Italians must now deal with this. The Brescia and Pavia Divisions
would take up position at El Mreir just to the north of Bab el Qattara
and keep an eye on the northernmost New Zealand positions, while
Ariete Armoured and Trieste Motorised Divisions drove south along
the route previously allocated to the panzer divisions as far as the
spot marked on the map 'Deep Well'. There they would watch for
XIII Corps reactions and attempt to block them if a general withdrawal developed.

But it was not to be quite as easy as that. For one thing, if 90th Light
had passed a quiet night, the panzer divisions around Deir el Shein
had suffered continuous and heavy bombing throughout most of the
hours of darkness, and although the panzers themselves had not
suffered much damage, their supply columns had been badly hit and
totally disorganized. It would take a considerable time to gather them
in, and only then could the tasks of refuelling the panzers and
restocking the ammunition racks – usually carried out at night –
begin. D.A.K. would not be ready to move off until mid-afternoon at
the earliest, and not even Rommel's insistence, his mounting anger,
his attempts at cajolery, and eventually his tight-lipped, eagle-eyed
surveillance could make the slightest improvement in the timings.

It was 1500 by the time the two divisions set off along the sandy, scrub-covered slopes of Ruweisat Ridge, the twenty panzers of 21st Division on the left and the seventeen of 15th Division on the right; and within an hour they were in trouble. Heavy artillery fire from the south disrupted 15th Panzer's movement almost from the start, and the British and South African squadrons of the Desert Air Force occupied the skies above them almost without interval, bombing and strafing – with, admittedly, little practical effect but adding considerably to the nerve-strain, the desperation and longing for rest of men already stretched to the limits of physical endurance.

Then at 1623, 21st Panzer on the northern flank reported the advance towards them of at least a brigade of British tanks containing in their opinion thirty Grants and another twenty mixed Stuarts and Valentines, and moreover – to some consternation at Battle Headquarters – they stated that the British tanks, instead of charging towards them with customary amateur hunting-field élan, were holding off at the extreme effective range of the Grants' 75mm. guns. In addition, at least four batteries of artillery were efficiently co-ordinating their fire with that of the tanks from a position well to the south at Alam Nayil.

In some ways this section of the panzer divisions' reports was the most sobering news to reach Rommel's headquarters that day, although later reports indicating a rigid refusal of either panzer division to go to the other's help or to that of 90th Light to the north – also under merciless air attack while endeavouring to make some headway against the nearest of the South African positions – added to the worries of an already deeply concerned staff.

As for the effect of the day's fighting on the troops themselves, the War Diary of the 90th Light strikes a most unhappy note:

> The German forces, badly exhausted by the heavy fighting and the hardships endured (moving day and night) during the preceding days and weeks, seem unable to take this last English fortress before the Nile Delta with the forces available. The enemy throws the whole of his available air force into the battle against the attack of the Afrika Army. Every twenty or thirty minutes, 15, 18 and sometimes even 20 bombers, with adequate fighter protection, launch their attacks. Although the material achievements of these heavy and continuous bombing and low-flying attacks is negligible, owing to the dispositions of the fighting and supply units, the moral effect on the troops is much more important. Everyone prays for German fighter protection . . . Sometimes German fighters appear singly, greeted by the roaring applause of the troops, but naturally they are not in a position to attack such large bomber formations. The last hope that remains is the Italian Divisions (X and XXI Italian Infantry Corps and XX Italian Motor Corps) which have seen but little action so far and are, therefore, more fit. However, from such comrades there is little to be hoped.[39]

By nightfall on July 2nd, the Afrika Korps had thus hardly shifted forward from their positions held at daybreak, and there was that much less ammunition in their supply trains, that much less petrol for their fuel tanks . . . and that much less energy and resolution for the battle. According to his memoirs, Rommel that night decided that the offensive could only continue for one more day at such a pitch and only a successful breakthrough tomorrow would justify the continuation of the battle.

Not that he revealed those thoughts to anyone else at the time. His orders to Panzerarmee Afrika for July 3rd were that the offensive was to continue, the axes of the drives remain unaltered and that one more grand effort by everybody would almost certainly shatter the opposition and open the way to the Delta, to Cairo and Alexandria, to rest and due reward. The panzer divisions would again drive eastwards and then up to the coast, 90th Light would hold the South Africans in front until the panzers were past them and then join the advance on the left flank; XXI Corps would keep up the pressure on the west side of the El Alamein box, XX Corps hold their position at El Mreir while Ariete and Trieste continue their drive down to the south to cut off the New Zealanders.

But it was no good. On the previous afternoon the later attacks eastward by the panzer divisions had been growing weaker and weaker, and on the morning of July 3rd they showed no recrudescence of strength or purpose. They now had only twenty-six panzers between them and when they moved off from their night hedgehog south of Deir el Shein, they found awaiting them on the southern slopes of Ruweisat the bulk of both 4th and 22nd Armoured Brigades, who between them deployed thirty-eight Grants, over sixty Stuarts and a dozen Valentines. The result was hesitancy and delay, and most of the morning was spent by the panzer commanders in requests to each other for more support, and rather unpleasant recriminations when this was not forthcoming. Tired men become waspish.

As for 90th Light, during the previous evening some of their forward troops, their curiosity aroused by unexpected sounds from in front, had gone forward to find that the nearest South African position had been evacuated – so they settled down there for the night; but dawn brought the advance of a British column which drove them out and took twenty of them prisoner, and 90th Light did little for the rest of the morning but shell the newly arrived column until it, too, pulled back.

No matter how Rommel railed, or what orders he issued, his faithful but exhausted men could do no more against what was obviously becoming a more solid and better-conducted defence with every hour that passed. And then came news of a further set-back which visibly stirred the Commander-in-Chief.

Ariete, the one Italian formation in whom he felt some confidence, had set off just after 0900 on their drive down to Deep Well, but unescorted by Trieste who claimed to be pinned down by 'incessant aerial bombing attacks'. Just short of Alam Nayil, Ariete came under heavy shell-fire from the same batteries which the previous day had co-operated so efficiently in halting the panzer divisions, and while the Italian gunners were endeavouring both to answer the fire and dig themselves in, they were suddenly struck in flank first by mortar, anti-tank and machine-gun fire, and then by a storming bayonet charge by a complete battalion of New Zealanders (19th Battalion, 4th Brigade) which overran them, captured forty-four of their guns, took three hundred and fifty prisoners and large numbers of soft-skinned vehicles . . . and as the rest of the Ariete Division drew back, it was caught again in flank by 4th Armoured Brigade. By noon Generale di Divisione Balotta was despondently reporting to Rommel that his command had been reduced to five M13 medium tanks and two guns.

The cold fact of this catastrophe was that an armoured division – and the best formation his Italian allies could supply – had been virtually destroyed by one infantry battalion and attached artillery; and with this news, Rommel knew that the operation which had begun at Gazala five weeks before was now at an end.

Map 24   July 3rd

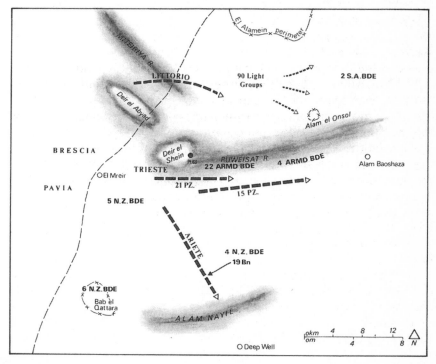

But there were still the closing rites to perform, the last benefits to extract from an operation which had, after all, administered a resounding defeat on superior enemy forces, and advanced his own army three hundred and fifty miles to bring them from the edge of the Jebel Akhdar deep into Egypt.

All was not yet finished, and at 1250 he signalled to the whole of the Panzerarmee, 'I demand energetic action by the whole of D.A.K.' He sent 90th Light forward once more and ordered Littorio to move up close in support, detached his reconnaissance battalions to cover the gap left by Ariete, and drove over to lead the panzer divisions forward himself on this last, dying spasm.

It reaped a small but worthwhile reward. The northern wing made little progress, but along the Ruweisat Ridge where Rommel was present, the two panzer divisions went in together under a co-ordinated bombardment, found a weak spot south of Alam el Onsol and drove through it to reach Alam Baoshaza, beyond the eastern end of Ruweisat Ridge. It would leave the forward troops penned in along a narrow salient, and 21st Panzer were quickly to complain that they were under fire from all sides – but a salient resolutely held can be a telling embarrassment to an enemy who wants freedom to manoeuvre.

At 2256, D.A.K. were ordered to dig in and await the British counter-attack, and that evening Rommel signalled Kesselring that for the moment he was halting the offensive:

> With the present fighting strength and supply situation an attack on a large scale is not possible for the time being. It is hardly possible to supply the army by night, as the roads are almost completely denied by enemy air activity . . . the intention [now] is in the first place to hold the front and regroup in such a manner that 2nd New Zealand Division can be encircled and destroyed.[40]

For this purpose he would need immediately more artillery, especially 88mms, more ammunition, more men, more fuel. But the first stage of *Operation Aida* had now come to an end. How soon the second stage could be launched and the triumphal march to the Nile resumed would depend upon support and encouragement from Rome and Berlin, and reinforcement and supply for the great-hearted, valiant but exhausted men of the Afrika Korps.

7 · First Alamein

It is generally agreed that the day upon which the British position in the Middle East lay in greatest danger was Wednesday, July 1st, 1942, and although the immediate cause of that danger lay on the battlefields to the south of El Alamein, there was also grave cause for concern throughout the entire area of the Delta where in some quarters something close to wide-scale panic existed.

What later became known as 'The Flap' was triggered by the evacuation of the Royal Navy from Alexandria during the last days of June. Faced with the possibility of attacks on the harbour by bomber fleets escorted by fighters from nearby airfields, Admiral Harwood (who had taken over from Admiral Cunningham when the latter was sent to Washington to head the Royal Naval delegation there) had dispersed his main force to Haifa, Beirut and Port Said, sent merchant ships and naval auxiliaries through the Canal to the Red Sea and even managed to expedite the repairs on H.M.S. *Queen Elizabeth* so that she could be floated up off the harbour bed and sent to Port Sudan, from which haven she made her way in due course to the United States for complete refitting.

These were, in the circumstances, undoubtedly prudent steps to take, but the speed at which they had been carried out, coupled with inadequate organisation, created an impression of panic which did nothing to cool the already febrile Alexandrian atmosphere, notoriously unstable since before the days of the Roman Empire and now rendered almost incandescent with nervous excitement. Rumours of the imminent arrival of the Afrika Korps fluttered the cosmopolitan hearts of the Levantine populace, for these immediately to be chilled by details of a 'scorched earth' policy to be put into effect by the retreating British as they fled back into the doubtful security of the Sinai Desert – both rumours being unfounded but assiduously cultivated by agents of the Axis Powers, with whom the Delta had long been well seeded.

But if the rich Levantines in Alexandria and Cairo could intrigue avidly to switch the emblems of their sympathies at the appropriate

moment from Lion and Unicorn to Swastika, there was a considerable section of the Delta populace whose hopes of successfully
executing such a volte-face were non-existent. Since the outbreak of
war, Egypt had become a collecting area for refugees from all over
Europe and especially from the areas bordering Russia – Poles who
had refused to accept the tragic fate of their country, Greeks and
Cretans who had fought against the invaders and then fled to fight
again, Serbs, Croats and Montenegrins who had escaped the mesh of
politics at home to begin weaving another abroad but with so
anti-fascist a vein that their fate would be most unpleasant once the
shadow of the Gestapo fell upon them. Above all, Jews from all over
Europe, whose lives had already been clouded and often shattered by
personal loss and tragedy, had flocked to the Delta in the hope that
eventually a homeland for them would be set up in nearby Palestine –
and to these this sudden close reappearance of danger assumed the
menace of an apparently implacable fate. Not surprisingly, among
them a degree of justifiable panic arose, first with the news of the fall
of Matruh and then with the Berlin announcement of the defeat of
the Eighth Army at Alamein; the embassies of any nation which
might be able to offer the remotest chance of further escape were
besieged, and the railway stations and exit roads from both Cairo and
Alexandria were flooded and inevitably choked.

Among the ordinary Egyptian traders and shopkeepers, un-
interested in who won the war but eager to make a profit from
whatever circumstances ruled, a cruel dilemma existed. Torn between a desire to keep open and sell high to a public uncertain how
long the piastre would hold, and a cautious instinct to board up their
shop-fronts against the attentions of a possibly panic-stricken mob,
they oscillated between the two attitudes with each changing rumour
and thus added considerably to the general uncertainty. There was a
run on the Bourse, the Egyptian Cabinet was said to be in continuous
session, the cotton market closed, and a rumour spread that the
students at the University, considered a hotbed of political agitation,
were planning action of an unspecified but probably violent nature.

The one note of brightness in this gloomy picture was provided,
oddly enough, by that indestructible element on the Egyptian scene,
the *fellahin*, who behaved with a sardonic impartiality which compelled admiration and increased the abrasive affection which existed
between them and the ordinary British troops. They might scream
and shout at each other, and 'black bastard' was the ordinary term of
both address and reference of the latter to the former, but they
frequently found themselves laughing at the same things together –
generally the antics or predicaments of their respective superiors –
and had remarkably little difficulty in communication.

At this juncture, once any immediate opportunity for loot had been seized (and at Sidi Bish, one of the Royal Navy camps outside Alexandria, the 'wogs' were into the area rummaging through the tents and store-huts even before the White Ensign had been lowered), the grinning, white-clad natives assisted with relish the efforts to escape of those who but recently had regarded and treated them with disdain. They carried the enormous trunks and suitcases along the streets to the railway stations, fought for places for their clients on the grossly overcrowded trains leaving for Palestine or Luxor, roped unwieldy packages and crates on to overloaded and dishevelled trucks and cars – all with gusto and high spirits and in an atmosphere of amused tolerance which was one of the few redeeming features of an otherwise unseemly interlude.

It cannot be said that officialdom did much to help. The Egyptian Army and Gendarmerie disappeared from the streets which were patrolled instead by English officers self-consciously wearing their revolvers, and groups of other ranks equally self-conscious because they were headquarter clerks and orderlies suddenly enrolled into emergency units to keep order, and with but little idea of how to set about it. Other groups of soldiers on the Cairo streets were also self-conscious – and worried too, for they were from fighting units which had been at Gazala or one of the intervening battle-areas, had during the retreat overshot the stop-lines at the frontier, Matruh or El Alamein, and were now anxiously avoiding the eyes of Authority – especially those of the Military Police – as they had for the moment no wish or intention to return 'up the Blue'.

And above both cities during that epochal day, especially over the centre of Cairo where the main Allied Military Headquarters lay, towered a black cloud from which drifted down into the streets a perpetual rain of charred paper, from the bonfires of official and confidential documents which a worried Command had ordered to be destroyed. As had happened in Tobruk during the last hours before capitulation, office staffs interpreted the order with widespread enthusiasm, and masses of ordinary administrative files went up in smoke in addition to the documents which might genuinely have been of use to an occupying enemy force. For months afterwards chaos existed at such ordinary levels of military life as pay, equipment returns, and acting, unpaid promotions, and one South African officer was able to boast afterwards that during the holocaust he had put all the documents relating to nineteen Courts of Inquiry to the flame, thus bringing relief to a few doubtless undeserving wrong-doers.

'Ash Wednesday', as the day inevitably became known, was to live for many a day in the memories of those who were present, and time has done little to diminish a remarkable legend. But even more remarkable was the speed with which the panic died. By the evening of July 3rd the packed exits had emptied, the crowds of refugees

returned – shamefacedly in many cases – and the somewhat mere-
tricious life of the Delta was resumed, the only physical reminder for
the civilians being the soot waiting to be washed away by the next rain,
for the headquarter personnel the empty files and the destroyed equipment, and for the Royal Navy when they returned the looted and
gutted establishments which they had so hastily abandoned.

It is very difficult to explain this sudden cooling of the emotional
climate except in terms of Mediterranean volatility, for it had not yet
become evident, even at the front, that the scales of war were tilting
back in favour of the Allies.

There are several descriptions of the condition of the Eighth Army and
the situation it faced during those critical days of July 1942, ranging
from Churchill's 'brave but baffled' to John Connell's more extended
delineation in his biography of Auchinleck:

> Some great, decisive battles have been fought at a campaign's be-
> ginning, and in history's light there is about them a strange morning
> freshness, an air of innocence and youthful ardour . . . But there are
> other battles, even more far-reaching in their consequences, which are
> fought at the latter end of long campaigns, in a wintry, grey Arthurian
> dusk, or in some stony pass beneath a torrid, unsparing sun that knows
> no romance and no illusion. The soldiers in such battles are trained
> fighters, lean and sinewy men, toughened by many hardships, disappoint-
> ments and losses . . .
> The first Battle of Alamein was of this latter kind . . . [1]

It would seem that John Connell was rather nearer the truth of the
matter than the Prime Minister (certainly in speaking of the 'disappointments and losses'), for although the men of the Eighth Army
were as brave as any soldiers were likely to be after such a run of
defeat, they were not particularly baffled in the sense of being
puzzled as to the reasons for their plight.

From their ranks when they had stood at Gazala nearly 70,000
were now missing, mostly as prisoners (33,000 at Tobruk alone), and
they had been forced to witness with ever-increasing frustration the
destruction or abandonment of tanks, guns, trucks, ammunition,
food, petrol and water – all having been brought to the battlefield at
enormous cost and expense of energy (much of it their own) – upon a
scale which appalled them. The vast majority of them had led lives of
narrow circumstance, and the sight of waste upon such a mammoth
scale both shocked and infuriated them. And they put the blame for
this colossal waste of valuable resources – of both men and material
– squarely upon the shoulders of their commanders.

It is often forgotten that there had been compulsory education in
the United Kingdom for over a hundred years which at the very least

had taught a large number of the commonalty how to think. Even more often overlooked by those who considered themselves well educated was the possibility that those who had not had the benefit of their own advantages might compensate for their lack with a basis of sound common sense. It did not need a course at a Staff College to perceive that matters had gone sadly amiss for the Eighth Army during the recent desert battles, and although the precise targets of the criticisms by those who had suffered most may not have been identified with total accuracy, the general direction in which they were aimed was not greatly off course.

The men knew that they were as tough physically as their opponents; they believed (rightly) that their adaptation to desert conditions was better than that of the Germans for they both knew of and believed in their national inheritance; and they knew that their own native intelligence and shrewdness were enough to withstand enemy onslaught, if they were not shackled by impracticable precepts imposed from above.

And this they had seen happening at every turn of the battle. Even at the most immediate levels they were commanded by eager and enthusiastic young men who, though undoubtedly brave and idealistic, quoted to them and were guided in their first (and often fatal) actions by unrealistic concepts of battle; and if their company and battalion commanders were adapting themselves to the realities of desert warfare in 1942, it seemed that any new expertise these were acquiring was not percolating very far upwards; the most reasonable explanation of the recent unbroken run of defeats was that the High Command were as out of touch with the realities of battle as were the subalterns they had recently trained.

In contrast to their own defeats of the last few months and the inadequacies of the men who commanded them stood the successes attending the efficiency and co-ordination of the Afrika Korps under their now-legendary commander, Rommel – all of which the fighting troops of the Eighth Army had closely observed, and with which they had been only too closely involved. And they wished that they were commanded by such as Rommel, and controlled by as efficient an organisation as that under which the Afrika Korps had won such conspicuous success. 'Organisation' had long been associated – often disparagingly – with the German temperament and with a supposedly Teutonic rigidity of mind and practice; but men of the Eighth Army could in July 1942 see that it had given to their opponents advantages which had proved superior to the individuality and initiative which, according to their instructors, were their own birthright – which in any case had not been much in evidence of late. Less slack 'jolly good show' amateurism and more tightly controlled professionalism was needed if the tide of war was to be turned.

'Rommel thinks it all out and takes whatever he needs with him,' stated one hard-faced infantry sergeant at this time. 'Our lot! Christ, they couldn't organise a piss-up in a brewery!'

This criticism undoubtedly constituted a gross slander against the faithful supply and administration services which saw that the troops were properly fed, that weapons and ammunition reached at least the forward supply dumps, that mail from and to home was safely delivered, that medical and dental services, hot baths, music and entertainment were all available in the rear areas for those who could get there. But the sergeant's complaint reflected a feeling throughout the entire army that this efficiency did not extend to where it was most needed – on to the field of battle. Infantry facing attack without adequate artillery support and whose promised shield of armour had failed to appear, found little consolation in the fact that their pay and cigarette rations were safely waiting for them ten miles to the rear, especially when it seemed most likely that they would eventually be enjoyed by the enemy.

The spirit of disaffection was by no means confined to the lower ranks. On July 4th, the day following Rommel's decision to dig in and concentrate on holding the ground won, Auchinleck ordered XIII Corps to drive north-westwards through the El Mreir positions across Rommel's communications; but the only formation to make the slightest effort to obey was 5th New Zealand Brigade, who came up against the Italian X Corps, were heavily dive-bombed and in due course fell back to their start line. Commanding officers of other formations seem hardly to have given this instruction serious consideration.

However, Rommel had seen the movement and moved 21st Panzer back and down towards El Mreir leaving 15th Panzer and 90th Light to fill the gap on Ruweisat Ridge, and these movements were in turn seen and reported by 1st Armoured Division – now in XXX Corps. In the hope that the Afrika Korps might be withdrawing, Auchinleck ordered both XXX and XIII Corps forward in the early afternoon, and the 1st Armoured Division with two squadrons of Grants overran 15th Panzer's Rifle Regiment and were in the process of taking nearly two hundred exhausted men prisoner when some of the leading Grants blew up on mines and a single 88mm. gun opened up on them – at which they hastily retreated, leaving the Germans to be captured later by a weak marauding column.

That day's fighting had several unlooked-for sequels. It reinforced Auchinleck's opinion that, despite his reputation, Gott had lost both confidence and energy; and that night in Norrie's caravan, the commander of 1st Armoured Division, General Lumsden, argued with Norrie for the immediate relief of his division in terms, according to one witness, 'almost insultingly insubordinate', on the grounds that they were exhausted. How they could have been considered more drained by battle than the infantry they had so often failed to support is difficult to understand, and they certainly had less valid claims for relief than the men against whom they were fighting.

Norrie, himself a cavalryman (11th Hussars), calmed Lumsden down and persuaded him that his division must remain where it was – but two days later he was himself relieved by Auchinleck of his command at his own request as he felt that, like Gott, he was over-tired. His place as XXX Corps commander was taken by Ramsden, but so many changes at top level exacerbated the confusion and genuine exhaustion throughout Eighth Army, and little happened actively to wrest the initiative from Rommel for a few more vital days – during which time he built up his defences largely in the form of interlinking minefields filled with British mines brought forward from Matruh.

Two days later an attempt was made to repeat the XIII Corps attack north-westwards from El Mreir but it met the same fate as the one on July 4th, though on this occasion 7th Armoured Division scored one notable success. It was being reorganised as a 'Light Armoured Division', its 7th Motor Brigade being joined by 4th Light Armoured Brigade consisting solely of armoured car regiments, and these cut through behind the German and Italian lines to reach Fuka on the evening of July 7th where they shelled the airfield and fuel tanks before withdrawing. At the same time, David Stirling and Paddy Mayne were out raiding with their S.A.S. patrols, and the Long Range Desert Group were running their usual highly effective taxi-runs back towards the frontier and Cyrenaica beyond.

And now, gradually, plans discussed between Auchinleck and Dorman-Smith began to show signs of fruition. Two further principles of action had been decided between them – first that the bulk of the artillery would be grouped together and operate directly under Auchinleck's control, and secondly that instead of attempting as in the past to destroy the most *powerful* enemy formations opposite – Rommel's panzer divisions – the opening attacks of the next offensive would be directed at his *weakest* link, the tired, static, under-equipped and not over-enthusiastic Italian infantry.

Rommel had already withdrawn his Afrika Korps formations to the neighbourhood of Deir el Shein and Deir el Abyad in order to rest them, leaving the line from the coast west of El Alamein down to and across Ruweisat to be held by the Sabratha and Trento Divisions of XXI Corps, with the Brescia and Pavia Divisions on their right; opposite them and into the El Alamein positions were now arriving, from Syria and Palestine where they had been training, Morshead's 9th Australians – lean, fit, bored and quite confident of their ability to deal with Rommel's Germans, let alone the Italians.

On the night of July 7th/8th a raid was mounted along the southern flank of Ruweisat by men of the Australian 24th Brigade, which hit 15th Panzer Division in leaguer and so worried Rommel that the next morning he replaced 15th Panzer's commander with Colonel Menny – and under cover of the raid and with purely deceptive intentions, the New Zealanders evacuated both El Mreir and the Bab el Qattara box to take up position some three miles to the south-east, releasing the bulk of their artillery to go further north. Little happened the following day, for apparently no one reported the move to Rommel for over twenty-four hours, but during July 9th the New Zealanders were able to watch appreciatively as a full-scale attack preceded by a heavy bombardment was mounted on their recent positions, 90th Light coming down and occupying El Mreir while the tanks, guns and lorries of the Littorio Division rumbled into Bab el Qattara. There was thus even less German or armoured support now for the Italians in the north.

Moreover, it seemed that Rommel had swallowed the bait completely and believed that his long-hoped-for breakthrough south of El Alamein was imminent; that night he gave orders for the panzer

Map 25   July 10th

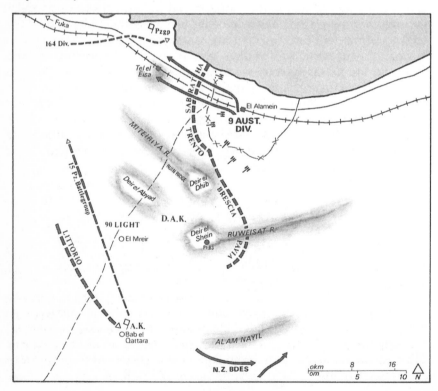

divisions to be ready the next day to sweep south-eastwards behind the Littorio and 90th Light, while he himself spent the night in one of the concrete shelters at Bab el Qattara recently occupied by the New Zealanders. His armour was now all in the southern half of the Alamein gap, as were all his German troops, while north of Ruweisat and totally unprepared for their fate, waited the hapless Italians of XXI Corps.

At 0330 on the morning of July 10th, Rommel was woken by the sounds of a bombardment which even at the distance of fifteen miles reminded some of his older companions of the dreadful First World War barrages, and he suddenly realised that he had been out-manoeuvred. By 1000, the Australians of 26th Brigade supported by thirty-two Valentines had attacked westwards out of the Alamein defences, advanced abreast the road and railway and captured the commanding feature of Tel el Eisa, having en route virtually destroyed two battalions of the Sabratha Division who, unfortunately for themselves, had been in the process of taking over part of the northern sector from the 7th Bersaglieri Regiment.

Panzerarmee headquarters were only three miles further back along the coast road and von Mellenthin, having also been woken by the bombardment, was soon shaken by the sight of hundreds of Italians fleeing past in panic and rout, having discarded their weapons and in some cases their boots in order to run faster. Fortunately, the leading formations of the first reinforcements to be sent to Rommel from Crete (164th Division) had just arrived in the neighbourhood, and from these von Mellenthin managed to form a defensive front to guard the headquarters, but by this time Rommel had abandoned all his plans for a sweep to the south-east and the Delta beyond, and come hurrying north with a battlegroup from 15th Panzer which he picked up on the way – to run immediately into 'terrific artillery fire from El Alamein' which effectively brought them all to a halt:

Next day, the 11th July, the British continued their attack south of the coast road, using powerful artillery and air support, and several more Italian units, this time of the Trieste, were overpowered and taken prisoner. Increasing numbers of troops had to be drawn off from the southern front and thrown into the fighting south of the coast road. Soon the whole of the Army artillery was brought into action, after which the British attack slowly petered out.

The British drive along the coast had brought about the destruction of the bulk of the Sabratha and a large part of the Trieste, and important sectors of the country had fallen into enemy hands. We were forced to the conclusion that the Italians were no longer capable of holding their line. Far too much had already been demanded of them by Italian standards and now the strain had become too great.[2]

More important, for the first time for many months, Rommel had been forced to dance to his enemy's tune. He made an immediate attempt to regain the initiative with an attack by 21st Panzer on the Alamein box but this failed in the face of blanket bombing of the assembly area by the R.A.F. followed by the shattering power of Auchinleck's massed artillery as the panzers tried to move forward, and in the evening Rommel broke off the attack 'in an extremely bad humour'. Next day he threw 21st Panzer in against the Australians with similarly depressing results, and by evening of July 14th he was facing the facts that the better part of two Italian divisions had been destroyed and that his precious armour was even further worn down – all to no avail.

Then during the night of July 14th/15th the second phase of Auchinleck's plan was launched – another attack on the Italian front-line infantry, this time aimed at sweeping them from Ruweisat Ridge and attacking the vital Deir el Shein area behind, in which 15th Panzer were then assembled together with the bulk of Panzerarmee's reserve artillery, several supply dumps, a strong concentration of anti-aircraft guns and the headquarters of D.A.K. and the Italian X Corps. Auchinleck was in fact repeating Foch's tactics of 1918 – a tattoo of hammer-blows on different parts of the enemy line designed not only to bludgeon the point of impact, but gradually to wear down the reserves both by casualties and exhaustion.

Unfortunately for Auchinleck, his immediately junior commanders had not attained the expertise or control of the British or French under Foch so many years before, and his plans went sadly awry because of this. Although XXX Corps were intended to exert some pressure in the north, the main attack on the western end of Ruweisat and Deir el Shein was to be carried out by the New Zealanders of XIII Corps and it does not seem that the corps commander, Strafer Gott, concerned himself very much with their plans of attack. Perhaps this was because Dominion troops always had the right of appeal over the heads of their British commanders to their own governments if they felt a lack of confidence in their orders, and after recent events many were threatening to use this right; but on this occasion Gott seems to have left everything to the New Zealand brigade commanders without question (Freyberg was still in hospital) and afterwards at least one of them, Howard Kippenberger, admitted to some poor planning.

Their 4th Brigade on the left was aimed at the western end of Ruweisat and had an approach march of six miles, of which the last three would be through enemy positions. If all went well the advance would put them on their objective (Point 63) at daylight, but by that time they would be out of range of their own supporting artillery and totally dependent for flank protection upon whatever heavy armament they had been able to carry or drag forward themselves. The obvious remedy was for armoured support to accompany the attack or at least to follow it closely, and General Lumsden ordered 22nd Armoured Brigade with its thirty-one Grants and forty-four mixed Stuarts and Crusaders to rendezvous with the New Zealanders at Point 63 by dawn – and with this agreement, the infantry went forward with great courage and considerable expertise on a silent night attack.

By daybreak, the New Zealanders had reached all their objectives, the ridge was in their hands, some companies had fought their way into Deir el Shein, over a thousand prisoners had already been taken and in Deir el Shein itself the Italian headquarters (including four generals) were about to surrender; but then 15th Panzer appeared behind the New Zealanders, having circled around them, and abruptly reversed the situation. As 15th Panzer's total strength amounted to fewer than twenty-five mixed Mark IIs and IIIs and their rifle regiment was down to fewer than three hundred men, the presence of 22nd Armoured Brigade at that moment would have made an appreciable difference – but they had not moved from their leaguer at Alam Nayil. In desperation, Kippenberger went back to fetch them:

> After ages, perhaps twenty minutes, we reached a mass of tanks. In every turret someone was standing gazing through glasses at the smoke rising from Ruweisat Ridge four miles away. I found and spoke to a regimental commander, who referred me to his brigadier. The Brigadier received me coolly. I did my best not to appear agitated, said that I was commander of 5 New Zealand Infantry Brigade, that we were on Ruweisat Ridge and were being attacked in the rear by tanks when I left an hour before. Would he move up and help? He said he would send a reconnaissance tank. I said there was no time. Would he move his whole brigade?
>
> While he was patiently explaining some difficulty, General Lumsden drove up. I gave him exactly the same explanation. Without answering he walked around to the back of his car, unfastened a shovel and with it killed a scorpion with several blows. Then he climbed up beside the Brigadier, who was sitting on the turret of his tank . . . The General asked where we were and the Brigadier pointed out the place on the map. 'But I told you to be there at first light,' General Lumsden then said, placing his finger on Point 63.
>
> I jumped down and did not hear the rest of the conversation but in a few minutes the General got down and in a soothing manner which I resented said that the Brigade would move as soon as possible.[3]

But by the time they did move, it was much too late. The New Zealanders had lost 1,500 officers and men before the situation stabilised, and in nobody's eyes were the 1,600 Italian prisoners they had taken a worthwhile exchange. Nevertheless, Ruweisat Ridge remained in the hands of the New Zealander survivors and the two brigades of the reconstituted 5th Indian Division which had attacked on their right, for the counter-attacks insisted upon by Rommel failed in the face of concentrated XXX Corps artillery which, with Auchinleck close by, was again being used in mass.

The material captured and the commanding positions won by Eighth Army between July 5th and 17th were sufficient to drive home to Rommel the fact that the forces now under his command were not strong enough to attempt any further advance towards the Nile, and that they would be extremely fortunate if in the near future they were not driven back to the frontier:

> On that day [17th July] every last German reserve had to be thrown in to beat off the British attacks. Our forces were now so small in comparison with the steadily growing strength of the British, that we were going to have to count ourselves lucky if we managed to go on holding our line at all.[4]

Kesselring and Cavallero arrived at Rommel's headquarters that afternoon and a long wrangle ensued which made very clear again just how near the bottom of the barrel they were . . . 'It can't go on like this for long, otherwise the front will crack!'[5]

It seemed that at last Rommel's fortunes were on the decline.

Unfortunately for the British, very few people in the Eighth Army possessed Wellington's intuition of affairs 'on the other side of the hill' and so to many among them matters still looked much more serious on their own side. Undoubtedly the grip which Auchinleck had taken on the army was much firmer than that to which it had been lately accustomed, but it seemed to some observers that the very stuff of which the army was composed had become so friable and denatured by disappointment that it was crumbling in his hands.

That week Auchinleck had been forced to signal Whitehall asking that the death penalty be reintroduced for desertion, in order to stem the flow to the rear of men who had decided to soldier no more – at least under the reigning authorities. In the event Whitehall refused Auchinleck's request, knowing that only Parliament could grant it and that the revelation there of the circumstances in which the request had been made would cause such a public outcry that chaos and confusion would result. They also knew that the correct cure for the condition was not death for those at the bottom but professional competence at the top and time for confidence in it to be restored.

In fact, the discontent which was causing such malaise throughout the British and Commonwealth fighting troops in the Middle East was not now so much attributable to the High Command, for already that one small victory – albeit defensive – had raised morale. But there were other factors which caused dissatisfaction, not least among them the contempt felt by the infantry for the armour, rising according to Kippenberger almost to hatred in the case of the New Zealanders. It had begun after Sidi Rezegh, increased during the retreat from El Agheila, was by no means assuaged by events during the Gazala battles, and by July had reached such a pitch that, to quote one embittered rifleman, even the cavalry were beginning to notice it.

And in itself, this situation aggravated another almost fortuitous cause for malcontent throughout Eighth Army. For what had seemed excellent industrial reasons at the time, it had been decided many months before that the Dominions and Commonwealth would contribute only infantry divisions to the war effort, and that Great Britain would provide armour. Thus the opprobrium which fell upon the armoured divisions from the ranks of the Australians, the New Zealanders and the South Africans tended to spill over on to the British infantry formations as well, even though their own attitude to the armour coincided with that of the Dominion troops. 'Pommie bastards' was a common term of reference to any troops from the United Kingdom, and it reflected a dislike and distrust which did not make for confidence at any stage of a battle.

Not that the Dominion troops had all that much confidence in each other, the relations between the Australians (in particular those of the 9th Australian Division) and the South Africans being especially strained. Many months later a group of the former were sitting in a well-known establishment in Cairo when a party of the latter entered. As the leading South African came abreast of their table, one of the Australians stood up and offered him a chair.

'Sit down, cobber, and take a drink,' the Australian said. 'You look all in. What's the matter – just run all the way from Tobruk?'

The resulting fracas was one of the more spectacular bar-fights the Middle East has seen (even taking into account the destruction of Shepheard's Hotel many years and one war previously) from which the author, who had been incautious enough to start laughing, was fortunate to escape with nothing worse than a split lip and two badly cracked ribs.

Even among United Kingdom troops there were 'tribal' dissensions. The Scots and Welsh have always had their differences with the English, among whom there was anyway an inherent coolness between southerners and those born north of the Wash; the Irish had an outlook entirely their own as had the Guards battalions, while men of the Rifle Brigade had a tendency to talk only to other Green Jackets. There were differences between the regular infantrymen and the 'hostilities only' troops, each blaming the other for recent defeats and united only in their detestation of tanks and all who rode in them – and neither were they particularly enamoured of the artillery whom they were only just getting to know. What *esprit de corps* there was therefore stopped short at battalion, battery or squadron level except among the Dominion troops, and even here it was restricted to their own formations.

None of these differences, of course, would have mattered or given rise to anything more than competitive ribaldry in a victorious army, or even one that knew clearly and throughout its entire being the direction in which its immediate aim and purpose lay. But in addition to the dreary history of the last few months, the Eighth Army was now suffering from a lack of clear guidance and especially of a clarion call to action which it would have positively welcomed, even had it been a 'Backs to the Wall' declaration calling upon it to stay where it was and either win or die.

Unfortunately, Auchinleck was in a painful dilemma and could not provide this, for although he undoubtedly sensed the benefits to morale which would follow such a call, he also knew that his prime duty must be to keep the Eighth Army in being.

For some time after he took command, Eighth Army intelligence continued to overestimate Rommel's strength, and according to the papers on Auchinleck's desk in early July his own uncoordinated and dishevelled forces could still be outmanoeuvred, and if trapped as at Tobruk or as had nearly happened at Matruh, it would be destroyed. In such a case England's only army in the field would be gone and the Middle East – perhaps even the war – would be lost. Auchinleck's situation at this time strongly resembled Jellicoe's at Jutland in 1916 where, although the best he could do would be to damage the Kaiser's High Seas Fleet severely, if he made a mistake he could lose the war in an afternoon.

Auchinleck had therefore to be very careful and to lay adequate plans for the further escape of Eighth Army by yet another retreat should this prove necessary – and there was no way of taking the essential precautions and keeping the troops at El Alamein in ignorance of them. This had been quickly demonstrated during the latter days of June, when Howard Kippenberger had been called back to take temporary command of the New Zealand Division in the absence of Inglis (the senior brigadier who was in command in Freyberg's absence) who had gone back to Cairo.

In search of information, Kippenberger had called upon his immediate superior, Gott, whose command post was nearby and whose reaction was to walk with Kippenberger out of earshot of others in the post and hand him a communication from G.H.Q. This began, 'The Chief has decided to save Eighth Army,' and went on to detail the precautions taken in the Delta – the defences being dug west of Alexandria, those at Wadi Natrun and Mena to shield Cairo, the building of boat bridges across the Nile – and also the routes to be taken by the various formations should the worst occur and a general retreat be ordered. The South Africans, for instance, were to retire through Alexandria, the New Zealanders down the 'Barrel Track' to Cairo, then up the Nile and eventually – according to Gott – back to New Zealand. According to the corps commander, Inglis had gone back to arrange the immediate evacuation of the New Zealand rear echelons and hospitals down to the Sudan – and to Kippenberger's protests that his countrymen at least were ready and fit to fight and that it would be criminal to abandon Egypt and a quarter of a million base troops in the face of 25,000 Germans and a hundred panzers (*sic*), Gott sadly replied that only the New Zealanders remained battleworthy, and that the real situation was as bad – if not worse – as that indicated by the letter.[6]

This was not only a gross exaggeration, a repetition of the tragic misinterpretation of affairs made by Gott at Matruh, but a fearful example of the state to which even a man of Gott's integrity and courage could be reduced by the strains of two years' continuous conflict. And it was to have serious repercussions throughout the army, for although Kippenberger determined not to mention the matter to anyone except his closest colleague (who also agreed to keep silent) it would seem that there were others who shared Gott's pessimism – among them Dan Pienaar who proclaimed quite openly that the only possible line of defence against Rommel was the Suez Canal.

And there were other reasons, deeper and on a strategic level, which prevented Auchinleck from committing Eighth Army to a 'win or die' posture at Alamein.

On June 28th, Hitler had launched his great summer offensive, splitting the Russian front on either side of Kursk, driving east towards Voronezh and eventually Stalingrad, and, even more dangerously from Auchinleck's point of view, south-east towards Rostov and the Caucasus. This offensive was one of the causes of Rommel's critical shortage of reinforcements and supplies, for Hitler's attention was now riveted upon Russia and not Africa; but this advantage for Auchinleck was outweighed in a signal from the British Military Attaché in Moscow with the information that the Caucasus was expected to fall within a month, which would put German armies on the borders of Persia – still contained in the area of Auchinleck's command.

And whatever Mr Churchill and the British people might think, Auchinleck was well aware that in the opinion of the Chiefs of Staff, the oil-fields of the Middle East were in the final analysis more vital to the Allied cause than any other asset in his charge.

Even if Rommel and the Afrika Korps were now held at Alamein or even beaten back to the frontier, events in Southern Russia might still necessitate the abandonment of Egypt, of the Suez Canal, perhaps even of Palestine and the Eastern Mediterranean ports, in order to protect the oil-fields at the head of the Persian gulf and the ports through which they could fuel the Allied war effort. In such circumstances, the defence of Egypt would become an irrelevance and the commitment to it of the only effective armed force in the area a perhaps fatal irresponsibility.

Whatever the advantages to morale of a 'Win or Die' call to the Eighth Army in July 1942, there was no way in which the Chief of the British Middle East Command, as it was then constituted, could make it and preserve his integrity.

The best solution to the problems posed by both Eighth Army's morale and the defence of the oil-fields would of course be the destruction of the Afrika Korps – a course of action being pressed with increasing fervour upon Auchinleck by Mr Churchill, whose reactions to the events of the last few weeks had varied between violent anger and brooding melancholy. In a signal to Auchinleck which was originally couched in such critical tones that the C.I.G.S. Sir Alan Brooke tried to persuade the Prime Minister not to send it (it was, in the end, modified) he wrote:

> The only way in which a sufficient army can be gathered in the northern theatre is by your defeating or destroying General Rommel and driving him at least to a safe distance. If this were accomplished before the middle of September, the Australian and New Zealand Divisions could return to their stations in Palestine and Syria and the 41st Division could be sent to the northern theatre direct.[7]

It then went on to detail other troop movements which were in train to help Middle East Command, but the plain fact emerged that the fate of the area lay in no one's hands but Auchinleck's and that if he wished to avoid an attack on both fronts, the one nearest to him must be eliminated as quickly as possible. He must, in fact, launch another attack against Panzerarmee Afrika.

By the time the fighting on Ruweisat Ridge had died down on the evening of July 17th, all Eighth Army's infantry divisions were closed up along the front and in contact with the Italians, while both 1st Armoured Division and 7th Light Armoured were held in reserve at the rear or on the flank. A second Indian Motor Brigade (161st) had arrived from Iraq and joined 5th Indian Division which had now become very weak, and there was in the neighbourhood an extra reinforcement for the armour. The 23rd Armoured Brigade had arrived at Suez on July 6th as the first instalment of the 8th Armoured Division, and by July 11th its 156 Valentines (still armed with 2-pounders) had been fitted with desert filters and judged adequate for action. Their crews, however, were obviously still unacclimatised to a Middle East mid-summer, and no one knew how much of their training in England would stand up to the realities of a desert battle.

None the less, their addition to 1st Armoured Division would raise the tank strength at Auchinleck's disposal to 323 of which 61 would be Grants and over half the still useful Valentines. On the face of it the possibilities of dealing the Afrika Korps a heavy and possibly lethal blow were thus not as low as might have been expected, though it was a pity that time did not allow Eighth Army to be built up to even greater strength, while Rommel was left to languish at the end of his extended supply lines.

The plan now adopted was basically similar to Auchinleck's earlier attacks – left- and right-handed blows delivered in quick succession – though better co-ordination between them was hoped for and this time XIII Corps would strike first in the south and XXX Corps second in the north. Operational orders were issued on July 17th, instructions for pursuit on the 20th, and for army/air co-operation the following day, just a few hours before the first attack was to go in.

The original plan was for XIII Corps with 1st Armoured Division

Map 26 Auchinleck's final plan for July 22nd–25th

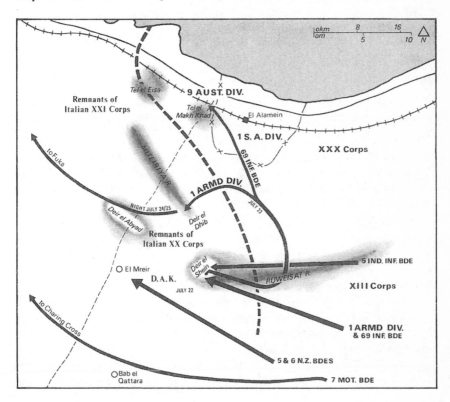

to drive north-westwards into Deir el Shein, Deir el Abyad and El Mreir and thus either scatter the German core of the defence or, more likely, draw in all Rommel's reserves. The timetable called for the New Zealanders and the Indians to be at El Mreir and Deir el Shein respectively by dawn on July 22nd, and in such firm control by the end of the day that the armour could then be released to go north to join XXX Corps on the 23rd, who would attack on the 24th/25th across the south-eastern end of Miteiriya Ridge, break open the rear defences of Rommel's army and allow the 1st Armoured Division to race through for the Fuka bottle-neck. The Motor Brigade of 7th Armoured would converge with it from the south while the armoured cars of the 4th Light Armoured Brigade sped towards Mersa Matruh. Thus even if part of Afrika Korps fought their way back out of the trap, the entire Italian element should be captured.

The whole plan of attack depended upon the close co-operation of the XIII Corps infantry with the armour from the moment the battle began, on the efficient disengagement of the armour immediately that stage was fulfilled (and it would be on a very tight schedule), and on its rapid transfer to the north followed by its equally close co-operation with XXX Corps infantry, some of whom would have opened wide gaps in Rommel's minefields to let the armour through.

In this regard, the *Official History* comments that the opening phase had at least the advantage that it would be under the control of one corps commander, but Kippenberger, whose brigade would provide support for the 6th New Zealanders attacking towards El Mreir, reveals a significant difference between theory and practice:

> I was very unhappy at the divisional conference. Again there was no Corps conference although this was a Corps battle, and we knew only at second hand what the other formations concerned were to do . . . It is essential, and elementary, that such details as starting-time and start-line, axes of advance, objectives, boundaries, lateral communications, artillery support, siting of headquarters, should be co-ordinated, if commanders are to help one another and do the best for their own troops. We knew very little indeed on these points.[8]

The brigadier commanding the supporting armour – newly arrived from Britain – was present at this conference, and although he promised that his armour would be at the right place to protect the infantry at their most perilous time – dawn – he resolutely refused to consider moving his tanks during the hours of darkness. No matter what might have been claimed for the performances of Rommel's panzers (and he gave the impression that he believed all those stories to be gross exaggerations) armour just could not move at night; but the infantry should not worry, for he was quite sure that his tanks would cover the necessary distance before the Germans would be able to mount any worthwhile attack upon them. And nothing that

Kippenberger or Brigadier George Clifton, 6th Brigade, could do or say would make him change his mind. As Gott was not present the New Zealanders had to accept the position, but when Kippenberger returned to his headquarters, he told everybody but his senior staff officer to leave and then dictated the following memo: 'The Brigadier has returned from the divisional conference and says there will be another bloody disaster.'[9]

As an omen to support this sad prognostication, both General Lumsden and Brigadier Briggs of 2nd Armoured Brigade had been wounded on July 18th in a Stuka attack, and Major-General Alec Gatehouse – a veteran of the early desert fighting – brought forward from the Delta where he had been training 10th Armoured Division, did not arrive to take Lumsden's place until the evening of July 20th, far too late for him to make any adjustments to the plans even had he considered them necessary.

And the following day brought yet another set-back to Auchinleck's plans. Ramsden, commanding XXX Corps's sector, had long felt that the South Africans now lacked the necessary aggressiveness and enthusiasm for so strenuous a task as breakthrough and pursuit, in addition to which his relationship with Pienaar left much to be desired. From the first he had therefore suggested and counted upon the Australians for the main burden of the fighting in the north when the XXX Corps break-out commenced, and to this Auchinleck had willingly agreed.

The Commander-in-Chief was therefore considerably dismayed and angered to be met at XXX Corps H.Q. on the afternoon of July 21st by a white-faced Ramsden announcing that General Morshead was objecting to the part his men were expected to undertake on the grounds that they had already played the stormtroops' role in too many actions, and that the plans showed too wide a dispersal of his troops for them to have much chance of success. Morshead had also stated that in his opinion there had already been so many changes in the timings of the attacks as to sow seeds of doubt in his mind as to the clear-sightedness of the planners themselves, and Ramsden added the gratuitous information that he thought Morshead's real reasons for objecting were that the Australians had no faith in the British armour, of whose reputation they had learned from the New Zealanders. He concluded with the announcement that Morshead was insisting upon reference to his Government before further action.

After the months of strain to which Auchinleck had been subjected it is hardly surprising that his first reactions were violent and extreme – he 'went through the roof' according to Ramsden – but he quickly calmed down with the realisation that he could not fight this battle without everybody's co-operation, that Morshead was fully entitled to what he was claiming, and after the events of the last few months could hardly be blamed for doubting assurances from corps or Army commanders with regard to armoured support.

Morshead was invited to 'come for tea' that afternoon, and a polite but tough session of bargaining took place at which it was finally agreed that only one Australian brigade should be employed, that the South Africans would operate on their inner, left flank clearing minefields, and that the British 69th Brigade, which was temporarily under command of 7th Armoured Division, would be brought up from the south at the same time as the armour came up from XIII Corps, and this would precede the armour through the gap and join the Australians for the break-out and pursuit. The three generals then parted, leaving Auchinleck with Dorman-Smith who had been taking notes throughout, and who now announced quite clearly that in his opinion the whole operation was unsound and should be called off.

It would take, in Dorman-Smith's opinion, at least forty-eight hours for 69th Brigade to move from their positions after the XIII Corps attack, up into the Alamein box in order to play their part in the vital break-out – and during that time Rommel would have been able to regroup his forces to meet it; and at this stage there was no time left to put in train elaborate deceptive measures to disguise from Rommel that Auchinleck was shifting his weight.

But military plans seem often to possess a momentum of their own. Perhaps Mr Churchill's exigence was weighing heavily on Auchinleck's mind, while far away to the north Rostov was already under heavy attack, and with its loss the Caucasus would be open to a flood of German armies. After but the slightest pause, Auchinleck shook his head. The operation must go on as now planned.

Just before dusk on the evening of July 21st, a brisk bombardment opened up along the whole length of the front (for the Australians were creating a diversion in the north so as to give XIII Corps as much advantage as possible) and the two XIII Corps infantry divisions – 5th Indian on the right along Ruweisat Ridge aimed at Point 63 and Deir el Shein, New Zealanders on the left coming up first from the south and then swinging left and into El Mreir – began their advance. The flank formations along the inter-divisional boundary would concentrate on gapping the minefields so as to let the supporting armour follow through – 23rd Armoured Brigade with their Valentines supporting the Indians in the north, 2nd Armoured Brigade with their mixed Grants, Stuarts and Crusaders following the New Zealanders. It was a close, moonless night and the thunder of the guns drowned out the crunch of gravel under trucks and carriers, the crash of grenades, the shouts of anger and fear, and the continuous muffled tramp of marching feet.

Then the bombardment ended, the attacking infantry ran clear of the shell-bursts and charged on towards their dawn objectives, taking them both after hard but valiant fighting. By 0500, the three New Zealand battalions and Brigade Headquarters were at their turning-point 2,000 yards east of the El Mreir depression, while 3rd/7th Rajputs were fighting furiously in Deir el Shein and 1st/2nd Punjabs had taken Point 63. Now was the time for the armour to come up, especially as General Nehring – despite the opinion of the new Royal Armoured Corps brigadier – had not thought it necessary to wait until daylight before sending in his panzers and the New Zealanders were under heavy attack by both 5th and 8th Panzer Regiments less than a quarter of an hour after they arrived. Many of their anti-tank guns had been blown up on the minefields as they came through, as had a lorry-load of sticky bombs which might have been of some use in the hands of men as desperate as the New Zealanders then became.

Kippenberger was back at his own Brigade Headquarters, waiting for news of his compatriots:

> Soon after daylight, from wounded and a few stragglers who had got in, it had become clear that there had been another disaster . . . There had been no appearance of the tanks. The German tanks moving in the darkness, and some of them actually following the brigade through gaps in the minefield, had attacked at first light and the survivors, quite helpless, had surrendered . . . There was nothing left of the rifle companies of the Twenty-fourth and Twenty-fifth except one company of the Twenty-fifth which had lost direction and had not reached the depression; little was left of the anti-tank battery and there were heavy losses in transport. Most of Brigade Headquarters was missing with the Brigadier . . . Worst of all, we had again relied in vain on the support of our tanks and bitterness was extreme.[10]

According to the *Official History*, two regiments of the 2nd Armoured Brigade did try to get forward to give aid to the New Zealanders, but one was held up by anti-tank fire and the other ran on to the minefields which had not been properly gapped by the infantry as they went through, for the techniques of minefield gapping had been forgotten since the days of O'Connor.

But one armoured brigade at least was determined to keep its promise of support. At 0800 – three hours after they had been required and without, apparently, a word of warning from anybody watching – the Valentines of 23rd Brigade with their young and unblooded crews formed up, with 40th Royal Tank Regiment on the right and 46th on the left, and attended by a total breakdown of its wireless communications charged forward with all the exultant courage and lack of tactical wisdom of the innocent and unrealistically trained.

For about a mile and a half, they swept forward not unlike a flotilla of destroyers at sea and certainly impelled by the panache of a cavalry charge; but then they came within killing range of the German anti-tank screen whose crews had by then had time to recover from their astonishment at such a scene after three years of war. There was a crash of gunfire, the leading tanks disappeared under a cloud of smoke and sand, the ones immediately following swung around past them and ran straight on to a minefield. Nevertheless, fifteen tanks from 40th Royal Tank Regiment broke through and reached their first objective – to find themselves flanked by anti-tank guns which unhurriedly picked them off; five eventually pulled back into safety. Of 46th Royal Tank Regiment's Valentines, thirteen were lost in the minefield, a few fell back but some pressed onwards after fanning out, disappeared to the west of El Mreir and were never seen again. Within two hours of setting out on its first action, 23rd Armoured Brigade had lost 93 of the 104 Valentines with which it had begun its advance (many had broken down on the way up from the Delta) and over 150 of its officers and men.

In the meantime, 22nd Armoured Brigade, whose task had been to protect the southern flank of the New Zealanders, had been sitting about in front of Howard Kippenberger's 5th Brigade positions, and out in no-man's-land beyond:

> They had several tanks hit and after a while realized they were doing no good and departed. One angry regimental commander saw me and stopped to apologize about the affair. He said that he felt bitterly humiliated but I am afraid that I did not answer very graciously. When they had gone, the charred skeletons of about forty of 6 Brigade's vehicles remained on the sky-line.[11]

The fighting on XIII Corps's front went on for the rest of the day, 5th Indian Division fighting back and forth along Ruweisat Ridge (for with the destruction of 23rd Armoured Brigade they too found themselves attacked by both German armour and Italian artillery) and in the end they were forced back almost to the positions from which they had set out in the morning. And below them along the inter-divisional boundary, the 9th Lancers and the 7th R.T.R. of 2nd Armoured Brigade tried to reach any New Zealanders who might have still been holding out at El Mreir (it seems unlikely there were by that time), lost five more tanks and had to reverse the others back out through the narrow lane in the minefield which was all they had been able to find. Kippenberger's closing comment on the action is understandably bitter, and not wholly unjustified:

> Two infantry and two armoured brigades had been employed. They had made three unrelated attacks from different directions at different times. A single small Panzer division of some twenty or thirty tanks and a fifth-

rate Italian infantry division easily dealt with all three attacks in succession and inflicted crippling losses.[12]

And yet, in one way, the object of this action had been achieved; Rommel's attention had been refocused in the south, his armour had been brought down there and although he had undoubtedly scored a success he would now be off balance for an immediate heavy and determined attack in the north. Although Auchinleck was shaken by the evidence of the inefficiency, the lack of co-ordination and the plain amateurism displayed throughout his army, probably wondering like Wellington whether there was anybody holding a position of responsibility in it who was both willing and professionally competent to carry out his orders, it nevertheless looked as though there was nothing to prevent the overall plan of battle from being carried through.

The Australians had not only leaned hard on the defences (mainly Italian but well 'corseted' by units of 90th Light) around Tel el Eisa, but they had broken out across Tel el Makh Khad in very tough fighting indeed during which one of the private soldiers won a posthumous Victoria Cross, and by nightfall were pushing towards Ruin Ridge on the southern side of Miteiriya. As the defences had been unexpectedly stubborn the advance was running late, and it was early evening before fifty-two Valentines from 1st Army Tank Brigade, which had been waiting in close attendance for most of the day, were on their start line ready to go forward on the last stage, carrying infantry and engineers to deal with mines on the way.

It was thus nearly 1900 before they set off, to run very quickly on to an unknown minefield in which some twenty tanks were put out of action, after which they became lost in the dark, found a ridge with a ruin on it which they quite understandably believed to be their objective, decanted their infantry, waited to give support to the next battalion to come through, after which they withdrew leaving the infantry to dig in on the reverse slope. It was not until the following morning that it became obvious that in the darkness they had stopped some 2,500 to 3,000 yards short of their objective, and that beyond the Australian infantry now lay a line of well-sited German positions with at least twenty guns well dug in amongst them. There was nothing they could do now but wait until the reinforcements arrived from the south.

This was the position at dawn on July 23rd; no further large-scale attack would be launched until midnight July 26th/27th and thus for eighty-four hours the defenders, already strongly positioned in front of the Australians, were able to sow more mines, dig in more guns and fill the gaps in their ranks from replacement units which, although not 'fit for tropical service' yet, were all thoroughly imbued with basic German Army doctrine, and had been trickling into the lines over the past few days at an ever-quickening pace.

The only misjudgment in Dorman-Smith's warning had been an under-estimate of the time the armour and extra infantry would take to come up.

The sad story of the last July attack is quickly told.

All through July 26th a heavy sandstorm cloaked the battle area but despite this the South Africans did not begin gapping the minefield south-east of Miteiriya until darkness, and by midnight there was still no clear way through. Soon after midnight, 24th Australian Brigade launched their attack towards Ruin Ridge and by 0300 had at last taken the south-eastern end of Miteiriya Ridge, at which they swung right towards the break-out area expecting the Durhams and East Yorks of 69th Brigade to come up on the left and drive towards Deir el Dhib. These had been delayed by the uncleared minefields behind and arrived late, and were then further delayed by the necessity to clear more mines themselves as they fought their way forward – and their technique was faulty. Carriers, trucks and men were blown up in a chaos of explosion and disorder, but by 0800 the bulk of the men of 69th Brigade were at Deir el Dhib, with the Australians slightly ahead of them on their right.

But missing from the 69th Brigade's ranks were the anti-tank gun flank screens who had all lost their way in the darkness, some being blown up and only one arriving at dawn within a mile of the men they were intended to protect. Needless to say, their predicament was quickly appreciated by 90th Light, who moved in, first of all by themselves and then supported by one of the reconnaissance battalions whose heavy armoured cars and light panzers, unopposed by either anti-tank guns or tanks, easily overran the unprotected British infantry and began rounding them up.

On this occasion at least, the British armour cannot be accused of not trying to help. Enough obloquy had been poured on the men of 2nd Armoured Brigade – and indeed on all those who wore the black beret – during the preceding weeks for them to be very eager to recover their reputations; but tanks which run on to uncleared minefields blow up, and there is nothing the crews can do but bale out as quickly as possible. The minefields in those crucial gaps had been immeasurably thickened during the eighty-four hours' grace given to the defenders, and neither the South Africans nor the British had the time, the men or the expertise to lift them.

Three Grants blew up within a few minutes of 6th R.T.R. starting through, while behind the Australians the faithful Valentines of 50th R.T.R. pressed on despite much greater losses, for they were endeavouring to take the Australians' heavier supporting weapons up with them. But they lost thirteen Valentines before they eventually fought their way through to the last known positions of the 2nd/28th Battalion in front – to find that these had been completely overrun and even the prisoners had been marched away.

The same fate had by noon overtaken the two 69th Brigade battalions – 6th Durham Light Infantry and 5th East Yorks – whose casualties were even higher than the Australians, with the result that the brigade was taken out of the line. By the time Ramsden, with Auchinleck's agreement, called the battle off, the Eighth Army had lost yet another thousand men and over thirty tanks – and if such figures seemed small compared with the losses during *Crusader* and the Gazala battles, the trouble was that Eighth Army could no longer afford them.

By July 28th, the Alamein front was quiescent – on Rommel's side, so it afterwards became clear, because he was short of ammunition; on Auchinleck's side, because he was short of men. The July fighting had produced one success and one failure for each of them. Auchinleck had halted Rommel's drive to the Nile – but the Afrika Korps was still in existence and Auchinleck dared not transfer any of his men to the northern front.

During the following twenty-four hours, Dorman-Smith completed an analysis of the situation throughout the Middle East with re-commendations for a thorough reorganisation of the Army, and having read it through and agreed to it, Auchinleck sent off his regular report to Whitehall, containing the sentence, 'We must therefore remain temporarily on the defensive and recruit our strength for a new and decisive effort.'

This, he added, was not likely to become possible before the middle of September. It was not a forecast to find much favour with the Prime Minister.

8 · *Churchill Intervenes*

It had seemed at the immediate moment an especially cruel stroke of Fate that Mr Churchill should have been with Mr Roosevelt when the news came through that Tobruk had fallen. They had been drawing up a programme of talks and discussions in Washington when General Marshall, American Chief of Army Staff, had entered the President's office with a telegram which, after glancing at it, Roosevelt handed without a word to the Prime Minister.

'Tobruk has surrendered', it read, 'with twenty-five thousand men taken prisoner.'

It was, Churchill later wrote, one of the heaviest blows he was to receive during the war, not only because it exposed the emptiness of the assurances he had lately received from Auchinleck that there was no intention of allowing Tobruk to be isolated, let alone captured, but by its reflection upon the fighting capabilities of the British forces. Only four months before, eighty-five thousand men had surrendered to an inferior Japanese force at Singapore and this melancholy repetition seemed to cast doubt upon the British will to fight; it was indeed a bitter moment, and he was not to know then that thousands of miles away the men being marched towards their prison-camps were feeling the disgrace as keenly as he was.

The kindness now extended to him by Mr Roosevelt and his advisers stands as a landmark in human generosity and compassion. 'What can we do to help?' was the first question the President asked, and with its answer put in train movements which were to send three hundred Sherman tanks and a hundred self-propelled 105mm. guns in six fast American ships to the Suez Canal. This extraordinary gesture of faith was even more remarkable in that the tanks had just been issued to American armoured divisions who had until then been training on obsolete equipment, and they had now to be withdrawn . . . and an argument that they would better serve the Allied cause by being left where they were would have been hard to counter.

But there are, incredibly, advantages to be drawn even from so unpromising a situation as that in which Churchill now found himself.

He had flown to Washington in order to accomplish two tasks. (This was the first time so important a personage had ever flown the Atlantic; it had taken nearly twenty-seven hours and before he had left, Mr Churchill had advised the King that in the event of his death on the journey, His Majesty should entrust the formation of a new government to Anthony Eden.) The first task had been to agree joint United States and British co-operation in the development of an atomic bomb, and the second was to try to persuade both the President and his advisers that an attempt to invade France across the English Channel was an impracticability in 1942, perhaps even in 1943, and that a more advantageous project would be a joint Anglo-American invasion of North Africa. This would be just possible in the time and with the shipping available, and it would also threaten Rommel from the rear and thus help to make not only Egypt but also the essential Middle East oil safe – at least from attack from the west.

American opinion at this time was focused on the need to help Russia which they felt overrode any possible requirements of the Eighth Army, and the most direct way to do that – and incidentally to finish the war rather more quickly than the British seemed to think possible – would be by a direct strike through France aimed at the heart of Hitler's Reich; and American optimism and confidence would brook no arguments that at least the first part of that programme, *Operation Sledgehammer*, to put a force of six divisions across the Channel, could not be achieved by the end of 1942. They were unimpressed by British warnings that the English Channel was most unlikely to provide weather calm enough for a large-scale operation at any time after September, unwilling to accept that even American technology and industry could not produce in time the necessary shipping and landing-craft for such a task, and frankly disbelieving when it was suggested that the defenders of Hitler's *Festung Europa* were both brave and competent enough to fling an American assault force back into the sea within hours of its attempt to land.

Now the fall of Tobruk focused all attention on the Middle East, simply by the apparent scale of the catastrophe. Military opinion in Cairo and perhaps elsewhere might argue the unimportance of the fortress from a tactical point of view, but public opinion throughout the world from Berlin to Washington was solid in its belief that the fall of Tobruk constituted the most telling blow to British and Allied prestige in three years of war, and in Washington they knew something must be done quickly to retrieve it. And logistic calculations would probably demonstrate that if shipping were used to take men and weapons to the Middle East in worthwhile numbers, there would be too little left to build up American forces in Britain for an early cross-Channel operation. It says a great deal for the good nature of George

Marshall, who was firmly set upon *Operation Sledgehammer*, that he did not allow this development in any way to sour his relations with the British.

To Mr Churchill, therefore, the last days of June 1942 were packed with contradictory emotions – humiliation at the military débâcle, flooding gratitude for American generosity, relief that an operation which in his own opinion and that of his advisers would be doomed to disaster was now less likely to be pressed.

But there were, of course, other dangers. If the events in the desert had weakened General Marshall's case for a cross-Channel operation, it had strengthened the hand of Admiral Ernest J. King, Chief of the Naval Staff and Commander-in-Chief of the U.S. Navy, who felt that the right strategy for his country was to turn its back for the moment on Europe and concentrate all available forces in the Pacific. For him, the Japanese were the chief enemy and Hitler could wait . . . even if this entailed the subjugation of Great Britain and the destruction of the British Empire. Fortunately, Roosevelt had little or no sympathy with this attitude, and wished – especially in view of forthcoming Congressional elections – that American troops should be in combat with German forces before the end of the year. Events seemed to indicate North Africa as the only possible theatre – but all Churchill's persuasiveness would be needed before it was certain and he had to return home before a decision was reached.

There were, of course, even more problems at home for him to face. In democracies, the position of a war-time leader is obviously affected by military events, and the run of desert defeats had brought a ground-swell of political dissatisfaction to the surface, resulting in a by-election defeat for his Government, and the proposal of a motion in the House of Commons, reading, 'That this House, while paying tribute to the heroism and endurance of the Armed Forces of the Crown in circumstances of exceptional difficulty, has no confidence in the central direction of the war.'[1]

This was the political situation which confronted Mr Churchill upon his return to England on June 27th, the problem which had to be resolved first.

'This is Tobruk,' he had said glumly when told of the by-election defeat, but doleful prognostications from Sir Stafford Cripps about the vote of No Confidence he would face in the House were dismissed with some contempt.

'You can't run a war as if you were in a laboratory,' Churchill growled at some of the complaints which Cripps suggested would be brought against him, and his faith, not only in public support but in his own powers to persuade and control Parliament, were fully justified when after a superb speech at the end of the two-day debate the motion was defeated by 475 votes to 25.

But it had all taken up valuable time and energy, and would not have occurred had Eighth Army held Rommel at Gazala; if, in Mr Churchill's opinion, Auchinleck had either been in command from the beginning or had taken command much earlier than he did.

Even after his parliamentary success there were other large matters to divert the Prime Minister's attention temporarily from events in Egypt. As the figures for shipping losses in the Battle of the Atlantic ('The only thing which really frightened me during the war,' as he was afterwards to write) came in, they revealed that over 400,000 tons had been lost in the early days of July and that of one 35-ship convoy to Murmansk, U-boats had sunk 24; and in Russia itself, the great German drive towards the Don and the Caucasus had begun. Stalin's demands for a Second Front grew every day more strident and abusive, and soon their effect upon Washington became only too evident. On July 18th, General Marshall, Admiral King and the President's friend and close adviser Mr Harry Hopkins arrived in London, and after a brief colloquy with the American Service Chiefs there (Generals Eisenhower, Clark and Spaatz, and Admiral Stark) took up again with the British the arguments for *Operation Sledge-hammer*.

Their instructions from Mr Roosevelt (although of course Churchill did not know this at the time) were to fight as hard as they could for *Sledgehammer* in 1942, for in the case of a Russian collapse Mr Roosevelt considered the operation imperative, but if they could make no headway against British opposition, then they were to 'determine upon another place for U.S. troops to fight in 1942'.

In this regard, they were to consider such factors as the effect upon the Allied War Effort of the loss of Egypt and the Suez Canal, the loss of Syria and the Mosul oil-wells, the loss of the Persian Gulf and access to Persian oil – and the concomitant risks of German oc-cupation of the whole of the northern coast of Africa and much of its western coastline as well.

> You will determine the best methods of holding the Middle East. These methods include definitely either or both of the following:
> (a) Sending aid and ground forces to the Persian Gulf, to Syria and to Egypt.
> (b) a new operation in Morocco and Algeria intended to drive in against the back door of Rommel's armies. The attitude of French colonial troops is still in doubt.

And the President's directive ended:

> Please remember three cardinal principles – speed of decision on plans, unity of plans, attack combined with defence but not defence alone. This

affects the immediate objective of U.S. ground forces against Germans in 1942.

I hope for total agreement within one week of your arrival.

FRANKLIN D. ROOSEVELT
Commander-in-Chief[2]

In support of Mr Churchill in the arguments which then ensued were his own Chiefs of Staff of whom Sir Alan Brooke as Chief of the Imperial General Staff was spokesman, and for three days the arguments for and against *Sledgehammer* were wearily repeated. Against the American statement that an immediate cross-Channel operation would be the best way of helping Russia by drawing westward a large part of the Luftwaffe, the British argued its impracticability.

Even if the minimum required force of six divisions was ready and waiting to go at that moment (and everybody agreed that this was not so) it was doubtful if the landing-craft would be ready by September which was the latest date at which reasonable sea conditions might still be expected. And in the extremely unlikely event of American optimism in the matter proving justified – how would the six divisions be fed and supplied throughout a winter when they would be under attack by German troops still confident of eventual victory?

In the British view, even if six divisions could be put afloat on the Channel before the end of the year, they would inevitably be lost, perhaps at sea, and if not, then either during the landing operations themselves or at some time during the following winter; and as hour followed hour, it became evident to the Americans that nothing they could say would change that opinion. There was an exchange of cables with Washington on July 22nd and 23rd, and then to Churchill's enormous relief, an acceptance by Roosevelt that there could be no *Sledgehammer* that autumn, followed by instructions to his representatives to plan for an 'expanded *Gymnast*' – a series of landings in North Africa which would include British troops as well as Americans, with the British taking the greater risk of landing inside the Mediterranean at Algiers and accepting the danger of the Axis closing the Straits of Gibraltar behind them.

Overjoyed, Churchill christened the expanded operation *Torch* and set about agreeing details of the composition of the ground, air and naval forces to be engaged. General Eisenhower would be Supreme Commander with a combined Anglo-American Staff, and Churchill suggested that the Deputy Commander should be the British General Sir Harold Alexander. Commanding the British task force should be Lieutenant-General Sir Bernard Law Montgomery, who at that moment was commanding troops in south-east England.

With all these vital matters at last agreed and in train, the Prime Minister could turn his mind to what was still the only active theatre in which the armies of the Western Allies were engaged, the desert.

As has already been related, the Prime Minister's high and romantic hopes for sweeping victories once Auchinleck had replaced Wavell in June 1941 had been quickly dashed, and within but a few weeks Churchill had been wondering if the change he had insisted upon had been the right one. His admiration for his new nominee consequently plummeted, and was not increased by Auchinleck's steadfast rejection of his own recommendation for command of the Eighth Army during *Crusader*, Maitland Wilson, and the appointment of Cunningham instead. (Churchill seemed to have a prejudice in favour of Green Jackets or, as they have lately become known, the 'Black Mafia' – as had Anthony Eden who had served with the 60th Rifles during the First World War; Wilson's original regiment had been the Rifle Brigade.) And Cunningham's performance during *Crusader* had done nothing to increase Churchill's confidence in Auchinleck's judgment.

But at least *Crusader* had been a victory (once Cunningham had been replaced) and had eventually moved the flags on Mr Churchill's War Map a satisfactory distance in the right direction; and Mr Churchill was sufficiently realistic and magnanimous to repress his disappointment when Rommel's riposte swept the desert army back so soon to Gazala.

But by March his impatience had been proving stronger than his sympathy, and cables flew between Whitehall and Cairo opening further a rift between the two men, despite the fact that each was to retain a high regard for the other. This regard, however, did not curb Churchill's language, and Sir Alan Brooke had had on many occasions to use all his cajolery to persuade the Prime Minister to remove such phrases as 'Soldiers are meant to fight!' and 'Armies are not intended to stand about doing nothing!' and clothe his vehemence in more diplomatic words.

Auchinleck's blank refusal during March and April to consider an early attempt to retake at least the nearer airfields in Cyrenaica had especially infuriated Churchill, whose historic terms of office at the Admiralty had given him a particular affection for the Royal Navy and its associations.

'The bloody man doesn't seem to care about the fate of Malta,' he exploded. 'Anyway, we can't settle this by writing letters'[3] – and he had requested Auchinleck to come to London for further discussion.

This invitation, for what he doubtless considered adequate reasons, Auchinleck declined – and the Prime Minister's first reaction was to suggest Auchinleck's immediate replacement by the general then serving as Governor-General of Gibraltar; and when Brooke and the other senior military advisers stood firm against this, Churchill relapsed into a state of bottled anger which found vent many years later in his memoirs, when he accused Auchinleck of refusing to come to London because it would be easier for him to reject Churchill's reasonable demands from Cairo than in Whitehall.

Matters between them had thus become increasingly strained during April, and by early May Churchill's eagerness for offensive action having at last been matched by Brooke's and that of the other Chiefs of Staff, Auchinleck had been sent a cable which was in effect a demand upon him either to attack Rommel at Gazala in the near future or to resign his command. A few days then passed while Whitehall awaited the reply, and when Auchinleck's agreement came to attack in early June, Churchill's relieved response contained the sentence, 'I should personally feel even greater confidence if you took over direct command yourself as in fact you had to do at Sidi Rezegh.'[4]

The outcome of this seemingly reasonable request reveals the wide divergence in view between the impulsive, romantic Prime Minister in London and the professional Commander-in-Chief in the Middle East.

Churchill looked upon the desert as a battleground upon which military glory was to be won by the defeat of a famous corps under a brilliant general – the victory then to provide Eighth Army with a springboard from which to seize North Africa, reunite Great Britain with at least a part of that world of France which he so passionately admired, and then from the Tunisian coastline to threaten Sicily, to invade Italy and thus to attack the main enemy 'up through the soft underbelly of Europe'.

But to Auchinleck (and to Wavell before him) the desert was nothing but the western flank of a theatre of war extending from Afghanistan, via Persia and Iraq (which had reverted to Middle East Command in January 1942), Syria, Palestine, Egypt and Libya as far as Cyrenaica, to which the greatest menace lay on the north-western flank through which might break German armies driving down through the Caucasus towards the essential Persian oil-fields. To both Commanders-in-Chief, the conflict in Libya was a tangential affair to be conducted by subordinates, while they themselves kept their eyes firmly on the main area of threat between the Black Sea and the Caspian. As a result, Auchinleck's reply to the Prime Minister's request contained the paragraph:

> Much as I would like to take command personally in Libya I feel that it would not be the right course to pursue. I have considered the possibility most carefully and have concluded that it would be most difficult for me to

keep a right sense of proportion if I became immersed in tactical problems in Libya.[5]

It was this last phrase which particularly stuck in Churchill's gullet. He did not regard the conflict with the Afrika Korps as a 'tactical problem in Libya' and according to his physician, Sir Charles Wilson, he twice spat the phrase out with great scorn.

'Rommel! Rommel!' he had raved. 'What matters but beating Rommel?'

And the events of June and July, once they had occurred, had seemed to justify his more narrow perspective. Now, at the end of the month which had seen the halting of Rommel's offensive, the decision for *Torch* and his political victory in the House of Commons, he felt he had time to review the whole situation in the Middle East and make any necessary adjustments to guard against further defeat and disaster.

He had already agreed that Sir Alan Brooke should go out to Cairo at the end of July in order to carry out his own investigation as to what had gone wrong, and with the news of another developing stalemate and the suspicion that soon he would be presented with arguments to the effect that several more weeks must elapse before another offensive against Rommel could be launched, Churchill decided that he would go out too. He felt in any case that it was now his own unpleasant duty personally to inform Stalin that there would be no Second Front in Europe that year to lift pressure off the Russian armies, and to try to convince him that an October invasion of North Africa, especially if preceded by a resounding victory in Egypt to sway the loyalties of the French and thus give the Americans a perhaps rapid and bloodless route through Algeria and Tunisia towards Sicily and Italy, would go far to rectify the omission.

Cairo would be a half-way stop en route to Moscow.

Churchill and the C.I.G.S. travelled by separate routes to Cairo – Brooke via Gibraltar and Malta, Churchill in an American Liberator which also called at Gibraltar but then made a long sweep south across the Sahara to reach the Nile at Beni Suef, and then fly north to land at one of the Cairo airfields. Nevertheless, they arrived within half an hour of each other just after dawn on Monday, August 3rd, and a few hours later Churchill was installed in an air-conditioned room in the British Embassy in Cairo, exhilarated by movement, travel and the sense of being 'the man on the spot'. He knew he was right to be there; at Gibraltar he had learned of Auchinleck's latest report containing the declaration that no further offensive action could be taken in the desert until mid-September, which would not suit at all. Even were such action spectacularly successful, time would be required for its impact on the French in North Africa to affect their attitude to *Torch* – more time than that between mid-September and the end of October, which was the present target date for the Anglo-American invasion.

The Middle East Command must be spurred to greater efforts, and if necessary sweeping changes made; and in this respect he was greatly heartened by the arrival in time for lunch of his old enemy and now great friend, the South African Prime Minister Jan Smuts, who had flown up from Pretoria. Churchill hated sacking people however much they might have deserved it; Smuts had a quality of ruthlessness which would support him if and when the knife had to be wielded. He had also a sharp tongue and an abrasive wit which added to the gaiety of lunch and left everyone in fine fettle for the labours of the evening – for Mr Churchill was a great believer in the benefits of afternoon sleep, and would not be available again before five o'clock.

It was in fact six o'clock before work commenced, when Sir Alan Brooke arrived at the Embassy from G.H.Q. with Auchinleck who had come back from the front for the meeting. It was the first time Prime Minister and Commander-in-Chief had met since the latter's appointment just over a year before and many differences had occurred between them since; but each could still appreciate the other's great qualities. It was not, however, a meeting to please Churchill for it was quickly evident that nothing he could say would change Auchinleck's opinion that the Eighth Army could not be ready to launch a major attack for at least six weeks; and for the moment Churchill did not feel inclined to reveal the plans for operations at the other end of the Mediterranean and the resultant political factors which made an earlier desert victory so desirable. In any case, he doubted whether Auchinleck would be swayed much by such considerations.

But when the meeting broke up and during the dinner which followed, Mr Churchill pondered the next moves; and at midnight he sent again for the C.I.G.S. Upon one point Brooke and Churchill were now in agreement – that Auchinleck's place was in Cairo and not at the front, and that a competent and energetic general must quickly be appointed to command the army in the field. It would seem, from everything Mr Churchill had heard, that the most distinguished, most highly thought of general in the area was Strafer Gott who, as Mr Churchill pointed out, 'had not earned the title "Strafer" by nothing'. Gott was also, though this does not seem to have been mentioned at the time, a Green Jacket, his original regiment being the King's Royal Rifle Corps (60th Rifles).

Mr Churchill, however, had never met General Gott, and from what Brooke had heard it seemed likely that Gott, after so long in the desert, might be rather tired. Brooke suggested instead that General Montgomery should be transferred from the *Torch* Task Force to take over Eighth Army, but to this Mr Churchill objected on the grounds that instant action was required and Gott was already in Egypt whereas Montgomery was back in England; perhaps a better solution would be for Sir Alan Brooke himself to take over Eighth Army – a suggestion which tempted the C.I.G.S. most damnably, but which upon deep reflection he forced himself to refuse. During eight months of often excoriating nervous strain he had managed to learn some of the techniques by which his turbulent master could most easily be handled, and he felt that he would thus serve both the army and his country best by staying where he was. It was nearly two o'clock in the morning, after a long and eventful day, before either of them got to bed.

Not surprisingly the Prime Minister, never an early riser by choice, was not seen during the following morning; lunch was again spent in relaxed but invigorating company (they were joined by General Wavell who had flown over from India) but at six o'clock Churchill presided at a meeting of the most authoritative British and Commonwealth personalities in the area – Brooke, Auchinleck, Wavell, Smuts, Admiral Harwood and Air Marshal Tedder, and the Minister of State for the Middle East, Mr Richard Casey. For nearly three hours they discussed the situation throughout the entire Middle East Command, but even when Churchill revealed the Anglo-American plans and explained the political necessity for an early and spectacular desert victory, Auchinleck remained obstinate in his declaration that the Eighth Army could not launch a major attack for at least six weeks. Mr Churchill was very ill content.

The meeting broke up in time for dinner, but afterwards Churchill talked again into the night with Brooke. The C.I.G.S. still pressed Montgomery as the preferred choice for Eighth Army commander, reinforcing his argument with evidence he had collected that Gott really was tired, and adding another of his day's discoveries – that despite some old antagonisms between Auchinleck and Montgomery, Auchinleck was nevertheless prepared to accept Montgomery as his commander in the field.

But Churchill would not agree and became a trifle testy. Gott was on the spot and could take over within days, Montgomery was three thousand miles away – and while such matters as changes in command were being discussed, why was no more important task being found for Maitland Wilson than command of a virtually unemployed army up in Syria, and occasional chairmanship of Boards of Inquiry?

Fortunately for Brooke, visits to the front were scheduled for the following day and even Mr Churchill would have to rise by 0445 – so argument did not continue long and they were in bed by one o'clock in the morning; though the unfortunate C.I.G.S. did note that as a 59-year-old professional soldier he was already feeling the strain of four days and nights of incessant travel and argument in hot, humid and thoroughly unfamiliar conditions, whereas the 68-year-old Prime Minister seemed to be more and more in his element.

They flew up to Burg el Arab at first light the following morning, and Sir Charles Wilson who accompanied them wrote in his diary:

> Very early this morning the P.M. drove with Auchinleck to his head-quarters behind the Ruweisat Ridge. There, in a kind of wire cage, we breakfasted with some men burnt brown by the desert sun. There were flies everywhere. When they were disturbed they rose in a cloud with a buzzing sound.[6]

However admirable Auchinleck's determination to endure the same discomforts as his troops, these conditions were not such as to recommend him to Churchill, and the subsequent session of argument with Auchinleck and his equally unyielding Chief of Staff, the enigmatic and (as Churchill discovered) unpopular Dorman-Smith, in a hot, cramped caravan, with desks and maps covered with sand and no air-conditioning or even an efficient fan to clear away his cigar-smoke, did nothing to ease the discontent. Nothing Churchill could say seemed to make the slightest impression upon these two determined, self-contained, assured professional soldiers who kept him stiffly at a distance, replied to his exhortations with cold facts and figures, and remained unmoved by his pleas. Coolly (despite the conditions in the caravan) and politely (though once or twice there was a gleam in Dorman-Smith's eyes which may have betokened a sardonic reply trembling on his tongue), they rebutted every argument with logistics, every call to action with lists of ration strengths and reinforcement tables.

And in the end, thoroughly displeased, he had to leave.

However, he did cause them some slight inconvenience, for Auchinleck had called a Corps Commanders' Conference for later that morning but Churchill upset this by insisting that Gott accompany him on the journey back to Burg el Arab for lunch with the R.A.F., as he wished to talk with the famous desert warrior.

He arrived in somewhat better mood. Gott had impressed him, and had himself been affected by the Prime Minister's enthusiasms. He had admitted that after so many years away from home he was looking forward to leave – about three months would be very acceptable – but in the circumstances he knew that this was impossible, and if Mr Churchill felt that he was capable of fulfilling satisfactorily the onerous duties required of the Commander of the Eighth Army, then he would willingly accept them. To both Mr Churchill and Sir Charles Wilson, Gott appeared to possess both the physical attributes and also the reserves of mental and spiritual strength to carry out the job.

The reception at Burg el Arab improved the occasion. Here was no wire cage filled with flies, no imprisonment in heat and sand; here was an open beach cooled by Mediterranean breezes, white napery, gleaming silver, brandy in goblets, and in due course (it had been delayed by mechanical breakdown en route) an excellent luncheon sent out from Shepheard's Hotel. Here also from the Air Force officers, all of group captain's rank and above, was confirmation of many of Churchill's beliefs. Here, as Sir Charles Wilson wrote that night:

> It is a new atmosphere. These men have not taken a bad knock; they are on top and know that they are on top. In an impersonal war of millions they remain individuals. These fellows were not groomed in a mess before the war. Their thoughts are not borrowed from others and their speech is forthright. They are critical of the Army, they say what is in their minds without batting an eyelid . . . Certainly the Army's shortcomings were set forth succinctly. It is not to them that one will look for a recommendation for mercy when the Commander-in-Chief stands in the dock . . . As we retraced our steps towards Cairo at the end of the day, the P.M. remained sunk in his own thoughts. He did not speak once, but I have a feeling that it is all settled.[7]

There seems to be no record of what exactly the R.A.F. officers said at that undoubtedly portentous lunch-time session, but some indication was provided many years later when Lord Tedder's memoirs were published. In a letter written at that time to his superior at home, Air Marshal Portal, he had written:

> The difference between those Army meetings and [our own] meetings is the difference between a funeral breakfast and a wedding breakfast. There's no life about them. Too many old men and 'nice chaps'. As Auck. remarked to me, the Army is suffering from 'good fellows'.
> Some commander should have been shot after the bolt from Agedabia. I wish he [Auchinleck] was a better judge of character and more ruthless in judging people solely by results. I also wish he had the ability to inspire the Army here. I am afraid he hasn't.[8]

Undoubtedly, Mr Churchill had a great deal to ponder on his way back to Cairo on the evening of August 5th, 1942.

That evening was spent quietly, and to the surprise of some people, Mr Churchill, although he had obviously been excited by the day's travel and sight-seeing, was not particularly talkative and wished to retire quite early to bed. But the following morning he burst into Sir Alan Brooke's bedroom while the latter was still dressing with the announcement that his thoughts had taken shape during the night, and that after breakfast he and Brooke would thrash them out.

The Desert Army needed a new commander, and a change in Commander-in-Chief would also bring in new ideas and new blood –

a point which Auchinleck had himself suggested over a month before when, at the nadir of British fortunes immediately after the fall of Tobruk, he had offered his resignation should Whitehall have lost confidence in him. But Churchill had not wished to remove Auchinleck then, and did not wish to do so now – but he had thought of a new solution to all their problems which would keep the best men in responsible positions, and side-step the failures. This solution he now explained to the C.I.G.S.

The chief complaint Churchill had against Auchinleck was his preoccupation with the northern front at the expense of the war in the desert – and he accepted that this was a preoccupation which, in Brooke's opinion and those of the other Chiefs of Staff, was thoroughly justified. Very well, perhaps the oil at the head of the Persian Gulf was more important than Egypt, but nevertheless Rommel must be beaten – and beaten sooner than Auchinleck thought possible.

Therefore Auchinleck must be allowed to concentrate wholly upon the front which he considered most important, and another Commander-in-Chief appointed to take over the area in which the battle against Rommel was being fought. In effect, Churchill proposed to split the present Middle East Command into two – Near East and Middle East. The new Near East Command, extending only as far east as the Canal, would have a new Commander-in-Chief and a new Army Commander under him, while Auchinleck would command the new Middle East theatre consisting of Syria, Palestine, Persia and Iraq, with whoever could be agreed by mutual consent commanding the forces there.

As for personalities, why shouldn't Brooke stay in Cairo as Commander-in-Chief, and as he seemed to favour Montgomery as Eighth Army commander, very well, Montgomery could be sent out as quickly as possible and someone else be found for Force Commander for *Torch*? To the Prime Minister, elated by success and inspiration, it all looked perfect.

It did not look so good to Brooke, and a long day's tactful manoeuvring to change some of the Prime Minister's ideas ensued. Much though he would have liked to accept the post of Commander-in-Chief, Brooke still felt the best service he could render his country was to stay at Churchill's side; moreover, he would not like Auchinleck to think that he had come out to Egypt to supersede him. And another point at issue was the detail of the division of the commands, for in Brooke's opinion the Suez Canal would make a very poor inter-command boundary.

Mr Churchill did not take too kindly to these blocks to his flow of inspiration, and his temper was thus somewhat uncertain at a morning meeting with some of the G.H.Q. staff; he was especially short with one of Auchinleck's favourite staff officers, Lieutenant-General Corbett, who a few days previously had been undiplomatic enough to inform Churchill that he himself had already been briefed to take over command of Eighth Army. He was soon to regret his temerity for when at the end of a day's discussions and bargaining a long telegram was sent to the War Cabinet in London, the suggested changes in command were as follows:

1 General Auchinleck to be offered the post of C-in-C of the new Middle East command.
2 General Alexander to relinquish the appointment of Deputy Commander, *Torch* and become C-in-C. of the new Near East Command.
3 General Montgomery to succeed General Alexander as Deputy Commander, *Torch*.
4 General Gott to command Eighth Army under Alexander.
5 General Corbett to be relieved of his appointment.
6 General Ramsden to be relieved of his command of XXX Corps.
7 General Dorman-Smith to be relieved of his appointment.[9]

Eighth Army would require two more corps commanders, but these choices could be made when the more senior appointments had been agreed.

The following morning (August 7th) was spent quietly, recovering to some extent from the previous day's travails and awaiting the War Cabinet's reply which arrived about noon. They agreed the changes in personnel but questioned, as had Brooke, the dividing line between the two new commands; and they were quite firmly of the opinion that the term Middle East Command must be retained for Egypt and the Western Desert. Whatever else the new command should be called, in the public mind 'Middle East' included the area of the present battleground and it would be unwise to change this.

But these were minor points, and were quickly dealt with. Confirmatory telegrams were despatched, key personnel sent for and for a few hours it seemed that all would now progress smoothly and Mr Churchill's plans for a new command structure, with the key positions held by the men in whom he felt most confidence, would be fulfilled. But then fate took a hand.

That afternoon, as Gott was flying back from the front to take up the reins of his new command, the Bombay aircraft in which he was travelling was attacked by German fighters and forced down. Despite the fact that it was on the ground and burning, the fighters attacked again and again and only three members of the crew, a medical orderly and one passenger – already wounded – escaped. General Gott and sixteen other passengers all perished in the flames, and by eleven o'clock that evening Churchill had been informed that he must choose again.

Whether or not his tiredness would have prevented Gott from making a first-class commander for Eighth Army, whether or not he possessed the intellectual abilities for such a post, his death deeply affected the army – and indeed the personnel of the whole Middle East Command. He was the last of the legendary figures from the early days of the desert war, the days of 'Wavell's Thirty Thousand'. Those days were now gone and a new era was heralded.

The changeover in command was to take place officially on August 15th, and there would inevitably be a certain measure of upheaval and disjuncture that not even the studiously polite and civilised behaviour of most of the participants could disguise.

On August 8th, when the final changes as a result of Gott's death had been agreed with the War Cabinet, Mr Churchill wrote to Auchinleck:

Cairo
8th August 1942

Dear General Auchinleck,
1   On June 23 you raised in your telegram to the C.I.G.S. the question of your being relieved in this Command, and you mentioned the name of General Alexander as a possible successor. At that time of crisis to the Army His Majesty's Government did not wish to avail themselves of your high-minded offer. At the same time you had taken over effective command of the battle, as I had long desired and suggested to you in my telegram of May 20. You stemmed the adverse tide and at the present time the front is stabilized.
2   The War Cabinet have now decided, for the reasons which you yourself had used, that the moment has come for a change. It is proposed to detach Iraq and Persia from the present Middle Eastern theatre. Alexander will be appointed to command the Middle East, Montgomery to command the Eighth Army, and I offer you the command of Iraq and Persia including the Tenth Army, with headquarters at Basra or Baghdad. It is true that this sphere is today smaller than the Middle East, but it may in a few months become the scene of decisive operations and reinforcements to the Tenth Army are already on the way. In this theatre, of which you have special experience, you will preserve your associations with India. I hope therefore that you will comply with my wish and directions with the same disinterested public spirit that you have shown on all occasions. Alexander will arrive almost immediately, and I hope that early next week, subject of course to the movements of the enemy, it may be possible to effect the transfer of responsibility on the Western battlefront with the utmost smoothness and efficiency.

3   I shall be very glad to see you at any convenient time if you should
so desire.

>Believe me,
>   Yours sincerely,
>   Winston S. Churchill

This epistle was conveyed to Auchinleck that same morning by one
of Churchill's staff, feeling 'as if I were just going to murder an
unsuspecting friend', and after Auchinleck had read it with typical
impassivity he asked a few questions and indicated that he doubted
whether he could accept command of the new theatre for a number of
reasons.

These reasons he detailed during a 'bleak and impeccable'
interview with Churchill the following day, Sunday, August 9th.
Although he accepted the grounds given for a change in command,
Auchinleck felt that the reduction of his responsibilities to such a
small proportion of those he had lately been shouldering would look
to the public too much like the appointment of an unsuccessful
general to an operational sinecure – a policy of which he would
thoroughly disapprove had it happened to anyone else and which he
could therefore not accept himself. He also voiced strongly the
opinion that such a division of the Middle East Command would
prove impracticable, as the new zone would rely for its supplies and
reinforcement upon passage either through the new Middle East
theatre or through India and a crisis in either of those areas would
affect delivery, however crucial the situation in Iraq or Persia might
be.

In the circumstances he asked to be allowed to retire into oblivion,
though at Churchill's urgent bidding he agreed to give the matter a
few more days' thought; but he warned the Prime Minister that he
would be unlikely to change his mind between then and Churchill's
return from Moscow in ten days' time. In the meantime, he would
return to the desert to hand over his command.

Epilogue

Auchinleck's retirement into oblivion was to last but ten months, all of which were spent in India – far more a 'home' to him than England had ever been. The first few months were spent as guest of the Governor of the North-West Frontier province, after which he moved down to Delhi where he tackled the job of writing his despatch on his Middle East Command.

Even with the fact of the return to his beloved India, it could not be a particularly happy time for him, tainted as it was with failure, with the thought that a lifetime of soldiering had ended with disregard and unemployment during a time of war. That became, in time, the bitterest factor – that wherever he turned he was surrounded by old friends and service comrades all busily engaged upon matters deeply concerned with his own profession, yet there was nothing for him to do. Out of sight of Authority, he felt sure he was also out of mind.

In this he was mistaken. Despite their differences during the time of his command in Egypt, despite the circumstances of his removal from that command, he was still regarded with great respect and indeed affection by the Prime Minister. His refusal to accept the Persia/Iraq command had disappointed Churchill but had by no means enraged him, for he understood the validity of Auchinleck's reasons for the refusal; but the Prime Minister regretted the waste of knowledge and experience which Auchinleck's unemployment represented and deplored the unhappiness which that unemployment must be causing.

An almost insuperable problem existed for further military employment, however, in Auchinleck's very seniority. He had been Commander-in-Chief, India, until 1941; he could hardly now be asked to accept a field appointment junior to the India Command, even though its present holder was his old friend Field Marshal Wavell. Perhaps some high non-military appointment could be found, and Churchill first suggested that the Governor of Bengal, Sir John Herbert, should be moved to make room for Auchinleck – and when that suggestion proved impracticable, he sought around for other Indian Governorships.

The solution, when it came, was simple. At the 'Trident' conference in Washington it was decided that vigorous and aggressive operations must begin against the Japanese in Burma and, as Churchill's disappointment in Wavell's performance had continued, it was decided that a younger man should take command of active operations in the theatre. Lord Mountbatten was appointed Supreme Commander, South-East Asia Command, and Wavell given the highest appointment within the Government's gift: but civilian – that of Viceroy of India.

This left the Indian Army, now growing rapidly to its maximum size of 2,500,000, without a Commander-in-Chief. Who better to occupy the position than the man who had spent his entire life in the sub-continent and almost his entire professional life in its service?

The re-appointment of General Sir Claude Auchinleck as Commander-in-Chief of the Indian Army took place on June 20th, 1943.

'I was very grateful,' was his simple comment.

The next twenty-one months passed quickly and were far happier and more satisfying than could at first have been expected. Though Auchinleck was not in operational command of the formations he recruited and saw trained, he was nonetheless fully engaged in the building of a huge fighting machine; and its eventual use was in the hands of Mountbatten, who acted throughout with understanding and sympathy so that co-operation between the two men and their staffs remained an example to all.

This was fortunate, for between them they had many obstacles to overcome. Even though the forces in the theatre were expanding all the time, their supply rating was on a very low priority. Throughout the last half of 1943 the fighting in Italy held the attention of the British and European publics, and thus of Whitehall, and 1944 was the year of the Normandy landings, which dominated thought and attention everywhere both before and after. Burma thus remained the forgotten front, and the Fourteenth Army rightly nick-named itself the Forgotten Army; in the excitement of D-Day even the end of the epic siege of Kohima was hardly noticed outside official circles in London. As for the problems posed by Chinese dilatoriness, 'Vinegar' Joe Stillwell's Anglophobia and Orde Wingate's egomania and sudden death, the British public was hardly aware of them until well after the war had ended.

Nevertheless, morale among the British and Indian troops in Burma remained high – and for this Auchinleck was greatly responsible. He was at home with Indians, whether civilian or military, and could talk with them all with ease and naturalness; and the Indian Army knew, throughout all ranks, that he was their benefactor and true friend.

When the end of the war came it was, of course, much more sudden than had been expected, the atomic bomb saving months if not years of conflict, and untold lives. And then, ironically, it became Auchinleck's job to dismantle the structure he had served all his life and which he had built up so magnificently during his last command. With the partition of India came the partition of practically every formation of the Indian Army.

From the early days of the Indian Army the British, as a matter of security, had ensured that its corps, regiments and departments had been manned half by Moslems, half by Hindus. Auchinleck's own regiment, the 1st Punjabis – an old regiment dating back to the Duke of Wellington – was half Moslem, a quarter Sikh and a quarter Rajput; and now Auchinleck was to be instrumental in its destruction. The Moslem historian of the regiment later wrote 'With great sorrow and midst moving scenes, the several battalions of the Regiment bade farewell to their Hindu and Sikh brothers in arms. . . . What had taken two hundred years to build was dismembered in three months.'

It was a bitter period for Auchinleck; though not, of course, as bad as the chaos and horror which followed so soon afterwards – though for this at least, Auchinleck was free of all responsibility. But he could not stay as Commander-in-Chief of what was left in India, and on December 1st, 1948, he left the sub-continent for good to live for a while in Italy, then in London, and eventually in Morocco, where he passed the last thirteen years of his life in countryside that reminded him of his beloved North-West Frontier home. Here he died in early March, 1981.

He had been offered a peerage in 1947 but had declined it, later commenting, 'I can't afford to buy coronets and robes and things. I prefer beer!' – an attitude which could well explain the devotion he had inspired throughout the rank and file of the armies he had commanded.

He was certainly a soldier's soldier.

Appendix I:
Forces Engaged in Operation Crusader

British and Commonwealth Forces

Commander-in-Chief, Middle East   General Sir Claude Auchinleck

EIGHTH ARMY
Lieutenant-General Sir Alan Cunningham (until November 26th)
Lieutenant-General N. M. Ritchie

Army Troops:

2nd South African Division – Major-General I. P. de Villiers
  3rd South African Infantry Brigade – Brig. C. E. Borain
  4th South African Infantry Brigade – Brig. A. A. Hayton
  6th South African Infantry Brigade – Brig. F. W. Cooper
  Divisional artillery, machine-gun company and reconnaissance
  squadron

Oasis Group – Brig. D. W. Reid

Tobruk Fortress
70th Division – Major-General R. M. Scobie
  32nd Army Tank Brigade – Brig. A. C. Willison
  14th Infantry Brigade – Brig. B. H. Chappel
  16th Infantry Brigade – Brig. C. E. N. Lomax
  23rd Infantry Brigade – Brig. C. H. V. Cox
  1st Polish Carpathian Brigade – Major-General S. Kopanski
  Divisional artillery and machine-gun battalion

Matruh Fortress
  2nd South African Infantry Brigade – Brig. W. H. E. Poole
  Fortress artillery

Long Range Desert Group – Lieutenant-Colonel G. L. Prendergast

XIII Corps – Lieutenant-General A. R. Godwin-Austen

Corps Troops:
  Medium, heavy, anti-tank and anti-aircraft artillery

4th Indian Division – Major-General F. W. Messervy
    5th Indian Infantry Brigade – Brig. D. Russell
    7th Indian Infantry Brigade – Brig. H. R. Briggs
    11th Indian Infantry Brigade – Brig. A. Anderson
    Divisional artillery, reconnaissance squadrons and Sappers and Miners

1st Army Tank Brigade – Brig. H. R. B. Watkins

New Zealand Division – Major-General B. C. Freyberg
    4th New Zealand Infantry Brigade – Brig. L. M. Inglis
    5th New Zealand Infantry Brigade – Brig. J. Hargest
    6th New Zealand Infantry Brigade – Brig. H. E. Barrowclough
    Divisional artillery, divisional cavalry, machine-gun battalion and 28th (Maori) Battalion

XXX Corps – Lieutenant-General C. W. M. Norrie

Corps Troops:
    Light anti-aircraft artillery and one reconnaissance squadron

7th Armoured Division – Major-General W. H. E. Gott
    4th Armoured Brigade Group – Brig. A. H. Gatehouse
    7th Armoured Brigade – Brig. G. M. O. Davy
    22nd Armoured Brigade – Brig. J. Scott-Cockburn
    7th Support Group – Brig. J. C. Campbell
    Divisional medium, anti-tank and light anti-aircraft artillery, and eight reconnaissance squadrons

22nd Guards Brigade – Brig. J. C. O. Marriott

1st South African Division – Major-General G. E. Brink
    1st South African Infantry Brigade – Brig. D. H. Pienaar
    5th South African Infantry Brigade – Brig. B. F. Armstrong
    Divisional artillery, machine-gun battalion and three reconnaissance squadrons

German and Italian Forces

Comandante Superiore   Generale d'Armata Ettore Bastico

PANZERGRUPPE AFRIKA
General der Panzertruppen Erwin Rommel

Deutsches Afrika Korps – Generalleutnant Ludwig Cruewell

    15th Panzer Division – Generalleutnant W. Neumann-Sylkow (died of wounds December 9th)

Panzer Regt 8 – Oberstleutnant Cramer
15th Rifle Brigade – Oberst Menny
Reconnaissance Battalion 33 – Oberleutnant Héraucourt
Divisional artillery

21st Panzer Division – Generalleutnant J. von Ravenstein (taken prisoner November 29th)
Panzer Regt 5 – Oberstleutnant Stephan (died of wounds November 25th)
Rifle Regt 104 – Oberstleutnant Knabe (1st Battalion of this regiment was commanded by Major the Rev. Wilhelm Bach at Halfaya)
Reconnaissance Battalion 3 – Oberstleutnant Freiherr von Wechmar
Divisional artillery and engineers

Division zbV Afrika (later *90th Light Division*) – Generalleutnant Max Sümmermann (died of wounds December 10th)
Infantry Regt 155 – Oberst Marks
Afrika Regt 361 – Oberst von Barby
Sonderveband 288 – Oberst Menton
Reconnasissance Battalion 580 – Oberleutnant Hohmeyer
Anti-tank Battalion 605

Corpo d'Armata XXI – Generale di Corpo d'Armata Enea Navarrini (H.Q. El Adem)
Bologna Division – Generale di Divisione Gloria
Trento Division – Generale di Divisione Stampioni
Pavia Division – Generale di Divisione Franceschini
Brescia Division – Generale di Divisione Zambon
Savona Division – Generale di Divisione de Giorgis (H.Q. Bir Ghirba)
Arko 104 (Artillery Group Böttcher) – Generalmajor Karl Böttcher (H.Q. Belhammed)

CORPO D'ARMATA DI MANOVRA XX (under direct command of Comandante Superiore)
Generale di Corpo d'Armata Gastone Gambara

Corps Troops:
Medium and heavy artillery and a reconnaissance unit

Ariete Armoured Division – Generale di Divisione Balotta
132nd Armoured Regt
8th Bersaglieri Regt
132nd Artillery Regt

Trieste Motorised Division – Generale di Divisione Piazzoni
65th Infantry Regt
66th Infantry Regt
9th Bersaglieri Regt
Divisional anti-tank and anti-aircraft artillery, plus machine-gun and mortar companies

Appendix II:
Forces Engaged at the Battle of Gazala, May 26th, 1942

Allied Forces

Commander-in-Chief, Middle East   General Sir Claude Auchinleck

EIGHTH ARMY
Lieutenant-General Neil M. Ritchie

XIII Corps – Lieutenant-General W. H. E. 'Strafer' Gott

1st South African Division – Major-General D. H. Pienaar
  1st South African Infantry Brigade
  2nd South African Infantry Brigade
  3rd South African Infantry Brigade

2nd South African Division (in Tobruk) – Major-General H. B. Klopper
  4th South African Infantry Brigade
  6th South African Infantry Brigade
  9th Indian Infantry Brigade

50th (Tyne and Tees) Infantry Division – Major-General W. H. C. Ramsden
  69th Infantry Brigade
  150th Infantry Brigade
  151st Infantry Brigade

1st Army Tank Brigade – Brigadier W. O. L. O'Carroll

32nd Army Tank Brigade – Brigadier A. C. Willison

XXX Corps – Lieutenant-General Willoughby Norrie

1st Armoured Division – Major-General H. Lumsden
  2nd Armoured Brigade
  22nd Armoured Brigade
  201st Guards Brigade Group

7th Armoured Division – Major-General F. Messervy
    4th Armoured Brigade
    7th Motor Brigade
    3rd Indian Motor Brigade
    29th Indian Infantry Brigade Group
    1st Fighting French Brigade Group

German and Italian Forces

Comandante Superiore   Generale d'Armata Ettore Bastico

PANZERARMEE AFRIKA
Generaloberst Erwin Rommel

Deutsches Afrika Korps – Generalleutnant Walther K. Nehring

15th Panzer Division – Generalleutnant Gustav von Vaerst (until May 27th)   Oberst Eduard Crasemann (from May 27th)
    Panzer Regiment 8
    Infantry Regiment 115
    Panzerjäger Abteilung 33
    Reconnaissance Battalion 33
    Artillery Regiment 33

21st Panzer Division – Generalmajor Georg von Bismarck
    Panzer Regiment 5
    Infantry Regiment 104
    Panzerjäger Abteilung 39
    Reconnaissance Battalion 3
    Artillery Regiment 155

90th Light Division – Generalmajor Ulrich Kleeman
    Infantry Regiment 155
    Infantry Regiment 200
    Sonderverband 288
    Panzerjäger Abteilung 190
    Reconnaissance Battalion 580
    Artillery Regiment 190

Corpo d'Armata di Manovra XX – Generale di Corpo d'Armata Ettore Baldassarre

Ariete Armoured Division – Generale di Divisione Giuseppe de Stefanis
    132nd Armoured Regiment
    132nd Artillery Regiment
    8th Bersaglieri Regiment

Trieste Motorised Division – Generale di Divisione Azzi
   65th Infantry Regiment
   66th Infantry Regiment
   9th Bersaglieri Regiment

Gruppe Cruewell – Generalleutnant Ludwig Cruewell

Corpo d'Armata X – Generale di Corpo d'Armata Benvenuto Gioda
Brescia Division – Generale di Divisione Giacomo Lombardi
Pavia Division – Generale di Divisione Antonio Franceschini

Corpo d'Armata XXI – Generale di Corpo d'Armata Enea Navarini

Trento Division – Generale di Divisione Getti
Sabratha Division – Generale di Divisione Mario Soldarelli

Notes

Crown copyright material throughout this book is reproduced by permission of the Controller of Her Majesty's Stationery Office.

1 Auchinleck Takes Command

1 Chester Wilmot, *Tobruk*, copyright © Chester Wilmot 1944, reprinted by permission of Angus and Robertson Publishers, Sydney, p. 255.
2 Quoted in Wilmot, op. cit., p. 205.
3 Quoted in Wilmot, op. cit., p. 200.
4 Quoted in *The Sidi Rezeg Battles 1941*, ed. J. A. I. Agar-Hamilton and L. C. F. Turner, Oxford University Press (Cape Town) 1957, p . 64. This and all subsequent extracts from this title are reprinted by permission of the Government Printer, Pretoria, South Africa.
5 Quoted in *Sidi Rezeg*, p. 64.
6 Quoted in *Sidi Rezeg*, p. 65.
7 Quoted in *Sidi Rezeg*, pp. 110, 66.
8 *Sidi Rezeg*, pp.110–11.
9 Quoted in *Sidi Rezeg*, p. 90.
10 Quoted in *Sidi Rezeg*, p. 92.

2 Crusader: The Clash of Armour

1 Quoted in John Connell, *Auchinleck*, Cassell 1959, p. 336.
2 Major-General Sir Howard Kippenberger, *Infantry Brigadier*, Oxford University Press 1949, p. 81.
3 Alan Moorehead, *African Trilogy*, Hamish Hamilton 1944, p. 220.
4 Brigadier G. M. O. Davy, *The Seventh and Three Enemies*, Heffer (Cambridge) n.d., p. 146.
5 Quoted in *The Sidi Rezeg Battles 1941*, ed. J. A. I. Agar-Hamilton and L. C. F. Turner, Oxford University Press (Cape Town) 1957, p. 136.
6 Earl of Onslow, *Men and Sand*, St Catherine's Press, 1961, quoted in Michael Carver, *Tobruk*, Batsford 1964, p. 53.
7 Alexander Clifford, *Three against Rommel*, Harrap 1943, pp. 131, 132.
8 Quoted in *Sidi Rezeg*, ed. Agar-Hamilton and Turner, pp. 161–2.
9 Quoted in *Sidi Rezeg*, p. 173.

10 Quoted in *Sidi Rezeg*, p. 194.
11 Quoted in *Sidi Rezeg*, p. 175.
12 Davy, op. cit., quoted in *Sidi Rezeg*, p. 177.
13 Major R. H. W. S. Hastings, *The Rifle Brigade in the Second World War*, Gale and Polden (Aldershot) 1950, p. 85.
14 In *The Royal Artillery Commemoration Book 1939–1945*, published for the R. A. Association by Bell 1950, p. 196, quoted in *Sidi Rezeg*, pp. 180–1, and reprinted by permission of the Royal Artillery Institution.
15 Quoted in *Sidi Rezeg*, p. 182.
16 Hastings, op. cit., p. 58.
17 Quoted in *Sidi Rezeg*, ed. Agar-Hamilton and Turner, pp. 199–200.
18 From *42nd Royal Tank Regiment* 1938–1944, published privately by the Regiment 1951, p. 10, quoted in *Sidi Rezeg*, p. 203.
19 Brigadier A. F. Hely, in *R. A. Commemoration Book*, p. 189, quoted in *Sidi Rezeg*, ed. Agar-Hamilton and Turner, p. 211.
20 'Preliminary Narrative', quoted in *Sidi Rezeg*, p. 212.
21 Cyril Joly, *Take These Men*, Constable Publishers 1955, p. 199.
22 Brigadier George Clifton, *The Happy Hunted*, Cassell 1952, pp. 129–30, quoted in *Sidi Rezeg*, ed. Agar-Hamilton and Turner, p. 217.
23 Hely, in *R. A. Commemoration Book*, p. 189, quoted in *Sidi Rezeg*, p. 214.
24 Joly, op. cit., pp. 203–4.
25 Quoted in *Sidi Rezeg*, ed. Agar-Hamilton and Turner, p. 220.
26 Quoted in *Sidi Rezeg*, p. 225.
27 D. Frazer Norton, *History of the 26th Battalion*, War History Branch, Wellington 1952, reprinted by permission of Historical Publications Branch, Department of Internal Affairs, Wellington, New Zealand. Quoted in *Sidi Rezeg*, p. 223.
28 Quoted in *Sidi Rezeg*, p. 233.
29 Quoted in Brigadier Dudley Clarke, *The Eleventh at War*, Michael Joseph 1952, p. 202.
30 Quoted in *Sidi Rezeg*, ed. Agar-Hamilton and Turner, p. 237.
31 Quoted, loc. cit.
32 Quoted in *Sidi Rezeg*, p. 255.
33 Heinz W. Schmidt, *With Rommel in the Desert*, Harrap 1951, p. 108.
34 Quoted in *Sidi Rezeg*, ed. Agar-Hamilton and Turner, p. 261.
35 Quoted, loc. cit.
36 Quoted in *Sidi Rezeg*, p. 262.
37 War Diary of 22nd Armoured Brigade, quoted in *Sidi Rezeg*, p. 264.

3 *Crusader: The Infantry Take Over*

1 *The Rommel Papers*, ed. B. H. Liddell Hart, Collins 1953, p. 163.
2 Afrika Korps War Diary, quoted in *The Sidi Rezeg Battles 1941*, ed, J. A. I. Agar-Hamilton and L. C. F. Turner, Oxford University Press (Cape Town) 1957, p. 305.
3 *Sidi Rezeg*, p. 306.

4 *The Rommel Papers*, ed. Liddell Hart, p. 164.
5 Quoted in John Connell, *Auchinleck*, Cassell 1959, pp. 364–5.
6 Major R. H. W. S. Hastings, *The Rifle Brigade in the Second World War*, Gale and Polden (Aldershot) 1950, pp. 92–3.
7 Heinz W. Schmidt, *With Rommel in the Desert*, Harrap 1951, p. 118.
8 Quoted in *Sidi Rezeg*, ed. Agar-Hamilton and Turner, p. 386.
9 Birkby, Carel, ed., *The Saga of the Transvaal Scottish Regiment 1932–1950*, Howard Timmins (Pty.) Ltd (Cape Town) for Hodder and Stoughton 1950, p. 348, quoted in *Sidi Rezeg*, p. 332.
10 Quoted in *Sidi Rezeg*, p. 332.
11 Quoted in *Sidi Rezeg*, p. 376.
12 *Sidi Rezeg*, pp. 376–7.
13 General Norrie's Report, quoted in *Sidi Rezeg*, pp. 392–3.
14 D. Frazer Norton, *History of the 26th Battalion*, War history Branch, Wellington 1952, quoted in *Sidi Rezeg*, p. 396. This and the following extract, from Borman, *Divisional Signals*, are reprinted by permission of Historical Publications Branch, Department of Internal Affairs, Wellington, New Zealand.
15 C. A. Borman, *Divisional Signals*, War History Branch, Wellington 1954, quoted in *Sidi Rezeg*, p. 412n.
16 *The Rommel Papers*, ed. Liddell Hart, p. 170.

4 *Embattled Spring*

1 Crown copyright, quoted in John Connell, *Auchinleck*, Cassell 1959, pp. 420–1.
2 Crown copyright, ibid., pp. 423–4.
3 Major-General F. W. von Mellenthin, *Panzer Battles: A Study of the Employment of Armor in the Second World War*, Ballantine (New York) 1971, copyright by the University of Oklahoma Press, pp. 104–5.
4 Quoted in Major-General I. S. O. Playfair *et al.*, *History of the Second World War* (hereafter referred to as the *Official History*), *The Mediterranean and Middle East*, *Vol. III*, H.M.S.O. 1960, p. 154.
5 Vladimir Peniakoff, *Popski's Private Army*, Pan 1957, p. 127. This and all subsequent extracts from this title are reprinted by permission of the Estate of Vladimir Peniakoff.
6 Quoted in Philip Warner, *The Special Air Service*, William Kimber 1971, p. 50, reprinted by permission of the S.A.S. Regimental Association.

5 *No Drums, No Trumpets*
(with acknowledgement to T. S. Eliot)

1 *The Rommel Papers*, ed. B. H. Liddell Hart, Collins 1953, p. 194.
2 Ibid., p. 195.
3 Crown copyright, quoted in John Connell, *Auchinleck*, Cassell 1959, pp. 506–7.
4 Crown copyright, quoted, ibid., p. 515.
5 *Rommel Papers*, ed. Liddell Hart, p. 206.

6 Ibid.
7 Ibid., p. 208.
8 Major-General G. P. B. Roberts, personal account of May 27th, 1942, unpublished.
9 Quoted in *Crisis in the Desert*, ed. J. A. I. Agar-Hamilton and L. C. F. Turner, Oxford University Press (Cape Town) 1952, p. 32. This and all subsequent extracts from this title are reprinted by permission of the Government Printer, Pretoria, South Africa.
10 J. A. Pitt-Rivers, *The Story of the Royal Dragoons, 1938–1945*, William Clowes n.d., p. 44.
11 Birkby, Carel, ed., *The Saga of the Transvaal Scottish Regiment 1932–1950*, Howard Timmins (Pty) Ltd (Cape Town) for Hodder and Stoughton 1950, pp. 464–5, quoted in *Crisis in the Desert*, ed. Agar-Hamilton and Turner, p. 34.
12 Quoted in Desmond Young, *Rommel*, Collins 1950, p. 124.
13 Quoted in *Crisis in the Desert*, ed. Agar-Hamilton and Turner, p. 38.
14 Quoted in Correlli Barnett, *The Desert Generals*, Pan 1962, p. 154.
15 Crown copyright, quoted in *Crisis in the Desert*, ed. Agar-Hamilton and Turner, p. 39.
16 Quoted in Antony Brett-James, *Ball of Fire: The Fifth Indian Division in the Second World War*, Gale and Polden (Aldershot) 1951, p. 177.
17 Major-General I. S. O. Playfair *et al.*, *Official History, The Mediterranean and Middle East, Vol. III*, H.M.S.O. 1960, p. 233.
18 Ibid., pp. 234–5.
19 Roy Farran, *Winged Dagger*, Fontana 1954, p. 144.
20 *Rommel Papers*, ed. Liddell Hart, p. 217.
21 Ibid., p. 218.
22 Crown copyright, quoted in Connell, op. cit., p. 540.
23 Playfair, op. cit., pp. 238–9.
24 Crown copyright, quoted in *Crisis in the Desert*, ed. Agar-Hamilton and Turner, p. 68.
25 *Royal Artillery Journal*, April 1948, quoted, ibid., p. 69.
26 *Rommel Papers*, ed. Liddell Hart, p. 222.
27 Crown copyright, quoted in Connell, op. cit., p. 430.
28 Winston S. Churchill, *The Second World War, Vol. IV*, Cassell 1951, p. 331.
29 Crown copyright, quoted in Playfair, op. cit., pp. 246–7.
30 Crown copyright, quoted, ibid., p. 247.

6 'A progression of avoidable disasters'
(General W. G. F. Jackson)

1 *The Sidi Rezeg Battles 1941*, ed. J. A. I. Agar-Hamilton and L. C. F. Turner, Oxford University Press (Cape Town) 1957, p. 225. This extract is reprinted by permission of the Government Printer, Pretoria, South Africa.
2 Draft history of the Rand Light Infantry, quoted in *Crisis in the Desert*,

ed. J. A. I. Agar-Hamilton and L. C. F. Turner, Oxford University Press (Cape Town) 1952, p. 81.

3 Birkby, Carel, ed., *The Saga of the Transvaal Scottish Regiment 1932–1950*, Howard Timmins (Pty) Ltd (Cape Town) for Hodder and Stoughton 1950, p. 487, quoted in *Crisis in the Desert*, ed. Agar-Hamilton and Turner, p. 82.

4 *Crisis in the Desert*, ed. Agar-Hamilton and Turner, p. 91.

5 Ibid., p. 115, footnote.

6 *The Rommel Papers*, ed. B. H. Liddell Hart, Collins 1953, p. 225.

7 Quoted in *Crisis in the Desert*, ed. Agar-Hamilton and Turner, pp. 122–3.

8 Heinz W. Schmidt, *With Rommel in the Desert*, Harrap 1951, p. 144.

9 Major-General F. W. von Mellenthin, *Panzer Battles: A Study of the Employment of Armor in the Second World War*, Ballantine (New York) 1971, copyright 1956 by the University of Oklahoma Press, p. 144.

10 Field Marshal Lord Carver, *Tobruk*, Batsford 1964, p. 212.

11 *Crisis in the Desert*, ed. Agar-Hamilton and Turner, p. 150.

12 Quoted, ibid., p. 194.

13 Crown copyright, quoted, ibid., pp. 194–5.

14 Crown copyright, quoted, ibid., p. 209.

15 Ibid., p. 210.

16 Quoted, ibid., pp. 210–11.

17 Crown copyright, quoted, ibid., p. 214.

18 Crown copyright, quoted, ibid., p. 217.

19 P. Caccia-Dominioni, *Alamein*, Allen and Unwin 1966, p. 137.

20 M. W. Brown, 'For You the War is Finish', in *History of the Second World War, Vol. III*, ed. Barrie Pitt, Purnell 1967, p. 1003.

21 Quoted in *Crisis in the Desert*, ed. Agar-Hamilton and Turner, p. 237.

22 Francis Tuker, *Patterns of War*, Cassell 1948, p. 89.

23 Crown copyright, quoted in Major-General I. S. O. Playfair *et al.*, *Official History, The Mediterranean and Middle East, Vol. III*, H.M.S.O. 1960, p. 286.

24 *Crisis in the Desert*, ed. Agar-Hamilton and Turner, p. 248.

25 Quoted, ibid., p. 255.

26 Major-General Sir Howard Kippenberger, *Infantry Brigadier*, Oxford University Press 1949, pp. 132–3.

27 Ibid., p. 135.

28 Lieutenant-Colonel G. R. Armstrong, in *R.A. Commemoration Book*, pp. 220–1, quoted in *Crisis in the Desert*, ed. Agar-Hamilton and Turner, p. 261.

29 General W. G. F. Jackson, *The North African Campaign 1940–43*, Batsford 1975, p. 243.

30 *Rommel Papers*. ed. Liddell Hart, p. 238.

31 Armstrong, op. cit., p. 222, quoted in *Crisis in the Desert*, ed. Agar-Hamilton and Turner, p. 263.

32 *Crisis in the Desert*, ed. Agar-Hamilton and Turner, p. 266.

33 See Barrie Pitt, *The Crucible of War: Western Desert 1941*, Cape 1980, pp. 458–9.

34 *Rommel Papers*, ed. Liddell Hart, p. 239.

35 *Crisis in the Desert*, ed. Agar-Hamilton and Turner, p. 291.
36 *Rommel Papers*, ed. Liddell Hart, p. 246.
37 Quoted in *Crises in the Desert*, ed. Agar-Hamilton and Turner, p. 296.
38 Quoted, ibid., p. 300.
39 Quoted, ibid., p. 310.
40 Quoted, ibid., p. 314.

7 *First Alamein*

1 John Connell, *Auchinleck,* Cassell 1959, p. 626.
2 *The Rommel Papers*, ed. B. H. Liddell Hart, Collins 1953, p. 253.
3 Major-General Sir Howard Kippenberger, *Infantry Brigadier*, Oxford University Press 1949, p. 169.
4 *Rommel Papers*, ed. Liddell Hart, p. 257.
5 Ibid.
6 Kippenberger, op. cit., p. 139.
7 Crown copyright, quoted in Connell, op. cit., p. 618.
8 Kippenberger, op. cit., p. 183.
9 Ibid., p. 184.
10 Ibid., p. 188.
11 Ibid., p. 189.
12 Ibid., p. 190.

8 *Churchill Intervenes*

1 Quoted in Winston S. Churchill, *The Second World War, Vol. IV,* Cassell 1951, p. 352.
2 Quoted, ibid., p. 400.
3 Quoted in Lord Moran, *Churchill, The Struggle for Survival 1940–65,* Constable 1966, p. 46.
4 Churchill, op. cit., p. 277.
5 Crown copyright, quoted in John Connell, *Auchinleck*, Cassell 1959, p. 500.
6 Moran, op. cit., p. 50.
7 Ibid.
8 Lord Tedder, *With Prejudice*, Cassell 1966, p. 313.
9 See Churchill, op. cit., p. 414.

Index